Brief versus
Long Psychotherapy

Brief versus Long Psychotherapy
When, Why, and How

James P. Gustafson, M.D.

JASON ARONSON INC.
Northvale, New Jersey
London

This book was set in 10 pt. Berkeley Oldstyle by Alpha Graphics of Pittsfield, New Hampshire, and printed and bound by Book-mart Press in North Bergen, New Jersey.

Library of Congress Cataloging-in-Publication Data

Gustafson, James Paul.
    Brief versus long psychotherapy: when, why, and how / by James P. Gustafson.
        p.   cm.
    Includes bibliographical references and index.
    ISBN 1-56821-470-7
    1. Psychiatry—Differential therapeutics.   2. Psychotherapy.
3. Brief psychotherapy.   4. Psychotherapy—Failure.
5. Psychotherapy—Philosophy.   I. Title.
    [DNLM: 1. Psychotherapy.   WM 420 G982b 1995]
RC480.52.G87   1995
616.89'14—dc20
DNLM/DLC
for Library of Congress   94-49234

Manufactured in the United States of America. Jason Aronson Inc. offers books and cassettes. For information and catalog write to Jason Aronson Inc., 230 Livingston Street, Northvale, New Jersey 07647.

Contents

Preface

There is no adequate book about what can be accomplished briefly in psychotherapy versus what takes a very long time in psychotherapy, because the author would have to be equally adept at both subjects to appraise the subject evenhandedly. In general, the brief psychotherapists know a lot about springing their patients out of present traps, and the psychoanalytic psychotherapists have had the claim on long-term development in psychotherapy. Neither group is willing to afford much validity to its opposite group, so there has been no synthesis.

The main subject of all psychotherapy is interpersonal relationships. An adequate book about brief versus long psychotherapy would have to have an adequate account about the repair of relationships. Yet, there is none available, again, because of specialization. The marital and family therapists know the subject from having the couples and families together, usually briefly. The brief individual therapists know the subject from the individual patient reporting the fix he is in, briefly. The group therapists watch the trend of an individual patient with a number of other strangers in the room, usually over a long time. The long-term individual therapists know the subject from waiting for the transference of the family of origin into the relationship with the doctor himself, usually slowly.

The majority of psychotherapists in practice perform most of these operations, as it were, eclectically. They are in need of a book, which the specialized world of medical schools and schools of brief, family, and long-term psychotherapy cannot give them. The niches nowadays go to the specialists, and so the experts are mostly fierce partisans of a single class of operations. How is the general practitioner of psychotherapy going to learn when to do what operation in his own consulting room? He is going to be a general surgeon, of psychotherapy, as it were, simply because his patients need him to be this generalist.

So, this book is devoted to the daily problems of the generalist of psychotherapy, by an author who has worked for over twenty-five years in all of the relevant fields, brief and long, individual, marital, family, and group. I happened to come up into the academic world of psychiatry when psychoanalytic psychotherapy was the chief training on the coasts. I began this study as a medical student at Harvard, and continued in a residency at Mount Zion in San Francisco, which was taught almost entirely by the psychoanalysts from across the street at the San Francisco Institute. I had an analysis in classical terms (four times a week for five years), in Madison, from a training analyst of the Chicago Institute. I've had a practice of long-term patients in Wisconsin for over twenty-one years, which is about half of my practice.

Yet, I was also fortunate in the late '60s to be drawn into the foment of group studies, so that I became a consultant in conferences on group relations for about fifteen years, learned group therapy and taught it here at Wisconsin for the last twenty-one years. Also, I insisted in the late '60s on learning marital and family therapy, began my training with one of the Palo Alto group, and resumed it here at Wisconsin when I began my Wisconsin Family Therapy Team over ten years ago, strongly influenced by the Milan team at first, and the narrative work of White and Epston later.

Finally, I decided soon after I came to Wisconsin to begin studying brief psychotherapy, starting from Malan's departure from classical psychoanalysis (Gustafson 1981), and began my Brief Psychotherapy Clinic in 1980 for which I am best known (Gustafson 1986, 1992, 1995).

Thus, I have been fortunate to stay clear of the usual specialization that has become the lot of the leaders of the different psychotherapies. Probably, I needed to develop my own work for twenty-five years before I could have a sufficiently long perspective on the advantages and disadvantages of the different procedures. As youths, we are enthusiasts, and do not yet know, as Freud liked to say, that "nothing is half so great as it first appears." It takes time to see this, and it also takes being free of the force of an orthodoxy bent on persuading more adherents.

I have been helped to write this book principally by three readers and friends, Ruth Gustafson, Michael Moran, and Peter Miller, with some additional help from Lowell Cooper, Mike Wood, Vance Wilson, and Myron Sharaf. My students in the Brief Psychotherapy Clinic of 1993–1994 contributed lively discussions on the first six chapters. They include: William Ayetey, Shirley Dawson, Suzy Freedman, Tamar Kelson, Donna Kiley, Maureen Leahy, Sara Long, Deborah Lynn, Michael Maze, Karin Ringler, and Steve Sutherland. I am indebted to Dee Jones for her skills in typing the manuscript with wonderful accuracy, speed, and organization.

Introduction

I have written this book so that it begins with the chief and necessary preoccupation of all beginning practitioners of psychotherapy, namely, being clear about who benefits from being understood and who gets more disturbed the more time you spend with them. Part I is everyone's book on the common interpersonal problems of all psychotherapies, brief and long, individual, marital, family, and group. Yet this subject of reading the difference between benign and malignant responses to understanding is also a subtle subject for the most experienced of experts. As Malan (1979) justly pointed out, you can hardly sort out who needs what operation in first sessions unless you are deeply familiar with all of the operations. Otherwise, you are going to recommend what you happen to know, like the surgeon who did appendectomies on all of his patients because he was good at them.

The middle part of this book is somewhat more demanding of the reader, because it involves him or her more in theory as well as practice. In order to sort out brief from long from impossible jobs, I have gradually developed a field theory (in *The Dilemmas of Brief Psychotherapy* [Gustafson 1995]), which is probably a variation on the chaos theory that is so important in the physical and biological sciences at the present time. I believe it is very simply presented here in Part II, as allowing either temporary exits, slow exits, or no exits from the dynamics of the patient. I show these three things in long-term, brief, and perpetual therapy, and I concretely illustrate an hour of consultation, my visualizations of the dynamic field with the patient, and how I put it into letters for them.

The last third is certainly the most difficult, because it is about the liberal education in psychotherapy and in Western civilization that is mostly lacking in the training of our period. Readers lacking this education will find it hard to know what they are missing, while readers having some of it may be very glad to discover what can lie ahead for them in their own studies. I am aware that I am running against a shared prejudice of the field of psychotherapy when I argue that understanding the maps of someone like Tolstoy in his two great novels is more important than this narrow specialization, which is mainly useful for getting a qualification and less useful for our patients. Yet I do not want to air notions of culture, as if one were better at this work because he is higher and broader and better read. Certainly, well-read doctors could be useless if they could not connect to the problems of their patients and map the way downward or upward, and accompany the patient along the way.

Thus, this book has three levels, ascending and allowing a wider view: the first common to all of us in reading interpersonal unhappiness, the second in reading what it takes and how long it takes to exit from the dynamics that hold the patient in place, and the third in seeing all of these dynamics in the context of the shared history of Western man, the group animal.

PART I

Selection and the Most Common and the Most Impossible Interpersonal Situations

Patients and psychotherapists spend much of their time discussing the difficulties that crop up with other people. In the days when psychoanalysis was the leading paradigm of psychotherapy, the therapist could just let the patient run on about these interpersonal reports, say very little, and trust that they would be enacted with him or her in the transference and there mastered. Nowadays, there is seldom the expensive time for this acting-in to complete itself, nor is there such assurance that the interpersonal fixes in the world correspond to what is eventually played out with the therapist.

With little time, we can't wait to find out, and are called upon to respond to the quandaries that the patient finds himself caught up in. For this we need accurate maps, for the patients expect us to show them the way through.

Often, however, there is no good way through. We had better be very clear about this, or we will promise too much, and be blamed for not delivering. Therefore, I have divided these six chapters into three pairs, each pair concerning the three common interpersonal fixes we are asked to solve. The first of each pair points out when the territory is highly likely to stay the same or get worse, while the second points to possibilities for change for the better.

The first fix, dealt with in Chapters 1 and 2, concerns the interpersonal territory of patients who have been hugely let down as children by their parents, or sometimes by other crucial caretakers, or sometimes later in life by being subjected to unbearable violence in war, or sexuality, or even in daily life. I refer to the entire class of situations that are extremely traumatic as basically faulted situations. By this, I mean, very specifically, that the subject is either violently intruded upon, or abandoned by any kind of protection, or both.

The famous Garden Island study of 698 children from prenatal care to their thirties (Werner 1989) showed that about a third grew up in these basically faulted situations of violent, alcoholic, and insane parents. The 3rd of the third who did not get away from such family situations became ruined, while the 3rd who did get away next door, or to relatives or interested teachers and so forth, did relatively well. The middle third, half in and half out of ruin, had mixed results. In Chapter 1, I discuss taking care of those who stayed in such malignant situations, and in Chapter 2, I discuss those who got out, but are still wounded from their stays.

In Chapter 1, "The Malignant Basic Fault," I discuss the dilemmas involved in taking care of people who will get worse, the more you give them. As Balint (1968) discussed, these patients do not feel satisfied when you spend an hour understanding their plight. They insist you do more for them. When you respond with more literal gratification, they become even more demanding, in what Balint called a malignant regression. This is to be expected with many schizophrenics, with most drug, alcohol, and other addicts, with most borderline personalities, with most paranoids, with most manics, with most false selves, antisocials, and patients seeking medical legitimization for ailments. See Chapter 16 for the most complete data on this subject from the Menninger Psychotherapy Research Project (Wallerstein 1986). The inevitable dilemma is this: they cannot bear to go on with getting more degraded, but they also cannot bear to do what is necessary to get to a different place. This becomes our dilemma to manage, and this is the chief subject of Chapter 1.

In Chapter 2, "The Benign Basic Fault," I discuss the dilemmas involved in taking care of similarly wounded and deprived patients, who are comforted and calmed by understanding, in what Balint called a benign regression. There are many, many different variations, as demonstrated so beautifully by William James, Binswanger, Balint,

Winnicott, Melanie Klein, Sullivan, Guntrip, Greenacre, Semrad, Kern-berg, Kohut, Masterson, Havens, Wallerstein, and many others. I con-fine myself to three topics, commonly neglected by the clinicians of this subject. The first is concerned with reading a basically faulted external world. These patients commonly long for a better world, over-look the old story, and crash back into its jaws. The second topic is the special requirements of basically faulted patients for a certain degree of interest, which if withheld, makes them suffer greatly, and unneces-sarily. The third topic is the reliability of giving the patient one hour of treatment per month, or twelve sessions per year, in many cases.

The second pair of interpersonal problems, presented in Chap-ters 3 and 4, deals with intimacy or marriage. My subject is not so much couples therapy per se, with both partners present, which tends to be a discipline all its own. Rather, it is the subject of intimacy and mar-riage, which the individual therapist has got to understand if he is to be helpful to the half of his patients who come because they are stuck in this area. Without a map, it is pretty hard to be of much help. My map is of the central dilemma in all intimacy, which is that what is needed by the first partner is miserable for the second partner, and vice versa. This is what Haley (1966) called the perverse triangle, in which any third thing, such as a friend, relative, interest, or idea, is helpful to one partner and perverse to the second. I would prefer to characterize it as a dilemma of diverging interests .

In Chapter 3, "Malignant Couples," the divergence of interests is so absolute that there is no hope of compromise. One wins, the other loses. That's it. Regularly, these couples invite the therapist to find a modus vivendi or solution. If he misses the harshness of the dilemma, he will try to find a solution and then be blamed for his futile efforts. These couples often stay together, as in *Who's Afraid of Virginia Woolf?* (Albee 1964), and devour third parties, including therapists, who try to mediate between them. The dilemmas are unsolvable when one or both members in the couple is a shaky character and must keep up their usual operations at the expense of the partner. These are their terms, without qualification. Thus, some characters have to play doormat, and are worn down to the threads. Some characters have to play half-in and half-out, so the coldness sets in, and the boredom, and the curling up like an old leaf. Some characters have to be congratulated for their every wish, or they hit the ceiling. Paradoxically, it is sometimes possible to do something for these couples, when they are doggedly determined to get help, by describing to them that they cannot possibly do what is necessary. I try to make this clear in the first session, whether it is with the couple themselves, or with one member of the couple in individual therapy. In fact, many patients I see individually are married to impossible and shaky characters such as I have described, and it is pointless to bring them in, when they will only demonstrate how prevailingly unpleasant they are. Therefore, I do a great deal of individual marital therapy with the somewhat more workable partner.

In Chapter 4, "Benign Couples," I discuss similar divergent dilemmas between the partners, when they are not so impossibly rigid in their requirements. These are the garden variety miseries of everyday life between well-meaning people, who do not grasp the divergence of their aims. I discuss the three I find most commonly. First is the kind of couple in which one dominates, and the other goes along. The dominant partner is more often male, like a coach, or an entrepreneur, or a policeman, who is entitled to give orders in the patriarchy, by divine right, but it is often the female who is the dominant partner, by divine right in the matriarchy. In either event, the director is almost always failed by the sidekick, because of the dilemma built into the situation. If she tries to stay on top of her feelings, she has to go distant, into a culture of silence, and becomes less gratifying. If she comes out with her feelings, she alarms the director. A second kind of couple secures fidelity to each other, but excitement diverges. A third kind of couple diverges over their range of interests, the first being wide-ranging and the second narrow. Misery is guaranteed unless the dilemma is negotiated, because her wide-ranging will not be backed by him, for whom it is miserable to follow in things that give him no pleasure, whereas her staying at home with him is miserable because she is so confined and deprived of what is her pleasure.

The final and third pair of interpersonal problems, presented in Chapters 5 and 6, concerns children. As with the two previous pairs of such problems, I believe it is of dire importance to distinguish "Malignant Families," Chapter 5, from "Benign Families," Chapter 6. Otherwise, one will be drawn into attempting to solve the impossible. I refer to such cases as children who will be walked on perpetually, who will delay responsibilities perpetually, and who will be antisocial perpetually. Sometimes, something modest can be accomplished once the difficulty is gauged for what it is. This is discussed in Chapter 5.

In Chapter 6, I discuss the rather big changes that can occur in families, by addressing the dilemma accurately in managing as a parent. Again, I do this sometimes with my family therapy team, but most often, I can do it with one parent or both. The three most common problems are the teenager out of control, the little ones as avengers for a wronged parent, and the overly controlling parent. I have placed the dilemmas of benign families into the context of growing up in America and getting help at a mental health center, because I find there is a great deal of ordinary good work there waiting to be done.

1

The Malignant Basic Fault

If I believe certain problems are malignant, I do not believe we are useless to help our patients with them, no more than oncologists are useless with malignant cancer. We will be worse than useless, however, if we underestimate their severity, for we will set up hopefulness that is dashed. This is a grave disservice, for these patients have only little hope when they begin these devastating careers of illness.

I have had my share of such failures. I never learned anything critical without getting it wrong first and losing a patient. In my defense, I can say that I have learned, and I can also say that I have had few teachers who warned me adequately. Few writers map this territory. (A short, but decisive list, in historical order: Freud on negative therapeutic reaction [Asch 1976], Jacobson on mania [1953], Sullivan on paranoia [1956], Main on the ailment [1957], Balint on malignant basic fault [1968], Winnicott on antisocial problems [1971b], and Kernberg and colleagues [1988] on borderline personality.) I will show a number of these failures here, to illustrate underestimation. What is finally crucial is to see what they have in common, so that we are ready for the entire series. Then we will have eyes for the next variant that comes along in our practices.

The Entire Series as Variations of the Malignant Basic Fault

Perhaps there is no substitute for the experience of failing with these grave disorders a certain number of times, thus correcting one's youthful therapeutic zeal. At some point one has had enough pain to want to bend one's mind around the way in which severe problems persist. Fortunately, they all work in pretty much the same way. This similarity of structure in all severe cases is not well marked out in the literature. It can be inferred from the data of the Menninger Psychotherapy Research Project described in Wallenstein's book, *Forty-Two Lives* (1986). Even there it remains a list of difficult topics (I will return to this data fully in Chapter 16).

The reason for this lack of description of a common structure to grave disorders, I think, is that you need a dilemma concept (Gustafson1995) to grasp the double jeopardy of these disorders, and dilemma has never been more than a word used in passing, without a grasp of its general theoretical significance. These severe disorders are not only based on dilemmas, but tragic dilemmas, which have no easy way out. As in tragedy it is too late for turning back and for rescue; yet something can often be accomplished when the dire situation is fully grasped.

A tragic dilemma is one in which the patient is sliding into ruin, but the alternatives are worse. The patient always complains of this drift to disaster, but is never prepared to do anything else. The first reason for the disaster is that the patient cannot manage by himself, and the reason for refusing help is that it brings him too close to the helpers as persecutors. Thus, it is what I call a far/near dilemma, as in my first diagram.

The reader may want to turn to Chapter 11 for a full exposition of my representations of the topology of the mind, and to Chapter 16 for a theoretical comparison with the mathematics of catastrophe theory and chaos theory. Here I will outline a few key points about my mapping, so that the reader may get a better glimpse of what these figures are designed to show.

First of all, the reader may think of the two horns in the diagram as the horns of a dilemma. In Figure 1–1 the far horn slopes into perishing alone, while the near horn falls rapidly or even precipitously into the perfidious hands of the so-called "helpers." The heavy and dotted

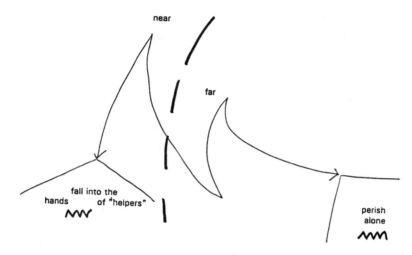

Figure 1–1. The Far/Near Tragic Dilemma of the Malignant Basic Fault.

line between the two horns indicates the hiatus or disjunction between the two halves of the map: it signifies that you are either in the conscious mind to the right, which is conscious of terrible loneliness, or you are in the unconscious mind to the left, which is unconsciously terrified of "help," which is actually betrayal. The unconscious dread of the left half of the map is so terrible that the patient is likely to flee to the right where the other peril gets him.

Thus, the mapping generally has coordinates of the external world and conscious mind to the right, which is smaller in energy, and thus drier, and earthbound in its metaphors, like Dr. Jekyll, discussed in Chapter 11. Conversely, the unconscious mind is mapped to the left, which is far larger in energy, and thus wetter, and oceanic in its metaphors, like Mr. Hyde, also discussed in Chapter 11. In other words, the vertical dimension of these diagrams is a coordinate of the size of the energy involved.

These diagrams allow me to picture for myself and for my patients and students the force field in which the patient exists, which is highly non-linear or abrupt in its sudden changes from gradual to steep rates of change. Without such a pictoral assistance, it is hard for us all to reckon the difference between standing on the banks of a huge river, where one can move freely without falling over, and being up to one's waist in the river, where a single step can subject oneself to overwhelming torrents. Thus, we are inattentive to the differences in territory, between the dry and relatively linear conscious mind, and the wet and overwhelming forces of the unconscious mind. This is why I often picture clouds over this force field, which obscure the situation, in which the patient is imperiled for lack of reckoning about what is coming next.

The verbal and mostly conscious means we have are too weak to grasp these typical situations. This is why the unconscious, which can correct the conscious, utilizes pictures in dreams. As Jung (1963) argued, the #1 self of the conscious mind is in grave difficulty if it cannot heed the #2 self of the unconscious mind. The #1 self mostly is familiar with words, while the #2 self mostly is strange with its night-portraits of how things stand, or fall. This is why these drawings are of grave importance to my patients. Winnicott (1971b) found the same thing with children.

The reverse or near/far dilemma is equally tragic: the patient clings to the doctor, and cannot bear separations. I will divide what can be done with such situations into three broad categories. The first is to decline psychotherapy, but remain available for emergencies. The second is to manage the situation, by facing with the patient that it is very bad either way. The third is to get the patient to make a huge change that transcends the terms of the dilemma.

Declining Psychotherapy, While Remaining Available for Emergencies

One common presentation is the patient with the ailment (Main 1957), who can't work, can't study, or can't relate to other people. This can be complained about bitterly, because it leaves the patient without money, qualifications, or friends; yet he throws the entire burden on the doctor to fix it, while he is prepared to do almost nothing but make efforts that are certain to fail. Almost always, he is angling for a disability income from the government, or a sinecure from the family.

A Case of Making Messes

A middle-aged man lived with his aging parents, and complained that he had been fired several times from jobs. He was very nice and made such a good first impression that he was easily hired, but it was getting harder with his record. He just made endless mistakes. Somehow he lost his concentration, and forgot things important to the boss. For example, he was supposed to watch over some children one day, became bored, turned on the radio, and one child wandered away and was lost for many hours, causing a tremendous panic. Needless to say, he was fired, but his attitude was that the boss had made too much of a little thing that had turned out all right! Always, it was someone else's fault.

I spent five years with this man going from one fiasco to another and never learning anything, despite my best efforts. He lived in a kind of cloud, which he could actually describe as surrounding him. He had learned as a child to tune out his baleful parents, by becoming absent or simply absent-minded. They could scream all they wanted; he hardly heard them. The trouble was that he could not come out of the cloud to engage fully with anyone or any task or anything. To come out would be like blowing in the wind. So he never did. He sank perpetually in one job after another, and never got near anything. Finally, no one would hire him, and he started receiving disability.

A Case of Unbearable Flashbacks to Incest

This patient, like so many others, complained of unbearable body memories like abdominal pain and genital pain and vomiting, which she believed were due to incest with her father. She was extremely suicidal, and had no ties to anyone but the mother who had always overlooked her troubles and told her to shape up. She had no work and no interests that anyone had been able to find. (I suspected they were wrong about this, since she was not yet dead.)

Whenever she began to tell her resident doctor about any of these memories, she would become overwhelmed, more suicidal, and come to a dead stop; yet she insisted that the resident relieve her of her terrible distress. She would take no responsibility for her safety between sessions, saying that was for the resident to figure out. All of this was presented to me for consultation.

I saw her with the resident and found exactly the same situation reported to me, except for one difference. I saw the dilemma was impossible. She could not go on like this, yet probing her trouble made her worse. So I told them that the treatment was even worse than the disease. (See Malan [1979, Chaps. 21 and 22] for some harrowing cases of treatment both declined and undertaken with pa-tients like this. I always remember as well his case of the social worker seeking treatment "to come alive in her work" [p. 213]. He cautiously asked about previous disturbance, and found to his hor-ror that she had smeared carbolic acid on her face in protest to a therapist, had threatened suicide on his doorstep, and had had to be committed.) I recommended they stop, with the proviso that the patient could discuss what to do with the resident if an emergency arose. (It is far preferable to do this in the first session, than after a year of pointless psychotherapy. Kernberg and colleagues (1988) and Malan (1979, Chap. 17) are very sound about letting the patient know at the outset their responsibilities in the psychotherapy. This is especially important in basic faulted cases, where the fault will yawn open if the therapy is getting anywhere. The treatment ought not to be begun if this is not planned for in advance.) Her suffering went into a lower key. (Patients who will get worse in psychotherapy are best managed, usually, by a team of people, because it is not too close and not too far. See Beels's Dilemma, later in this chapter, which enunciates this concept of space to traverse the near/far or far/near dilemma.)

Managing Tragic Dilemmas

Sometimes it is possible to manage in malignant situations, and some-times one has little choice. For example, our second year residents in the emergency room are forever having to manage dilemmas with bor-derline patients of the following sort.

The Case of Yet Another Borderline Patient in the Emergency Room, or The Malignant Helping Profession Syndrome

A young female is brought in by police, after she alarmed her room-mates by cutting on her wrist. She is stubbornly quiet, and resentful that she has to answer annoying questions. The resident locates her chart and finds this is the twentieth episode of this kind in the last year, and that three hospitalizations have accomplished nothing, except to anger the staff who do not want her back.

The resident calls me on the telephone, and is in the usual dilemma. If he takes her into the hospital, he feels used. If he sends her out, he is apt to be woken up later when she comes back in the middle of the night. I reply that this is the usual dilemma, and that he is going to suffer one way or the other, so which suffering is he going to prefer? He decides to put her in the hospital.

Since I am also covering the inpatient service, I get to see her for a staffing the next day. She is a little more communicative, having gotten her way, but emits the usual air of resentful tolerance of inquiry about her affairs. I find that she used to be a social worker herself, but this broke down when she could not set any limits on the funds she was giving out. She had been terribly nice, and complete advantage was taken by her clients.

Now, she is in a hopeless fix. Without her helping profession, she feels worthless. She can't really go back to it, because she can't stand up to anybody about anything. So, she makes suicide attempts, and gets worse with each fiasco. For example, her roommates are fed up with her, and she with them.

In this particular interview, I neglected the most important question, which is what did *she* want to do about all this? This is most important, because such cases go nowhere without the patient wanting to do something herself. (Malan's [1976] chief finding with long-term therapy is that motivation is the greatest limiting factor.) Without self-motivation, patients get us to take the initiatives, and subsequently prove they will not work. (The helping profession syndrome is Malan's coinage [1979], and the malignant version is my adjective.)

I fell for this one. In my cleverness, I pointed out that she could only take back her profession if she could refrain from being so nice. This annoyed her, because she felt being nice was her best point. It was just that the clients had misused her; so it was their fault.

I did have the sense to warn her of the hazard of changing her nice, helping stance. I told her she'd be apt to swing the other way, and let loose of her aggression. It would be difficult to find a middle way, and take a long time. Well, she soon showed the futility of my ideas, by storming violently at her visiting roommates, and leaving against medical advice!

Her proof was complete, and fits the tragic dilemma. She goes on and is betrayed by being nice. She engages help, becomes violent, and breaks off treatment. Next time I see her I will not make a move until

I find out what she prefers to do, and then I will, as Sullivan (1954, 1956) would say, make the unpleasant implications perfectly clear, that is, the two ways that she is very likely to fail: by being taken advantage of, or by blasting people.

A Generic Paranoid Patient in Psychotherapy

I have had somewhere near ten paranoid patients in psychotherapy in the last several years. Of course, I do not want to describe any one of them, because I will be obliged to seek their consent, and I do not want any legal arrangements with any of them. In any event, the same unpleasant sequence of events occurs in every single case, and that is what I have finally grasped, and will relate.

These cases are not grossly and obviously paranoid at the start, or I never would have been tempted to begin. The patients are actually appealing, because they suffer terribly. As Reider (1953) suggested, they come into psychotherapy in a state of "positive paranoia," or the delusion that the world is out to help them. Often, they have had dreadful childhoods of torture and abandonment. A little kindness got in there just enough that they believe in it with a vengeance.

I go through an early phase, in which my understanding eases their terrible isolation with their unbearable pain. Often, there is a great letting go of tears. This brings me closer, and this is too dangerous. I am now regularly attacked over the smallest misstatements, failures of empathy, or insinuations that I had never intended. The positive paranoia has shifted to its shadow side of negative paranoia. If I have my wits about me, I do not allow myself to be provoked into an outburst, which will discredit me completely and allow them to get their distance back by walking out on the spot. I do allow them to regain some distance, by being somewhat unpleasant in return. "Thus, while the therapist ordinarily should try to make things run rather smoothly, with the paranoid person he should go to some trouble to make all implications, especially the unpleasant ones, very clear" (Sullivan 1954, p. 232).

Since they all have a genius for discovering things that are slightly wrong, I always grant them their point. I follow with disagreeing with the conclusion drawn, and I tell them they are determined to put me in a bad light because they were getting very anxious about seeing me in a good light. For example, one such patient hounded me about being too distant when she cried, another for how my department handled her crazy mother, and another because she felt worse after draining sessions. Some of them get enough distance from my being accurate about their dilemma, and some have to quit to get far enough away from my help. For a fantastic account of a brief psychotherapy with an extremely paranoid, but capable, patient of this kind, see Balint's "Stationery Manufacturer" (Balint et al. 1972). The first half of the therapy concludes with the patient's dream of curling up with Balint as a big snake, and the second half ends in an unrelenting attack on Balint in an attempt to extrude him altogether. Balint barely survives it, while being absolutely clear about what is going on.

The dilemma of paranoids is yet another variation on the tragic dilemma. Alone, they are unbearably isolated. Connected, they are defenseless. Reider (1953) was one of the first to grasp the double nature of paranoia, when he wrote that there is both positive and negative paranoia. Positive paranoia is the belief that someone is out to help you, and negative paranoia is the belief that someone is out to harm you. When we play into the first, we get too close and bring on the second.

A Case of Manic Sport

Like borderline and paranoid patients, those who suffer from mania have interludes which are deceptively pleasant. This is where we get hitched, unwittingly, to what will turn out to be a shooting star. One such patient was very appealing in a boyish way, but had a terrible track record of false starts. At the time I began his treatment, five years ago, I was interested in what Michael White (White and Epston 1990) called unique outcomes, especially in the dreary lives of chronic careers of mental illness.

This young man might have been seen, alternately, as a chronic paranoid schizophrenic, or a schizo-affective disorder, or a paranoid personality. These diagnoses tend to overlap to a great extent. He was excitable, and that was the big thing. He was driving a girl crazy with his enthusiasms, which she could not get him to stop. Finally, her parents went to the police, who sobered him up a little. Then he came to me.

He spent most of his days thinking about this young woman, and her puzzling refusal of his great love. I ought to have left him in this great quandary. Instead, I proposed he might do something more useful. He began yet another job. This got his parents' hopes up that he finally had found a competent psychiatrist. Soon, he became mad again, convinced that the boss was gay and out to seduce him. He quit. After this, the parents gave me a good deal of grief.

Again, we were in a tragic dilemma. In his high states, the patient was untouchable; he was in a cloud like Jehovah (Jones 1923). But he would bother the young woman and this brought on the police. If he wasn't solipsistic like this, and actually got engaged in work, he felt too deficient and vulnerable, and could not bear the pain.

A Case of Manic Rage

As every experienced psychiatrist will testify. the really frightening thing about mania is the booming rage. Whenever I am in charge of the inpatient service, I hope I do not have too many of them sounding down the halls and putting everybody on edge. Even in our back room, we hear their ominous ranting.

> One patient came to me on a good dose of lithium, pleasantly enough, wanting help to get through medical school. The picture was very simple. She had very high ideas about correct behavior. When these ideas were refuted, she had a fit. For instance, she believed in fairness. Three times a day something unfair could be counted on to come along and set her off, and set her friends', professors', and parents' teeth on edge.
>
> I saw her about once a month for two years in a long brief psychotherapy. The therapy was long in lasting two years, but brief in its number of sessions (Gustafson 1986). I confined myself to countering her amazement at these impingements of unfairness. For a long time, I saw little effect. She kept reporting more of the same, with more of the same outrage. She did quiet down in each session, and so her response to understanding was benign. (See the final case of this chapter, "The Case of Danny Boy," for a discussion of mixed malignant and benign basic fault.) Finally, after a year, she began to anticipate at least what I was going to say about her incredulous reports. "Oh, yes, you're going to say it is really amazing!"
>
> What finally got to her was that two close friends sat her down after one of her rampages and told her they had almost given up on her. This shook her. The following session, she had faced about ten different situations that were unfair, and kept her composure through all of them. I had told her in the previous session that even

if she could not help feeling frantic when these things happened, she would feel less so if she were not surprised, and she might need to take a hike to keep from bursting out, until her adrenal cortex calmed down in an hour. In the next session, she said I was right about everything, except it took her three or four days and not an hour to settle!

Gustafson's Thesis

When I was a medical student, I went to the Royal Edinburgh Hospital to study chronic hallucinating schizophrenics for my thesis (Gustafson 1967). I had about ten such patients, who were willing to keep journals about what the voices told them. One even took dictation from the voices on a typewriter. I found that all of them listened to the voices when their lives had broken down, and the voices comforted them. Later, as they came to rely on the voices, the voices got extremely mean and punishing. Here was the tragic dilemma played out in a hallucinatory world!

For example, one woman had felt terribly alone in the world, and began to hear voices of helpful doctors watching over her. As soon as she trusted them, they began to experiment on her, give her orders, and tamper with her body.

At the beginning of the summer, she was relieved that someone was interested in her world, but by the end of the summer she pulled back from me as if I might become like one of those doctors. All ten of the patients did the same thing. They were dreadfully alone with their hallucinatory worlds, and really quite eager for my company, but they then began to fear my company as if it too would become persecutory.

This becomes the cycle of paranoid schizophrenia. Beset by their voices, they come toward the staff. This is a brief relief, before they fear depending on staff, and pull away to depend on their voices. This solitude becomes harrowing, and they go back toward staff, and so on, in a perpetual circle.

Beels's Dilemma

Twenty-five years later, I read an interview with Chris Beels (1991) that explained the implications of the schizophrenia cycle I had noted, and the tragic dilemma of these patients between being far away or near.

Beels said that schizophrenia was a housing problem. By this he meant that schizophrenics did best in small boardinghouses where they could keep their distance, such as from dinner table conversation, yet there was always somebody up to have some slight company. In short, the patients had a space in which to traverse between far and near as they needed to, every day, as illustrated in Figure 1–2.

A Case of High Expectations in Schizophrenia

One patient was brought to me with her husband and little son, because she was getting worse and worse for several years after a psychotic break. The husband was a severe man, who outlined for me her countless household blunders. Some were actually quite dangerous, such as leaving things burning on the stove. The patient was barely audible, and hung her head.

In striking contrast, the boy was full of life, and looked like he was well taken care of. I made much of this, and suggested she

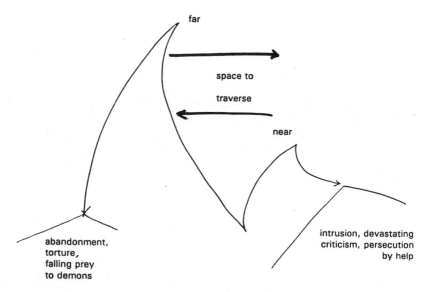

Figure 1–2. Beels's Housing Dilemma With Schizophrenia.

must be a pretty good mother. She replied that she was hardly her old self, and her husband nodded in agreement.

I replied that this was a very dangerous idea she had about full recovery of her old self. She was thinking much too big. That was always very dangerous, and she would have to fail. Nobody ever got anywhere with this unless they did little things. That was the consultation.

About a year later, a woman grasped my hand in the hall and thanked me profoundly. It was she, looking so great that I had not recognized her. This too passed in the subsequent year, because she let her church think she could run the place, which she could not. Then she felt guilty, hung her head, and got back to where I first saw her.

Finally, she had another child, and got so paranoid she would not come out. Her husband asked the resident to come see her, and she did. The resident had learned something from me about the far and near dilemma of these patients. She came only for a half hour. There she found the patient very fearful that she would have her child taken away from her as a bad mother.

The other supervisors of the resident advised her to prescribe more antipsychotics, but the resident was fearful of what was already coming out in the breast milk. I had different advice. I thought she was having the usual postpartum disaster of mothers who lack mothers themselves or the equivalent, and who only get criticism instead. She was unduly isolated, yet feared intrusion, in the tragic dilemma we have discussed in all of these cases. "Oh," said the resident. "Let's have the church grandmother come, *she* will be welcome."

Of course, any company is dangerous. The trick is to allow some room, yet not too much; always with the understanding that both near and far turn sour. That is the gist of Beels's Dilemma.

Transcending the Terms of the Tragic Dilemma

I have had a few patients transcend the terms of the tragic dilemma in long-term work. All of them had a malignant exterior, which hid a very benign response to understanding. In the language of psychoanalysis (Kohut 1971, Ornstein 1974), there is a vertical or horizontal splitting of the psyche, and the two halves operate very differently. In these cases, the malignant demands for literal gratification hide the quiet, comforting, trusting, and benign response to understanding that is felt to be too hazardous. The patient appears and acts much worse than he is at the core. He has a kind of antisocial crust, to keep him out of the jaws of trust (Winnicott 1971b).

Tragic Antisocial Cases

The antisocial trend can become so much of a rut that the patient cannot give it up. It has simply gone on too long, and gotten too much of a set of connections in the world, and the possibility of trust just fades into marginal improbability. Trust is not for this world. (See Winnicott's [1971b] case of Mrs. X, and my discussion of Winnicott with Mrs. X [1986, Chapter 7]. Winnicott barely finds her behind her barrier of a ruined life.) So there are countless antisocial cases—criminal, drug-abusing, alcoholic, prostitutional—that are tragic in this very same dilemma, because it is too late to get near them. They are all variants on Winnicott's formula. The child is hurt, trusting. He attempts revenge, to take his own back. Nobody stops him. He keeps on going in his cynical distance. Finally, he becomes unreachable.

The variations that look malignant, but turn out to be benign, go like this: the authorities stop the child; the doctor then can reach behind the crust, to the hurt child. The trusting connection is reestablished. I will return to this subject in Chapter 6, because it is one of the chief activities of garden variety family therapy.

False Positives

Before I show how the tragic dilemma is sometimes transcended, I would like to discuss falsely positive situations. Often, the patient wishes to be delivered from a tragic dilemma, but it is impossible. As I say, often, it is contrary to physics.

The Case of the Wizard of Oz, and Semrad's Comfort

One of my male patients had a wild business career until the age of 35, which ended because he was in several drunken car crashes. Because of his near-death experiences, he was persuaded to go into the hospital for long-term treatment of his alcoholism. In other words, he hit bottom. He admitted that he was powerless on his own with alcohol, and accepted the Alcoholics Anonymous helping community with God, in the hospital. If far was tragic, near seemed possible.

I saw him ten years later. He was dry, but very depressed. He was barely dragging himself, with low energy, through days working in a bureaucracy. At home, he was so exhausted that he was of almost no help to his wife or his teenage children.

He had flashes of his old expansive genius, which had propelled him in business. Mostly, these took the form of telling war stories from the good old days, of his big investments, which had mostly crashed. He could make this very funny. He would gather energy entertaining this way, which brought light into his face, and force into his gestures. Then, ending a story, he could be seen to fizzle, like the Wizard of Oz shrinking into a little man.

For about three years, I saw him once a month. Every session was the same. He would come in dead, rise to life about two-thirds of the way into the hour, go grey and small, and then go out like ashes once more. I told him he was a miracle, like an Egyptian religion of one, a Phoenix who rose from the ashes, which I witnessed once a month. This went on and on. Eventually, it became clear that he imagined I would get him further. As my old teacher, Semrad, used to say, I was, unwittingly, in collusion with delusion.

In our discussions of his Egyptian religion, he told me that his resurrections were all too fleeting. He was but a Friday Phoenix. Mostly, he was exhausted, frightened by having to face work, and a complete failure at home. He cried. I replied as gently as I could that he had hoped to be much more than this. He said he was absolutely nothing.

I disagreed, pointing out some good reports on him at work. He said it wasn't really him. I disagreed and told him he had done these things. He said that nobody knew what rotten feelings he had inside. I agreed. The worst was, I submitted, that I was not magic. Now, he wept. Yes, he had hoped I would deliver him. Perhaps, I said, there is a little comfort in bringing out this pain. I was thinking of Semrad, who did precisely this, and this is what relief I can give this man.

False Selves

The trouble with these people is that they have been abandoned and intruded upon unmercifully as children. This man had been sexually and violently abused, and had no defenders. He had gotten a very high idea of himself as an entrepreneur Wizard, like Citizen Kane. It was so extravagant an image (Binswanger 1963) he could not live up to it: hence, the alcohol, and finally the crash. He is little better being dry. He requires extravagant images of himself to counter his meager self-respect, yet he cannot measure up to these claims at all. He is either dispirited, or having a comeback that lasts like a ten-minute flight up into the air. His modest accomplishments feel like a false self to him, while his true self is rotten (Winnicott 1971a, Chap. 2). It is extremely painful, and it is too late, as in tragedy. He is far away, because near is terrible to bear. He let me go there a little with him, like Semrad would do, and Winnicott.

A Case of Danny Boy

I have had a handful of patients who have transcended the tragic dilemma, like a patient I have described at length (Gustafson 1976b). I will just summarize it here, as a striking contrast to the case of the Wizard of Oz, and the reader can refer to the original report for full technical detail of how to conduct a long-term psychotherapy of that very difficult kind. The reader may also refer to Goldberg (1975) for two clear examples of split off well-being behind an external crust of sexual perversion that appears malignant. The eating disorders, anorexia, bulimia, and obesity, and the obsessive-compulsive disorders, need also to be distinguished between malignant and secretly benign. The decisive thing is whether you can reach the pain behind the crust so the patient is comforted (Winnicott 1971a), but it also helps a great deal if the patient has a *competence* to show his or her abilities in a non-pathological way (Masterson 1988).

On the surface, he was similar to the Wizard in having been terribly let down as a child, in being extravagant in his claims, and in requiring alcohol to keep him up in the air. He too had had a terrible, nearly tragic car crash. His demeanor was very antisocial. He lied, cheated, sang, and even danced drunk on rooftops. He was also very cynical.

Behind this was a capacity to connect and bloom that had been split off. I reached it most movingly, after he had told me about smashing a leprechaun when drunk:

> When I asked him in the next hour about the leprechaun and what it had meant to him, he told me it reminded him of a song he had always loved and which he had listened to before he had gone to the bar that day. The song was "Danny Boy," which he went on to explain was a song about a father saying good-bye to his son, sending him to war. When I asked the patient what the father says to the son, he replied that the father says, "I love you so much," and then the patient began to sob and shake. [Gustafson 1976b, p. 79]

We reached back to his well-being here, long lost. It was a well-being in which he could be simply loved for himself. It was sound, and did not have to make claims, like the Wizard's, that would inevitably collapse.

2

The Benign Basic Fault

A benign basic fault is a perpetual vulnerability to abandonment and intrusion, which responds with calming to an understanding of the particular incident (injury). The tendency to fall back into the abyss remains like a scar that comes apart. The outer surface of such patients can be anything. In other words, they can appear subservient, delaying, or overpowering as characters (Gustafson 1992, 1995). The shadow side is this abyss, which yawns open when the patient is hurt again.

These patients tend to be overestimated and underestimated. Because they are so responsive to understanding, they are taken into brief psychotherapy. There they improve, and then fall back into the abyss at the conclusion of the twelve sessions, or soon thereafter. Then, they feel tremendously disappointed, and usually blame themselves for not responding correctly to a correct psychotherapy.

Often, they are then underestimated, as if they cannot be helped, especially as if they cannot be helped when time is limited. Now, they must have five or ten years of psychoanalysis, four times a week, to establish a merger or idealizing transference and work it through (Kohut 1979). They are no longer considered neurotics, but they are now self-disorders who require the long-term couch.

Indeed, like every other proposition in psychotherapy, this one is half right. There are many patients who benefit from such a long-term procedure, and get a huge consolidation of self. I just presented such a case, of "Danny Boy," to close Chapter 1. I have had many other similar cases. If they did not require five visits a week for ten years, they often required one or two visits a week for five years.

I have also found that many of these patients can make a big change when time is limited. I mean as little as one hour per month. They usually require several years of time passing, so the psychotherapy is brief in terms of hours, long in terms of time passing. I call it long brief therapy (Gustafson 1986, Selvini-Palazzoli et al. 1978).

Usually, these patients prefer to come twice a month or four times a month if they can afford it. Some like the spacing of several weeks between meetings. I generally let each patient decide his or her own rhythm. We experiment with one, two, three, or four week intervals at the outset, and adjust as we go along.

This is similar to Winnicott's policy of being available as needed. I did pick it up from him, after talking with his long-time editor, Masud Khan, in London in 1981 (Gustafson 1986, p. 61). Khan told me that Winnicott got his best results from this intermittent schedule, so I began trying it out myself. When I think of it now, in terms of the benign basic fault as a profound vulnerability to abandonment and intrusion, I see that this availability on the patient's terms of time is corrective of abandonment, without becoming intrusive. The patient does not have to fit into our schedule, which is not his need.

There is a good deal more to this method than schedule, and this good deal more is my subject for this chapter. I divide my propositions into three, as usual. The first concerns readiness for the world, which these patients all lack. Because they long for responsiveness that is there when they need it and that gets out of the way when they do not need it, the world is forever striking them hard and leaving them in the lurch. My first topic is readiness for such a world.

As Balint proposed in the 1930s, following Ferenczi, these patients do badly with an analytic technique that is a blank screen. Thirty or forty years later, psychoanalysis finally came around (Balint 1968), when self-objects became fashionable and holding environments were allowed as a so-called parameter or adjustment to classical technique. Now, the key is mirroring, allowing idealization, and taking up all the (narcissistic) injuries to this rebuilding of a self, so it can be consolidated (Kohut 1979). Therefore, my second topic is the crucial matter of giving interest, and being ready for slights that we set off in these patients unwittingly. Many of these patients are driven from psychotherapy by therapists who fail to perceive nonverbal cues to these needs for attunement. This turns out to be a dilemma, for attunement can turn out to be collusion. The dilemma is how to be attuned without colluding in delusion, as Semrad used to warn us in Boston.

My third topic is how we get these patients to make the jump, like Bateson's dolphin, from the series of particular disturbing incidents to readiness for the entire class of (narcissistic) injuries. The jump is often sudden, but we can do a great deal to prepare it, and that is my third topic.

Seeing the Next Train Coming

These patients have gotten just enough parenting to believe the world can be good to them. Indeed, they use it well, to take comfort. Their very openness is what imperils them, daily. They all have a dilemma about whether to be near or far, just like the patients of Chapter 1 suffering from the malignant basic fault. The current reply of psychoanalysis to this dilemma is to take them into a good enough relationship, which repairs the (narcissistic) injuries that occur in being near, one by one, as they occur.

My reply to the dilemma is to take on their selective inattention to a hostile or indifferent world first. In this way, I eventually get them to see the next train that is coming, and step out of the way. I note this cloud of amazement to dispel it, and to help the patient to clear sight. What is particular to these patients about missing, or seeing, the social world coming?

Routinely, these patients are living with someone, or married to someone, who runs over them regularly, and leaves them crying alone. It would seem to be a contradiction to their very needs. However, it is better to have this than nothing. Also, they manage to be continually amazed by the crudity of the partner. This helps to stabilize a miserable drift of the relationship. They stay with an amazing partner, which is bad, because going away is more desolate. This dilemma needs a name, for it is legion. It is like a Pinter (1977) play, so I will call it "Pinter's Dilemma."

A Machine For the Suppression of Time

The partner is either mean, or on another planet, like one of the philosophers of the asteroids in *The Little Prince* (St. Exupery 1943). The patient is usually a woman who cannot quite believe it, because she gets a little gratification occasionally, especially when she is about to give up, which draws her back in. The drift in time is to turn her off, especially in the sexual sense, because her body is not fooled like her mind. She goes through a period in which she is open to him, a period in which she is only sometimes open to him, and in which she is not open to him at all.

She is a perfect machine for the suppression of the drift of time, which is just what Levi-Strauss called the chief effect of a myth (Leach 1970, Chap. 7). That is, her cruel dilemma is suppressed by a mythical solution, which is a life-lie to her (Ibsen 1890) in its promises. The dilemma is between staying on a slim hope, and going on a worse hope. The mythical solution is that her subservience will be rewarded. The reward will get less and less, in fact.

What am I to do? I help her to be less amazed, so she is not hit by his crudity each time right between the eyes. Whether she will go or not depends upon whether her ecology offers her a better landing (Gustafson 1995, Chap. 15). I can often relieve her of guilt. For example, one patient dreamt she had done her duty sexually as a wife, and woke up with the heavy guilt that she in fact had not. She wished to, but she could not bring herself to, and this she knew was the death knell of the marriage; nor could she tell him, without his hitting the ceiling. That she would not risk.

Her dilemma was indeed dreadful, but I could face it with her. Going on, she turned off, and could not tell him, so she would be blamed for being unavailable. Telling him would be violent, so she did not. If her dilemma could only drift into worse and worse, she could at least externalize it as a fate in which she chose one bad thing over another. This reduced blaming herself, for the alternatives were a given.

The Dilemma of the Wounded Helping Professional in a World at Fault

The wounded helping professional often gives what he hardly got— empathy without demands attached. His very availability keeps him looking for the same for himself in a world that is highly conditional. Routinely, he looks to be himself, as an individual, and be accepted. He even expects to rebel, and be congratulated by the establishment! Establishments are highly conditional, rewarding those who are presentable on their terms. Spouses can be likewise.

Very accepting psychotherapeutic relationships may, paradoxically, lead to a more secure self, which is increasingly hurt and angry
about the establishment and the spouse. I have had many patients come
to me from previous psychotherapy who continually told me what a
marvelous accepting doctor they had before me. The previous doctor
had become a shibboleth for finding the world at fault.

Thus, a man who was a very successful farmer decided to join an
agricultural bureaucracy to help family farms. He had a very nice doctor who backed him in his new helping profession. However, he could
get no backing in the bureaucracy for his earnest programs. The old-
boy network of the bureaucracy was not about to fund any project but
its own. The patient was amazed and hurt so many times, that he became heartbroken. I saw him ten years later, when he was still amazed,
on disability.

Naturally, his wife had gotten tired of hearing his saga in its innumerable variations. He therefore turned to another woman who listened well. This broke up his marriage. Of course, the new woman
turned out (surprisingly) to have her own agenda, namely, to marry
him. Thus, he was let down by her as well. Now, he was holed up alone.
He was not being utilized. His only connection was looking after some
beautiful trees, assisted by a little neighbor boy.

He was stuck being far away, because being near got him into
collision with the reality that his agenda was not going to be backed by
people who prefered agendas of their own. That is a pretty good definition of the world. After all, everything turns out to be somewhat egocentric. Bureaucracies are purely egocentric. Their rationality is not in
the service of helping, as this patient imagined, but in the service of
help that uses *their* formula. After all, this was their only trick, this
formula, and they would not readily consent to their own extinction.

I told him that he could not afford to make a comeback into the
world until he could read the formula that was surely coming with
everyone he had to deal with (of course, with the exception of his previous doctor). Otherwise, he had better stay far away with his beautiful trees, and his little helper, neither of which would talk back and
contradict his beautiful agenda. I have just met this patient, so I have
no more to say for now about what will happen with him. With twenty
or thirty others just like him, the results vary over a wide range. Some
stay far away, and experience less hurt. Some keep trying, and keep
being amazed by the lack of backing they receive. Some finally make
the jump and transcend the dilemma. Before I describe some of these

jumps, I need to finish this first topic of reading the world, and show the second topic of providing interest.

A Case of Integral Calculus in a Bipolar Existence

Reading the world is most difficult when the emotional platform you are standing on is swinging through huge ups and downs of bright hypomania and dark despair. You almost need a theory of relativity to translate your readings. When you are up, you are ready to tackle anything, and so you make sweeping decisions that involve you up to the neck. When you are down, you are hardly able to drag through a day, and so you want to drop everything you agreed to do in your high-flying period. This is the ordinary existential dilemma of so-called bipolar disorder. Psychiatry is convinced it is a periodicity caused by the biochemical tides that respond to seasonal light (SADS) and other impersonal triggers that remain mysterious. I do not doubt the biochemical tides, which are impressive in these patients, but I can pretty well tell when they are going to turn in terms of the patient's dilemma.

My patient complained bitterly of her little existence as a social worker in a small hospital that just plain used her up. When this just about broke her, she would swing into pursuing her big existence—going out West and buying a ranch with her cowboy boyfriend. Almost set to go, she would get sleepless and panicky. Then she would call the plan off, and go back sheepishly to her cramped and bitter quarters. I would tend to sink with her and fly with her, losing my own perspective in the process. I was in collusion with many foolish decisions that could not be sustained. They were either too big or too small. So she was continually reversing herself, driving her boyfriend crazy with indecision, and jeopardizing the good will of her boss. He had taken her back several times, but could not be counted on to do this indefinitely.

After I had gone around this cycle with her for several years, I was finally able to conceptualize the dilemma, quite as the concept of dilemma was coming along for me in other cases. If she decided things in the throes of her little existence, she would have a bleak meaningless prospect. If she decided things on the wings of her big existence, she would fly off the map to destruction. The only decisions that could stand up as halfway reliable lay somewhere in between. They too would be faulty, neither being low-key enough for the dark periods, nor highly keyed enough for the bright periods. However, she might be able to get through.

I told her that her advanced training in mathematics might supply an apt metaphor for her topology or territory. The integration of the slope under the little curve was too cramping, while the integration of the slope under the big curve was too vast to cope with for very long at all. She might last better by a calculus that integrated the average territory. This interested her, even as it appealed to a middling concept of herself. The last time I saw her, she had told the boyfriend she wasn't going West with him, though she loved him, and she had told the boss she would stay on, though she needed more time off to cultivate her garden. I don't expect this outcome to be without unhappiness. Indeed, it will still be too little at times, and too much at other times, but I am guessing she can at least keep it going, and can at least stay out of low and high disasters. Already, she feels less guilty about driving the key people in her life crazy. This makes her a little more secure.

Interest without Collusion

I do not want to go over the familiar ground of the vulnerability of these patients to slights for very long, because the topic has become a truism. I do need to mention it, however, because these patients need to be handled differently from ordinary neurotic patients. How so?

First of all, you need to expect that you will often hurt their feelings, unwittingly. If you aren't expecting this, you will miss the hurt that is passed over rapidly. All you have is a far away patient, who suddenly has no interest in continuing. You need to catch these sudden disappearing acts. Then you go back to what it is you did or said that hurt. Then, you apologize. Often, it can be a little phrase, that seemed derogatory. It came across as a put down.

Secondly, you need to be very careful about any changes in the schedule, or phone calls, or notes. These are laden with meaning, chiefly about the patient's importance. I try to respond promptly with these patients, whereas I can wait a week or two with ordinary patients until the next session. Not so with these patients. They plunge very fast. Yet, as Balint (1968) showed so beautifully, they come back very fast if they are attended to promptly. I often write back brief notes, and take brief telephone calls from them, so they can let me know where they are, and so they know I am with them psychologically. The regression, as Balint argued, is in the service of being understood. I find, as Balint did, that this contact is not over-used and it is not addictive in the sense of leading to increasing demands (of course, it is precisely addictive in cases of the malignant basic fault as described in Chapter 1).

Thirdly, and lastly, the need for responsiveness is further heightened by a terrible history of trauma, as in cases of incest. Not only has the patient been intruded upon, and not only has the patient been abandoned, but the patient has undergone a kind of torture, usually as a small child in the hands of a huge perpetrator. These experiences are so terrifying and overwhelming, that the child dissociates them into compartments in order to go on at all. This is the last defense before having to go psychotic as a recourse to deny the pain. Sometimes there are brief psychotic moments in these patients, when you are getting them to take down their wall. (See Winnicott [1971b] and his case of Mrs. X for a very graphic moment of such madness. See also Gustafson [1986, Chap. 7] for a discussion of how Winnicott handled it so beautifully. Sullivan was very adept at translating madness back into ordinary experience. See Chatelaine [1981, pp. 427–441] for a nice example.)

Routinely, the experiences are too overwhelming to talk about directly. I have to allow for substitute modes of expression. Drawing can be done, so the patient is talking with me as an adult, while drawing as a child. Dreaming is a kind of drawing that alludes to unbearable aspects of the torture with a little bit of disguise. We circle in, and back off, and circle in again, breaking off another piece of what is enormous in itself. Sometimes, the raw terrible events come through overwhelmingly, and the patient becomes absolutely frantic. As Balint (1968) argued, there is no substitute in such terrible passages for the patient to be able to sit closer on my footstool and hold my hand for a few minutes until the horror passes. (In this age of so much misuse of the physician relationship, such a maneuver is fraught with misunderstanding, yet it would also be wrong to act as if the symbolic gesture can be dispensed with. It is certainly not to be utilized in an erotic and malignant basically faulted situation.)

We have already passed over into the realm of long-term psychotherapy when there is this kind of trauma, and where this kind of attending is absolutely necessary. Before I leave the topic of necessary interest, however, I need to bring up the attendant problem of collusion with delusion.

When a patient has been hurt so badly, as in incest, or the equivalent torturing of a child, there is a great tendency for the patient to seek psychic compensation in one grandiose way or another. In other words, the child wants to force back into his own hands what he has lost (Winnicott 1971b). This is seeking gratification on demand, which is tantamount to malignant and addictive regression. A benign basic fault can have such elements, almost surely has such elements, when the experience has been this overwhelming. Thus, there are cases that are both benign and malignant.

For example, the patient may respond well to being understood in sessions, but be quite unwilling to take responsibility for securing herself between sessions. She may inflict very malignant demands upon her husband. (In so-called multiple personality disorders [MPDs], some of the selves are benign, and some are not.) It is best to look for these dangerous tendencies in every case of incest or its equivalent trauma at the outset, so we do not find ourselves down the road in collusion with a delusion about what we can do for them.

Which Is More Dangerous: Treatment or No Treatment?

Regularly, with such patients, we are in the predicament or dilemma in which the patient is going to pieces without help, but will place impossible demands upon us if we take them into psychotherapy. If this dilemma is faced clearly, we can get crucial leverage that may make the difference between getting through and disaster, in or out of therapy.

For example, the patient is crying all the time, and feels terrified. Her remote and egocentric husband is continually failing her with his distance. Since she feels entitled to great interest, she attacks him with a vengeance. This drives him farther away. She is all alone and suicidal, and apt to get worse by the day.

The treatment that discusses her incest is apt to send her into worse tailspins. She is barely able to keep going, anyway. She will have none of hospitals. She has no friends. So treatment looks even more dangerous than lack of treatment. It would have no floor under it, and the doctor would be called upon to save the patient without any way to do it. This is a rather commonplace dilemma with extremely wounded patients.

I outline the dilemma of treatment versus lack of treatment. She is apt to get worse without treatment, but she is apt to get worse faster with treatment. Only if she is prepared to get herself to a safe place when she is taking a nose dive can I take her on. I simply lack the powers to keep from setting off overwhelming experiences and to bring her back from them. Hours or days just have to pass for her to come through. If she cannot agree to such a procedure for a safe place, then I will not start psychotherapy. She can do without treatment, and come to the emergency room as necessary. This proposal stays clear of collusion with the delusion of omnipotent help (Kernberg et al. 1988).

One Session a Month and Jumping to Another Level

I have spent some time on these extreme cases to provide a contrast to more modest cases that have a lovely place in long brief psychotherapy. It is disastrous to confuse the two.

A Case of a High-Flying Man

A patient of mine had big ideas about being a professor, having a great lover, and several other grand ideas of this kind. He came to me when his great love left him. She had gotten an offer at another university to be a professor in her own right. He was crushed.

It turned out that he would become very wounded, like a lost child, when left or when he was not appreciated. He sunk fast, yet he insisted on forcing his way in a very difficult graduate program. He counted on help from several illustrious professors.

He found a new girlfriend, a kind woman, to back him up. She was not as grand as he wanted, but she was good to him. He was inclined to look for something more suitable to his stature. He became disconsolate when he tried to give her up, and could not even do his daily work. Then, the illustrious professors turned out to be less interested than he supposed. They were looking for duplicates of themselves: strange, but true.

I saw him once a month, also, for two years, until he took his jump. He decided that he needed the simple backing of his girlfriend, and he decided that these professors were killing him. In other words, he grasped the divergence of backing and grandiosity. They just didn't go together, as he had long hoped. He could grasp the sounder of the two.

Binswanger and Sound Construction

Binswanger (1963) wrote a very beautiful essay called *Verstiegenheit* ("Extravagance," in English). The German word means to climb too high, as in the Alps, so some search party has to bring you down. Binswanger's metaphor is that we often have to bring patients down from mountains where they do not belong.

Often they are stuck up there like my patient because they are fleeing from a narrow little existence like the one they had as children, with parents who cared for them not at all but only for money as in *Grimm's Tales* (1819). This is very commonplace. The child dreams, romantically, of a quest and of a mate. Indeed, the fairy tales encourage this sort of thing. Thus, there are two constructions of an existence, one pitifully small, and one beautifully bright.

What happens in the long brief psychotherapy (long in duration, brief in number of sessions) is that the patient rocks back and forth between the two pictures of his existence that will not do, neither one. The little existence is reliable, but too dreary. The big existence is exhilarating, but cannot be backed up. Time seems to be necessary to crystallize some third thing of a manageable size, and of sound construction. It really is a third world needing to be created, and worlds do not get born overnight. (Yet they *can* be born in a day. Many of Malan's star cases [Malan et al. 1975] on a ten-year follow-up of a *single visit* are of this kind. Jumps are hard to predict! This contradiction of sudden versus slow timing can probably be understood by mapping that shows slow development of a third thing, slow clarity about the two impossible things, and a sudden discontinuity when all of this crystallizes.) It is a third world needing to be created between the divergence of sound backing and big scope. It takes a lot of grief to see that these two are not the same, after all. Then the jump comes.

3

Malignant Couples

A doctor with a patient in the malignant basic fault is a malignant couple, of the particular kind we could call a malignant psychotherapeutic couple. The two are a malignant couple because the patient will insist on gratification in an ever angrier spiral. The doctor is going to be ferociously at fault, whether he gives nothing or he gives a lot. If he says no, he is depriving. If he says yes, he hooks the patient to a higher dose of gratification.

The doctor himself becomes malignant when he tries to make this impossible couple work out (Main 1957). If he is flattered into trying, he will become exhausted by rendering his endless, increasing services. If he tries, then, to pull up short, he is apt to be revengeful on the patient for not getting better. His zeal is apt to result in punishing the patient with heroic intrusive measures, like psychosurgery, ECT (electroconvulsive therapy), or with abandonment, for not responding properly to his extraordinary efforts.

A Case of a Savior Husband with a Fallen Wife

Now imagine such a couple as this living together! The husband likes to save deserving women (Freud 1910). This is his vanity, his sexual excitement, his character as a savior. Like all characters, this myth of himself is a machine for the suppression of seeing the effects of his dilemma over time. While at first his wounded beloved is responsive, and he becomes hooked on saving her, very soon her demands begin to exhaust him. Her rage now surfaces as he falters in repairing the queen. He becomes very disappointed at her lack of appreciation. He had imagined she would be different from his mother. Actually, she is different from his mother, who was more of a shut-in wounded. This wife gallivants. She'll hook a lover wherever she can turn one up. So, now, the husband has got to try to control her as well.

Dicks's Hypotheses as a Single Malignant Dilemma

This machinery works with relentless precision, according to three mechanisms outlined by Henry Dicks (1967), to wit:

> *Hypothesis* (1). Many tensions and misunderstandings between partners seem to result from the disappointment which one or both of them feel and resent, when the other fails to play the role of spouse after the manner of a preconceived model or figure in their fantasy world. [p. 50]

In the light of this case Hypothesis (1) receives a special rider which looks almost like an inversion: Tensions between marital partners can result from the disappointment that the partner, after all, plays the marital role like the frustrating parent figure, similarity to whom was denied during courtship. This often collusive discovery leads to modification of the subject's own role behaviour in the direction of regression toward more childish responses to the partner. (1A) [p. 62]

> *Hypothesis* (2). Subjects may persecute in their spouses tendencies which originally caused attraction, the partner having been unconsciously perceived as a symbol of "lost" because repressed aspects of the subject's own personality. [p. 63]

Thus, the savior husband is disappointed by the failure of the fallen wife to respond (Hypothesis 1). He is also disappointed because this is just like his pathetic mother (Hypothesis 1 A), rather than the exciting courtesan he pursued. Finally, he persecutes her for her very licentious-ness that caused the attraction, which was a lost (shadow) aspect of his own personality (Hypothesis 2). He ends up depressed, withdrawn, bitter in the good little house of his existence like he had with his mother. The big existence, which enlarges his own personality by bring-ing in his own repressed license, collapses.

Naturally, there is another side to this picture, which is the mir-ror opposite of the three relentless mechanisms working in the fallen wife. Her hopes for a big existence are crushed, similarly, by the falter-ing devotion of the savior husband, who turns out to lack commitment to her (Hypothesis 1), which is, after all, quite like her father, who glit-tered but lacked any depth (Hypothesis 1A). Finally, in her rage she attacks his mildness (which is different from her father's cruelty), driv-ing it away, and even driving him to lapse into the very cruelty of her father (Hypothesis 2).

Of course, it is an impossible couple to repair. The situation got worse and worse. There were flare-ups that nearly exploded the house, when they tried connecting over their miracle. Then there were dead periods that were very desolate, when they gave up. Neither was tenable.

My job with the husband was simply to indicate the necessary suffering. Either way, it was impossible. After a series of terrible ex-periments trying again and after a series of desolate months he became convinced in my school of suffering (Freud 1909) that he lost no mat-ter which way he went with her. Basically, he got more interested in his job, which gave him a little more scope, on a stage that was defen-sible, given his degree of competence in his profession.

Levi-Strauss's Myths—Three Machines for the Suppression of Time

I will distinguish the machinery of malignant couples by the different myths that drive them. In "Dicks's Dilemma," the small existence put up with in childhood is going to be fulfilled by the ideal, which will bring into existence whatever was previously excluded, as in the say-ing: "Ships at a distance have every man's wish on board" (Hurston 1937, p. 1). This ideal, which drives the coupling (with the missing half, as in Plato's *Symposium*), turns out to be a myth precisely as defined by Levi-Strauss. There are a number of steps to his demonstration ex-plained most lucidly by Leach (1970, Chap. 4). The reader will probably be familiar with myth defined as a "sacred tale" (p. 58). Levi-Strauss shows that the innumerable variations in which a sacred tale exists turn out to be a secret code: "to exhibit publicly, though in disguise, ordinarily unconscious paradoxes of this kind" (p. 79), for example, "if society is to go on, daughters must be disloyal to their parents and sons destroy (replace) their fathers" (p. 88).

Thus, loyalty and disloyalty diverge in these "irresolvable unwelcome contradictions" that we cannot bear to look at directly. The myth proposes to solve them, when they are in fact insoluble. Some myths cover up the contradiction, while some let it through more baldly as a story about other people (not us). Thus, the Oedipus story is bald, showing that undervaluing the blood line is a disaster (killing the father), while overvaluing the blood line is also a disaster (insisting on the truth coming out). More precisely, it is tragic to oppose the clan, or to uphold the clan. (Essentially, all dilemmas have this structure: it is punishable to oppose the group [anti-group horn] and it is entropic to uphold the group [pro-group horn]. See the conclusion to Chapter 18, "The Group Animal.")

Thus, the sentimental myths propose to solve the contradiction of being in the clan versus being out of the clan, by making it all come out happily ever after: you marry out (exogenously), and get all the virtues missing from your own clan (living endogamously). The trouble is that the spouse is not the perfect completion after all, turns out to be like the old familiar partner, and is punished anyway for any departures that are truly different from business as usual. In other words, the sentimental myth is destroyed by the machinery of "Dicks's Dilemma." Nevertheless, the coupling has been effected, and offspring often follow. So the clans are perpetuated, at the expense of the pair that enacts the myth. They are its victims. As Whitaker (personal communication) liked to say: "Marriage is when families exchange hostages."

So far, I have been stating what all coupling has in common. The differences come from different pictures of the perfect completion. I distinguish three kinds or classes: devoted, stable, and directive.

The Devoted Spouse as Perfect Completion

This used to be the universal ideal of the wife as helpmate to the power quest of the husband. She is to supply the perfect kindness, warmth, and excitement, to supplement his ferocity, coldness, and patience in the hunt. Now, they have the complete range of virtues, united.

How do these opposed terms actually get on? Well, they contradict each other. She fails to keep the household on his terms. He fails to be a companion to her at all. How could it be otherwise? The virtues *repel* each other in daily life, if they are drawn together in the dream of perfect completion that arranges their coupling.

The Clan Machine for Shaping Up the Wife

So soon as the rosy consummation is fulfilled, the husband will find the wife faulty, and grind her into the dust for it. He will do this, unwittingly, in the service of the machinery that must bring the exogamous virtues into line with the household economics that are the dominant mechanism.

I could cite a hundred different variations, but they all amount to the same cruel thing. Let us say the husband is English and proper, and marries a South American woman for her warmth. You know where the crunch will come. She will be attacked for examples of her laxity, like getting up late, being too open with the neighbors, and having sloppy parents. She is apt to doubt herself to pieces. Now it is her turn to decimate him, if she can muster the strength, for his cold stiffness, which could never be attractive! Whether the marriage survives this cruel period (in this sense, there are cruel, malignant periods in a marriage and more kind, benign periods, rightly breaking up a rigid distinction between malignant and benign types) depends upon whether there is anything that remains in common of value that has not been done in.

What do I do consulting with her? Let's suppose she still likes and respects her husband, but it is now seven years later and she is still resentful, mean to him, and guilty of weakening him. He is not his former self, but is depressed.

She comes to me puzzled about her distance from him and about her resentment, which will not let up. She knows this isolates her further from him, and drives him further down. Yet, she can't relent. Interestingly, she is in the same stance with me for the first two sessions of distance *en garde*, while she cries her heart out at home. When I pose this as interesting, I find that she is tremendously suggestible when close, going up with interest, and going down with criticism. This is how she was nearly destroyed by her husband's putting her in line. The resentment works to keep him at arm's length, where he cannot send her down again.

I can give to her her dilemma. The distancing operation is slowly ruinous, while nearness can only be resumed if she is ready for the dire effects of his suggestions on her suggestibility. I do not think malignant coupling is fatal to the couple in every case. This couple may have enough friendship to pull through, when they have an adequate map of their territory, pointing to what has been overlooked with disastrous effects. This couple reached a benign later phase, but, perhaps, too late to repair the wounding.

The Stable Spouse as Perfect Completion

When the child has experienced dreadful chaos, she will often dream of perfect completion as a kind of stable father figure, or, conversely, he will dream of perfect completion as a kind of stable mother figure. Often, the stable spouse is all stability, to the exclusion of most other virtues, like an ice professor in a Bergman film, or an ice queen in Grimm's *Tales* (1819). So, the virtue sought exogamously is gotten, but it turns out to exclude everything else. It stays around, forgoes chaos in affairs, forgoes intrusion by staying in its ice world. It is a dreadful dream come perversely true. The chill gradually finishes off the couple like an advancing glacier.

The Sacred and Profane Love Machine

She was married to a regular guy for about twenty-five years and they sent off three sons into the world. He painted the outside of the house, listening to football games, and then he painted the inside of the house, listening to basketball games, and so forth. Her only clue that anything was seriously wrong was that he gradually drank more and more until he was often drunk in the daytime.

He did his sacred duty, but he had a shadow side that was beginning to seep out with the disinhibition of drink. Actually, he had had a mistress for ten years, before he broke out with it and smashed up the marriage suddenly, like wrecking a car beyond repair. The sacred love machine had outlived its day, and the profane love machine was now having its day, publicly.

We have a little epidemic of these cases in Madison among 40- to 50-year-old men. Evidently they are well known elsewhere, as in Iris Murdoch's (1974) novel, *The Sacred and The Profane Love Machine*.

Usually, they get to me too late to alter the fate of the couple. My job is to help the wife do what she can with the pieces.

Ordinarily, she has a grave dilemma. Staying with the husband when that is even possible is very toxic because of the need to hold back so much bitterness. Going is often worse because of the prospect of an unending solo existence, with half or less of the income. Often, both hells are made nearly intolerable when they throw her back into child-hood grief of the same kind. As a child, she also had to hold back rage, and she was also unendingly alone. So, the dilemma is near tragic, if not altogether tragic. The difference is that I may help her to bear it, to let out the feeling, and to see that suffering is great either way, and, therefore, not her fault. This externalization of her fate relieves a tre-mendous amount of guilt. She is secretly grandiose in believing she could have brought her icy husband around. So, she has a kind of existential choosing to do, which has its own dignity and relief, as in Figure 3-1. The dilemma for the wife is put unforgettably by Robert Frost (1923) in "Fire and Ice": the fire of toxic rage, versus the ice of perpetual isolation.

A Case of Custard for Comfort

The wife had a long series of dreams about this dilemma that were extremely painful. I could say simply that they were a way of get-ting to the pain with me, so she would not be locked in ice. A typi-cal dream in her series was as follows: She is on a scale, which is descending, in jerks, while she is eating custard. The pointer, which is over her husband's head, points to her ever-increasing weight. She cannot stop eating. She called this her custard hell. It aptly pictures her inability to stop eating for comfort. While she consciously thinks she can do without comfort, she unconsciously knows she is driven to take it in to allay her pain.

A turn in this hell came when I got her to explain her vocabu-lary of custard. She had taken it from her uncle, who had a cache for his ulcer. It was the only nice thing she had, and she kept steal-ing it. Punishment in the form of beatings could not stop her! (See Winnicott [1976], especially the Case of Mrs. X, and my discussion [Gustafson 1986, Chap. 7].) I responded that this was a terrific sign of her spirit as a child that saved her from despair. It was still very much with her. She was extremely pleased that I found her out, and

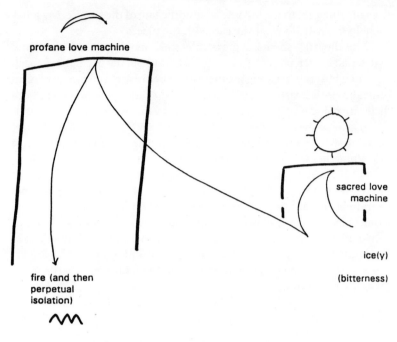

Figure 3–1. The Sacred and Profane Love Machine.

relieved that I found her badness good. She went from looking like a girl half dead to a powerful woman with much light in her face. "So, you mean," she said, "I still need to take something for myself?" I nodded, "Look at the difference in you when we get to this." It was a revival. Yet it is not a fairy tale. For her, taking risks fire, just as with her uncle. Just as her cooling herself out with custard risks ice. A previous dream was of her own funeral, in which she kills herself with salt (a preservative).

The Director Spouse as Perfect Completion

A lost child often seeks direction, as from an advisor, a mentor, or a spiritual guide. Her myth is of perfect completion by a father superior. There are innumerable variations, from "Father Knows Best," to Henry Higgins, to the master therapists who are paraded everywhere as all-knowing directors. Again, the missing direction is swallowed in the exogamous coupling.

A Case of the Director Silencing Machine

One patient of mine was a frantic, disorganized woman with two frantic, disorganized daughters from a previous marriage. She was subsequently discovered by her second husband, who had plenty of ideas of how her life could be rectified. He took charge of her, which was exciting for him, and a relief for her.

Of course, once the coupling was arranged, all hell broke loose. He began to show the extent of the pettiness to which he could go to have the household run correctly. This was a great disappointment to her, for she had fallen back into the clutches of her own cruel father. Rebelling from her father had been the impetus to create the chaos that she had become an expert in living in. Now, she set her daughters loose on this new husband, in order to drive him crazy, and they did: coming home at three in the morning, leaving their dirty underwear in his bathroom, and so on.

For a while, I saw them together, but this was a fiasco. Out of his chaotic childhood, he was driven like Citizen Kane to rule his world. This meant depositing his ideas in her, and there they were supposed to come to fruition. Freire (1970) calls this the banking method of education. The object or student is just supposed to swallow the deposits of the "director culture." This makes the student disappear into a "culture of silence," for she no longer exists except as a receptacle.

If she somehow manages to rebel by finding her own voice, she will be put down with violence. (See Gramsci [1973] for a cogent description of this hegemonic strategy of rule. You rule with words, with tanks waiting in the wings. See Dürrenmatt [1962] for a savage farce, in which three physicists in turn kill the nurses who are in love with them.) Of course, I naively invited her to voice her situation. The more she did, the more despotic he got. Finally, they broke off the marital therapy. They had to. It was getting violent.

I have since corrected what I attempt with "The Director Silencing Machine." Now, I pose the dilemma before I am silenced. This has a chance of catching the attention of the director, who is the key player in the game. I tell him that I do not think he can stop suppressing his wife. This is too bad. Suppressed, she will disappear behind her wall into a culture of silence. Then he will have no company and will feel desolate. Yet, if he tolerates her voice, it will shake him. He has a terrible dilemma. Sometimes, I find he is stubborn enough to struggle with it or frightened enough of being left altogether alone; sometimes not. That is his decision, once I have posed his dilemma accurately. It is a very difficult liberation.

The Three Malignant Machines as One Machine for the Suppression of Time

A myth is a sacred tale. Those who follow it are an army that conquers territory with its formula under its sacred banner, such as "progress is our most important product." That, of course, was the myth of General Electric, promulgated on General Electric Theater every week by Ronald Reagan in the 1950s. Of course, the myth is a machine that suppresses its shadow truth. This shadow is about the *destruction* by progress. Progress is actually a very tricky dilemma, for it is often difficult to say when it is more helpful and when it is more harmful. It is a secular religion. This is a contradiction in terms, but a suppressed dilemma is a contradiction in terms that is kept covert. It is secular in content, but sacred in form. You have to follow it, religiously, or you are out.

This positivistic religion gathered shape in the late nineteenth century, proposed by Comte (1830) and many others. Now, it is taking over the world, because of its technological powers. It runs governments, communications, science, art, publishing, athletics, and just about everything. Its opposition is relatively feeble, and has to take to remote Buddhist temples in the hills of Japan to hear its own voice (Snyder 1990), or resort to throwbacks to progress like fundamentalism in all its forms: Christian, Muslim, Romantic, and so forth.

The formula of the positivistic religion is that *more is better*: more data, more money, more GNP, more research, more students, more products, more housing, more jobs, etc. If you add to the numbers, you are in. If you don't, you are out (see Gustafson 1995, Chap. 4, on increase packs).

Naturally, families are drawn into replicating the myth, for they supply its soldiers. The economy of the family becomes a sacred object. (Of course, the classic example is *Death of a Salesman* [Miller 1950], but Ibsen preceded him in *Hedda Gabler* [1890].) Christmas letters become a list of the family's GNP of accomplishments by every member. Those who have nothing to report are glossed over. The shame is suppressed:

> What we really have in this city are able people, competent people, who as they rise in the world have more and more complicated professional lives. Quite logically, that eats them up, and the monstrous residue that is left behind is beyond emotion, but with an appetite for it, and a terrible and terrified longing and unsuitability for it. . . . the cold ambition is, I repeat, unlivable. [Brodkey 1994, p. 77]

The mythical machinery of positivism has to suppress knowledge of the drift of this emptiness into numbers. The three machines I distinguished for this suppression are just increasing degrees of violence. The "Clan Machine for Shaping Up the Wife" merely dresses her down to size. The "Sacred and Profane Love Machine" betrays her to someone else. The "Director Silencing Machine" cuts out her tongue. "The Marguerite of the future could alone decide whether she were better off than the Marguerite of the past: whether she would rather be a victim to a man, a church or a machine" (Adams 1881, p. 447).

If the reader interested in gay couples has not given up already, let me say that they operate when they are malicious just like the couples outlined above (an early report is Sullivan's [1956, pp. 243–246], which is tragi-comic). If the reader interested in female dominance in couples has not given up, let me say that they operate perfectly well with women in charge instead of men. The machines are but machines for the suppression of time (its drift, its divergence, its shadow). This is the definition of myth (Levi-Strauss, in Leach 1970, Chap. 7).

Myths instill conformity, but they are also instruments of transcendence (Campbell 1949) (Peter Miller, personal communication). This is the subject of our next chapter.

4

Benign Couples

Relatively benign couples are *less* violent. They have less need to sacrifice, say, the wife to the husband, or vice versa. This means that negotiation is viable. There can be a give and take on both sides. One might ask why the give and take is not adjusted naturally in the couple, without calling in outside help. Things can get pretty far out of whack, for one or both parties, without being addressed. If addressed, there can seem little room to compromise.

My reply is that coupling is thoroughly driven by myth, and myth converges everything to come out right. "Myths think themselves out in men" (Leach 1970, p. 53). By this, Levi-Strauss means that men and women are vehicles for myths, unwittingly. The polarities that are played out within us are things like in-group and out-group, right and wrong, tasteful and disgusting, cooked and raw. In the narrative of the myth, the hero and heroine come out beautifully (right).

The narrative both alludes to impossible oppositions that diverge in the course of time, like in-group and out-group, and converges them in the story line. Since couples mostly couple along the lines of the mythical story, they terribly want to believe in its promise and desperately want to overlook the actual divergence between their struggle and the myth (ideal). This leads to selective inattention to their actual dilemmas. They can hardly be discussed, or negotiated, if they are not admitted to exist.

The Myths of Coupling

What are the myths of coupling? Bion (1959) calls them basic assumptions. He distinguishes them by the instinct that fuses them. Instincts have a way of melting down oppositions in their heated fantastic furnaces. Thus, sexuality is a pairing of opposites that become one as if their differences now mean nothing. Bion calls this *basic assumption pairing* (baP), which assumes or presumes that the couple serves to create some third thing like a great idea or a child. This is the main myth of couples.

Yet it is obvious that other couples combine in the sway of dependency, or *basic assumption dependency* (baD), which assumes that everything will be taken care of in their shared longing to be looked after. Still others combine in the fire of fight, or *basic assumption fight-flight* (baF), which assumes that they only need to fight their shared enemy for everything to come out perfectly. By their shared enemy I mean their parents, or the system, or Western Culture, etc. These couples often take flight elsewhere for their ceremony.

Of course, all three instincts, with their heated assumptions, can work together in the most delirious of marriages. The couple come from opposite ends of the earth to marry, say, north and south, and have so much in common that they will take care of each other perfectly, and at the same time, they battle the establishment they both hate with a fury. This is an excellent myth for second marriages, which are going far afield to correct the narrowness of first marriages. They have tremendous energy, from all three instinctual sources. This is enough to dissolve the entire world, as in *Antony and Cleopatra* (Shakespeare 1607). Actually, such coupling hides its own demise only from the couple, who are in its tremendous delirium. (The inflation of claiming everything proves indefensible, as Caesar and Pompey, the two rivals of the triumvirate with Antony, are driven to overturn the couple of Antony and Cleopatra.)

Between the simple pairing assumption (baP) that unites the football player and the cheerleader who have nothing else in common, and the extravagance of sex, dependency, and war (baP, baD, baF) of Antony and Cleopatra lies any degree of complexities of coupling. A myth is a set of polarities, and the number of polarities that are resolved in the narrative of the hero and heroine varies with the culture and with the particular couple.

Probably, all coupling myths have *some* articulation of sexual, dependency, and fight assumptions. If the sexual pairing is most developed as romance, there is some latent understanding of depending upon each other to bring up children, and there is some latent understanding of how they will conduct the fight to earn a living, jointly. Conversely, an emphasis on mutual dependency will have latent understanding about sex (perhaps to have very little) and about the fight for money (perhaps to have very much). Dicks (1967) believed that concurrence on all three of these chief subjects creates the steadiest marriages, and Wamboldt and Wolin (1988) recently demonstrated empirically that agreement about each other's parents in the period of engagement had a very sound effect on the marriage lasting. Such agreements integrate all three instinctual modes, for the couple agrees to depend on the parents in some ways, fight them in other ways, and stay apart from them to make love. See "The Corset" (Connell 1945) for the same success worked out in terms of the neighbors.

Perversity and Dilemma

In any event, the coupling myth makes all of these matters come out right, and is thus a machine for the suppression of time. In very little time, however, the concurrence begins to come apart. Any third thing, person, idea, pleasure, interest is perverse when it is desirable for one partner while at the same time harmful for the other. In time, these perverse thirds (Gustafson 1992, Chap. 8, Haley 1966) crystallize out as gravel or as mountains in the path of the mythical machinery that thrives on mutual thirds that satisfy both partners at once. The machinery can come to a halt.

Naturally, some perverse thirds are more massive like mountains and some are annoying like gravel. In general, the instinctual needs are loaded. There is dangerous and explosive trouble when sex, dependency, or the fight to get a shared living stop being mutual pleasures. Indeed, all three instinctual situations drift in time to become perverse. When vital interests are so opposed, the couple is in a dilemma. This dilemma will diverge, unless it is faced, and handled. Of course, the myth suppresses this attention and, thus, the repairing work. I will now take the three great divisive instincts in order of sex, householding (dependency), and careers (fight).

Sexual Dilemmas

Sexual combination seems to be triggered as an innate releasing mechanism (IRM) by sign-stimuli in herring gulls or in dogs, Certainly, this is familiar in human beings, who are set off by certain looks, or gestures, or colors, which signify a releasing opportunity. Yet there is something about symbolism as well as signs.

While authors as different on the subject as Freud and Jung will point to different symbolisms, all seem to suggest that the symbolism of making love is a curious potion of being the same and being different. If not enough the same, there is no easing in. If too much the same, there is little thrill. So, sex is a kind of cooking in which the play teeters between these dangers. The ingredients vary widely. Thus, Freud emphasized a potion of the good man saving the bad woman. Jung proposed something more like Shakespeare's romances, where the object becomes the missing complement. Thus, Desdemona is purity to the rough Othello (1604). Perhaps, Freud's bourgeois men seek the bad woman, also as a complement, to free them from their straightjackets. Yet, the complement can go too far, and repulse. This is the symbolic dilemma in sexual adventures. The word concoction is apt, I think, because it catches the transitory triumph of sexual climax, which tails off into the prosaic afterwards. It comes from the Latin *concoquere*, which means to boil together. So the term has traditionally male and female allusions, to the cock and to the cook. They make heat, with pleasure.

Sexual Failures in Brief Psychotherapy

The subject of sexual failures is a huge subject that bears directly upon the likelihood of coupling. It is a subject that comes up looking for brief psychotherapy. It encompasses everything from impotence to sexual perversion to frustration in mate seeking. While I cannot digress here to write a book on this subject, I can suggest an outline of what I find regularly when I look into these sexual complaints.

Referring to the dilemma of sexual union, I can point to several places that are apt to go wrong. Some cannot get out of the prosaic compartment. They complain of dullness, impotence, and the inability to arouse interest in prospective partners. In general, they are stuck because they practice being prosaic, which is nice and far away from other people, while they shun what is arousing, which is terribly close to other people.

There are three lovely cases of such inhibition in one of my previous books (Gustafson 1992, Chap. 2), which happened to be told as problems in the subjective world seen in dreams. In "A Case of Something Wild," the subject is stuck in a Victorian house. In "The Case of the Orange Seaplane," the subject is stuck at an "average, basic, regulation picnic." In "The Case of a Man in His Fortress," the subject is stuck in an unassailable fortress of being fat, which he represents as the famous fortress in South America called Cartagena. All three of these subjects dread arousal because of the dangers of openness into which the subject is thrown. The reader can refer to all three, but I will retell the briefest, which will serve as a paradigm.

The Case of the Orange Seaplane

The patient was a woman complaining of dull, restricted living and the lack of a man. In her tenth session she presented a dream in which she was on the ground and heard a plane overhead. The CB radio said it was in trouble. It crashed immediately. She felt glad she was not in the plane. To make a long analysis of the dream much more to the present point, it turned out that the plane was an orange seaplane like she had once seen as a child at a lake in northern Wisconsin. This meant a glamorous pilot taking her somewhere, and had been the dominant metaphor of her erotic passages. Yet the orange seaplane falls like rain, which is her grief perpetually of being let down by them. This was the substance of a series of adventures with men.

I was able to look at this neglected subject of men in orange seaplanes to find what she amazingly overlooked in all of them. She could not tell if they had orange seaplanes that were put together badly, so-so, or well! She assumed they were sound, and they crashed. Indeed, she was on the verge of trusting another such pilot with all of her money when we looked at the warning of the dream together. The project with the new pilot was going to save her from dullness at the average, dull, regulation picnic, only to fall like rain. From our work, she declined going for the next ride. It is only possible for this woman to allow herself to be aroused when she can stop overlooking the construction of the vehicles that will transport her (see, in Figure 4–1 the hole in her selective inattention pointed to by the finger).

Some patients can look at this hole in their selective inattention in arousal, and some cannot bear to do this. Why not? This brings up the dilemma of sexual union. Some patients are full of arousal, but this arousal is so extravagant in its claims that no one less than a god or goddess could possibly play the partner. While not prepossessing themselves, they yet presume a double for themselves that is perfectly gratifying. I have had many patients who are tremendously malignant in this insistence. They go through two phases. The first is the invention of his erotic double and placing it over a particular object like a superimposed photograph. The second is his outrage at the particular ob-

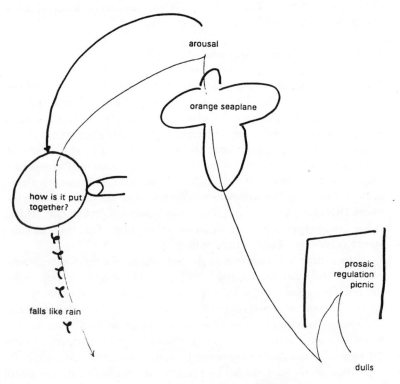

Figure 4–1. The Case of the Orange Seaplane.

ject being found out to be much poorer than the invention. Now the particular object is punished, often with considerable cruelty. Sometimes, the inventor attacks himself, as well, and ends up in our emergency room with a suicide attempt. The two phases are illustrated in Figure 4–2. It is not only our poor borderline patients who live this cycle, and fall regularly into their malignant basic faults of hell. In Shakespeare's (Hughes 1992) plays, the princes like Hamlet do it as well and ruin their Ophelias, and the queens of hell, like Lady Macbeth, finish off their husbands. All it takes is an invention out of line with the object, and the punishment will surely come. Some patients have such extravagant concoctions that they can never find anyone to fit them. Some just mope about their paltry lives complaining of their stupid husbands. They know very well that their conception is not of this earth, so the husbands just get it in the ear in and out of season. It is surely miserable living with a Queen of Hell, or a Prince of Hell.

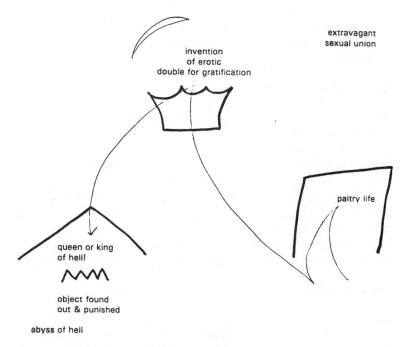

Figure 4–2. Extravagant Sexual Union.

The routine problem in coupling is the distance from the extravagant conception to the poor object. (See Figure 4–2 again.) If love selectively inattends to this fall with its hot eye on the mythical convergence of all virtues in the goddess of complete being (Hughes 1992), the unconscious will sight the divergence with its compensatory cold eye and even in advance of the foolish coupling.

A Case of Being Hot to Mate

A 20-year-old woman was seeing me about her anxieties to settle down. Because of her religious beliefs, she had never made love before. She had a dream in which she had nothing on but her panties, and a football player she knew had nothing on but his underpants. She took hers off and his, but then he stopped. . . . Because she is an intellectual woman and he not at all, she had nothing whatever to say to this man, but discovers herself in the dream placing herself entirely in his hands. This woke her up to the power of her urge for sex. Sex was one power, and good company was a second power, and the two might diverge wildly. I told her that she was lucky to be so clear about this dilemma, for many her age are muddled by the myth that the two are one.

Householding Dilemmas

The second great instinct that drives coupling is dependency. The myth is "and they lived happily ever after." The trouble is that everything being taken care of is extremely dull and dispiriting. As Jenny the Dog says in *Higglety Pigglety Pop!* (Sendak 1967) as she runs away from home: "I am discontented . . . I want something I do not have. There must be something more to life than having everything" (p. 4). Yet it is good to have a home. Herein lies the dilemma of what Gandhi called householding. It is good to have a home, and it is good to be free of home. While Jenny's story is a melodrama of coming through, the very same dilemma can be highly tragic, as in *Anna Karenina* (Tolstoy 1875).

The Tragic Householding Dilemma: Anna Karenina

Tolstoy opens with a comic and pedestrian version of a small soul named Stiva Oblonsky, Anna's brother. He feels trapped by the endless drudgery of his large household in which his wife, Dolly, is sinking and wearing out at double his rate. Of course, that is because she carries the entire burden. Smart Stiva will have his childish pleasures, especially dining on things like caviar and mistresses. Ironically, Anna comes to get him back in line, and to comfort Dolly's anguish at her discovery of Stiva's latest betrayal.

In a single line, Tolstoy shows his grasp on Stiva as a prisoner of his own pleasures: "Matthew (the servant) blew some invisible speck off the shirt which he held ready gathered up like a horse's collar, and with evident pleasure invested with it his master's carefully tended body" (p. 5). Stiva is but a stud of society. While he appears to fly free of home, he is a horse who is completely dependent on his stable for sustenance. He slips back in, shamefaced, but really shameless.

The irony is that Anna is in the same fix, in reverse, in that she is strapped to the repulsive Karenin. Again, Tolstoy shows the entire problem in a physical detail, which is what Anna first notices when she returns from Stiva and Dolly's household in Moscow to her home in Petersburg. The first face she sights getting out of the train is her husband's face:

> "Great heavens! What has happened to his ears?" she thought, gazing at his cold and commanding figure, and especially at the gristly ears which now so struck her, pressing as they did against the rim of his hat. When he saw her, he came toward her with his customary ironical smile and looked straight at her with his large tired eyes. An unpleasant feeling weighed on her heart when she felt his fixed and weary gaze, as if she had expected to find him different. She was particularly struck by the feeling of dissatisfaction with herself which she experienced in meeting him. It was that ordinary well-known feeling, as if she were dissembling, which she experienced in regard to her husband; but formerly she had not noticed it, while now she was clearly and painfully conscious of it. [p. 95]

Here is Anna's repulsion to the bed she has made with Karenin who is so reputable. She has managed to overlook (by selective inattention) her repulsion, which now sticks out in his gristly ears! The detail is telling, for Karenin is all ears for his advancement in the bureaucracy, like the famous Nose of Gogol (1836), which was all nose for advancement as well, so it cut loose and ran about Petersburg on its own steam!

The myth of comfort in householding correctly breaks down, when its selective inattention can no longer suppress the shadow of repulsion. Now, Anna breaks out like a horse with her lover, the horseman Vronsky. Tolstoy prefigures her fate in the ride of Vronsky on the most beautiful horse, Frou-Frou:

> She leapt the ditch as if she did not notice it, seeming to fly across it like a bird. But at that very moment Vronsky, to his horror, felt that something terrible had happened. He himself, without knowing it, had made the unpardonable mistake of dropping back in the saddle and pulling up her head . . . Owing to Vronsky's awkward movement she had dropped her hind legs and broken her back. [p. 182]

So it will be with Anna, whose spirit is broken by Vronsky and who dies throwing herself in front of a train. Anna's tragedy is the extreme one, while Stiva's is the trivial one, but they occur, Tolstoy shows us, as sister's and brother's on the same terrain or topology. This terrain or topology is the householding dilemma that Jung outlined so accurately in his essay on "Marriage as a Psychological Relationship" (1925) in which one partner needs a smaller domain, while the other needs a larger domain.

For the wide-ranging of the pair, the little domain is stifling. For the stay-at-home, the big domain is frightening. So, if they stay in the little domain, one is stifled, one content, while if they range in the big domain, one is free and the other very insecure. So either range is perverse for one of the pair. This is Jung's "Marital Dilemma," as illustrated in Figure 4–3.

The Standard Wisconsin Marriage of Karenin and Dolly and Its Routine Householding Dilemma

Usually, Dolly the worrier is not married to Stiva the epicurean, nor is Karenin the bureaucrat married to Anna of great longing. Ordinarily, Dolly worries to a husband like Karenin who cannot bear listening to her fret. Karenin putters with his important papers to his wife Dolly who cannot wait for him to go back to his office. Indeed, I saw three such couples the day before writing this passage.

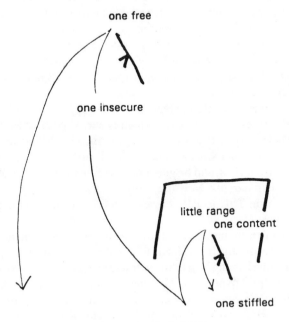

Figure 4–3. Jung's Marital Dilemma.

One of the three was presented to me by a resident, and the other two were virtually the same dilemma. All were miserable, and could not grasp why. The husband complained to the resident that he could not stand his wife. All she did was complain to him about her boss. He had two bad options. His inclination was to suggest solutions, such as, "Why not talk to the boss?" This option annoyed his wife, because she only wanted the comfort of sharing her suffering. If he went along with this, he felt filled up with her troubles, helplessly. He became angry, and then withdrew into having six beers.

In his six beers, he could not get out of his mind the image of how fat she had become as she sat and complained. He felt like quitting the marriage. Well, "Why not?" the resident asked. Because she was a partner, after all, and he found being alone even worse.

The resident now advised him that he had an alcohol dependency and sent him for evaluation. The man said he wasn't coming back. Now the resident was asking me what had gone wrong with his help.

As expected, the man's mother was a fat and pathetic lady, and the man's father was a get up and go hunter, so the man was in the very fix of his parents. In Wisconsin, we have these marriages repeating themselves through so many generations that it is impossible to say when they began, or when they will end.

Of course, the wife's perspective is the opposite. For her, she is being failed in getting company, which is why she has to eat for comfort. She is saddled with a useless companion, who disappears into his beers, or annoys her with advice she has heard too many times. She finally gets hysterical, and he goes crazy with really being helpless, and puts her down harshly. Now they both feel like quitting the marriage, for it is hellish. This usually passes, and they resume being partners who are unsatisfactory.

What can be improved? It did not help to recommend alcohol evaluation to the husband, for it is was like his father telling him to shape up while leaving him in the helpless lurch with his mother. I find it is more helpful to pose the dilemma back to such a husband. He prefers having a partner to being all alone, but he is apt to be downed by his wife dragging him into a mire. He imagines a better wife, who briskly takes care of business. He is combining two of his favorite virtues, having a partner and having a vigorous helpmate like himself, which do not go together. It is an excellent idea (myth), but it denies his actual dilemma. Now what would he like to do?

A similar man who posed a similar dilemma later in the day decided he did not want to get on thin ice with his Helga's worries, but he would be willing to scheme with her about their curling team (thicker ice). She could get something more of a presence, without his feeling too helpless.

A similar woman was frantic about her husband's tirade when she became hysterical, amazed at how mean he was to her. I noted it was only the four hundredth episode, always set off by her getting frantic, and alarming him. Of course, she had gotten frantic, because *she* was feeling helpless in getting him to share *anything*. She, naturally, concludes that she can get nothing, or will get put down if she tries something. I disagreed. She had a better chance asking him to do something for her that did not make him feel helpless. He was actually anxious to give her something, especially to make up for this last fiasco. If she used a calm and matter-of-fact tone to suggest a discrete option that he was good at, he'd do it and therefore relieve his guilt!

Work Dilemmas

Every family is in a fight for its economic sustenance. For most families, this is an endless and dreary war (Terkel 1972) that turns the household into a bunker. The myth (baF) is that the beleaguered battler retreats there to get whatever he needs to go back refreshed to the fight. Since the soldier is sacrificing himself for his family, the family will be grateful and listen to his reports of these far off battles, and congratulate him on his victories, and meet his every need.

The Lomans in the 1990s

This was Willy Loman's (Miller 1950) expectation of his family. The great guy returns home to be celebrated. Indeed, he returns home quite the same forty years later, from selling, coaching, or shuffling papers. He expects to have his way on his home territory, as he has had to comply on the territory of the corporation. God help the passing dog who defiles his lawn!

A couple of things have changed on him in these forty years. You can see it in reports from Japan:

> Your life probably follows the conventional path. You go to elementary school in your hometown, learn the lists of historical figures, memorize your English words. You study hard after class so that you can get into the right high school, and then the right college. After spending four pointless years in college, you join a corporation. If you are a man, you marry in your late twenties and have a kid the next year. You get promoted or transferred a few times, maybe even become a manager . . . Then you die . . . What is the point of life? [Tsurumi 1994, p.20]

In brief, the myth of the warrior is breaking down in its promise. Willy crows less about his firm, and his exploits in it. Willy has less of a stage for glory, and twice as many hours. He is in a hell of a pickle. It is better to be stuck on first base, than to be off base altogether; yet it is tedious to bring home the news of being stuck at first base. The family turns off to the lack of news.

Besides, Mrs. Loman and the boys have similar pickles in their struggles even to get to first base. They like attention as much as Willy likes attention. It is all so difficult to have a satisfying conversation. If he talks, they put up with it. If they talk, he puts up with it. The reports are from different special battles, of interest to specialists. They do not satisfy nonspecialists listening, nor the reporter himself.

A Case of Being Compensated by the Family for the Daily Battle of Work

Nowadays, both Mr. and Mrs. Loman have jobs that are confining and repetitive and tiring. Both are seeking compensation for their all day battles on behalf of the family. By about six o'clock in the evening, you have two people who want to be taken care of, and no one left to take care of them. When you add tired and cranky children who want to be taken care of—for they have not seen their parents all day, and they too feel put upon by the demands of their jobs, of schoolwork—there is no one left to take care of them.

This situation cannot possibly go well as it is constructed. (See Figure 4–4.) The terrain is untenable. There are only a few possibilities about where the longing for compensation will go: into anger; into giving up; into distraction such as television or newspapers; into substitutes for the spouse—like pals at the bar, or affairs; into turning to the children for being taken care of by them.

Yet, routinely, couples expect it (somehow, mythically) to work for them. This is the crowning myth of the family. I put a (purple) crown in my drawing, which shows that self-sacrifice in the daily battle *will* converge with being compensated by the family! They overlook (the hole, pointed to) the glaring absence of anybody to bring about the fulfillment of the myth.

Thus, it becomes my (routine) job to pose the dilemma back to couples that they wish to overlook. One or both partners is taking a tremendous beating in the world of work and importing it into the family to be compensated, which will *never* work. Where did they get the idea (myth) that it ought to work? Of course, I always find that the husband's father knocked himself out, let us say as a coach with many

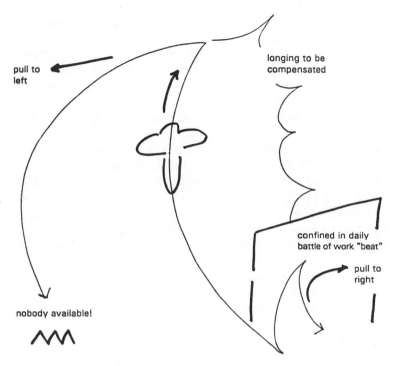

Figure 4–4. The Dilemma of Compensation for Confinement in the Daily Work Battle.

games on the road, while his mother faithfully waited with supper hot and his pillow pressed. The myth comes from the previous generation.

Now, the husband *knows* it is nearly the twenty-first century and that women like his wife have careers. Yet, he *feels* the longing to be compensated like (he imagines) his father was. He is very angry at his wife's going her own way, while he also thinks he has no legitimate right to object. The turmoil inside him goes underground, until it surfaces in his affair. (The worlds of power flatten men like Loman with bogus, inflated attention ["I wowed them in Boston," says Loman], which is addictive [malignant]. He is in withdrawal coming home. The family has the ugly and malignant dilemma of feeding his addiction for inflated attention, or frustrating and getting his violence. The cross-over from an ordinary, benign family to a malignant family is only a matter of degree.)

Now, the wife has a terrible fix. She is apt to oscillate between her anger at the betrayal, and her anxiety to make up her lack to him. The first alarms him, so he runs away, and the second robs her of her own independent initiatives.

Of course, only a third thing will work, for her, or for him. This, however, will require a revision of the myth. He cannot have a headlong career *and* be completely compensated by an independent wife. Those two great things do not converge. She cannot have a headlong career *and* be completely compensated by an independent husband. When I pose this dilemma as a matter of physics on their terrain, some obvious revisions come into view. He or she may consider reducing the need for compensation by reducing the load of the career, or by arranging to be compensated elsewhere like going for a workout at noon. This can take the pressure off the spouse to supply the impossible! Of course, this runs the risk of distance. What will they share that they actually find of mutual satisfaction? This is a crucial question, but they will hardly get to it when pinned down by impossible claims.

Left and Right

This dilemma of career and compensation has a different topology for every couple, and the unconscious always renders it with greater precision and beauty than the conscious mind. In general, the demands of career appear as pulls to the right. (I am indebted to Peter Miller for first bringing this right/left dimension of dreams to my attention.) To go to the right is to comply with what is right. To go to the left is to deviate and risk exclusion from the economies of the increase packs.

These polarities of right and left acquire different shadings in European languages, but they all put the correct to the right, and the incorrect to the left. Each language has somewhat different connotations about the rightness of right, and the leftness of left. In English, left comes from the Anglo-Saxon *lvft,* which means weak, while the French *gauche* means awkward, which is similar to the German *linkisch,* which also means awkward (Weekley 1967). Conversely, right in English comes from Anglo-Saxon *riht,* which means straight, erect, just, while the French *droit* brings in the connotation of a correct claim, as of the king, and the German *rechts* is also a legal right.

The myths of coupling subordinate the left to the right. Thus, the medieval commentary of the great scholar Rashi (1040–1105) upon the Talmud renders this commentary on *Genesis 2:18:* "If he is worthy, she will be a help (mate)" (Ben Isiah and Sharfman 1949, p. 24). Or the opening line of a beautiful recent novel (Wilson 1986): "And as long as he sought the Lord, God made him to prosper."

This pull to the right is rendered specifically in dreams as a tremendous force. While the conscious bows to it, the unconscious renders it as also very dangerous.

A Case of Huge Wind to the Right

A young graduate student in the humanities was contemplating getting on track (the right track) as a would-be professor, but he was (somehow) reluctant. He was deviating (to the left), but did not know why. He dreamt:

> I go to an outdoor theater of my professor. He has a set, which is of grey cardboard teeth, for his new play. They are huge, like the figures at Stonehenge. Obviously, he is concerned about rain on his cardboard teeth, so he has erected [e-recht-ed (*recht* means right in German), *sic*] three brown Army surplus parachutes over them as a temporary shield from storms. Unfortunately . . . and this part is ridiculous, because parachutes would not stay up of their own accord. They naturally are for falling! . . . the parachutes are being driven by a great wind from below upward, and to the right! So they do not cover the grey cardboard teeth at all, which will be ruined by the next rain. I wake up very anxious.

The wind turns out to be the tremendous drive of his professor to go to the top. Yet it frightens my patient, the graduate student, who cannot fail to see that the emperor's clothes (Stonehenge is primitive royalty) are but grey cardboard. This semimilitary and Army surplus operation is a fiasco! Instead of taking a fall from his grandiose drive with parachutes, he is forcing them upwards to cover up his huge grey teeth which are mere cardboard. My patient finally notes " . . . and his wife is leaving him!"

Of course, the dream makes it perfectly clear why. Anybody pulling for collusion with such a preposterous pull to the right is going to place a spouse in a very difficult dilemma, as illustrated in Figure 4–5.

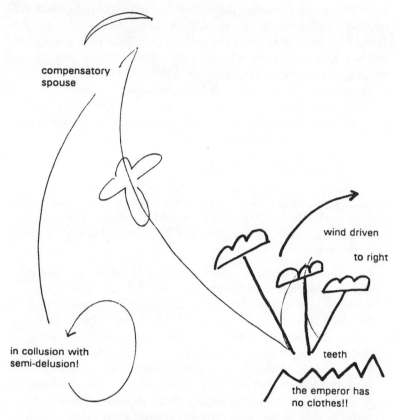

Figure 4–5. The Topology for the Spouse of the Playwright Professor.

Either she announces her alarm, or she colludes with his pretense and is taken prisoner. My patient obviously was being warned about embarking into such territory, which is impossible for a couple. He had been pondering two things after all, which diverge terribly: the rightward course of following in the footsteps of his professor, and the leftward course of running off with his girlfriend.

5

Malignant Families

Malignancy in Families as Ritual Sacrifice

It is not fashionable to say that families are malignant, yet they often are precisely so. Sacrificing daughters to incest, for example, for the compensation of their violent fathers is literally malignant. The survival of such a father is extended at the expense of his daughter, who is ruined. One lives, the other dies. This is psychic murder, just as a malignant tumor destroys its host body.

Of course, this sacrifice, especially of the female as currency between men, is ancient and extremely widespread and it continues, certainly in my state of Wisconsin. Greek tragedy portrays it, Elizabethan tragedy portrays it (remember Ophelia, Desdemona, and Cordelia), and modern tragedy portrays it (I recommend Durrenmatt's *The Visit*, 1956).

Yet incest is but one terrible variation of the theme of *ritual sacrifice*. Wives become victims of shyster husbands, who hold up the entire family at a kind of psychic gunpoint. Teenagers, even "teenagers" who are 40 years old, can become tyrants who hold the family hostage with their suicidal threats. Mad, shaky, brittle parents, similarly, suspend the lives of everyone else in the household. Those are some of the worlds of malignancy in families.

Of course, there are variations to the therapy, which are evident in the different languages adopted and promulgated and swallowed by the families in a kind of conversion. Some will be converted to comic absurdity, some to a new structure from a new papa or mama figure, some to being caught at their game, some to the marvelous simplicity of feeling things together long covered up, some to an elaboration of their unique outcomes into a new and celebrated story of the family reborn.

Given the fashion of family therapy, writers like Selvini-Palazzoli (Selvini-Palazzoli et al. 1989) seem too negative. She writes that the families that bring about such ruined children as chronic anorexics and schizophrenics play dirty games, which they adroitly cover up under a veneer of cordiality. This is terrible news for a fashion that strives to be entirely sentimental about the family, which is seen as basically good, but sometimes has to be saved by a technique from some monster error of communication, or structure of rules, or story about itself with a bad ending. Like all myths, this fashion is a machine for the suppression of time (Leach 1970, Chap. 7), which hides the dilemma of the family that will emerge in time, despite the cover-up.

The malignant dilemmas of these families are historical and economical and driven by the huge anxieties of rising or falling in the hierarchy of social class. If the family is going to avoid sinking, or catch a wave to rise on, key family members have to be kept going. This will be accomplished by sacrificing other family members as compensation to the key player: wives, children, husbands, and so forth. This is the ritual sacrifice. Of course, all families make sacrifices, as we say, but what is dangerous is the extent. For example, parentified children are commonplace to propping up a family in which both parents are exhausted. This parentification is benign if the daughter has some life of her own to return to, and if the sacrifice is temporary. It becomes malignant when she has only a false self of serving at her own expense.

The Schreber Case of a Dog in Hell

The Bavarian Supreme Court Justice Schreber became famous because of the autobiography he wrote to justify his mad visions. Freud (1911) analyzed the autobiography, and Schatzman (1963) analyzed the family context much later. For me, it is the typical scenario of the malignant sacrifice in a family.

Schreber's father was a famous pedagogue in Germany, known for inventing torturous instruments of education such as desks into which children were strapped to force them to learn. Schreber was the experimental dog for this set of experiments that were to propel the father into his glory. He had the usual terrible dilemma, of submitting to degradation or objecting, and being threatened with exclusion from the family.

The responses of children to such nightmares vary enormously (Werner 1989), from descent into schizophrenia, to developing eating and obsessional disorders, to borderline personality organization, to a benign basic fault, depending on whether or not they have somewhere else to go. How vigorously they search for somewhere else to go is probably a matter of hardiness, which is constitutional (Werner 1989).

Schreber himself was a loyal dog in hell who seemed all right until he became Chief Justice. At that point, he was very sensitive to being left by his wife, and began to hallucinate a God who was obsessed with putting rays into his female body. The psychosis (Freud 1911) returned him to his father's mad possession. Perhaps his loneliness as a successful adult was unbearable.

This is typical of an onset of schizophrenia in form, even if it is later in onset than the usual adolescence (Gustafson unpublished, a). The first stage is a kind of dreaming for the longed-for savior. Then the savior proves punitive, exacting the surrender of the soul. Then the patient alternates between longing and dreading and fighting with the delusional object (Gustafson unpublished, a). As demonstrated in Figure 5–1, this infinity of the cycle can lock up a patient forever, if there is no exit that is bearable for re-entry into the world. The world as it exists for the patient may be too lonely, or too paltry.

Other Variations of Ritual Sacrifice

There are many, many variations of this malignant dilemma for a child. The dog in hell role may be played for the father, for the mother, and for siblings, and for other relatives in determinative positions of power. Usually, the adult forcing compensation through a child is at a loss in the economic world or in the world of the extended family (which is equivalent), and is unable to get help from the spouse.

Thus, the father may have been a captive of his mother and becomes a captive of the corporate president. His independence is sexualized, and his wife is stone cold. Probably she is cold because of his infidelities. He forces himself on his little girl. She is tortured by this

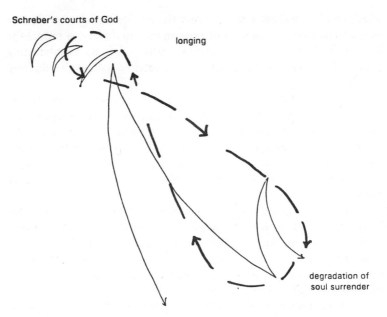

Schreber's courts of God

longing

degradation of
soul surrender

Figure 5–1. The Psychotic Inner World of Schreber.

use of herself, but is strong enough to dissociate the experiences. She later experiences, like so many other women, flashbacks in the form of gruesome body memories.

The mother may be a dutiful servant to her own cold and punitive mother, and may marry a man for form, who gallivants as far from her as possible. She pulls her daughter into tow, to compensate herself. The daughter's position is servile. Serve mother, and get crumbs. Don't serve, and get her cold hatred. The daughter plays this false self role until adolescence, until she rebels a little, and is rejected. Then, she starts slashing and burning herself in the borderline career.

The stories could be multiplied endlessly, but they only repeat a plot of bare bones, as I have already illustrated in Figure 5–1. The child is in what Laing (1959) called an untenable position. The gist of it is that servility results in becoming degraded, and objection is exclusion. There is no tenable position in such families for children placed in such positions by more powerful adults or siblings. The child suffers unbearable intrusion, or unbearable abandonment. Oddly, he or she becomes used to the first, scapegoat position. It becomes the only known form of security. It is better to be a dog in hell, than a dog flying through the black void (Gustafson 1986, pp. 207–211, 388–391). Thus, Schreber is disoriented when he loses his familiar and degraded place.

Selvini's Maps of the Sacrifice

Selvini-Palazzoli (Selvini-Palazzoli et al. 1978, 1989) is one of the few writers to take this sacrifice as a terrible necessity in the pathological family that is not to be underestimated. She is fully aware of the g's or gravitational forces involved. (See pp. 70–72 [1989] for an apt account of herself caught in such force fields.) Her mapping of these dynamic systems introduces several points of great practical importance.

Myth in History

First of all, the myth of the extended family or clan has a history, in which its pretensions are more delivered in some generations, and more fantastical in other generations. For example, the Casanti myth (Selvini-Palazzoli et al. 1977) of a Tuscan tenant farm family presumed that the only strength was in staying together under the iron fist of the *capoccia,* or feudal father of the clan. Deviating resulted in the disaster of having no one to look after you.

There was a kind of truth to the need for this subordination, which extended in a line down through the five sons, with their wives descending in a corresponding rank at a lower level. However, once the five sons moved into the city with their five wives and countless children to form a building construction firm, the myth of "one for all" in strict hierarchy began to depart or diverge more and more widely from the actual different interests of the five nuclear families in the clan,

The third generation becomes openly competitive, yet the myth of unity pretends it is not so. This is bewildering for Nora, the beautiful 13-year-old daughter of the fifth son, Siro. Turned against by her nasty cousin, Luciana, she can get no confirmation from Siro or her mother, Pia, who contend it cannot be so. Nora goes into anorexic protest and nearly finishes herself off.

The Milan family therapy team nearly assists her in doing the job by backing her against the clan, before they grasp the dilemma of Siro,

Pia, and Nora in its full malignancy. Siro and Pia have to quiet Nora to keep in place the myth of the clan, yet they have to back Nora to keep her from going mad. The team finally grasps this and has the family talk in secret about the clan, while redoubling outward loyalty. This relieves Nora of her untenable position of being assaulted by the cousin and abandoned by her parents, *without* jeopardizing the standing of the family in the clan machinery necessary to their fortunes.

This idea of the myth of the extended family diverging from the actual and social and economic trends of the times is well known to novelists. It is one of their chief engines of tragedy. I am thinking of writers as diverse as George Eliot in her portrait of Dr. Lydgate going down in the provincial town of *Middlemarch* (1865) because of his high ideas, or the tenant father in Faulkner's "Barn Burning" (1939) going down in the rural South, because of his low ideas of revenge. The fervor of the myth in each story (family) obscures the actual course of things running rapidly downhill.

Imbroglio

Selvini seems to drop her historical grasp of myth in the family after this single essay in 1977. Yet the idea of myth as machine for the suppression of time comes up later under a different name. This is the term *imbroglio*. The gist of the idea is that one of the parents creates a mythical alliance with one of the children, to compensate him for his spouse failing him.

When the child begins a protest against the key player in the family, believing in the backing of the ally parent, the myth is shattered. The ally parent actually has his bread buttered with the dominant wife. He betrays his daughter. She cannot believe it, and ups her challenge, and the plot goes from bad to worse to catastrophic (Selvini-Palazzoli et al. 1989).

Selvini insists that the cover-up of the mythical alliance and its plunge into disaster is usually complete. The surface is pseudo-dumb, or pseudo-urbane, or pseudo-something. Only a doctor with a map to look for it has a chance to turn it up. The surface will be that the daughter is crazy, and no one can make any sense of her demise. (Whenever a child commits some drastic crime in Wisconsin, the newspaper always interviews the family and the neighbors who always purport to be completely surprised. She was [always] a very nice girl.)

Thus, Nora of the Casantis, in retrospect, can be seen as a casualty of an *imbroglio* in which her naive faith in her alliance with her proud father, Siro, crumbles in the face of his greater loyalty to Casanti solidarity. The two big ideas of Selvini can be taken as different aspects of the disaster of myth. The first aspect is the tie of the myth to past success of the family, which obscures its widening divergence from daily reality. The second aspect is the tie of the child to compensating a downed parent, which obscures its own collapse to come. These two ties of myth finally snap when stretched too far. The most famous and summarizing line in *Ulysses* (Joyce 1914) is about this terrible divergence: "'History,' said Stephen, 'is a nightmare from which I am trying to awake'" (p. 34).

The force field in such families is simply tremendous. One pull is outside and to the right into history: "Behind the shining modern rocking-horse, behind the smart doll's house, a voice would start whispering: 'There *must* be more money. There *must* be more money'" (Lawrence 1933, pp. 857–858).

The opposite pull is into the dream of the mythical power to the left, which seizes the child to compensate his parent: "'Well, anyhow,' he said stoutly, 'I'm a lucky person.' 'Why?' said his mother, with a sudden laugh. He stared at her. He didn't even know why he said it. 'God told me,' he asserted, brazening it out" (p. 859). Children are pulled to pieces by such cross-currents. Here is an example of my own.

A Case of an Italian Daughter

A young graduate student in Italian Literature, Nora, came in because she felt terribly hurt by her parents. They were of peasant stock, dominated by the mother, who lacked formal education altogether. She was a formidable force, bowed to by the father. In other words, this daughter came from a very common situation in southern Europe.

Backed by her father, Siro, she did well in school. So far, they were still on fine terms. The trouble came when she got a boyfriend and moved in with him secretly. Mother suspected it, and began a mad campaign of calling the apartment to catch her boyfriend there. She left vindictive messages for him such as "I know you are living with my daughter, and I will get you for it."

Nora began to get an ulcer. While her boyfriend was marvelously patient with the mad mother, Nora herself could not believe the lengths to which her mother now proceeded to destroy her happiness. She kept on. The final blow that staggered her was the very one that Selvini predicts in her map of the *imbroglio*. Siro takes the mother's side against her. This breaks her heart, and brings her to us.

Unlike Selvini's cases, who became schizophrenic, anorexic, or something else of equal gravity, this young woman just felt utter amazement and great pain. (Thus, *imbroglio* as a malignant situation can create malignant patients like Selvini's, or benign patients like this young woman. As Werner [1989] shows, some children have a more vigorous constitution and find sound allies outside the family [as Nora found this boyfriend, teachers, and us] who help them come through the horns of the malignant dilemma.) I could relieve a great deal of it in a single session, if I did have to leave her with her serious dilemma. I could relieve her by tackling her amazement at her mother's ferocity, and at her father's complicity, so she could see for once that she was laying herself wide open to pain by looking for anything different from them. They had to behave exactly as they were behaving in defense of the traditional idea of a maiden's honor. Her problem was to depart from their system, and expect them to tolerate it well, and thus get clobbered. She had a dilemma:

If her mother is a queen of tradition, she is also a queen who will have it *both* ways: traditional and modern. Her realm is indefensible, because the two virtues cannot be held together. She either retreats to her mother's realm, or she advances to a little realm of her own under fierce attack. If she chooses the latter, she might as well get ready for the next onslaught. Indeed, the mother enacted a pseudo heart attack to force her daughter not to return to school. This old lady would stop at nothing! The patient was furious when the trick was caught, and came back here.

A Novelist's Family Therapy—the Problem of Language

While I am very grateful to Selvini for her helpful maps, I do not embrace her methods or recommend them to the reader without reservation. She is a kind of poker player who beats families (and colleagues) at their game. This is itself a mythical machine for the suppression of time by leaving the impression that her marvelous interventions leave them happy ever after. History is not gotten out of so easily. Its dilemmas remain arduous. I explain what I mean.

Like the entire fashion of family therapy, Selvini is obsessed with technique. She differs in not holding onto the first tool she finds and making a rigid system out of it, which is the usual thing. She is fertile of invention. She keeps apart from the fashion of the training circus, so she can follow the path of her own creations. She is not held back by her own teammates or students. (See Jung [1935, pp. 120–121] for a devastating picture of disciples who fix the truth in order to guard it.)

First, she conceives of the trick as one of communication, second, as a paradoxical bomb, third, as a series of tilts of the board to bring down the current winner and reinstall the current loser (Gustafson 1989). When I wrote an essay in 1989 about the first three phases of her twenty-year career of invention, she, of course, was already in a fourth phase. This was the invention of the invariant prescription, which tested the readiness of the parents to go out in secret from the domination of the psychotic teenager (Selvini-Palazzoli et al. 1989). I am sure this sentence itself is already out of date as a picture of her present method. She will be in a sixth phase by now.

My argument is not with her series of inventions. (Tomm's many papers [1984, 1987–1988] do a fine job of making technical operations of the Milan family therapy team as explicit as possible. Yet they miss the mapping of the territory on which the families must continue to live.) My argument is with the mythical machine that creates them. While I have benefitted from her tools. I do not believe that tools fix families. Families are dynamic systems, which are embedded in history. Interventions like the invariant prescription alter the dynamics, for example, of the parents being pinned down by a mad child. If the parents will follow it, they will break the spell of their subservience. This also breaks up the covert alliance of the *imbroglio* with one of the parents appearing to side with the patient, while actually betraying her. Yet the family remains in a grave dilemma set by their positioning in society. To illustrate the inevitability of a grave dilemma continuing in a malignant family, I'll cite a typical situation.

A Case of the Queen's Croquet Game

Much of individual psychotherapy depends upon an accurate map of the territory of the patient's family of origin. If the doctor thinks the territory is relatively flat, when it is actually mountainous, he is likely to send his patient over a cliff (Gustafson 1989).

This young woman's family was mountain country ruled by queens. Her mother was all right to her for the first several years of her life, until two momentous things happened for sure and a third thing probably happened. One was moving out of a neighborhood where her mother was comfortable to one where she became bitter. Two was her sister's birth. Three was probably her father's exile from the house.

Her mother now became the kind of mean queen who favored her sister in everything, while rubbing my patient's face in all the dirt. Her father did not defend her, and may have done worse to her. Like Cinderella, she scrubbed and scrubbed, and lay as low as she could to keep from compounding her misery. She got through because of school, where she was duly celebrated.

Her marriage was a disaster, because the prince in the pumpkin turned out to be even meaner than her mother. She comes to me in a kind of shell shock. Forever, she finds herself back in a field of combat. Private life gets mean with men, but working life gets just as mean. She went into nursing to be helpful, but even there there are continual attacks. The surgeons are nice only when they are having their way!

Naturally, the meanness catches her off guard because she looks for kindness to visit. Amazed, she is decimated, and falls into the abyss of her childhood.

If she reacts to her husband or to the surgeons with the tears and rage that she feels, it gets much worse. If she keeps her demeanor, she has tremendous turmoil to bear with inside her body. This is her dilemma on the malignant playing field of the Queen's Croquet Game (Carroll 1865). The reader may recall that the Queen of Hearts plays as she pleases, and reacts to any opposition with the shrill cry of "Off with her head!"

Alice gets in much trouble by reacting honestly. Yet, she is troubled by the servility of all the players to the whims of the Mad Queen. Only when the Cheshire Cat appears as a kind of ghost in a tree is Alice able to get any company to discuss what is going on, as illustrated in Figure 5–2. It is vital that the Cat be accurate about this madly tilted terrain for croquet, where the Queen is always on top. This gets Alice ready for the next piece of high-handedness. It is also vital that the Cat know what it feels like for Alice, so she can share with him what she dare not breathe in the direction of the Queen. Finally, it is vital that the Cat understand history, for Alice is like Stephen Dedalus

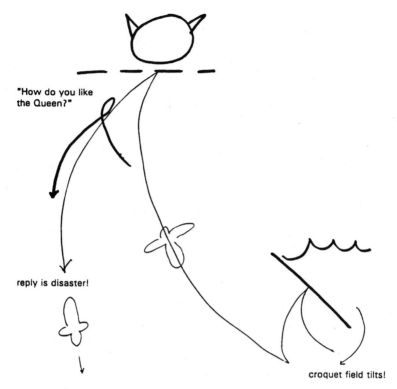

"How do you like
the Queen?"

reply is disaster!

croquet field tilts!

Figure 5–2. Queen's Croquet Field.

in trying to wake up from history as a nightmare. Like the poor flamin-
goes who try to get out of being used as mallets in the game by flying
into the trees, Alice has her flights. She imagines getting out of the
Queen's game, but continually finds herself back being shouted at.

I wrote her as follows:

You have been living in combat zones like the Queen's Croquet
Game all your life. You will note that Alice had to remain perfectly still not to make it worse, yet bear her pain (of what struck
her weaknesses) *and* her anger *and* her jealousy of the Queen. I
regret that the Cheshire Cat did not show up sooner, to help her
get through some of these horrid scenes.

The Cat is not going to go along with the illusion that she can get out of history. She will have to live on steep playing fields, where the players are in a kind of heat to play with the Queen. To go away, is to have no company at all. I have mixed up my fairy tales a little bit, putting Cinderella and The Queen's Croquet Game together. They are similar plots at the outset, because the girl (Cinderella or Alice) protagonist is caught in a cruel fix with a very bad mother (witch or queen). A rescuer comes along (prince in a pumpkin-carriage, Cheshire Cat) to save the day. The difference is in the nature of the help. The Prince will take the girl away to a better and higher world, while the Cat will only provide perspective on the game the girl has to play.

Desperate girls do need stories of deliverance to keep up morale, yet these very stories set them up with being delivered into the hands of worse princes. Thus, the pumpkin has to be deflated, eventually. Curiously, the Cat is orange like a pumpkin and deflates by its odd method of dissolving into thin air. When these patients from malignant families get a Cheshire Cat in their corner, they begin to cope ever so much better with their dilemma of being inside such a family, versus being outside. They are more ready for the dire events inside and get away as best they can, while they are not cast out alone into the void at the mercy of any petty prince. Many blunders are committed with this dilemma. If the pumpkin myth is deflated without anything to take its place, the patient can give up on life. Yet collusion with it as a delusion sets up a crash for the therapy. This usually takes the form of a belief that therapy will help the patient find a partner who is pure love (and no hostility). See Chapter 1 on "The Malignant Basic Fault" and Chapter 13 on "Training I." See Cameron (1961) for a case of a schizophrenic patient who hallucinated a cruel parental figure and gradually substituted the voice of Dr. Cameron instead!

Family Therapy as Description and Family Therapy as Intervention

The field of family therapy is much newer than the field of brief psychotherapy: forty years versus one hundred years. Yet I do not think that the next sixty years are going to make up the difference. This is because of the schools, which will govern the training.

A little history may make my point. The first kind of family therapy was descriptive. The idea was to describe to the family what was going on. The assumption was that the family could be analyzed like a patient in psychoanalysis. The family was supposed to welcome insight. You can well imagine that Cinderella's mother did not take well to having her realm looked into. She had power to lose, and she was not about to let intruders tamper with her control.

The second phase began, and continues to this very day, of finding ways around the cover-up (Skynner 1986). This is the phase of interventions. The family therapist gets within reach of the family, usually, because Cinderella's mother wants something done about Cinderella's not doing what she is supposed to do. The trick is to address her protest, engaging her, while taking on the hierarchy of the family that is going to keep the protest going.

Such families always want the impossible. Their playing field is so tilted that Cinderella is about to fall off; hence, her protest. The powers in the family want Cinderella to cut it out, without altering the tilt of the board. This is impossible. Yet Cinderella may not play unless the board is righted. This is also impossible, as illustrated in Figure 5–3.

This kind of impossible situation begets interventions that pull off the impossible trick. It takes a fast one to do this, so the techniques can hardly be replicated. These include being absurd with them, giving them paradoxes, proposing rituals that look trivial but alter the power, etc. The bottom line is that the powers give up some power in exchange for Cinderella cutting out some of her protest, and Cinderella gets some standing but hardly a revolution.

This juggling of the board occasionally happens as it is supposed to happen in the Annals of Interventive Family Therapy. It takes a kind of charmer who gets himself let in, and some of these sleight-of-hand operations that alter the balance of power. I am not going to try to teach it in a few paragraphs. See Skynner (1986) for the best brief summary of the favorite interventionists, or my chapter on the Milan Teams (1986, Chap. 16), or refer directly to Whitaker, Minuchin, Haley, Selvini-Palazzoli, Michael White, etc. See especially the Sala Case in Selvini-Palazzoli and colleagues (1989) for the most vivid sequence of the alternation of winners and losers as the board tilts wildly back and forth. It took me ten years with my team (The Wisconsin Family Therapy Team) and with study of these predecessors and with study of literature and history to be able to cope with these malignant families. Anything less is likely to underestimate the difficulty (Ruth Gustafson, personal communication). Mostly, it is unteachable. Also, it only works in

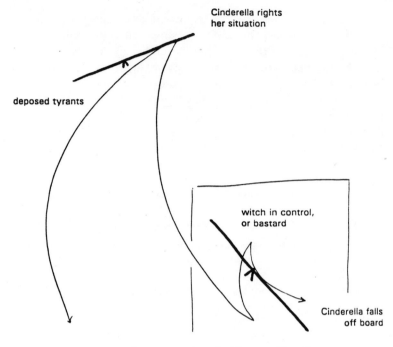

Figure 5–3. Big League Family Therapy Situations.

a few cases. I will conclude this chapter with discussion of these two limitations.

Unteachable Family Therapy with Malignant Families

The simplest way to say this is that the great method of the pioneer genius in family therapy becomes didactic. Once it is didactic, it no longer works. It is either going to join the powers to teach a lesson to Cinderella, which will turn her off, or it is going to join Cinderella to teach the powers a lesson, which will turn them off. It becomes a mythical machine for the suppression of time (that is, for suppression of the malignant dilemma of the family).

Why do followers become didactic? They like a system. They get a set of rules like structural family therapy, or group-analytic family therapy, or narrative family therapy, or whatever. Once they get the rules down, they teach families. It hardly ever works. These families are really impossible, and you simply cannot teach the possible to families that are bent on continuing the impossible.

Three Really Impossible Families

Even the great magicians of intervention are stopped by some families. It helps to see why. I will describe three of my favorites. The gain in practical terms is to help patients, individually, reckon what they are up against.

The gist of really impossible families is that key players need the sacrifice of other family members to keep their own existences going. They feed off the sacrifice, and cannot live without it. The sacrificed become so specialized in their roles that they are fit for nothing else. The thing is apt to be stable as long as nobody has anything better to do or anyplace better to go. The family is miserable, but it is familiar and beats the void.

The Case of the Human Football

I have seen many variants of the situation where you have one or more highly brittle parents, who are involved in a ritual of living that cannot be disturbed. Their spouses and children have to tiptoe around it and endure rages at any little thing out of place. It is simply not possible for anybody else in the household to have a definite personality, because this would disrupt the one personality that is paramount. So these are all variations of the Queen of Hearts. The fearless leader of such a family, of course, can be the father or the mother, or some deadly combination of both, such as often seen in joint alcoholism.

The most unforgettable for me was "The Case of The Human Football," because the daughter struck me literally as having such a shape. Now, this had to be my imagination. She surely had arms and legs and a head protruding out of her torso. Somehow she was tossed back and forth from the mother to the father, and finally to the psychiatrist. Nothing could be done with her. She would not even respond to huge doses of antidepressants and several series of electroshock. This is why the psychiatrist asked our family therapy team to see her with her brother and her parents.

The mother commanded everything. Naturally, she began the session with a harangue worthy of Fidel Castro, which I brought to a halt by raising my hand like a student in class. She then called on me like a teacher annoyed with the interruption of a student who missed the point. The father was perfectly servile, and the daughter was perfectly absent. These two rotated around the fiery sun goddess of a mother, the first clucking and the second with the perfect silence of a football turned into a vacant planet. The little brother seemed to have little to do with this trio at all. He amused himself with some of our toys as if he never listened to these people. (As Werner [1989] shows, the best spot in these families is near the back door for getaways.)

The most telling thing was the mother's continual left jab and her right uppercut. The jab was her harping on her daughter's not doing anything right, especially her not responding to the treatments of the psychiatrist. The uppercut was when we finally elicited a little life in the cold planet, which was struck within seconds with tremendous scorn. It was clear enough that no disruption of the status quo was going to be tolerable. The next hour was redundant.

A Case of Senior Shyster and Junior Shyster

These guys are also legion. They put on a very good show for doctors: supersincere, absolutely well-meaning, and completely unreliable. They drive their spouses crazy because nothing they propose can be counted on to take place. Usually, everything is self-excused because they are terribly important people with terribly important business, and the family will just have to wait.

When junior begins a kind of amateur hour in school of slugging kids and talking his way out of it with excuses, mother is the one who has to handle it all. If father is finally dragged in, he is enraged at his wife. With us, he is the soul of diplomacy.

The mother presents with amazement. She cannot believe this guy. This is apt to keep up for a very long time her endless travails of tears and rage. Worse is what she gets once she is not amazed. This is her complete lack of control, over senior shyster, and, increasingly, and distressingly, junior shyster, the understudy. The little fellow is impressed with how his father works his mother into a perfect frenzy. He just has to try it out for himself. This is apt to get worse and worse, so long as the mother fails to see her intermittent reinforcement of a budding (buddying) career.

The Case of Soiled Underpants Put Back in Mother's Dresser

Children get to be the key players in some families, and drive everybody crazy. While some of the geniuses of the field like Selvini-Palazzoli and Michael White show cases of bringing these mad capers back into line, the cases can be really impossible. One of my favorites was a girl who was off to a fast start as the fast girl of the high school .

Not only was she getting a big reputation for jumping into bed with the boys, she was also tossing the evidence back into her mother's dresser. She'd steal her mother's panties, take the boys, and invite mother to do the laundering. This outraged her mother, who regularly presented the evidence to her father. The father did absolutely nothing. He liked to be out hunting with his dogs, and refused to be drawn into these petty affairs.

I knew the girl was protesting a grievance, I knew it was very serious, and I knew it was ten years in the past. As Winnicott (1971b) notes well, the antisocial career always begins as a protest to actual injury. Yet the protest can get such a hard nose and a fast track that it is irreversible. I also knew her father was not about to come in from the cold. I finally knew that her mother picked up the pieces. It was going to go on and become the usual mess.

6

Benign Families, Growing Up in America, and Brief Psychotherapy in Mental Health Centers

I have conducted a number of workshops on brief psychotherapy in mental health centers around the country in the last several years, where I have had the chance to consult on cases the staffs are having trouble with. I always see variations on the same cases. They are typically American. Even when you come from a relatively benign family, it is difficult to grow up in America.

It is crucial for us to know where the hold ups are, because the patients can only hint at them before they cover them up from us and from themselves. I divide childhood problems very broadly into from birth to age 10, 10 to 20, 20 to 100. That is: childhood proper, adolescence, and so-called adulthood. I consider the latter a kind of childhood that is usually surrendered.

I show here ordinary people coming to a mental health center in the Midwest for help. The troubles they have are the same as the troubles of the staff.

The Hold Up of an Ordinary Childhood

I use the words *hold up* here advisedly, because it so beautifully alludes to something held up or delayed, and also something like a hold up that is a bank robbery. The story goes like this. A child with at least one good-enough parent has a difficult experience. It can be anything, from getting beaten up by a brother, to being forgotten on a birthday by a father. The child is hurt and angry.

The good-enough parent is usually there to receive the child and comfort her, and the pain is passed through, and the anger is let go (Winnicott 1971b). Yet there are some things this parent cannot bear to hear herself. So the child is stuck with her tears and rage, when it comes to some subjects. She'll do her best to lift herself out of the misery, by taking an adult attitude of not minding it and being brave (Reich 1931, 1933). A certain rigidity of character comes into being. The child has taken on a mask or persona of an admired adult, and the vulnerability is now in shadow (Jung 1935).

There are three kinds of masks or personae or characters, which I call subservient, delaying, and overpowering (Gustafson 1992). They are but variations of a single character, which has a little power, or some power, or much power. This acceptable character (with varying power), which makes you an insider in the family, in school, and later in work, is one of increasing the output of whatever group you are playing a part in. You do your chores, or your school numbers, or your work quotas (or scores in sports, or crimes in a gang, or confessions in church, etc.). Rice (1965) calls these outputs the primary task of the group. See Gustafson (1995, Chap. 4) for a discussion of increase packs.

Sometimes the child acts up. She will not take her subdued place. The hurt is too much to hide. Also, the child has enough confidence to make her protest known. She commits a little hold up of the family bank. They will have to stop their accumulation of capital to deal with her. She is taking back some of the family capital for herself.

Winnicott and Children Looking to Be Found Out

I have borrowed most from Winnicott (1971b) for finding such children. His approach can be described simply, but few can carry it out. See St. Exupery (1943) on the difficulties of a child finding an adult he can talk with and be understood. It takes a child's imagination, which adults mostly lack. A lovely collection of examples of this kind of imagination by doctors with adult patients is in Balint and Norell (1973). The doctors are general practitioners and their method is called *the flash technique*. I gave a lengthy account of Winnicott's method in my first book (1986, Chap. 7), which I will abbreviate here.

The gist of his method is what Winnicott calls meeting the challenge of the case. He begins with greeting the child informally, but taking careful note of his own (unconscious) offhand remarks. These remarks have an uncanny accuracy about what needs to be faced with the child. For example, one teenager told me her parents could explain her troubles better than she could. I responded that I was sorry they were not with us, for they could do the whole job! She and I both laughed as I put my finger on the problem we would be facing about their intrusiveness.

Next you get acquainted by an exchange over ordinary topics. If you are utilizing drawings, or completing each other's drawings as in the squiggle game (Winnicott 1971b), the pictures are first apt to be banal, like houses, dolls, stick figures, cars, trucks, etc. The child indicates in a veiled way what is troubling her, so she can see if you pick up the hints, or not. If you don't catch them, the interview will not develop behind or beyond its stock beginning.

If you have caught the hints, the child starts to get excited like Bateson's (1971) dolphin gathering energy. Now, you take a drop deeper, often asking for a dream. You say something like, "I bet you have had a dream about this" (whatever is hinted in the pictures, which get more exciting). Now the child takes you as a transitional object with her into the very territory of shadow that the good-enough parent could not bear to go into. If the child is to face something terrible, you often have to get there first, so she can gather your confidence for herself. (As Virgil did for Dante in hell.) Winnicott knew that the children dreamed of what they needed and he had to be it (the transitional object): "I was struck by the frequency with which the children had dreamed of me the night before attending . . . I was . . . fitting in with a preconceived notion. . . . Either this sacred moment is used or it is wasted. If it is wasted, the child's belief in being understood is shattered. If on the other hand it is used, then the child's belief in being helped is strengthened" (1971b, pp. 4–5). You will have to know and say something about what is around the next corner. Thus, Winnicott helps Mrs. X (1971b) with a terrible passage of being temporarily psychotic by saying, "You mean you *do* go mad, only it is done so quickly that it is all over. Your fear is that you will find you have done something awful while you have been mad" (p. 335). This extension by Winnicott now allows the woman (child) to tell him something she "never told anyone." She had almost strangled a child which got on her nerves.

The final phase is to come up from such unbearable things now shared, spent, and workable. I offer to write a little note summarizing our findings. I borrowed this practice from David Epston, who showed me in Auckland how he pulled up his typewriter after a consultation and shared his thoughts with his patient, instead of burying them in his file cabinet. I don't know if Winnicott ever did that, but it continues the exchange, for the child can write me back, or keep me posted, until she needs to run something further by me.

A Case of Aerial Defenses

This 5-year-old girl was so fearful at bedtime she had to sleep with her older sister in order to quiet down. She knew there was big trouble once she turned out the light. I saw her with her sister and with her parents four times in four months, and a fifth time for follow-up after six months.

I knew from her parents that they were having trouble corralling the big sister, who was 10 and rampant with hyperactivity. The big sister was obsessed with violent criminals from the television and from the movies, which are the usual fare of mass-police entertainment (Brodsky 1988). The parents were somewhat at their wits' end about her. The mother had more of the burden, being home. The father preferred not to deal with her, because he let himself be bugged, until he exploded.

I got my own fill of the big sister, who marched in and told stories about this killer of children with great glee. Mother would tell her it was time to stop, many times over, with little effect. Finally, she'd lose her temper, and that would bring some blessed silence from that quarter for 5 or 10 minutes, before it would start up again.

I had a pretty good idea from mother's reaction and father's reaction and my reaction that my little patient would also have a reaction to this hypomanic wind blowing out of the south. I could well imagine it might be very difficult to settle down with such a thing howling away at bedtime. I don't mean the big sister, who would be spent from her day's exertions. I mean the little sister being pent up with her own reaction. Everyone has had this experience to some extent, as in college when partying is proceeding next door late into the night. You go to bed early to get ready for your exam. They finally become tired and go to bed, while you are now wide awake.

The order of my sessions was to see the family together, then the two girls together or separately. There is not much to say about the first meeting with the little girl, except to say that we did some ordinary drawing together and she let me know there was some kind of monster keeping her up. We got on easily, and I responded that we could hardly arrest this monster and put it in jail until we had a picture of its face. She agreed to watch for it, very seriously.

By the second session, she was clear that the monster was the very one that her sister talked about incessantly. She liked drawing something like an SDI (strategic defense initiative) for intercepting this demon, who seemed to come out of the very dark sky. By the third session, she was eagerly building for the demon a jail of blocks. She picked him up out of her closet with an ambulance and tossed him somewhat rudely into the clinker. As I said to her parents: "This may help, but she and I need some more work to help her assimilate her own evil genius."

By the fourth session, she was doing just this. When we played the squiggle game (Winnicott 1971b), she just used every drawing to thrash me. Next, she set up the hospital again to lock up the demon. This did not satisfy her. She took him out again, put him in the back of an ambulance, and threw him off a cliff!

I might have guessed what she was working up to, for her first squiggle had been a star in the sky. I said, "Oh, Twinkle . . . " and she gaily sang it to me. Evidently, she loved being high and rich ". . . like a diamond in the sky" . . . which is where she dropped the demon from! By the fifth session for follow-up six months later, she was still drawing stars in the heavens and letting them loose in a Fourth of July of colors, from a Fourth of July tank! My work with her sister and with her parents is also relevant to this outcome. The sister needed help with her own helplessness, which was driving her furious hyperactivity, and her parents needed help to contain her, by fewer words and firm action. This took some of the pressure off the little sister.

This little girl had been stuck being nice. She had suitable aggression to coping with invaders, but she had to borrow me to bring it out, fiercely, but humorously. Her parents had been quite good enough parents in every other way, but it was hard for them to go with her into the night of the demon combat. For them, it got so serious. She borrowed me, and became a diamond in the sky! For a comparable example in Winnicott (1971b) see Rosemary, who was having black depressions for the lack of being able to share her aggression.

If I am in the realm of magic with my little patient, in a kind of Grimm's fairy tale (1819) form so typical of the reports of family therapy, I also want to step outside it in conclusion. I believe her troubles are not over by any means, as much as her parents and I might wish for her. She is a young female in a wicked culture of western man.

As Gilligan (1990) shows so well, she will be drafted strongly to the right to be a nice teenage girl with no being of her own. This is the right horn of inclusion as a trap. If she resists this pull, she will have to be fierce but good-natured to stay off the left horn of exclusion for being too individual. In other words, she must pass through the dilemma of growing up in America as an adolescent.

A Case of a Nice Boy Screwing Up in Junior High

This story is similar to the last story, but adds a complication and takes us further into the transition between childhood proper and adolescence.

The hold up in this case was not an intrusive sister, but intrusive parents. It was not their fault. They just had one piece of terrible luck after another, with jobs, health, housing, and so forth. The boy comforted them, because he loved them very much.

He kept it up, until junior high school, whereupon he stopped doing schoolwork. The usual cajoling, and rewarding, and punishing, did not get within a mile of him. He was brought to me by his doctor, with his parents.

I hit it off straight away with him, bringing in my big drawing pad and magic markers. He liked drawing very much as I do, so he borrowed my tools and set to work sitting on the floor to my left. I felt he was ready to plunge ahead, if anybody would meet him half way.

The resident who was taking care of this family essentially wanted to know from me whom to work with next in this family and about what. She had her hands full with the parents, and the boy, now 12, was getting earfuls of the endless troubles of those two. This continued his place of long-standing as pal and consolation to each of these unfortunate people.

The parents were obviously grieved. The father was a very hurt man, such as I often find in Wisconsin. He had believed in his company, gotten injured on the job, and was being let down terribly over compensation. This continued with the State Compensation Bureau, forever checking on his disability. The father was now very suspicious, and his suspicion extended to me. If he had been too trusting in his youthful hopefulness, now he was leaning far into cynicism. The mother was long-suffering as well, but less brittle.

She immediately answered the resident's question of what to do next by saying that something had to be done about this bright boy doing next to no schoolwork for going on two years of junior high school! I turned to the lad and noted that he was surely on protest, about something. He did not resist the suggestion in the least. He helped me a great deal to figure out what it was.

In fact, he claimed he was over his protest already, citing several pieces of work turned in in the last week. His mother exclaimed that she had seen these improvements once in a while but they did not last. So, I commented to the boy that his mother had seen comebacks before. Now that he was in day five, how long could he keep it up? He was sure he would keep it up from now on. His mother guessed about ten days.

I said I didn't know, but I imagined he would slip up, when he felt hurt again. Then, the comeback would be over, and the protest resumed. We needed to understand his hurt. The hole in the story I saw before me was this: since the family had been sorely troubled for the last seven years, how had this boy only begun his protest two years ago coming into junior high?

To make a long story short, the timing was very important. We reached to his pain, in losing both of his parents two years ago, in this way: he had been pals with father and with mother in doing things physically, but they had either become so laid up they couldn't wrestle (father), or they couldn't be at home much for having to work (mother).

I asked his parents to step out for a few minutes. Now, tears came to his eyes, as he continued drawing. I had reached back to the hurt behind the protest. Now, I wanted to get to the anger of the protest itself, and, looking down and to my left at his big drawing, there it was!

As shown in Figure 6–1 I saw a medieval fortress, and a drawbridge let down (letting him out), and, as shown in Figure 6–2, someone setting off a huge and colorful flare (his anger like the Fourth of July).

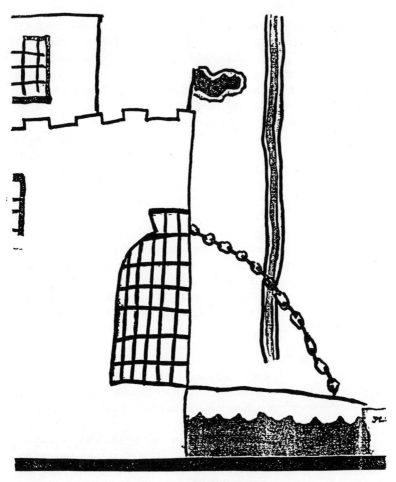

Figure 6–1. The Boy in Prison.

Now, we could conclude. I asked the resident to bring the parents back in, and I gave her and the family my reply. I felt the boy needed his own doctor, for he was now going into the world on his own. He would have to leave his parents to their own problems, yet he would want to keep his place with them. I felt he could decide with his parents when to come to their sessions, and when not to come to their

Figure 6–2. Fireworks!

sessions. I promised to write the parents, and I asked the boy if he wanted his own letter. He did, indeed.

The complication is that there is more than one thing going on. The boy is protesting his hurt, like my little 5-year-old patient, but he is also two years down the slippery slope of playing hookey, and finally, he is reluctant to separate from his foundering parents, for whom he is the mainstay. I have to tackle all three of these catches, or his hold up will continue. Any one of the three will suffice for motivation to stay truant. This is why family therapists fail so often with such familiar cases. Here is a lad aching to go forward, but he will not unless his three hang-ups are loosened. He isn't even a hard case, for really difficult teenagers also lack anything to attract them in junior high schooling. Those are "four-hang-up" children, and they are lucky if anybody gets one of the four! I described a similar family in the Milan Team's simulation (Cecchin, Boscolo) at Calgary in my first book (1986, Chap. 16). They picked up the separation catch beautifully, between the dropout and the parents, but the girl's pain and her game of hookey and her lack of vital interests did not come up. At the time, I was very impressed by the music of the interviewing, which was very engaging in its rhythm, language, and returns. Charm engages, but is often weak in carrying through, for lack of an adequate map. The charm wears off, when the passage grinds to a halt.

The Hold Up of Adolescence

This previous lad has already taken us over the border from childhood proper, which starts its decline at about 10 and is finished off in most by 20, when the previous child is hooked up into a responsible life, more or less. He has become a citizen at 20, who pays his bills and refrains from upsetting anybody important.

In between, however is the turmoil of adolescence. I like the Dulwich, Australia, writers best about this period (Smith and Tiggeman 1989, Tiggeman and Smith 1989), because they put their pointer right smack on the garden variety dilemma of teenagers and their parents (and parental surrogates like teachers, therapists, coaches, etc.). The dilemma is that the parental figures want control, while the teenagers want greed. I meant to write "freedom!" and my typewriter let through a slip of my unconscious, which illustrates the primitive nature of these collisions, by substituting "greed."

If the parents have their way, the teenager feels stifled. If the teenager has her way, the parents feel that all order and responsibility and hope for a viable future break down.

A Case of a Foster Daughter on Thin Ice

Here is a typical situation of a neglected teenager in peril on the horns of this usual dilemma. The girl's therapist presents her to me because she is afraid the girl is going to get herself tossed out by the foster par-

ents. It is the usual situation that the girl is hurt and angry about abandonment by her parents, which is compounded by the birth of a long-
awaited child to the foster parents who turn gladly to their own, and
away from her. The teenager, naturally, reacts with a protest, in scenes
at school.

The family therapist confirms that the foster parents have about
had it with the teenager, and (probably) *do* contemplate sending her
back to the agency where she came from. This will destroy the precious
relationship with the individual therapist.

The key point in the video interview of the girl by her therapist,
for me, turned around her amazement that making dinner for the foster parents, to show her good will, got no thanks at all. This crushed
her hope of being a good girl, and drove her back into protest. Following the Dulwich line of thinking, I proposed to the child's therapist and
the family therapist that the girl's amazement showed her underestimation of what it would take to get recognition from these foster parents. These people were probably down on her, and were not about to
respond to a single deed of reparation for all the trouble she had caused
them.

My consultation to the two therapists is summarized as follows:

Dear _____:

I am impressed at your reading of this situation of _____
with her aunt and uncle and cousin. _____ is being tuned into
beautifully. The surrogate parents are understood, exactly, in their
slim tolerance for this girl. So the peril is that they will get too
little back for giving her a home, and she will be out, and treatment wrecked.

It appears, _____, that if you meet with the surrogate
parents, they will confirm this. But this would allow you to let
_____ know that these parents actually *believe* that she is not
interested in pleasing them. Would she then be interested in proving them wrong by something shockingly positive (obviously,
helping out making a meal fails to get their attention, because
it just didn't make an impression!)? I enclose the essay by the
Dulwich writers, not because it is a panacea, because it is not. But
it allows the parents and the teenager a chance (if they want it,
and it is not too late) to correct the complete misunderstanding
in the other party. Of course, after you pose this to _____, you
need to pose to the parents that _____ actually *believes* there

is no way that they would recognize her efforts for them. Would they like to prove her wrong?

Of course, as _____ pointed out, they are angry, and maybe too angry to be willing to credit her at all. It may be too late, or they too rigid in their expectations. Then, her need to show some anger at her plight drives their anger at her not toeing the line, and gratefully!

Please keep me posted.

While I find the Dulwich ideas for coping with the central dilemma of teenagers and their parents very practical, I do not care for the fairy tale form to the stories they tell. To wit, " . . . and now they lived happily ever after." This myth of the reconciled teenager can be true in a way from this kind of intervention, but this machine suppresses the march of history itself. These teenagers are being harnessed to a slot, surrendering the infinity of their possibilities. As Reich would say (1933), they will lose their "bioluminescence."

Romance and Actual History

As I often dream about the subject of these chapters the night before writing them, and as I trust my unconscious to read the map, I will relate last night's dream:

> I was looking to go fly-fishing. and went up along Lake Michigan, to where a beautiful trout stream entered into the lake. However, a fishing boat captain had built his house over the stream at this very point . . . like Frank Lloyd Wright's "Fallingwater" house in Pennsylvania. This captain was like one of those Orvis guides, who supposedly will take you to the best fishing. He pointed out his beautiful back window onto the lovely trout stream, which was entirely controlled by him. It was a deep, dark color of good trout habitat.
>
> Annoyed with his dominion, I drove down a back road upstream, to a clearing, where I could look back on the captain's prize waters. They were a bright blue and almost neon color showing a completely empty bottom like a swimming pool at Las Vegas. I knew they were completely infertile, a very pseudo-bioluminescence.

Later, I wanted to ride my bicycle away from the conference center where I was talking about this very subject, only a
loud blast of a factory whistle stopped me as I put my foot on the
pedal, signaling that I must go back to my harness.

I do not take my unconscious (or anyone else's) literally, but only
as a correction, and often by caricature, of what the conscious mind
would overlook.

My unconscious is saying that the control advocated by parents
and surrogates and authorities, which is fought by the teenagers, wins
out, and the teenagers actually lose their fertility. Captain Orvis con-
trols the waters, setting up his factory. The waters in the dream were
serpentine or feminine in shape, and had become prostituted. This, in
brief, is the history of the last three thousand years, starting with the
destruction of Sumer and its goddesses.

I know all about unique outcomes (White and Epston 1990), and
I am all in favor of their extension into beautiful stories of resistance
that are successful against the panopticon of social control (White
1989), but they breed a dangerous romanticism, which, like all myths,
will create a luminous cloud over the actual territory of an extremely
controlling society. I will cite you three examples of misguided romance, which underestimates the physics of control. The first is a junior in high school at about age 18, the second a young woman who
works as a teacher at age 28, and the third a man who has gone into
early retirement at 48. This will illustrate the decimation of romance
at its early, middle, and late stages.

The gist of romance, whether in characters such as Anna Karenina
(Tolstoy 1875–1877), or in Walter Mitty (Thurber 1942) is to slip out
the back door of history and avoid its relentless march as a mythical
machine for the suppression of time. Romance is the alternative myth.
For example, in America, the '60s myth of cooperation was an alternative to our chief frontier myth of all-out competition. All societies seem
to have a dominant myth like ours, and an alternative like ours (Slater
1976). Youth who are balking at being harnessed into the machinery
of the dominant myth find ready mythical material lying around in the
shadows of the same dominant society. Thus, we find in the opening
of *War and Peace* (Tolstoy 1869), Pierre and Andrew refusing to coop-
erate with the advancement machine of Anna Scherer's soiree, and plot-
ting to do something else. Pierre goes drinking with his wild pals, who

drive him to drink a bottle of vodka standing in an open window as a bet. Andrew resolves to go get himself killed in the coming war with Napoleon. Later, both fall in love; and so forth. They just follow the alternative myths open to Russian youth.

The differences between my maps and those of most family therapists is chiefly about history, which outlines which parts our heroes can play. Those who do not know this history are condemned to repeat it. My heroes fall, as Jarrell (1941) knew, from the family into a very specific society: "From my mother's sleep I fell into the State."

A Case of Karl Marx

This case involved one of the brightest young fellows I have met in my consulting room. He was so smart that he had figured out that the ordinary laws did not apply to him. He had been arrested with his pals for car thievery, yet he did not think it was any big deal. That was the impressive thing, his cool attitude. From his superior perspective, his mother ought to stop fussing, and his father shut up. He knew what he was doing, and only needed to be let out of the stupid high school, which was no place for geniuses like himself. Just let him get his G.E.D. (high school alternative diploma), and everything would take care of itself, from then on out: nice fairy tale.

He certainly would not be coming to me on his own. He came in tow with his father and mother and little sister. The parents did not share his confidence in his own judgment. Indeed, they felt he was very far off base, and his sister violently nodded her agreement.

The interesting thing was that the father was similar to the son about going his own way. He had come out pretty well, as a kind of blue-collar aristocrat, who could set his own tempo and agenda of repair work. So, the father was passing on his own cultural capital (Bourdieu 1977, 1984, 1988) to the son. I could not tell if the son was going to take it too far, and get himself suppressed or not.

Naturally, mother and daughter had the reverse problem, of being the meek female helpmates to these male aristocrats. I was able to pose to them their fate as the meek, versus the alternative fate of making their presences known. As I wrote to them . . . "Curiously they [the father and son] have got what you [mother and daughter] need [knowing what they want] whereas you have what they need [knowing what others feel, getting the wider angle, and the drift of where things are going]."

The women also had a romance or myth that was apt to be misguiding. The helpmate deal was turning out to be suppression. Of course, that too is a historical fate of women in the lower class. This is why I was posing it as a problem for these two. They were pretty excited, but, of course, so were Thelma and Louise.

A Stuck Adolescence at 28, or Growing Up Female in America

The patient was introduced to me by her therapist. Her mother was in the position of the last two women, of long-standing helpmate. Like many women in the Midwest (C. Bly 1981), the mother had put off doing what she liked until about 45. She was now going about her own business.

The mother, however, was fearful for her daughter, now 28, who seemed to be running the opposite risk. This young woman was spirited, and was not going to be boxed in like her mother had been for so long. Indeed, a man had dated her a little and announced on one evening that she had until midnight to decide whether to get married. She got out of his car, straight away.

She did work she believed in as a teacher. She was pretty lonely. Here we were talking, brought together by her therapist who wanted my opinion about what could be done for this woman. The patient herself was inclined to ask me if hypnosis could get rid of her symptom of hair-pulling (trichotillomania).

Interestingly and typically, no one had any idea of what was triggering this obsessional routine. The patient had no idea and the therapist had no idea and the psychiatrist who gave her medication had no idea. Here was a hole in the story we would have to see into in order to reply to the patient's chief concern. All I had to do was take a little history of when it showed up, which was in high school, listening to "stupid teachers." They angered her so much, yet she could not come out with it, so she began pulling out her hair instead. I told her that herring gulls did the same thing! It was a displacement of her anger, that allowed her to sit through stupidity. Of course, it turned up subsequently to be useful with all manner of stupid situations.

Now, I could take the dive deeply into her dreams with her, and she told me about a dream taking place in the nearest big city in which she sat with a friend having lunch. Nine macho men in a row came in to bother her, and she killed all nine barbarously and yet offhandedly.

Her friend commented after the series, "They probably did something [wrong]!" We both laughed at this casual dismissal of nine murders. After she and I worked up the dream together, I was ready to give my opinion to her and to her therapist, which I summarized in my letter to the therapist to share with the patient:

_____ wants to know if hypnosis will relieve her hairpulling. If only it were so easy, to get rid of such an unhappy habit! Unfortunately, it will not work, because _____ needs such a habit to divert her rage in situations in which she feels trapped by stupid people (as in high school lectures). She panics in claustrophobic contexts. Her dream shows why: She has murderous feelings which she is too blithe about. Her friend says: "They probably did something!" to excuse nine murders. Now that is a caricature of being too accepting of a terrible thing.

So I am obliged to give her back her dilemma. She will need to stay far from people, and be lonely, if she cannot learn to have it out with people in a constructive way, that is, neither taking their control helplessly, nor murdering them. She missed out on this education, and the crucial question is whether she has the motivation to make it up. (If she wants something easy, and only has the motivation for that, she will not make it up, and be left in her dilemma until at least her mother's age.) While this is a classic indication for intense brief psychotherapy, even with the chronicity of the neurosis, the outcome depends on her readiness to undergo the education, which would surely include having it out with her therapist.

History lays heavy burdens on us all. For young women in America, the double burden is a pair of roles. They are both untenable myths that drift badly in time. The first is the helpmate myth of this young woman's mother. The second is the feminist and alternate myth of vigorous expression. The first presupposes the machinery of the one-down position, while the second presupposes a one-up position as a kind of Queen of Hell. I realize this is a caricature of what the feminist writers intend (Gilligan 1990). I mean to say that there is a strong pull to the right to become one kind of machine, and there is a strong pull to the left to become the opposite kind of machine. Either tilt of the board brings about a travesty, while equality is a remarkable feat.

This young woman and her mother occupy the two horns of the dilemma of growing up female in America. They lack the experience of give and take in relative equality, which would be necessary to have some third thing that could last. Naturally, I relate to her as best I can in this third way, and pose the problem of whether she has the fight in her for that kind of education. As Malan (1976a,b) discovered, the key is this motivation when the focus of selective attention points accurately to the path that will get you through the saddle of the dilemma. It needs to be added that being ready yourself still leaves you with a thin field of companions in the male species. Selection errors abound out of sheer wishful thinking (selective inattention to the shadow side).

A Stuck Adolescence at 48, or Growing Up Male in America

If I get the same plot/dilemma everywhere I go about growing up female in America, I also get the same plot/dilemma about growing up male in America. Both are about the cruelty of getting a slot in the hierarchies that are generating history, or about getting a companion as refuge from history.

One man was depressed and low-key and stuck living alone. His therapist was concerned rightly that he was pretty likely to stay there indefinitely. Of course, he was lying low because he had been badly hurt in engaging the world. Naturally, he did not have a clear idea about how the world hurt him and how he had lacked a defense. Here was the usual hole in the story about the most important thing. If we could sight his lack of defense, we could estimate if he could get an accurate education, so he could re-enter the field. Otherwise, he had better stay far away, and be kind to his little grandchildren who were no threat to this big man.

He could tell me the history, if he could not add it up for himself. The gist of it was that he had taken a job as a teacher for poor kids in faith that the higher-ups would hold up their end with supplies. They did not. He was more and more shocked, and outraged. They talked liberally, and padded their own projects. Finally, they had to take him away. He was so hurt and angry, and tied up in knots of self-doubt, that he could not think straight. He asked to be put on medical leave, and they were glad enough to be relieved of his irritating presence.

Of course, his wife had grown weary of a daily report of this misery. Like wives of oppressed husbands in Belfast or in Sarajevo, these wives begin to feel helpless hearing about their husbands as whipping boys. They often become shrewish with impatience that the old boy is not getting it and the family has to pay for his short-sightedness. The alienation divides the couple; the husband finds a moll who listens to him; and the marriage is also wrecked. Then, the patient is shocked that his girlfriend wants to marry him when he has in mind only comfort for himself. She turns away, and he is completely alone. To his amazement, or shall I say, to his consternation, bosses and women have their own covert agendas.

Obviously, he has missed this. He has been in a cloud of "Doing the Right Thing," like the pizza parlor owner, Sal, in Spike Lee's film. In such a cloud of semi-biblical righteousness, Sal can see almost nothing of what is going to happen! For he foolishly believes that other people are out to help the man who is doing the right thing. (Positive paranoia [Reider 1953].) He completely overlooks agendas so divergent from his own, which is why he ends up with others hating him and burning his very temple to the ground.

I summarized to my patient's therapist the dilemma over whether or not a comeback was going to happen:

> I think _____ can only come out of his corner in a comeback, if he can read situations in which his agenda is very different from the agenda of others, like the bureaucrats who hurt him so badly in the recent past, or like with his new girlfriend as of now. Otherwise, he will have to stay far away from people like a woodchuck. Can he complete his education on this absolutely crucial subject? I don't know.

I have met this man everywhere I go in the Midwest to do consultations at mental health centers. He is on the far horn of the dilemma of growing up male in America, because the near horn is indefensible for those in a cloud. Conversely, the men who do not come to me for help are those who engage by playing the game adroitly. They have little purposes of their own, so they readily take up the corporate game of increasing something (sales, status, goals, patients seen or publications secured, etc.).

Like the playing cards in Alice, they do not show their faces, but only their backs, when the powers, like the Queen of Hearts, pass by. They can be read out as K, Q, J, 10, and so on, and as spades, hearts, diamonds, or clubs. If they know their suit, and they know their numerical value, they can pass in the game as inside operatives. They become stale and repetitive, and so they wear out fast. Entropy sets in (Jantsch 1980) without challenge by the unfamiliar. Very often, I hear of them from their wives, who feel dreadfully alone for lack of company.

A Final Word of Late Childhood

The operative dries up in his increasing operations (St. Exupery 1943), and is no longer a child at all. He circulates like a playing card, or a postcard facedown with a correct stamp in the upper right-hand corner. He can be male or female. It hardly matters anymore, except females get paid less and excluded more.

Fortunately, some have gotten allies to keep them going with their dreams, play, and slow time. They operate in the fast tempo of the fast lane, but they know to get away. My older daughter and a friend just came up for the weekend in Madison, to get away from the pressures of Big City University. They complain that the place just tightens you up. One has a stiff neck, and the other a stiff lower back!

I reply that it is so everywhere in the operative society of universities and corporations and bureaucracies—that is, in the chief economic machinery of the country. The miracle is that some still thrive, and my daughter tells me of a professor who thinks slowly and aloud in class in an original way. While many of the high-strung students are jumping out of their seats with questions, the professor continues his line of thought to the delight of my daughter. He is fresh, is following his own fertility, and has a tempo that is strong enough in its own rhythm that it is not disconcerted by the jagged, jumping, frantic rhythms of the students hurrying for their places in the hierarchies.

I reply that I hope he gets his twenty papers written and accepted for publication, which is the only criterion for tenure. I hope he is playing the operative game with his right hand, while tracing his own thoughts slowly with his left hand. (See Yeats's poem "Long-Legged Fly" [1939, p. 178] for this beautiful, unhurried tempo.)

Often, I am called upon to help my patients through the horns of this dilemma called Adulthood in America. One horn is operating, so you circulate where all the rewards are given out for status, money, and so forth, yet you tighten and dry up there. The second horn is to follow your own fertility, yet you are in jeopardy of being cast out there. It is a dilemma about getting back and forth, between necessary operating and necessary fertility. Compare Japan to the United States. The operating mode seems even more desperate. Yet the alternate mode becomes chaotic, or protean (Lifton 1971). Getting back and forth can necessitate a literal and physical journey between the frantic cities for operating, and the solitude of the Buddhist temples in the mountains for fertility (Snyder 1990).

A Case of a Dolphin with a Stiff Back

I will close this chapter on growing up in America with a very brief tale of coming through the horns of the adult dilemma. The patient was a successful banker in middle age, who felt out of touch with himself. We spent about a year on his search for himself, which he did with dreams and with painting. It was slow going, with some beautiful epiphanies like rainbows, which faded fast. He complained of a stiff back, and a frantic feeling in his stomach, and of wearing out at the pace of his lists of responsibilities all carried out faithfully.

It was as if we quickened him in the sessions, and then he went dead again. (See Wilson 1986, *The Quick and the Dead*.) The machinery of his existence seemed to have him in its wheels like Charlie Chaplin in "Modern Times" and they whirled him faster and faster. A little break on my couch every two or three weeks was just enough to catch his breath, but hardly a strong enough measure against the tremendous pull to the right of his responsibilities.

After about a year of this labor, he came like Gauguin to say he had to get out of France for the South Seas. He did, coming back with beautiful serpentine blue and green portraits of a bay he had come to love as a place of Sumerian fertility for himself. The paintings he had departed from, by contrast, had been brown and orange and red humps of dry mountains. Naturally, he was a new being, with a light in his face. I could see the same serpentine forms that had been humped in his brown mountains now swimming in a kind of bioluminescence in his green and blue bays. Similarly, many of my women patients bring me chapters of Estes (1992), which encourage them to drop out into "running with the wolves," etc. In brief, drop out into the fertile domain of what Estes calls the "Wild Woman." This is pure mythology of the Cinderella sort. It is useful to encourage the hope of a world elsewhere (Poirier 1966), but it is itself a mythical machine for the suppression of the actual difficulties of returning to the operative world.

My patient told me he had to quit his job, and he had an idea of a consulting job that would leave him his liberty to get back to his bay in his imagination. In essence, this man was transferring himself from the harness of the lower upper class, to the liberty of the upper middle class (Fussell 1983), so he was working with the actual channels in the class apparatus. He was extremely pleased. The next time I saw him, I witnessed the actual difficulty of re-entry. The territory of the dilemma was not about to go away.

His superior had convinced him to withhold the news of his re-signing, to give the company time for some backstage preparation. He had gotten back into harness, and his back stiffed up so badly that he could hardly move! Angered, he resigned, and his back eased in a single day. Amazed, he told me this story. I was not amazed, as his paintings had already mapped the territory of his dilemma, and like Le Corbusier, I had a map for it, as shown in Figure 6–3:

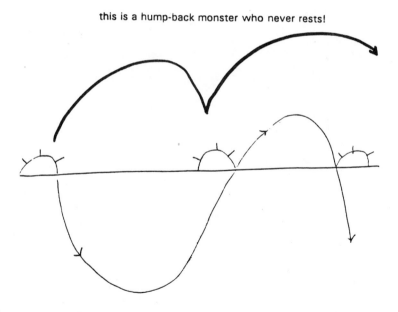

this is a hump-back monster who never rests!

this sets the rhythm of work for man

Figure 6–3. Le Corbusier's Dilemma.

I am not telling fairy tales, so I do not conclude with his living happily ever after. The pull is upward and to the right to the harness of increasing. The descent downward and to the left will risk exclusion. This is the territory to which we grow up in America, if we can get this far!

PART II

EXITS FROM THE DYNAMICS OF THE PATIENT: LONG, BRIEF, AND NEVER

As I have shown in Part I, there is a general tendency for patients with a benign response to understanding to change for the better, and for those with a malignant response to understanding to change for the worse. The timing of the change is now our second subject.

This timing depends upon the dynamics of the patient. I do not mean only psychodynamics. I believe it is more accurate to say that it is the dynamics of the patient's entire situation, inside and outside, that we have to look to. In other words, the patient exists within a force field.

I will not argue the scientific evidence for the relevance of the force field to outcome until I get to Chapter 16, "The Science of Long-Term Psychotherapy." The only substantial study of outcome in long-term psychotherapy, the Menninger Psychotherapy Research Project (Wallerstein 1986), is a continual argument for the patient's need for help to face the world and to make supportive arrangements within the world. Findings from the studies of generally briefer psychotherapy by Malan (1976a,b) and Luborsky and colleagues (1988) confirm this tendency.

Before I get to outcome in Part III, however, I need to show in Part II what I mean by facing the dynamics of the patient's situation with the patient. In general, all psychotherapists point to some dynamic that needs to be challenged for the patient to get better. The psychodynamic therapists may point to a conflict within, the interpersonal therapists to a bad effect on other people, and the behavioral therapists may point to a behavior, like avoidance, that will ensure a stalemate. As I have argued in my previous book (Gustafson 1995), and amply illustrated in Part I of this book, there is a great likelihood that the patient will overlook at least two dynamics that drive him, one outer, and one on the inner surface of his world. This will be the horns of his dilemma, on which he is apt to be impaled. Generally, his therapist will be more likely to sight one of these horns, while missing the other, because his training is specialized to inner, interpersonal, or outer worlds.

Over 150 years ago, Comte (1830) argued for the possibility of a "social physics" that would comprehend the forces acting upon men. Nearly fifty years ago, Lewin (1947a, b) attempted to carry out this program with his mapping of dynamic fields in social groups, which he called "quasi-stable equilibria":

> One of the fundamental characteristics of this field is the relative position of the entities, which are parts of the field. This relative position represents the structure of the group and its ecological setting. *It expresses the basic possibilities of locomotion within the field.* [Lewin 1947a, p. 14, italics mine]

In other words, an adequate grasp of the force field of the patient will discern where movement has a chance, what form the movement will take, and what are its dangers. Is the exit long, brief, or never? I will take up these different situations, separately.

In Chapter 7, I begin from standard psychoanalytic long-term psychotherapy (Gabbard 1994). I believe the central idea of this technique was argued by Rapaport (1959) in his classic systemization of psychoanalytic theory. The idea is that the patient is driven by dynamics, unless he can stand back from them in what Rapaport called "relative autonomy." He is driven outwardly, like a Pavlovian rat, and he is driven inwardly, like a dog in heat. He behaves reflexively. By looking at these situations in which he is driven, he is gradually able to substitute feeling the drivenness, while not having to act it out. This change occurs very slowly.

In Chapter 8, I show the possibility of a sudden change even in a single hour, or in very brief psychotherapy in "The Case of the Missing Lion." This is a full transcript, so that I can be as specific as possible about what I do to spring a change. In general, many patients like this one are stuck on an impossible form of control. In terms of chaos theory, this is the strange attractor around which their behavior revolves (C for control). The jump is to another strange attractor (R for romance), which, for this patient, is to become vocal about injustice. Of course, that is also fraught with problems, but it will release tension, and ease her from having to pull out eyelashes. Therefore, the sudden jump may be stable. Other patients jump back the other way. For example, a patient caught up in an impossible romance (R), as a kind of love fish hooked by a nasty fisherman, might jump back to being a distrustful bitch (C), as she put it to me.

Of course, neither (C) nor (R) works well in the long-run. Control dries up, and romance goes smash. Only some synthesis of the two is adventuresome in the name of a higher ideal and down-to-earth enough to be ready for the next turn in the road. I call this a third strange attractor (T), which is a slow development, and the subject of Chapter 9, "Thirty-Year Psychotherapy." It will be held back by cloudiness about any section of the map: concerning the emptiness of mere control, or the excessive climbing of romance, or the need for a suitable stage to play out transcendence, successfully.

Still, some things will not yield to the most profound discussion. This is our subject of Chapter 10, "Necessary Suffering." You cannot get rid of some connections to other people once made, or the suffering of the past, or having to compromise when your dilemma is bad versus worse. Finally, sin and death (and taxes) do not go away.

If the force field of a patient is mostly a given, and if cloudiness about it condemns the patient to be driven, unwittingly, then the natural antidote is to picture it as clearly as possible. For this, I find drawings indispensable, and here I illustrate them in Chapter 11, "Visual Maps." In particular, I draw upon the Jekyll and Hyde story of Robert Louis Stevenson (1886), because it is the most common fate of Western man, as Jekyll argues in conclusion. This is because he dries out in duty as the tireless servant, Dr. Jekyll, at (C), while he springs into the liberty of unrestricted romance (R) as Mr. Hyde. In general, the endless plots of mass-police entertainment (Brodsky 1988) of modern television and mystery reading follow this formula. They lead nowhere but in a daily circle of grind and daydream (Winnicott 1971a, Chap. 2).

Finally, I conclude Part II in Chapter 12, "Official Documents and Generative Letters," with the use of words to point to the map. Some language is official, which gets you paid. Some language is generative, like metaphor, which travels from one region of the map to a far-distant region, and thus integrates or pulls it together.

7

Long Psychotherapy

The beauty of long-term psychoanalytic psychotherapy is its simplicity (Gabbard 1994). The core idea is for the doctor to encourage the patient to drop some of his defenses that are necessary in the world, in the safe place of the doctor's consulting room (Havens 1989). If all goes well, the patient will gradually become more free to be himself in his feelings and thoughts and actions.

All of the technical measures of the doctor serve the relatively simple aim of freeing up the patient from the rigid part he has made his burden (Freud 1930). In other words, he labors under the requirements of his social duty, which he has internalized as his super-ego. He is driven by its requirements and becomes ill.

Yet, he is going to rebel against this onerous life by following his impulses (see Chapter 11, "Visual Maps," for the same concept in R. L. Stevenson's *The Strange Case of Dr. Jekyll and Mr. Hyde* [1886], which turns out to be no strange case at all, but Everyman). This too will take his self-governance from him, because he will be driven to love and fight and depend upon people willy-nilly, without regard to his actual self-interest. The psychotherapy will let loose this impulsive id in him, where it can be observed. Gradually, he will *feel* these urges, without being forced to *enact* them.

Thus, he will develop an observing ego that looks both outward about being driven to duty and inward about being driven by the instinctual drives. His ego will achieve relative autonomy (Rapaport 1959) from both kinds of drivenness, as illustrated in Figure 7–1. He will have a kind of poise or balance.

The Standard Technical Measures

Little has changed since Freud codified his technique (1912, 1913, 1914, 1915), as presented in Greenson's (1967) classic textbook of psychoanalytic psychotherapy. The doctor invites a certain freedom of association, notes resistances, and finds projections of the parental images onto himself. This happens over and over again, working through the two kinds of drivenness: of the super-ego and of the id.

A Case of Everyman

Everyman comes in for help, because he is anxious and depressed. He's got a very mundane job to do. He has trouble getting himself out of bed and putting his harness on, being depressed by the day's prospects,

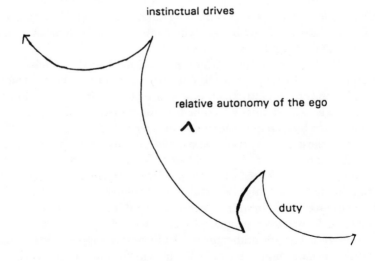

Figure 7–1. The Relative Autonomy of the Ego.

or lack thereof. He is also anxious about the job, because he fears he will forget parts of it that he'd rather not do.

He has few dreams he can remember, except the recurrent dream of not showing up for an exam in high school. He has daydreams, however, of beautiful women who give him what he wants (see T. S. Eliot's "The Love Song of J. Alfred Prufrock" [1915]). He tends to be chronically angry at his wife, for she is patently not this mother of all wishes. She is dull to him, and preoccupied with the children.

He comes to psychoanalysis or psychoanalytic psychotherapy and gladly puts his back to the couch. He is relieved to leave his burdens with his jacket at the door. When he is diffident, the doctor notes his resistance, and he comes out with something he was embarrassed about. For example, he has been imagining himself as a splendid public figure who is irresistible. He imagines that the doctor thinks this a foolish claim. It turns out his father did not like to hear about such things, so the resistance to telling about it is a transference resistance; and this projection of intolerance onto the doctor is clarified and moved off of him; and thus censorship is relaxed. There will be a little less drivenness from the super-ego.

Now, he swings the other way, in some excitement about a lady he has recently sighted. She responds to him, unlike his wife. He becomes anxious talking about her, which shows in his agitation of hands and feet. The doctor notices his rapid movements, and notes that he seems alarmed. The patient is relieved, and can talk about his fear of being carried away by his impulses to run to this lady and touch her all over. This could be the ruin of him. There will be a little less drivenness from the id. He can put words on the urges, so he can ride the words, in place of the urges running away with him. In Freud's metaphor, the ego rider has a firmer grip on the id horse.

However, the psychotherapy has to be long, for each relaxation of the super-ego to a more tolerating ego, and each wording of the id to a more manageable ego, is a small structural change that requires a very long series of similar changes to consolidate a relatively autonomous ego (Strachey 1934). This process is called working-through. In terms of the group selection theory of the brain (Edelman 1979, 1982, 1985), the id-group and the super-ego-group of cells are gradually won over to the ego-group of cells. The right group and the left group get smaller, and the center group gets bigger.

Another beauty of this simple way of working with this elegant theory is that the social world never really has to be faced. As Everyman comes to terms with his shadow mother of all wishes, he will be less harsh on his wife for failing to live up to this daydream (Jung 1925). As Everyman bears the pain of coming down from his glorious image of himself to his actual ordinary place (Bibring 1953), he will be less depressed and anxious. He will be less depressed at work because he can enjoy his wishfulness, without literally looking for it at every turn. He will be less anxious, because he can keep one eye on taking care of business, without fear of it wandering off into the daydreaming that is out of control. Thus, love and work will improve, without any specific attention to them, per se.

Additional Technical Measures

While a general theory like Freud's can have its typical case like that of Everyman, there are cases that are sufficiently different to alter the technical procedure. I will briefly go over these discoveries, in the order that they have been accepted. (See Gustafson [1986, 1995] for the discoveries by Reich and Jung that have not been accepted.)

Object Relations Theory

This theory has many sources, especially in the ideas of Melanie Klein (1959), but it gets its chief application in work with borderline and narcissistic patients through the work of Kernberg (1988) and Masterson (1988). The gist of it is that the ego is split by highly pathological situations in childhood, into a kind of false and often grandiose caretaker and a hidden and wounded child. Unless the caretaker is challenged, it will create a shallow situation that is a stalemate. Also, the desperate child will be unreached and continue to be terrified by any situation that suggests intrusion or abandonment.

Self Psychology Theory

This theory also has many sources, but it gets its chief application in work with patients who are also very sensitive to intrusion and abandonment through the work of Kohut (1971). Because many patients are less walled off than the borderlines and narcissists, they can be reached by a sensitive mirroring, and an attunement to their need to believe in someone (like the doctor himself). Failures in mirroring and attunement become advantages, when they are faced, for each overcoming of disappointment strengthens the patient against such injury. He is gradually immunized.

Other Current Theories

Other theories have gotten some interest, but are a little too difficult for general acceptance. For example, the control-mastery theory of Weiss (1993) suggests that patients test their doctors, by tempting them to act like the traumatic parents, or by putting them into the same position as the traumatized child (passive into active). For another example, the theory of developmental deficits in Gedo (1979) shows that patients may need to be shown how to reduce illusions, achieve a workable organization of their set of purposes, and reduce tension (Levels III, II, and I, respectively). For a third example, the complex theory of the uses of language of Havens (1986) suggests that patients need more than questions that threaten to pin the patient down. They need exclamations to encourage feeling, declarations to encourage boldness or correction, and so forth. (See Gustafson [1986, Chaps. 9 and 10] for a thorough discussion of the work of Gedo and Havens, and Gustafson [in press, a] for a review of Weiss's latest book.)

Limits for Psychoanalytic Psychotherapy

Certainly, there are discussions of selection for psychoanalysis and psychoanalytic psychotherapy (see especially Malan [1979] for the most thorough job upon which he expends six remarkable chapters). Little is written, however, about how little some patients change. Freud (1937) faced this topic bravely at the end of his career.

I will discuss this complex subject in many places in this book, notably in Chapter 9 on "Thirty-Year Psychotherapy," in Chapter 10 on "Necessary Suffering," and in Chapter 18 on "The Group Animal," where I take up the commonplace problem of the schizoid compromise, or being half-in and half-out. Before I take up any of those variations, I want to address the garden-variety failure in long-term psychotherapy.

The most relevant way I can think to do this is to take up the subject of long-term psychotherapists in long-term psychotherapy. Since they usually have had a lot of long-term psychotherapy, both as patients and as doctors, when they come to me for further help, they illustrate the limitations of what they know about themselves.

Long-Term Psychotherapists in Long-Term Psychotherapy

They mostly tend to be alike, in two ways. This is fortunate for the purposes of writing, because I can keep from discussing any one of them (and jeopardizing confidentiality, for any given patient of mine in this category may be the exception to the rule). The two ways are that they are very cloudy about the force of the outer world and about the force of the inner world. (See Chapter 9, "Thirty-Year Psychotherapy.") By cloudy, I mean something very specific. They are unclear, muddled, amazed. This means that the forces sneak up on them without any warning. When you are in a thick cloud, you cannot see what is about to strike you. You are relatively defenseless. (See *The Adventures of Huckleberry Finn* [Twain 1885] for unforgettable tales of Huck and Jim riding the big river in night and fog and storm.)

Why would a long experience in long-term psychotherapy leave a patient (doctor) in this condition? The reasons are relatively simple. Psychoanalytic psychotherapy usually is highly interpersonal in its focus, coming down most dramatically upon the catches that occur with the doctor himself (in the resistance and transference). When the theory calls for relative passivity in the doctor to wait for these developments *between* the patient and himself, there will be little discussion about the collisions the patient has with the world. Certainly, his feelings about such harsh events will be shared, but there is not likely to be a study of how these things keep happening. (Gedo [1979], provides a clear exception, in terms of developmental deficits, as discussed in Gustafson [1986, Chap. 9].) Neither will the patient be likely to study much about that other world that knocks him down, namely, the unconscious that is so powerful in dreams. Oddly enough, despite Freud's discovery of this royal road, it is hardly used in psychoanalytic psychotherapy to much advantage. Notice that Gabbard (1994) gives it one paragraph in his widely accepted text, namely, to note that it will reflect the themes of the discussion. The elements of the dream are to be translated from the manifest appearance to their latent associations.

Obviously, any given practitioner of long-term psychotherapy could depart from the rules of free association, resistance, and transference analysis. He could watch the collisions with the social world, like Sullivan (Gustafson 1986, Chap. 6), and he could watch the intrusions of the unconscious, like Jung, as described below (Chap. 17, "Jung's Individuation, Compared to Freud"). If he could do this, he would sight the two great vulnerabilities of my patients who are long-term psychotherapists.

The General Case of Being a Prisoner of an Unconscious Image

Almost all of these patients have a romance about themselves that is not quite explicit. For example, many are in love with love itself, and expect to be delivered from an unhappy life by a romantic partner. This almost never, never works. Nevertheless, it is apt to be endlessly hopeful. The therapy will prove to be futile, because the longed-for savior never appears.

If the patient will bring dreams, the dreams will illustrate the absurdity of the claim, as of romance (Jung 1933). For example, Jung's most extended case in this essay is of a woman who dreams of being rocked in the arms of a God of Wind (Wotan) overlooking wheat fields. The dream is the best way to grasp the huge power of the claim upon the patient. Gradually, it subsides as it is put into perspective. (See Gustafson 1995, Chap. 13, "Dreams as an Individual Map of Dilemma," for an ample discussion of technique.)

Regrettably, most of these patients will not consistently bring dreams. Then I am reduced to pointing out, less convincingly, the myth, say the romantic myth. Some of them can turn more to depending upon themselves, if they have an art, or a sport, or a political mission. Depending upon oneself in this world is apt to be much more reliable. Some have so little education in this that it may be too late to begin. Of course, the pursuit of a genuine passion that unfolds for at least a lifetime is about the only reliable way to win and hold love. Without it, one is apt to become boring.

The General Case of Being a Prisoner of the World

Psychotherapists tend to be idealistic people who know very little about how the world works. In this, they are abetted by a sentimental culture that supplies them with things like the movie "Field of Dreams." The moral of the story, you will probably recall, is that you need to follow your dream, such as to build a beautiful baseball field in a cornfield in Iowa: "Build it, and they will come!"

Of course, baseball teams do not come unless you can purchase the franchise from a league in which baseball is officially played. In reality, the United States is a land of salesmen, who will definitely come if you've got the money (or the credit) (Shorris 1994).

You are going to get hurt endlessly until you get this straight. Groups work quite simply, in terms of increasing something (see below Chapter 18, "The Group Animal"), whether it is baseball crowds, or papers for tenure. Many of my patients can't quite believe it, so they are continually amazed, unprepared, and injured. (See Gustafson 1995, Chap. 14, "Seeing the Social World Coming.")

A Static Theory Turns Out to Be a Disadvantage

Let us suppose the patient is ideal, and develops a relative autonomy of the ego from the claims of the world and the claims of the unconscious. Perhaps he will be assisted in this by a doctor who can show him the very mechanism of the world that he misses and the very mechanism of the god who makes him a puppet. He is poised, and in balance. Now, what will happen?

Well, he is apt to become bored, and boring, for the great struggle has gone out of his life (see Chapter 15, "Tolstoy's Fate," for a harrowing example of Tolstoy in midlife at a standstill).

This is the great disadvantage of the stability of the psychoanalytic theory. It is finished, but for minor tinkering. By getting rid of the outer world and the amplitude of the (collective) unconscious, it has its regular phenomena of resistance and transference in the interpersonal world of patient and doctor. Little more can be said about it. Of course, the nuances can be quite lovely (see Margulies [1989] for a fine appreciation of color, texture, tone, and so forth), and those who can just enjoy these sensory variations are apt to last the best in the specialty. It is a kind of maternal quality, which delights in the particular child–adult (see Winnicott 1971b).

Readmit the world and the collective unconscious as two huge realms of exploration, and the theory regains its vitality. Rather than that pale term of relative autonomy of the ego, the stakes now are a transcendence that can only come from the double adventure of a life-time of eluding traps in the world and in the unconscious, as illustrated in Figure 7–2. (See Gustafson [1986] on Odysseus and on *Moby Dick* [Melville 1851].) But that is our subject in Chapter 17, "Jung's Individuation, Compared to Freud."

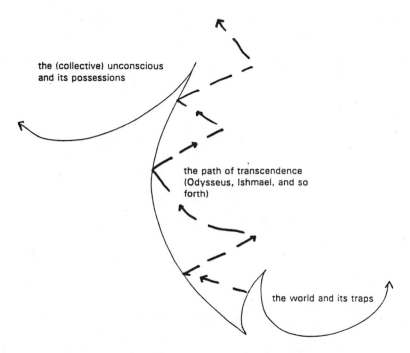

the (collective) unconscious
and its possessions

the path of transcendence
(Odysseus, Ishmael, and so
forth)

the world and its traps

Figure 7–2. The Path of Transcendence.

8

Brief Psychotherapy:
The Case of
the Missing Lion

Introduction

The single hour for me is the same in its structure, whether I am consulting to a resident or conducting a brief psychotherapy or a long-term psychotherapy. Thus, it is timeless (in its structure), while time bound (in its context of how many hours I have to give this patient) (John Strezlec, personal communication). I am showing this single hour of consultation in full, in order to show this structure, which characterizes all of my work.

In general, the single hour has an entry around the preoccupation of the patient or of the resident consulting me. Here, the resident is occupied with a missing piece in the cognitive-behavior therapy she is conducting with a student who complains of pulling out her eyelashes. They have had a handful of sessions, in which the patient has been taught how to control her fingers. Yet, the resident feels that she cannot reach the "piece" that has to do with how the patient feels about what is bothering her. The patient seems to be behind a wall (of her character armor).

So, there is something missing on the outside surface of the patient's reactions to the world. This gap, hole, or piece of selective inattention is usually my first concern to find. For, because the patient lacks clarity and access to this force, it perpetually drives her. Here, in this case, it is tension about her need to be perfect, and this tension is what keeps her pulling out her eyelashes.

Once the patient has some confidence in me, we drop into her shadow side where she is able to tell me about her dread of the unfamiliar. This surfaces as her dread of me as the unfamiliar person she is coming to meet—in other words, in the transference. Interestingly, I am able to link the outside surface and the inside surface in terms of our initial joke about the Missing Lion. First, the missing lion is her own anger when she is not perfect. Next, the missing lion is projected out onto me as the stranger (lion).

Sensing her pain about the unfamiliar, I am able to ride this feeling back with her into her humiliation in gym class as an awkward child, and link it to her fear being in my "psychiatric gym class." Now that we are in very deep, I take the dream dive like Winnicott (1971b) by asking her what she has dreamt about all this.

I will leave the reader in suspense about her dream, in which the missing lion definitely comes up from the deep to roar, and rattles and riles her with its strength. Here, we certainly have the missing piece of feeling, which the resident had sought at the outset. This has been the gap, hole, or selective inattention on the inside surface, which is my second concern in an hour.

Finally, I need to exit the hour by tying it back to where we began. The patient has not only been riled and rattled with great feeling, but she has also enacted pulling out her lashes in the throes of this missing force. I thus have met the challenge of the case for the hour by coming up with what has been missing, and sought. I conclude by summarizing the dilemma this leaves the patient in and how disturbing it has to be for her. My letter, included at the end of this chapter, goes over this same ground, so it is as clear a map as possible. This dilemma is usually missed by patients and by therapists, because it is painful to face how *some* trouble is inevitable. It is my third concern, therefore, in every hour.

For this patient, her dilemma (as summarized in the letter that follows the session by about a week) is that she wants to be perfect, but this only makes her tense. If she gives up on perfection, then she is apt to feel a great anger at the injustice she can no longer overlook. She fears her anger will be too much for others dear to her (like her fiancé).

This is why the lion has been missing (until I led it in). The lion is a mixed blessing, and this is her dilemma, which is ongoing.

In general, a brief psychotherapy is an arrangement to have six or twelve hours to go over this kind of ground, usually a single episode of trouble in the patient's life (this case has two episodes, concerning perfection at work, and perfection in marrying). A long-term psychotherapy usually goes over many different episodes from many different periods of the patient's life. In Chapters 9 and 10, I will discuss at length what it is about the patient's dilemma that prolongs it—thirty years, or perpetually.

The Case

As I went about final preparations for the following video consultation, the patient remarked that it was quite a studio. I replied that it looked like a department of psychiatry but *actually* it was owned by MGM (Metro-Goldwyn-Mayer films, of Hollywood). Archly, she quipped back, " . . . then where is the lion?" (alluding to MGM's trademark lion). As was usual for Winnicott, and for myself, the key and missing piece from the unconscious was supplied offhand and informally before we formally began.

The Reason for the Consultation

Gustafson: All right. So . . . as I said, you and I will talk about what you take your work to be, the two of you, and what you've achieved, and where you might feel stuck at all, if at all, and then [patient] and I will talk about it for an hour, and then I'll write her a letter with a copy to you [resident]. We'll try to understand this. I mean you hinted to me that you had gotten somewhere for a while and then it had slipped on you in some sense. That was sort of the caption to the story that you . . .

Resident: Right.

G: . . . that you sort of hinted at last week.

R: It started in January . . .

G: January.

R: . . . and at that time it felt like you had made a decision after struggling with this by yourself, first for about two years when you were in eighth grade, ninth grade?

Patient: It was like, actually the second year that I was in school, in college I mean . . .

R: Ya, but didn't you have . . .

P: Well, ya, but not [unintelligible] initially, and then there was a big, long time lapse and then . . .

R: Right, and a long time lapse and then you've had this for about four years?

P: Ya.

R: Ya, and so, I think from the way I heard it you [unintelligible] in a pharmacology lecture, which the School of Nursing had talked about this, and you became concerned and decided this is it, you wanted to come in, so she came in in January and we talked and pretty much started describing the behavior, and at that time it seemed like it was linked up with reading more than anything . . .

G: What? Reading?

R: Reading, study times.

G: Studying.

R: But the other part that made no sense was there were actually movie times, like if you were at the movies, or bored watching TV, and again you'd have that behavior. One thing that was kind of interesting was that just the call, just making the phone call and coming in the door had made a difference, and so she had started to get some success just because she picked up the phone, so by the time I saw her which was, what? two weeks later or something? her eyebrows had grown in and she was pretty pleased with that.

G: Ya. So how did you understand that?

R: Well, I felt like that was a decision for her, that she had decided this is it and that she had decided that I'm at my point now, I'm going to make a point of change.

G: She's ready.

R: Ya. We, you know, we did some interviewing, I talked with you a little bit about the family. The part that's been puzzling to me I think has been that I haven't seen a lot of how you deal with anger, or how you deal with feelings. From what you've told me, in your family it's okay to express angry feelings, like between your mom and dad and you and your sister, and your fiancé, you can tell him, but I've wondered if this has been an expression of how you feel stuck. What we talked a lot about recently, and I guess I'm jumping ahead now . . .

G: It's all right.

R: What we talked a lot about recently was that you put a fair amount of pressure on yourself to be a very good nurse and be a very good nursing student, and we've talked about the plucking as a way to get your own attention when you're read-ing, to force yourself almost to stay on topic and to understand everything. Because I've been a nurse, we've been able to talk about the fact that when you're passing medications or in any way related to passing medications, there's a real need to make no mistakes, make no errors, and . . .

G: Do you know that tennis players are the same way? Some of the world's famous tennis players? Have you ever seen . . .

P: I believe it.

G: Lendl and Boris Becker, they develop, there's so much pres-sure to do everything exactly right that they develop these little, Ivan Lendl was the world's number one tennis player, he was always plucking his eyebrows out, and right in the middle of . . . the match . . . the tension, he was so tense, I think it re-leased tension.

P: [unintelligible] that fits, ya.

G: It's a way of discharging tension. Boris Becker, he was the world's greatest tennis player for a while, he isn't anymore, poor fellow, and every time he'd play a point he had this little bark like a seal—he'd go uh, uh, you know, and it was just I think, just that the tension is very unpleasant, so a person's got to have some way not to be so tense, I mean one way or another one has got to find a way, so that's a crucial word, in other words if you don't have an outlet for tension, you might end up going back to this one, especially when your therapy is ending.

R: And you did say that last time . . .

P: Ya.

R: That what we had done is stretched out the time, since we had this eight session motto we had kind of stretched out the time from her last appointment to the most recent one, and it was pretty clear from what you've said that things have gone down hill.

G: Ya, well that would fit because in a way I would think talking, talking with Dr. R. would sort of unload some of this stuff for you, huh?

P: Um, hmm.

G: Make you a little bit more at ease with yourself, 'cause you, on your own you sort of bottle it up.

P: Ya.

G: And being quite a correct nurse, such a perfect nurse, huh? It's such a burden to be perfect. I would, well, it really is, isn't it? It's terrible, it's terribly hard.

P: I'm predisposed to it.

G: You are. Ya, because this urge to, for perfection is, it's very hard on a person, huh?

P: Um hmm, um hmm.

G: Especially if you get it early in life . . . you know, very early if you, very early in life you get on this track of pushing yourself as hard as can be, you know, oh [unintelligible] tightening yourself, huh? Ya. Okay, so just roughly speaking, it could be that, that, there's also something about carrying all of this on your own shoulders, huh? All this perfection you've been, it's quite a, you know, it's like having a knapsack full of trouble, carrying all this burden around, just being able to hand it over to somebody else would ease you up a bit . . . [T]hat's my hypothesis for this, that you found an avenue here that, an alternative route to lower tension and now you're withdrawing the tension-relieving device which would drive poor [patient] here back into the old . . .

P: The old behavior.

G: Her old behavior.

R: The piece that we sort of started with was kind of a cognitive behavioral approach . . .

G: Ya.

The Therapy Got Stuck (Missing Piece)

R: . . . and you kept records and paid attention to when this was happening, and we looked for alternative things to do with her hands, and she came up with something finally where she was holding two objects and that really made a difference, and she also, part of it was really related to schoolwork, and the pressure of knowing exactly the material she had just read, and so she attempted to manipulate the times, you know, stretch out times or change times when she was reading. Recently the reading load has gotten worse, which has made this, again, more difficult apparently. But the piece that's been missing from me, I think, has been more the affective piece of it . . .

G: That's what you were saying.

R: Ya. Because I have felt at times when we're talking, I mean I'm sure there were times when we were talking when I was saying, "Well how did you feel about this?" or "Tell me about this" or "How are you feeling?" and you kind of would look at me like . . .

P: I'm not really [unintelligible].

R: Well, no, a little bit like, almost like I was going down the wrong alley, and I felt at times that I was going down kind of a dark alley and not really seeing what was going on there.

G: That's interesting.

R: The other piece of that that you, you did talk about too is that your mom had some problem with panic attacks, but later in life.

P: Ya.

R: More like forties?

P: Um, hm.

R: And had . . .

P: Late forties.

R: Late forties. 47 or so, and, I haven't talked to you too much about that? Not too much?

P: No. Just the one day we explored it a little bit, but . . .

R: So there was that kind of piece of it, and I got the sense that she went on meds and that was helpful to her. In many ways I got the impression that you're more like your dad, more quiet like dad. I get the sense that dad's very caring about you, that you feel pretty comfortable with him. I just sort of picked that feeling up. My guess is that mom, mom's given you more advice about what you should do about all this . . .

P: Um, hmm.

R: . . . but I got the sense that dad was more of a quiet, caring individual in your life. But it feels to me like there's been some missing pieces and I wanted to come in when you came last week and I knew you were frustrated and I felt like maybe you could help us with the missing pieces.

G: Ya, well, the big missing piece for you then is why this pleasant young lady won't let you in on her feelings.

R: Um hmm, um hmm. Although we talked about it in terms of, I get a sense that [unintelligible] has been really good in her life . . .

G: Oh, there's no question of that . . . I've already concluded, I've already come to that conclusion, that was an understatement, she's been very good.

R: Very good, and it probably was hard for her to come in and ask for help because you've been managing so well in so many ways on your own and been very good, meeting other people's expectations I think, for a long time. And not a complainer at all.

G: Oh no. Self-reliance.

R: Ya. Absolutely.

P: Ya.

R: And successful.

G: And good at it.

R: Ya.

G: Ya. So to get to a point where you actually have to ask somebody for something might not come so readily for this young lady, huh?

R: Ya. I would think not, I would think it was difficult.

G: So maybe that's a partial answer to your question.

R: Ya, maybe.

G: She'll let you help, she'll let you help a little bit.

R: But not take her burden.

G: But not get too close, you know, not, you know, I mean she's going to let you offer a little but, you know, like, stay away lady, you know, I mean, don't get too close to me, or something, something like that?

P: Ya, I don't know what's there to tell because I feel very comfortable with you, I mean there's nothing that I've lied or hidden about, or anything like that so I mean I don't know what there is that I need to tell you that would, you know, fill that in, 'cause I don't feel there's anything there.

R: Ya, I know you don't, and I know you don't . . . I don't feel like you have lied to me in any way, but I feel like there is, I feel, what I think I'm feeling is this wall about, that I think you feel all the time, being not as in touch with your feelings. My guess is that I'm feeling a lot of what you, you feel, that you're kind of, there's something in there that you're not letting yourself feel, and that's what I think I've experienced.

G: What do you think it is?

R: Well last week when we, we started talking about this, I thought it was, this kind of rage about, we kind of talked about it this way, that there were sort of two voices on her shoulder, and this one voice sort of says: pay attention, make no mistakes, because you were talking about wanting to come out of nursing school and be very skilled and not make any mistakes, and that you had really admired your teachers, and we sort of joked about this because I can remember several nurses I worked with here that, they made no mistakes . . .

G: No, I know.

R: None.

G: I know, I've seen them.

R: They will not make a mistake because it would not happen to them ever under any circumstances.

G: Yes, I understand . . .

R: Okay.

G: It's perfectly clear.

R: And so we could really relate to that, but I think what I heard you saying was that part of you would like to get out of school and function like that. I mean it would really feel good to be that competent, and that that seemed to be one side of you, and then the other side there was a piece that was sort of saying, you know, but what about [unintelligible], you know, how much torture do you have to go through to function that, at that high level of performance, just graduating, impossible, and I felt like this other side of her sort of says well, what about the person here.

Where Is the Lion?

G: Where's the Lion? As you said, well, the unconscious will speak to me.

P: No, this shoulder.

G: It's on the other shoulder, ya, there's the Lion, where's the Lion, yes, I'm going to draw a nice big lion here for you, let's see, so let's see I, so here's the problem, we'll draw a picture here of the situation we have, we have a nice, this is, this is a crown here of perfection, no mistakes, this is, you know, you're very near getting, you know, you're rising towards the crown of perfection here, this is the kingdom of no mistakes. This is the King of No Mistakes here. The trouble with this, it makes people tense. They get tense, they sort of twist a bit here, they get tense ascending this pathway here to heaven, you know, to rise here, and then, that's one shoulder, that's the shoulder that's drooping, and then we'll draw, and then over here is the, over here is, that's the MGM Lion. It's mad that it doesn't know, it doesn't know, nobody can seem to find the damn thing, nobody can seem to find the lion. But he's around. Bounds up and down the hall, you know. But he's kind of, he's kind of an elusive lion this one. Draw a nice lion. That's as far as I can go with the lion right now, that's as far as I can see him. So, so this is, these are the two shoulders here. This is the drooping shoulder to the right, and then there's this other shoulder that's kind of missing, that's the missing piece. It's sort of the person that has to put up with all this perfection, things build up underneath, huh? You seem to know exactly what I mean.

P: Umm hmm.

G: So what about this, what about the burden, you know, what about this, see this is, how shall I do it here? ya, maybe, the world mostly sees the correct side of you, almost entirely, so this is all, you know, like, this is basically what appears to the world and in treatment is a person who is trying very hard to do everything absolutely right and it's getting tense. That's all the world sees, right? The other part is hidden and that's what you would like, you'd like to get a glimpse of this other side. For good reason because this kind of feeling that one is sitting on makes a person tense too. So, since you seem to know about what that is, let's talk about it.

P: That's the problem, I don't really think I'm angry, at least I don't know if I am.

G: Well, anger is probably too strong a word. Ya? I mean I guess the issue, if we start with words that would come more comfortably to you, I mean what is it like for you, I mean when you're working so hard to do everything so perfectly and getting tense, you agree to tension, feeling tense. Well, maybe if we look at where it gets the most tense, you know where the burden seems most hard to carry. Where would that be?

P: It's schoolwork.

A Problem of Quantity

G: Uh huh. And like . . .

P: Mainly school related.

G: So this tends to occur mostly around school stuff?

P: Umm hmm.

G: And where would you, where would the tension get to its most screaming pitch so to speak?

P: Where, I'm not clear what you mean?

G: I'm using too strong words for you. Where does the tension get the tightest, when do you get the tightest about schoolwork—toward the end of the semester or, are you there now or . . .

P: It depends, I don't, it depends.

G: Well I'd like, that's what I'd like to understand though, where, where, you know, I mean tension is, you know, goes up and down for you. I'm interested in when you're least tense, and when you're most tense . . . I mean you know, if we take this tension here, you know, we could graph it, you know, it goes up and down, I'd be interested . . . when it's, you know, when you can ease up a bit and when you're really tightened.

P: I guess the more projects I have to do, the more exams, it's, it's probably quantity related . . .

G: Very much about quantity—just the size of the load.

P: Ya. Than necessarily a certain part of the semester.

G: So when things pile up?

P: Umm hmm.

G: Then you're apt to get pretty tense.

P: Umm hmm.

G: Uh huh. Okay. So it's pretty quantitative, and then when there's less you're apt to be easier with yourself.

P: Umm hmm.

G: How would things stand with you right now?

P: Umm, they were tense last week, but they're less tense this week, but they're still tense.

Pleasing Herself

G: Still somewhat, somewhere in the middle this week.

P: Ya, not, not to the point where I have nothing to do and can just do whatever I want.

G: I see. So when you're, you're easiest when you're doing what you please. Is that right?

P: Umm hmm.

G: What do you like to do?

P: Sit, I like to, I sew quilts, and I like to do that.

G: So, what, when you're doing what pleases you, your quilting and sewing, what else do you like to do?

P: Social things with our friends.

G: Our friends, you were referring to . . .

P: My fiancé.

G: Your fiancé. You're how far from getting married?

P: Five months—October.

G: So when you and, what's your fiancé's name?

P: _____.

G: You and _____ are hanging out with your friends, this is easier for you?

P: Umm hmm.

G: What do you guys like to do?

P: We do nothing.

G: Do nothing?

P: We just drive sometimes or go see movies or, we have, I think we have unique friends in that we don't have to be doing something to be entertained, we can just sit and talk, or . . .

G: You can entertain yourselves.

P: . . . go look at houses or whatever. Ya.

G: Good. How nice. Where is, how do you, how does that work? I mean how did you find someone that you could be entertained with by not doing anything.

P: I don't know.

G: So the two of you are alike in that way, huh?

P: Ya.

G: Huh. That's interesting. These two people are so easily entertained. Maybe you weren't raised on television.

P: Oh I was though.

G: Were you really?

P: Ya.

G: So maybe you, the two of you just watch TV?

P: Ya.

G: I see. So when you, did you say [unintelligible]?

P: Ya.

G: So he, he seems to settle you down, huh, being with him?

P: Umm hmm.

G: It's pretty easy for you. It's kind of an easygoing relationship. So it sounds, from what we've talked about so far, it sounds pretty quantitative. When, you know, when the load is heavy you are apt to be tense, and when the load eases up and you can do nothing, you're apt to be a lot easier.

P: Umm hmm.

G: Is that about right?

P: Ya.

G: I see.

R: Can I throw a piece in there?

G: Sure.

The Resident Throws In a Key Piece

R: A piece that didn't fit, we've talked about this, was when she started to keep track of when the plucking would occur there would be times like during a movie, or times when watching TV that she'd have the urge again. It felt like, from what you told me, it felt like it was tension, kind of tension and then a release of tension.

G: Ya, sure, that's always what it is.

R: But that, when we were trying to make sense of when this occurs, what are the, who are you with, and what are the precursors, why is this occurring, sometimes at the movies.

G: Let's find out. Let's go to the movies together, see why this would occur, huh? Let's talk about a movie where you might get tense.

P: We didn't have success with that.

R: No, you know you didn't have success with that.

P: No.

G: You couldn't . . .

P: See she thought maybe it was that I wasn't allowing myself to go to a movie and just sit and do nothing, and that I had to be back working on something, and so that I was sitting there taking out frustration of, I guess, you'd say wasting my time watching this movie, even though I wanted to be there, even though maybe I had suggested it, and that I was, that I should be back doing something else. And I don't know if that's true or not.

G: Maybe you disagree.

P: I don't know.

G: Well you don't, you don't see the evidence for it, you're . . .

P: I haven't had a situation like that recently so I can't remember it to evaluate it.

The Transference (Unfamiliar People)

G: So you don't have the data.

P: No.

G: Am I making you nervous?

P: No.

G: Why were you, you were getting a little nervous there. What was that about?

P: No, she just smiled at me.

G: You weren't nervous?

P: I am now . . .

G: If I put you on the spot.

P: Ya.

G: It makes you nervous. If I sort of push you a bit, huh? That'll do it, that'll tighten you up a bit?

P: Sure.

G: So if I push this lady she'll get a little nervous, she'll get tense, right? Just trying to draw a map, you know, where this is and where it isn't. What are you thinking?

P: What am I thinking?

G: Ya. You're . . .

P: I'm waiting.

G: It's hard when I don't say things, isn't it?

P: Umm hmm.

G: Well just see what that's about. I'll just let you sit here without, well let's just see. Really, that might tell you something about, you know, what your tension is about. I'll just sit, I'm not going to say anything for a few minutes here, see what it's like for you.

P: It's probably going to make me nervous.

G: Ya. Well let's see what that's about. Let's just see what that, see what we can discover about your fear if I'm not busy. You still tense?

P: Getting less tense.

G: Ya. . . . What was that I was passing a little bit, what was that, it's something about my just being quiet or leaving you . . .

P: Partly 'cause I knew what your intention was.

G: What was my intention?

P: To do it on purpose to see how I'd react.

G: [unintelligible].

P: Well before then 'cause I didn't know that that's what you were doing.

G: Oh, I see, now that you know that I'm . . .

P: Now that I know that . . .

G: That I'm just doing it on purpose you're not so afraid of it.

P: No.

G: So you didn't know, when you didn't know what it was it made you nervous . . .

P: Umm hmm.

G: So unfamiliar things frighten you.

P: Umm hmm.

G: Ya. That's important I think.

P: Ya.

G: You like to know where you are, very strongly.

P: Ya, ya, that's actually . . .

G: A big thing.

P: That's a big thing, ya.

G: Let's just see where that goes, what, something about not knowing where you are that, that really leads into danger for you. Why don't you just see why, I don't know why, I mean I don't know why that is, I see that it is about you. What is it about unfamiliar area that's been so hard for you in your life?

P: Probably because I've been raised to have a plan, well, I like to have a plan to know what the goals are, to be in control I guess.

G: It's a way of being in control.

P: Yes.

G: So if you're not, you get, it makes you real uncomfortable.

P: Umm hmm.

G: That's, to put it mildly huh? Now we're getting closer, huh?

P: Umm hmm.

G: So if, you find yourself in unfamiliar territory then this, this education about having plans and being in control all of sudden is not working.

P: Umm hmm.

Her Dominant Perspective (Character, Security Operation)

G: Okay. I'm going to have to start a new drawing here. But these are important plans, these are important words for you, huh? Plans and control. So part of it is you, your whole upbringing has been to have plans and control, and then when you, when things are, when you don't know what's going to happen and it's unfamiliar, what's been your history with that. I know it's not the main history but you probably, it's happened to you anyway hasn't it?

P: Ya.

G: Where have you been, found yourself in unfamiliar territory?

P: I think that over the years I've been better at, have gotten better at just plunging into it and just going for it, whereas before when I was little I'd probably avoid it.

G: Would you?

P: Ya.

We Drop into the Shadow (Pain)

G: What sort of unfamiliarity would you avoid as a child?

P: Gymnastics class.

G: 'Cause you, because, what makes you laugh about that?

P: Just a funny memory, just 'cause I couldn't, I didn't, I was taller than everyone else and so I couldn't bend the way that they were bending and I lacked the ability.

G: You felt awkward.

p: Ya.

G: It was painful for you. Scary. That you would be embarrassed or something.

P: Ya, something.

G: So you would try to steer . . .

P: Ya, so I'd beg mom not to go.

Bravery (A Third Thing)

G: So that's one example of your history with sort of unfamiliar and awkward situations, huh? But now you try to brave these things.

P: Sometimes, ya, and sometimes it's actually kind of fun.

G: So you've gotten more bold in that sense.

P: Ya.

G: But it's very hard for you if, if you feel awkward or not in control or not at your best, huh?

P: Umm hmm.

G: You're a proud soul aren't you? You don't want to come across badly. I suppose coming here you, you know, is an example of being brave.

P: Ya, I was just telling her that I was really nervous about it.

G: And yet you sort of steeled yourself to do it.

P: Umm hmm.

Back to Transference (Psychiatric Gymnastics Class) and Bravery (Third Thing)

G: What were you afraid of coming here?

P: You.

G: Me? And what about me?

P: What about you?

G: Well, what about me is, was scaring you?

P: Oh that I'd, see that's, okay that's the funny part because I was telling _____ that I was really nervous about this, he goes well you weren't nervous when you went to see Dr. R. I'm like no, but I had met her before, so that, 'cause I had to come that day and they matched me up with you and then you happened to be there walking through and you just said hi, and so I, what

I'm getting at is that I hadn't seen you or met you and so I didn't know . . .

G: I'm an unknown.

P: Right.

G: Whereas you look familiar and . . .

P: Right.

G: Not too far out of a person and—she probably struck you as somebody you could be comfortable with and familiar with, but you didn't know me and so that's a threat.

P: Right.

G: The unknown is very threatening for you. So you were being brave to come face the Lion.

P: Umm hmm.

G: If I brought the other lion out then she'd really be afraid.

R: What was interesting is you said yes right away, that did surprise me that day. When I talked to you about this it was like ya, I'll do that.

P: Umm hmm, ya.

R: There was no part of you at that moment that seemed to . . .

P: No. See sometimes I think oh ya, that would be fun to just go . . . I was in that mood that day.

R: You were.

G: Ya, well you have this sort of braver side, you have kind of a brave side where you want to sort of chance it.

P: Ya.

G: [unintelligible] well, let's try.

P: That one side wasn't working and I agreed, and then like 'What did you do?'

G: And then later you began to shake at the thought of what you let yourself in for. Ya, how's it going? How's it going right now?

P: I still feel nervous 'cause there's people over there and the camera's on, but . . .

G: Ya, what makes you uncomfortable about that? What they might think of you or . . .

P: Sure.

G: What are you afraid of?

P: This is probably kind of a weakness to have this kind of a . . .

G: [unintelligible] hmm, sure, and if they see that you have a weakness then what? They might . . . what's . . .

P: Make some judgment on me.

G: I see. It's like going to gymnastics class and feeling like you don't bend too well.

P: Right, [unintelligible] best effort ya.

G: I see. And now you're in another gymnastics class. Psychiatric gymnastics. Back in class and not feeling like you're doing as well as you'd like. You feel afraid of people looking down on you.

P: Sure.

G: I just sense some pain about this issue for you.

P: Some what?

G: Pain. I sense you've been hurt about this.

P: Ya, I think I had some rough friendships in second and third grade or something.

G: Tell me about that.

P: Oh, just the whole popular–not popular, just finicky friends too . . .

G: Sure.

P: . . . which I realize now that, you know, at the drop of your hat your best friend could all of a sudden not be your friend.

G: Ya, that's how they are.

P: Ya, that's how they are.

G: Finicky friends, ya. So, but you got hurt, your feelings got hurt by this finickiness, this inconstancy.

P: Right. Because I wasn't one of those people, I wanted to find, you know, I didn't need a lot of friends, I just wanted to find a set few loyal people that you don't have to worry about the politics of making friends, you can just go out and be friends.

G: So your idea, what you are, you're the kind of person that makes a few really good friends and you're very loyal, right?

P: Umm hmm.

G: So these people would be hurtful to you.

P: Umm hmm.

G: 'Cause it's now they are, now they aren't, now you're in, now you're out.

P: Umm hmm.

G: You had a lot, you took a lot of pain from them.

P: Umm hmm.

G: It's still with you.

P: Sure.

G: So, what are you thinking?

P: I'm just looking at you writing.

G: Ya, you're waiting for me.

P: Ya.

Assimilating the Unconscious (Riled and Rattled): "The Other Shoulder"

G: Well we're getting to, this is your vulnerable side, I just sense it rattles you a bit, you know, to get to the side of you where you're vulnerable, you know, this is your vulnerable side, huh, this is the other shoulder where you're not as well defended, although you're getting braver.

P: Umm hmm.

G: You know, I mean you're, you've decided that you have to take some chances in life and that's good 'cause you, people that are afraid of unfamiliar situations can retreat from life. Do you know anybody like that? Have you known people that need to be in control, sometimes their lives get smaller and smaller because they, anything that's unfamiliar they won't take the chance, but you, you have some, you have some . . . oh, I know why I'm thinking of the lion . . . you know that other lion? you know the lion in the Wizard of Oz?

P: The Wizard of Oz, oh.

G: You're a little bit like that lion. You're frightened [unintelligible] is that right? You think that's funny?

P: Ya.

G: Well isn't that true?

p: Ya.

G: The Cowardly Lion.

P: Umm hmm.

Her Dilemma Mapped with Her

G: Now this is the, one could become a coward from these painful experiences with these finicky girls and the pain of that, and one could run away but after all here we are on a yellow brick road trying to become brave, huh? This is a, I'm drawing a yellow brick road for you here. The Cowardly Lion recovers. I'm not the Wizard of Oz though. Just so we get that straight. I don't particularly like him after all. Ya, so you're engaged in trying to be braver, but inconstancy and finickiness is, well when one is looking for stability like you have been, seems like all your life, this [unintelligible] to be reliable . . .

P: Ya.

G: If one looks for stability in the wrong places one gets wounded and that seems to be what happened, they were looking for stability among finicky people and that would be very wounding. Ya. You know what I would be most interested in?

Winnicott's Dream Dive

P: Hmm?

G: What your dreams are like.

P: You know she said that.

G: She's warned you about that, huh?

P: And I can't remember them.

G: I bet you haven't had a dream you could remember your whole life.

P: My mom would, [unintelligible] that she used to be more into it and so she'd want us to keep a journal, so for a while I did that, but . . .

G: I bet you can't remember a single dream from that journal.

P: Probably not.

G: She's been forewarned. I bet you didn't even dream, you know, from all that six hours dreaming last night I bet you, I bet you you don't remember one, one second of your dreams from last night. Huh? Not a single image. Not even . . .

P: Sometimes, usually I do remember images, but then I can't place where they were.

The Doctor Gives Himself Away

G: That's okay. I'm just interested in just an image that you might have in a dream. I'll tell you one of mine. Let's see what did I have last night. What did I dream? Oh, ya. I'm always dreaming on Hamlet. Do you know Hamlet?

P: Ya.

G: I was actually at Elsinore last night again, I'm always going back to Elsinore. What did I dream? I dreamt that I wasn't, I said that somebody else was going to have to do the funeral service for the King. That was my dream last night. That's kind of interesting. Um, so, no, I knew I was there, I mean I knew I was in, I knew I was, I'm always putting myself into plays and movies . . . do you do that at all? Do you find yourself in the middle of . . .

P: No.

The Patient Gives Back: A Non Sequitur

G: What sort of image might crop up with you?

P: Well I had a dream last week where, see mine are really bizarre and really non sequitur . . .

G: That's okay, but that's interesting you see because . . .

P: Like the grass turns into a field and then it's something else . . . I mean the dream, I think, I think I'm thinking about it and like ya this makes perfect sense, and then I wake up and I'm thinking like what in the world, that didn't make sense at all.

G: Well that's okay.

P: But . . .

G: I don't mind. Ya, what was this non sequitur last week?

P: All I remember is just that I was living with, our family was living with a murderer.

G: That was the dream?

P: Ya.

G: Okay. Well that's, that's enough, that your family, you mean your family that you grew up in?

P: Well no, see I don't know, it just felt like a family, it wasn't, I didn't see my mom, I didn't see my dad, but it just felt like a family.

G: Okay. So a family living with a murderer. That was the non sequitur. Okay. And that was the, it was like a, that was the scene so to speak.

P: Umm hmm.

G: Okay. Should we work on that, do you want to do that?

P: I don't remember any more than that.

G: That's all you need. That's all we need.

P: Okay.

The Translation of the Dream Elements

G: This will, this will, this is, that's all we need to work. Okay? Should we do just a little bit on it. It's a little dream but it's, I think it's probably enough to get to something important. So tell me about families, I mean this was a family right?

P: Right.

G: So tell me what your, tell me what families mean to you. You have a history with a particular family.

P: Right.

G: Can you tell me about your family? Or a family, or, what, I mean tell me your history with families, you know, when did you meet families and what about families. Tell me all about families for you, you know what I mean?

P: Ya.

G: You're a particular person who has a history with families. What is your history with families?

P: Myself has been supportive and kind of, I want to say adventurous as far as being open-minded and, you know whatever you want to do go for it, that whole thing. I know that families don't just have to be a mother and a father because _____ comes from a family that his father is not really their family as far as support goes and as far as who you would want to be associated with, so that, if you just surround yourself I guess that you feel comfortable with, that's kind of a family.

G: But in _____'s case the father is what?

P: Well he's actually the stepfather, but he's just, he doesn't fit in with the support network.

G: He's not supportive you mean?

P: Right.

G: What . . .

P: Well, mentally. Monetarily he . . .

G: He does.

P: He purports to be, but he's kind of a negative influence on the other two brothers.

G: I see. In what way? What makes him negative, in what way is he negative?

P: He is very oriented toward money and belongings. He has some past rendezvous, when he was married to _____'s mother, and that's partly the reason that the older brother and _____ don't really care to associate with him because they don't agree with his values and morals or whatever. He pretends to be a pillar of the community and he's in the Lions Club, you know, all those sorts of things community-wise . . .

G: Not the Lions . . .

P: Well I mean . . .

G: Ya, I understand.

P: Mr. Businessman, I have three kids, look at me I'm great. Whereas in his closet there's a lot of secrets that make him to be a real creep.

G: I see, you mean rendezvous with other women, is that it?

P: Like affairs, ya.

G: I see. So he appears, he's a person that purports to be upright, but actually is creepy.

P: Right. Ya.

The Dream Translated Agitates Her Non-Verbally (Riled and Rattled)

G: I see. Okay. He's makes you nervous.

P: Ya.

G: I notice you were more uncomfortable when you talk about him.

P: He's strange, 'cause I've never met, I mean nobody in my family is like that, I've never met anyone like that, but I've known about them, known about their past like that.

G: For you a family is a safe place . . .

P: Ya.

G: And so if there were somebody like that in it, it's kind of a contradiction in terms. Like having a murderer in a family. Right?

P: Right.

G: You see . . .

P: You can make sense out of anything.

G: She's very confident. She has great confidence in me, she thinks I can make sense out of anything. Just when I caught something that might be subtle here you see? So, I mean, in a way [unintelligible], I mean, the something about, the something disturbing to you about _____'s father being, you know, having to be in a family like that that's disturbing. It's like your unconscious exaggerates it, it looks like, you know, having a murderer in the family. I mean it just, it just doesn't belong. It's a contradiction in terms. Tell me about murderers? What's your history with murderers?

P: I don't have one.

G: Oh, you know you've known about them. When did you first learn about murderers?

Nancy Drew as Her Ideal of Childhood Courage

P: Oh, probably, I don't know, did people in Nancy Drew murder other people? I don't think that they went that far. I don't know. I always used to read mysteries when I was, I read all the time when I was little. I read all the Nancy Drew books like five times.

G: Ya, what happens in those? I didn't read those.

P: I can't remember. See. It's just so, they're pretty toned down I guess, I don't think there were ever any murders in [unintelligible].

G: But they are mysteries?

P: Ya.

G: They are about wrongdoing aren't they?

P: Umm hmm.

G: Isn't she tracking down wrongdoing, Nancy Drew?

P: Umm hmm.

G: Okay. So, I mean, your first thought about murderers is, in your history, is at least if not murderers, of badness . . .

P: Right, ya.

G: And what further experience have you with murderers?

P: Umm, probably just TV.

G: TV?

P: Ya.

G: There's a lot of them on TV.

P: There's tons.

G: They come in one side of [unintelligible] and go out the other. And what about murderers on TV? What's, how's that for you?

P: Kind of frightening just because I feel like people are getting desensitized to it and, I mean I assume I fall in that category too so that, I don't know.

G: It bothers you that it's, people are desensitized to something so horrible.

P: Ya. Ya.

G: Ya, it does bother you, I see.

G: What if they are? I mean what about that? What are you afraid of?

P: Umm. I guess that ultimately it's going to lead to some kind of moral decline or something as far as [unintelligible] of what's important.

G: That makes you, you know, unnerves you a bit, to think that that sort of . . .

P: Ya, well not [unintelligible] but in the long run.

G: In the long run, ya, okay. Well if there are murderers in families it's not good for families.

P: No.

Establishing the Conscious Standpoint, to Set Up the Dream as Its Correction

G: So, you had this dream last week?

P: Ya, I think so.

G: Do you remember which day it was?

P: No.

G: But sometime last week. What were you doing last week?

P: Probably talking a lot about _____'s Dad.

G: Were you? Why, who were you talking about it with, with _____?

P: Ya, and his mom.

G: Were you visiting with them or something?

P: On the phone. Talking to [unintelligible].

G: On the phone. And what would you all be saying about, just what a creep he was?

P: Ya, because he's decided now that he wants to file for custody of one of the brothers.

G: I see. So he's sort of back to his bad, bad doings. So you were talking with his mother about the trouble that this guy is causing.

P: Right.

G: So, and how did you feel about that consciously, I mean you were discussing it last week.

P: Right. I just felt it was wrong, not in the best interests of the younger brother.

G: Ya, does it make you anxious?

P: Uh, just . . .

G: Uneasy, [unintelligible] kind of squiggle around and you were just actually pulling at your hair . . .

P: Well I'm just trying to figure out what I want to say.

G: Okay. fine, fine, no rush.

P: I guess it would make me frustrated that, that he's even around and making problems and she's trying to, I mean she's a very supportive woman, she's hardworking and . . .

G: Trying to do the right thing.

P: You know, the pillar of that family and he's just chiselling away at it, you know.

G: Chiselling away at the person that's trying to hold that thing together.

P: Umm hmm.

G: Ya. There's some, ya, indignation on your part about this?

P: Ya.

G: Like how dare he?

P: Ya, it would get to that point I'm sure if he actually went through with it. He's just saying now that he wants to . . .

G: He's threatening.

P: He's said stuff like this before, so I mean if it actually got to the point where I thought he was really, meant something by it then I would probably start to feel real frustrated about it.

G: Ya, I see. Exercise, you might get, your feelings might get going around.

P: Ya.

G: To see this creep getting away with this stuff, with somebody who's basically good. I mean that [unintelligible] with outrage [unintelligible]. So your unconscious is in there saying now, you think, in a way you're, it seems to me, your dream means that consciously you don't like what's going on, your unconscious is saying I'll say I don't like it, it's like having a murderer in the family, I *really* don't like this, huh?

P: Ya.

G: So it's a way of sort of, your unconscious is saying now you really don't like this, I mean this is outrageous, huh?

P: Uh huh.

G: Is that right?

P: Ya.

The Disturbance in Her Dilemma

G: But you, when I sort of touch on this you do get more uncomfortable with having the outrage?

P: Ya, I don't know that I would ever confront him on it.

G: You would be scared of that.

P: There may be some day out of one week that I'm, I'm going to go do it right now . . . and then I, I probably wouldn't.

G: You'd be afraid.

P: Ya.

G: What would you be afraid of?

P: Him.

G: What would you be afraid of coming from him?

P: Umm, well the stupid, the stupid thing because I don't think anything of him, I mean I think he's a creep, and so why should I care what he thinks of me, so why can't I just tell him off or tell him what I think of him?

G: I don't know. Let's see if we can find out. I mean obviously that frightens you to even consider that you would tell off somebody like . . .

P: Ya.

G: You can say that again, huh? What's scary, what's the danger of telling off the creep? Have you ever done that before?

P: I've tried.

G: Have you?

P: I 'spose, ya. I guess I'm just, I get rattled and then I want to have something to come back at it, you know, I mean I want to have, have my thoughts all in mind so that they don't rile me up.

G: They don't rile you up or rattle you up?

P: Both.

G: Rile and rattle. You have to get so much emotion going that you get riled and rattled, but this kind of, so it's hard to keep your cool, it would be hard to keep your cool when you are really, like to take this person apart.

P: Right.

G: I see. Ya, okay. You're, you look thoughtful. Well you look like you're, just wondering what I'm saying, well I'm just writing down what you said basically that if something really, you have very strong feeling about this creep, and you, you knew you did, didn't like it, but your unconscious says you're outraged, and then I ask you about your outrage and you say, well it's a little scary to be outraged because if one told off somebody like that it would be very hard to keep one's cool, huh? And you've had that situation before evidently.

P: Ya.

G: Where does that take you to? Having to tell off a creep and getting riled and rattled, when did that happen to you?

P: When lately?

G: I don't know, when in your life did that, have to do that?

Widening the Domain of Her Dilemma

P: Umm, we had some neighbors that are kind of inconsiderate with their stereo and so I get pretty mad about that because I feel that they're just encroaching on my, you know, just common decency . . .

G: Ya, it sounds like they are.

P: So, but in those instances I think it's been a little bit better just because the guy that, the main guy that does all the problems, who we had the problems with is kind of irrational, so it makes me more, feel more rational so that I can actually sort out what I want to say so I don't just come off being, you know, tart little things I'm going to say what I want to say and then . . .

G: You can keep your cool with an irrational person, you can be the rational one.

P: Ya.

G: So you're afraid of being the emotional one.

P: Ya, and being out of control.

G: And being out of control with your, in a riled and rattled way.

P: Not being able to be, not being able to effectively communicate what I want to say without ditching the effort and saying oh, just never mind.

G: Ya, you might run away from it if you were getting, losing your, you were losing it so to speak.

P: Ya.

G: With your anger, you might duck it and say oh, forget it.

P: Ya.

G: So you're in kind of, see your dream image in a way shows something that, it shows that a situation which you're trying, which is bothering you, can bother you a lot more than you like to admit.

P: Ya, that's true, ya.

G: And the reason that you try not to admit how bothered you are is you, you don't want to lose it, you know, when you come forward with your feelings you, so that's interesting. See that's what we do with that dream, huh? Does it make sense?

P: Umm hmm.

G: How are we doing? We've got another 5 minutes. Well, what's all that got to do with the price of tea, huh? You guys had what? One more session or something?

Back to the Doctor's Dilemma

P: Well to talk about what happened here.

G: You don't have a, you have a session to talk one more, I mean just in terms of your insurance?

P: Ya, probably two more.

G: Two more, I see. Well, what have we learned from this, huh? Do you want to say something? How is this sitting with you, I guess, you know, I mean I'm the person that you're consulting to and you were wondering about the wall . . .

R: Umm, hmm, and it's clear to me that the two shoulders are really there, the two sides. I had thought last time that this behavior sort of reminds [patient] that this side is here too, it's like she maybe doesn't want to just be so compliant and be such a good girl and do the right thing and be that perfect nurse, because what price does it, what huge price does she have to pay? And I felt like this was a way of sort of getting her attention, getting in her face about that . . .

G: So that's like a question to me, I mean that's your hypothesis.

R: That's my hypothesis.

G: And you're asking if I agree with that?

R: Ya, I guess I'm asking how could we have gotten more in touch with that side? I felt frustrated at times, although I know [patient] was saying to me that she felt I wanted . . .

G: She was trying to be a good patient.

R: Oh ya, no doubt. Ya, I have no doubt about that.

G: Well, it's impossible that she could be otherwise, she even will take some risks for you and . . .

R: Ya, and come in here.

G: Ya, that was nice.

R: That was nice. But the hole, I felt the hole was there, the affective stuff was missing and I was wondering how I could have gotten around that differently. I mean I see what you did with the dream.

G: It's interesting, isn't it?

R: Yes.

G: That got down, that got behind the wall a bit.

R: That got behind the wall a lot.

P: But see I didn't think there was a wall, if you had asked me about that I would have told you, you know.

G: Ya, at first you didn't even think that you had a dream.

P: I knew I thought, well, of all the things that I, 'cause she said that you might ask me if that, well that's the only thing that I can think of to remember, so if you ask me that's what I'm going to say.

Blow Up (Correction of Selective Inattention)

G: Sure. So I mean, that's one way to get, I mean, it seems to me from that is one answer to the question, you know, that people think that their dreams don't make any sense or that a fragment of something doesn't have any meaning. That's generally what people think, when if you bring it into focus all of a sudden it's like a Nancy Drew mystery, I mean it's, there's a lot there. Did you ever see "Blow Up?" The movie "Blow Up." It's about, there was a murder in a park, this was a movie in the '60s, you might be interested in this, there was a murder in a park and there was a picture of the park, but in one little place they, and then they had to blow up this one part of the photograph in order to see. In a way I mean this little dream fragment about the murder in the family is like a, we just sort of enlarged it and took its history, and then took this into the kind of stuff that really disturbs you. Got closer to where you, you know, where your feelings run strong.

P: Right. But then where does that get you? I mean what do you do with that? Once . . .

G: What do you do once you've found it?

P: Ya. What do you do once you've made sense of your dream?

G: Well it seems to me that your conscious, my view is that the conscious mind sometimes misleads us, sort of living with one, you know, leaning from one shoulder all the time or, one might miss certain things, one might underestimate for example how much feeling one really has and how afraid one is to own it, you know, like you're going to get married in five months and it seems to me you're joining a family where you're going to be upset. In a way the dream looks forward to something that's going to disturb you, and you might need some practice facing your feelings so that, you are kind of a, I mean I think you can feel like the Cowardly Lion, and you'd rather be the MGM Lion, right?

P: Sure.

Coming Back to Where We Began: Lions

G: But that, I mean, you know, it's, we'll just extend the road here, here's the MGM Lion up here, that was where we began. You asked me where he was and here he is, the MGM Lion. Well, but in a way that would be nice if you could be more the MGM Lion you know, instead of a cowardly one. Right now you experience yourself as a cowardly one, and that means then you won't be ready for certain things in life, and life isn't always familiar, and marriage is full of, and marrying into a family that's fraught with a guy who's been a creep is going to bother you a lot, it's going to, so it seems to me an important thing for you to be able to admit when you're outraged and be able to own your feelings about that so that you can deal with it, 'cause you're not going to be able to avoid it.

P: Right, right.

G: I mean in the world of nursing everything is perfect, but, you know, in the world of marrying into a family who has a creep in it, it will be very imperfect, so that's something maybe the two of you can talk about, you know, I mean how, how your feelings actually do run and how frightened you are of your, your sense of injustice, I mean you have a very keen sense of injustice, don't you?

P: Ya, ya.

G: I mean that runs strong in you. And since you don't want to be cowardly, you know, you're basically trying to be a braver person, huh?

P: Umm hmm.

Her Dilemma Posed, in Conclusion, as Similar to the Herring Gull's

G: So you're going to have to be brave in this family I think, otherwise you'll be pulling your hair out and your eyebrows. Did Dr. R. tell you about the herring gulls, what I said about herring gulls? You know when herring gulls pull their . . .

P: I don't know who that is.

G: Herring gulls, gulls? Sea gulls.

P: Oh, okay.

G: When they, when they're in fights with other herring gulls, to avoid the fight they begin pulling, when they're coming up against another creepy herring gull that they'd like to, you know, take, you know, pull all its feathers out, you know what they do? They pull grass. They turn from each other and they pull up grass. And it's a way of avoiding the collision.

P: Oh.

G: You know when herring gulls will, all of them will troop into, or fly into a certain beach, you know, to lay their eggs, and it means they're in very close proximity, and some of the herring gulls turn up their stereos, and other ones are creeps, so some of the herring gulls get really mad as hell about how unjust their neighbor herring gulls, and then they basically do the equivalent of pulling out their hair. They pull up grass. So I think you can expect, whenever you're confronted with something, you know that, where you feel there's a lot of injustice, you're going to feel like running away and pulling up grass. It could be a signal to you that, you know, that feelings are running strongly. Then maybe you could, so that's what I think. That's what I think this is. It's a very, it's a very, it's a sign of that something bothers you *very* much, and consciously you don't want to be bothered at all, right?

P: Right, 'cause I have other stuff to do.

G: Ya, it's inconvenient, you know. It's very inconvenient.

P: I've got other things to do . . .

G: I have a rock and roll band that lives next door to me, and I feel like taking that house apart brick by brick. You know how inconsiderate that is. A rock and roll band in the next house, and then one rock and roll band dissolved, the older brother, and now the younger brother's got another one. I don't know if I'm going to get through the summer, I may have to go talk to Dr. R. I may be pulling my hair out. I'll start pulling the grass out.

P: Pull *their* hair out.

G: Pull their hair out! Well there it is, you see, that's what this is, it's a real displacement to get away from outrage. So. I'll write you a letter. You need to give me your address and I'll write your whole dilemma.

Letter Following Session

Dear _____:

The trouble with your excellent pursuit of perfection/familiarity . . . is that it always makes the pursuer tense . . . and more so when the load is greater. It also leaves a person very anxious in situations which are unfamiliar, finicky, awkward . . . and, as your dream shows, morally wrong. So, the general tendency is to shy away and become less and less able to cope with the irregularities of life.

Fortunately, you also have a brave side, which counteracts the retreating side, and brought you even to face me! So, if you are a Cowardly Lion, you are daring to go down the Yellow Brick Road . . . and, maybe, someday, if you keep going, you can become the MGM Lion you were asking after.

Your conscious mind tends to minimize your feelings, while your unconscious mind is ready to counteract it with full force (there is a murderer in the family!). The trouble with it is that it will indeed rile and rattle you, until you practice handling the big force so you remain self-possessed. It looks to me like your unconscious is warning you that you are joining a family which will not be perfectly familiar like your own, thus challenging you to become a capable Lion.

I would love to hear from you in a year, next April and perhaps have you visit me in May, to see how you are coming along with these struggles of yours. I enjoyed our work together.

9

Thirty-Year Psychotherapy

It is only fair, after showing the effectiveness of brief psychotherapy, to make the opposite case, that is, for situations that take thirty years to change. Nothing is understood, in psychotherapy, without understanding its negative. This is how we can grasp the forces involved.

The simplest way to state where the thirty-year hold up occurs is in Bateson's distinction between Learning I and Learning II. (See Gustafson 1995, Chap. 6 for my discussion of Learning I, II, and III.) To wit, many people learn to change a particular situation (n), which is Learning I, but never grasp the entire *class* of situations, so that the next instance will be dealt with summarily (n + 1), which is Learning II.

To take the case example I used in my first discussion of Bateson (Gustafson 1986, Chap. 15), "The Dog in Hell" was a man repeatedly mistreated like a poor dog, in an endless series of the same plot. The actors and scenes varied, from parents to girlfriends to professors, at home or dating or in school. Yet, he was always amazed by the next incident in the series, and fell down badly, and miserably, like the dog in hell that he was playing: in other words, a role of endless subservience.

The tendency of any particular session was to grasp the last incident, overcome his amazement at it, feel his suppressed feelings, and invent a different and preferred way to respond. Yet, he had tremendous difficulty grasping the absolute similarity and redundancy of one episode to the next episode. Of course, the analysts call this the problem of "working through," and simply indicate it takes a long time. This begs the question of what allows the Dog in Hell to jump out of the series of hellish incidents into a purgatory of something different. Why do some dogs take one lesson, and some twelve, and some twelve squared, and some twelve cubed, etc.?

Bateson suggested several ideas about the jump in learning from instances to the class (I to II), based on his observations of the dolphin at the Oceanic Institute in Hawaii. The idea was to stop rewarding the dolphin for previous training, but rather to reward only if the dolphin did something new:

> . . . each of the first fourteen sessions was characterized by many futile repetitions of whatever behavior had been reinforced in the immediately preceding session. Seemingly only by accident did the animal provide a piece of different behavior. In the time out between the fourteenth and fifteenth sessions, the dolphin appeared to be much excited; and when she came on stage for the fifteenth session, she put on an elaborate performance that included eight conspicuous pieces of behavior of which four were new and never before observed in this species of animal. [Bateson 1979, pp. 122–123]

The dolphin jumped from the class of old behaviors reinforced to a new class, by consistently being in the wrong and by some unearned fish so she could stand staying in the experiment (a little inconsistency).

I suggest that things are somewhat more difficult with the human being, citing my Dog in Hell, in two ways. For one thing, my patient had gotten whatever he had gotten by playing the dog. He had become a kind of genius of playing it to advantage, for example, making final exams into hell and getting his girlfriend to be unappreciative, so going home from college would be a relief. For another, he was like the sinners in the Fifth Bolgia of Dante's *Inferno:* skillful at the game of graft, and completely lacking a vision of heaven that he might aspire to, so that punishment had no educative effect that would lead him out of the pitch. (Educate means, from the Latin, *e-ducere,* to lead out.) There is no path out of hell, up the mountain of purgatory, without a vision of heaven. Also, you need a guide who has the heart for it, and the wit to keep finding the path when lost.

Indeed, my patient got some appreciation from me of his genius, and finished college, but has been stuck ever since, as I showed in my follow-up of him (Gustafson 1995). He could not climb further in the realm of work, nor in the realm of mating, but lives with his parents in the interstices of our Roman Empire. He got a subclass of Learning II, in school, but that was as far as he could go, unable to generalize it to other domains.

It occurred to me that some people like him take thirty years to make a jump (to Learning II), when I noticed some profound changes made by people about 50 years old. At 20, they never could let go of their insistence. This led me to consider the difference between 20-year-olds and 50-year-olds and to ask if maturation could be speeded up at all by an adroit education. I think it sometimes can. This chapter is about a change so great, Jung called it transcendence (see Chapter 17). This transcendence is well known in Eastern philosophy as *marga* (Campbell 1959, p. 164). It is obscured by four kinds of clouds.

The Cloud That Obscures Territory

The first cloud envelopes territory. So long as we are literally caught up in conquering, mating, and fitting in, we are driven by innate releasing mechanisms (IRMs), seeing only the points of light that trigger us to do what everyone else is doing. All else is shrouded.

In other words, we are complete creatures of the increase pack (Canetti 1960), in its various moods, of fight–flight, pairing, and dependency (Bion 1959). Or in the terms of classical Indian philosophy, we are driven by *karma*, or power, *artha*, or pleasure, *dharma*, or duty (Campbell 1959, p. 464).

Our perceptions, moods, and even thoughts are not our own when we are tied into territory. Orwell (1946) describes ordinary prose: ". . . prose consists less and less of *words* chosen for the sake of their meaning, and more and more of *phrases* tacked together like the sections of a prefabricated hen-house . . ." (p. 159). The purpose, says Orwell, is to keep things cloudy, so they are not seen, which is a defense of the status quo: " . . . a feeling which suddenly becomes stronger at moments when light catches the speaker's spectacles and turns them into blank discs which seem to have no one's eyes behind them. A speaker who uses that kind of phraseology has gone some distance towards turning himself into a machine" (p. 166). This is as true of patients as it is of politicians. When they repeat the phrases of other people, they turn into machines without eyes.

In the late twentieth century, reading the world may be less a matter of phrases, than images, which is what Kundera (1990) calls the shift from ideology to imagology:

> Some one hundred years ago in Russia, persecuted Marxists began to gather secretly in circles in order to study Marx's manifesto; they simplified the contents of this simple ideology in order to disseminate it to other circles, whose members, simplifying further and further this simplification of the simple, kept passing it on and on, so that when Marxism became known and powerful on the whole planet, all that was left of it was a collection of six or seven slogans so poorly linked that it can hardly be called an ideology. And precisely because the remnants of Marx no longer form any logical system of ideas, but only a series of suggestive images and slogans (a smiling worker with a hammer, black, white and yellow men holding hands, the dove of peace rising to the sky, and so on and so on), we can rightfully talk of a gradual, general, planetary transformation of ideology into imagology. [pp. 113–114]

If this was the beginning of imagology, it now runs all of public life under various names, like public relations, journalism, editing, political consulting, spin-doctoring, and so forth:

> Nowadays, the imagologue not only does not try to hide his activity, but often even speaks for his politician clients, explains to the public what he taught them to do or not to do, how he told them to behave, what formula they are likely to use, and what tie they are likely to wear. We needn't be surprised by this self-confidence: in the last few decades, imagology has gained a historic victory over ideology. [p. 114]

Truth becomes the facts, gathered by journalists, social scientists, with statistical significance:

> Public opinion polls are the critical instrument of imagology's power, because they enable imagology to live in absolute harmony

with the people. The imagologue bombards people with questions: how is the French economy prospering? is there racism in
France? is racism good or bad? who is the greatest writer of all
time? . . . And since for contemporary man reality is a continent
visited less and less often and, besides, justifiably disliked, the
findings of the polls have become a kind of higher reality . . .
Public opinion polls are a parliament in permanent session.
[p. 115]

Truth comes in a very small box, which allows an image, and a name.
For example, psychotherapy consists of a safe place, or a unique outcome, or a program. All have been shown to have statistical significance
and are, thus, beyond doubt.

Because people have such programs for everything, which are supposed to work, they are amazed, shocked, and bewildered when they do
not work. They are at a loss for describing the situation. A. S. Byatt (1988)
shows this paucity of language in her review of the poetry competition
one year for the *Times Literary Supplement:* "I had trouble finding six
poems I thought were good enough to print and I felt little, almost no,
pleasure. But I was, paradoxically, deeply moved by the bulk of the poems.
The subjects fell into readily distinguishable categories" (p. 174).

Byatt goes on to the several categories of triteness in poems, and
then blames the lack of expression on lack of interest and play with
the English language:

Then there were the poems of sex, reproach and indignation—
the most memorable, a poet's wrath at her mother-in-law for
sneering at her secret writing. There was a recognizable subcat-
egory of aging men inviting warm, responsive girls to share lonely
beds. . . . Most of the poems were bad because the language was
inert. Several began well, with a striking observation, and then
petered out in cliche. They were covered by a kind of kettle-fur
of imprecision. . . . [pp. 174–175]

For me, this serves just as well as a description of what people
tend to sound like as patients. They peter out in dull repetition, and
cloudy imprecision. Byatt calls them inert: "I found myself privileging
little poems that were inert. A poem about a failed marriage stays in
my mind because it worked it out in terms of a dry bed—no river of

life, no wet sex, no damp children" (p. 175). The general tendency is to have a program, which fails, and becomes inert, like a dry bed in marriage. The rest is darkness.

A Case of Forty Years of Service to the Borderline Dynamic

This woman, 44 years old, had been repeating the same formula of service for forty years, starting with serving her mad mother, continuing through a perpetual series of siblings, peers, teachers, men, bosses, children, husbands. Every trauma amazed like the previous.

I saw her for seventeen sessions over two years, that is, once a month or less, so it was a slightly elongated long brief therapy. She was in a complete cloud about her formula of service, which failed over and over, when it collided with what I call the borderline dynamic: to wit, if you do what I want, I will give you a scrap; if you neglect anything, or object, I will attack you unmercifully and/or abandon you.

Now, the chief perpetrator of this dynamic that pained her the most and brought her for help was her husband, but he was just the most recent perpetrator in a long line of predecessors. Still, he was a champion in his own right. He continually amazed her with his meanness. He could be a little nice, which kept her going, but always turned on her for any request that she might have, and always exploded if criticized about anything at all.

I took a very simple tack with her, as in Bateson's account of the dolphin repeating her old tricks. I just kept asking her what was so amazing about his being a jerk. He could be counted on to keep it up until doomsday. Of course, I had to give her unearned fish, to keep her going. This I did by noting that she, herself, was a generous person and, by implication, a person worthy of getting something back.

For a year and a half, she returned with the same story, time and again. She was suffering, but she did not chose to kick him out, for being alone was worse for her. By the second year, she was less amazed, and more ready for his meanness.

The Cloud That Obscures the Gods

The only way to see the series of failures in the social world is to step back far enough, with company, to see it at a glance. This very movement, of detachment from territory, now pulls the subject in a kind of riptide outward toward the huge forces of the oceanic unconscious.

A Case of a Dutiful Son

This man in his mid-thirties had spent only thirty years being correct in the way his parents wanted, winning athletic and academic contests. He was a good competitor, but he was also generous. He was continually amazed that his bosses were not like himself, but set out to humiliate their juniors. He would become enraged, tighten his fists, and nearly get himself thrown out of the company.

I only had to hear about this scene for about ten visits, point out to him that they were all in the same series, and he began to sit back with me and see the next one coming. This brought about a lull of complaints. I told him he could put his feet up on my couch and see what came up from the depths. A sea-change was coming, as pictured in Figure 9–1. He felt it as a queasiness. He didn't say anything for about a quarter of an hour. The surface was, thus, calm, but that is not how he felt. He wasn't talking because he was pouting. He had been queasy, and I had not come to his assistance! So, he was hurt and angry.

Of course, this is a transference of a lost and vertiginous child. So soon as he backs off his considered formula of a very active dutiful

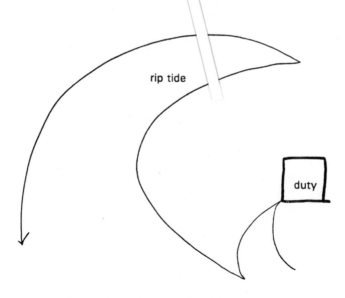

rip tide

duty

Figure 9–1. The Rip Tide of the Unconscious.

son in a mean world, he falls back into his childhood. Detachment drops him from active back into passive, and that is very frightening.

The Enveloping Cloud of a God

The unconscious is not just the repressed childhood, and children are not just children, at the mercy of parents. They are also great dreamers, who commune with godlike powers, and the gods themselves.

The most magnificent and terrifying example is Lawrence's story, "The Rocking Horse Winner" (1933). (I have a copy of *The Norton Anthology of Short Fiction* [Cassill 1986] on a table in my consulting room, and I joke that it is the chief textbook of psychiatry.) It shows the profound interaction of the economic outer surface, and the demonic turbulence of the inner surface. It is the story of a boy, Paul, who grows up in a family that does not have enough money for the superior tastes of the parents. The mother's heart turns to stone for the lack of this luck to bring in money. The boy's determination to give her the luck she longs for, and bring her back to life, is the very stuff that Freud told us about. Yet, the blue god who takes him over, is of religious import, and Lawrence says so, over and over again:

> "Well, anyhow," he said stoutly, "I'm a lucky person." "Why?" said his mother with a sudden laugh. He stared at her. He didn't even know why he had said it. "God told me," he asserted, brazening it out. [p. 859]

> "Master Paul comes and asks me, so I can't do more than tell him, sir," said Bassett, his face terribly serious, as if he were speaking of religious matters. [p. 860]

> She stood, with arrested muscles, outside his door, listening. There was a strange, heavy, and yet not loud noise. Her heart stood still. It was a soundless noise, yet rushing and powerful. Something huge, in violent, hushed motion. What was it? What in God's name was it? [p. 868]

The boy rides his hobby-horse in a frenzy, until he knows the name of the horse that will win the next race, and bring in the money. The frenzy finally kills him. I do not want to belabor how Jung demonstrated this so beautifully in what I believe is his most important essay, "The Relations between the Ego and the Unconscious" (1916). Perhaps, the simplest way to summarize Jung's discovery is to quote the dream that is the center of his argument:

> Her father (who in reality was of small stature) was standing with her on a hill that was covered with wheat fields. She was quite tiny beside him, and he seemed to her like a giant. He lifted her up from the ground and held her in his arms like a little child. The wind swept over the wheat fields, and as the wheat swayed in the wind, he rocked her in his arms. [p. 76]

This is the equivalent of the boy, Paul, in Lawrence's story, in the grip of the Horse God of Blue. Here, it is the God of Wind, a kind of Wotan. As Lawrence makes evident, this is a dangerous and demonic situation. It can kill a boy, in weeks, or it can run with him for thirty or forty or fifty years. While he may learn something from the collisions of the Blue God or the Wind God with the brown world, he is not likely to grasp the series, which will run with unabated furor.

A Case of a Prophet in the Temple Revisited

Perhaps the reader will remember the story of the resident I had as a patient twenty years ago, who had a dream of flying down the canyon of Wall Street astride the tail of a 747 (Gustafson 1995). This possession, naturally, drove him into flying over boundaries, time and again. I could not help him when he was 25, because I just did not know what Jung was talking about.

The sequel is fascinating, not only for demonstrating the sway of a God who was relatively undisturbed for twenty years, but also for showing what huge relief is gained from the assimilation of this unconscious mind by the conscious mind. This is Jung's chief idea of psychotherapy. It is altogether uncanny that this resident wrote me twenty years later to tell me he was finally in a Jungian analysis on the West Coast, which began with the following dream:

> The dream began as he packed his trunk for a flight called Flight 147 on a small airplane (the size of those little commuter flights). Oddly, his trunk fit into the nose of the plane, and protruded like an African lip, until it was folded in.

He and a shadowy double had to fly on the outside of the plane, which was now like a bicycle. Next, he has to pilot the craft himself, as the pilot cannot manage. The plane barely clears trees, and it is stormy, black, like a tornado. He is trying to cross the country in small hops, to get to Washington, DC (the capitol).

He decides the journey is too big and too hazardous and he turns back. At the hangar, he tries to remedy the fraud of the flight. The authorities agree to take $1000 in $200 bills, which is all he has in his wallet. He gives it, and realizes he has been cheated again. The authorities are very nice and tell him this is a lesson in cheating they have given him, and now he can teach someone else!

You can imagine my astonishment at this dream. In one way, I was relieved. No longer was he in a 747, but a 147. No longer did he blast down the canyon of Wall Street, but he actually turns back from his insistence on reaching the capitol. Even before he turns back, he is only going to cross the country in small hops, like a grasshopper.

In another way, I can see he is still in danger. He has a trunk that fits into the nose of the plane, which protrudes like an African lip, until it is folded in. Obviously, he still has a thing about magical powers. Also, he flies a bicycle in a black tornado (notice the African and black idea repeating). Finally, he has no great regard for his analyst, who fleeces him at $200 a session for all he's worth, and then claims that it is the usual procedure of medical school applied to a lesson in cheating, "See one, do one, teach one."

Yet this is progress. He has assimilated the vastness of his God and ambition and is scaling it down to size. He is overcoming the psychic inflation of being possessed by the Blue Flying God. Obviously, he has use of a fertile (female, black, African) imagination, which is enjoyable. Finally, he reads the analyst as ordinary, so that he must do the analysis himself; not bad.

Jung's Hazards

If we see here a man emerging from a numinous and godlike black cloud, which claimed him for twenty years before I saw him, and twenty years after, we need to understand that this education of forty years usually fails, and we need to know how it fails. Jung (1916) discusses two ways.

One is what he calls regressive restoration of the persona, which means to give up the god business and be a regular citizen, minus the swaying wheat fields. It's safer, but it is deadly dull. The other is to keep up the claims of godlikeness, seriously:

> Probably no one who was conscious of the absurdity of this iden-tification would have the courage to make a principle of it. But the danger is that very many people lack the necessary humour, or else it fails them at this particular juncture; they are seized by a sort of pathos, everything seems pregnant with meaning, and all effective self-criticism is checked. [pp. 119–120]

Or it can be done derivatively, as it were, like a dog:

> The disciple is unworthy; modestly he sits at the Master's feet and guards against having ideas of his own. [p. 120] . . . One feels the full dignity and burden of such a position, deeming it a solemn duty and moral necessity to revile others not of like mind, to enroll proselytes and to hold up a light to the Gentiles, exactly as though one were the Prophet himself. [p. 121]

The failures are these: to give up the numinous cloud and become a clod, or be carried away by it and be a phony god.

The Cloud That Obscures the Insertion

Let us suppose that a man or a woman had somehow gotten a pretty good education in the brown study of group life, and in the blue study of god-possession. He or she would be ready for the next (n + 1) deal of the cards, as Henry Adams (1907) wrote so beautifully of Thurlow Weed as if he were playing the deck of Alice in Wonderland: " . . . he appeared to play with men as though they were only cards; he seemed incapable of feeling himself one of them. He took them and played them for their face-value . . . " (p. 147). For example, he would understand how to play the absolutely banal and omnipresent game of cards among men called "The Prisoner's Dilemma" (Gustafson and Cooper 1990). This is a vast subject, but it can be simplified to this: a fellow I play tennis with arranged to play a week in advance but called on Saturday to tell me another game he had been unsure of had come through and so he couldn't play. I was being dealt with very rudely.

I hung up and he called me in the afternoon to say he wanted to play after all. I said, fine, I'll see you there. This little dialogue is an entire education in the cards played by men. For if I am amazed by his betrayal, I am lost, and very hurt. If I go along with it, he will make a habit of it. I simply play tit for tat, cutting him off in mid-sentence, but yet I forgive and gladly take his offer for the afternoon.

Kutuzov is the great virtuoso of this play in Tolstoy's *War and Peace*. He is like the great generals of the East, who form the commentary of the greatest book on the strategy of war ever written, *The Art of War*, written by Sun Tzu in the 6th century B.C. These generals are neither seized by the hot passions of territory, nor are far adrift with god madness, but they drift in between, watching for what is decisive: "That is why it is said that victory can be discerned but not manufactured" (p. 85).

They wait for the momentum in the favor, but assume the enemy will come in the meanwhile. In the meanwhile: "So it is that good warriors take their stand on ground where they cannot lose, and do not overlook conditions that make an opponent prone to defeat" (p. 90). All of this is possible, because of their belief in " . . . the ultimate meaninglessness of the greed and possessiveness that underlie aggression" (p. 29).

Kutuzov fits this Eastern tradition perfectly, because he gives ground when he cannot defend it, and goes to sleep. His hot lieutenants would attack, because they cannot bear to lose, and he will hear none of their foolishness. He even lets Moscow be burned, because victory is not yet to be discerned. He will not force its manufacture.

He has to be capable of going to sleep in his tent, alone, secure in his judgment, no one applauding, many caviling. This is hard to do. Most are lost in the cloud of forcing things, because they can't lose and they can't be alone and they can't wait for the turn of momentum back the other way, of East to West. Tolstoy himself could not (see Chapter 15).

A Case of Campion's Piano

I write a variation, clinically, of Jane Campion's movie, "The Piano," because this movie is an apt Greek tragedy of our time. An apt tragedy speaks for everyone. The story is of a woman who accepts being a mail-order bride to New Zealand. She arrives, like a goddess from the sea, conveyed by Maori outrigger canoes from the steamer to the beach, with her piano and with her daughter. There is great joy, as the two are left alone in the sunset, she playing, her daughter cartwheeling.

Her husband, arriving the next day with his men, will not take the piano because it is very inconvenient for him. Because she is dumb, she can only gesture, frantically, and hate him implacably and darkly. Here is our problem, which is that the god gift will not be fit into the economic machinery of this man and his rubber plantation. It will not go, and yet, tragically, she will force it to go. The means is a neighbor man she persuades to go get it for her, in return for piano lessons, which are in turn a barter for making love to him.

The husband finds out from the little girl, who is caught between the economy and the tragic romance, and he comes in vengeance and chops off, not her head, but one of her fingers. She gets to leave, with her lover, and the girl, and the piano—only she has arranged to topple it in the sea with a rope attached to her foot to drag herself down with it to a sea grave. It is the funeral barge of a goddess, come from and taken back to the sea.

My patient is 45 and similarly implacable about her piano. It is her god-given gift, which was supposed to insert her in the economic machinery of piano careers on the big circuit of rubber plantations. It didn't, for many reasons, and not for the lack of talent. It was a matter of starting late, having no connections, and being a complete naïf about the politics of music careers.

Like the goddess in the movie, she just believed in the beauty of her playing. If faculty in her school of music were bad, she sometimes told them. If they seemed good, she trusted them. A long series of fiascos was the result of this policy. The end result is that she is a magnificent musician, with no standing, in Chicago. She can hardly get a few students, because she has alienated nearly everyone and gained no one for her cause.

She came up to see me once a month for two years, with little to show for her visits. I just kept telling her that her beautiful music was one thing, and the rubber plantations were another thing, and they had almost nothing to do with each other. Finally, she got it, this series in a cloud, and decided that she didn't want any more of Jung's two hazards. If she gave up her piano, she was dead in his regressive restoration of the persona. If she kept insisting on its triumph at Carnegie Hall, she was going to bruise herself to death. She decided her beauty was one thing, worthy of concerts she would enjoy, and the economic circuit was quite another.

Every artist of the twentieth century has had to undergo this descent, from the blue sea of the dream to the brown of the wasteland of economics on the circuit. If you can't get back and forth, you are destroyed.

The Fourth Cloud

If the reader has followed me this far, and it is very far, indeed, then the fourth cloud is not as mysterious as it will seem to the uninitiated who have never begun. The idea is simply that there are three clouds you can be sure of, over territory, over the god, and over the insertion of the blue god into the brown world. The fourth cloud is just that something is always hidden by whatever clarity you have got, and it is best to assume you are missing something big, so others can educate you further. Humility has a chance to learn, further.

How do I decide whether these clouds can be dispelled or not, and how do I decide how long it is going to take? Essentially, a sound mechanics of inquiry will draw the relevant force field, in the three steps I have been describing all along: first, finding what the patient is looking for; second, finding what he overlooks and posing his dilemma; third, seeing what the unconscious has to say further in dreams.

A Case of Staying with the Wife or Leaving

I just happened to see this case last, so it will serve as typical of my mapping procedure concerning the space-time needing to be reckoned. The man married a lady he could talk with in college, but had no intense feeling for, and now, thirty years later, naturally had less. He had met a 30-year-old lady he liked to sport with. He was looking to make up his mind, which was stuck in psychic vacillation about staying with the old lady or going with the new lady.

I noticed several gaps in his account. First, he nearly crushed my hand in an iron grip. This told me he feared to ease up. Probably no one got very close to him. Second, he showed surprisingly little excitement for the second lady, although he professed to want to run off with her. These two gaps would argue a schizoid position as perpetually half-in and half-out. (See Chapter 18 below for a full series of the half-in and half-out story.)

I decided to check this picture of an insoluble dilemma by asking for a dream. He had none. This confirmed his distance not only from the outer world, but also from the inner world. Yet I gave him the chance to find one for our second meeting.

There are several possibilities, illustrated in Figure 9–2, that will be soon clarified. He had been in a thirty-year cloud of doing the correct family thing, householding, as Gandhi called this phase of life. That cloud was passing off to the East, leaving him under an open Midwest sky with a wife he would rather not be sitting with. His inner god was not yet evident. Without a dream, it would be hard to bring it into focus. It was clouded over, to the West as it were.

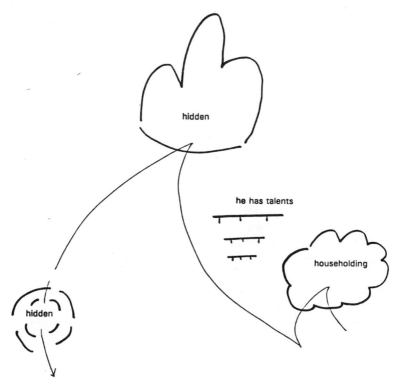

Figure 9–2. Can the Clouds Be Penetrated?

If he can bring it out, there is a chance for a renewal. I doubt that this would be brief, as his half-in and half-out stance looks very well established. If he cannot bring it out, we will be stuck with his conscious mind preferring staying or leaving when we have mapped the downsides of each. This will be brief.

Summary

The way to read the space-time of the patient's force field is to see if the clouds that obscure it can be penetrated. Some are so literally attached to the outer cloud that it will never pass by. Yeats (1918) puts this most economically:

> The sentimentalists are practical men who believe in money, in position, in a marriage bell, and whose understanding of happiness is to be so busy whether at work or at play, that all is forgotten but the momentary aim. They find their pleasure in a cup that is filled from Lethe's wharf . . . [p. 22]

They are determined to be in equilibrium, and to exclude the unconscious. They are apt to peter out after about thirty years, as entropy sets in.

If the man can get free of his outer territory that has worn him down, we will see if the cloud over his inner territory can be dispelled. Can he face the god that owns him? Perhaps not, if he would fall into the abyss of his childhood. Perhaps not, if the god is so far out that its virtue cannot be played into the world. Possible stages to play it on may be so faintly developed that they will take a hundred years like Rip Van Winkle with Henry Hudson and his men (Irving 1829).

I draw the map by seeing if the clouds can be moved. The most grateful parts to play are in those cases where the patient accepts that he has to untie his dream from a territory in the world that will not work, when he can face what is beautiful to him from the god, and when he has stages in which to play something new, and where there will always be fourth clouds with further discoveries. Keep the clouds in place over any of these findings, and you delay the unfolding of renewal for years or forever.

10

Necessary Suffering

If some suffering finally yields after thirty years, some never will, and this is our next subject. Psychiatry wants to be ameliorative and writes progress notes, so this science has little place for discussion of tragedy. This leads all of us in the field to have trouble facing certain situations that are not going to get better, only worse. There is much futile activity. Western medicine, in general, is weakest on this very point, of accepting limits (Spiegel 1994). Bateson's essay on alcoholism (1971) shows how this typical and difficult problem for doctors is driven by the assumption of fixing it, and relieved by accepting the weakness the patient cannot bear by himself. I am indebted to Myron Sharaf (personal communication) for pointing out to me that my own work (1986, 1990, 1992) has been overly optimistic and has given too little attention to this subject of suffering.

Conversely, a doctor who has an eye for what is not going to get better can relieve himself and his patient of much of the trouble of futile projects, which can allow the vitality to flow to where it can do some actual good. I ask then, which suffering is necessary?

Irretrievable Events

In tragedy, the protagonist discovers too late his error (Aristotle 1934). It will run its course, and he must bear his fate. For my patients, such an error was in choosing a mate, or in bringing up a child, or in taking a line of work. Usually, my patient has no idea in advance of the disaster that was being prepared. He was just doing ordinary things, and fell into it, quite naturally, as in the most terrible poem of the twentieth century, "The Death of the Ball Turret Gunner":

> From my mother's sleep I fell into the State
> And I hunched in its belly till my wet fur froze.
> Six miles from earth, loosed from its dream of life,
> I woke to black flak and the nightmare fighters.
> When I died they washed me out of the turret with a hose.
> [Jarrell 1941]

The abruptness of this poem is true, true to my patients, who seem to wake to black flak and the nightmare fighters. They have taken a fall, quite unwittingly, like being born.

A Case of Having an Involuting Spouse: Wild Strawberries

When I was a medical student, I read of involutional melancholia as a strange entity. *Involute* means, from Latin, to roll into itself, or curl up. Little did I know then that everyone who has only one idea will do just this. The idea will wear out, and curl up: like an academic career, or being a mother, or selling. Any person caught up and possessed by an archetype will undergo this fate. A new beginning depends upon two ideas, which, like sexuality itself, create a fresh being.

A great many of my patients find they are married to a leaf that is curling up. All are amazed. All become gloomy. All contemplate going their own way, but nearly all cannot do this, out of loyalty to their one-time partner.

Nearly all try to take these partners to marital therapy, which, by improving communication, is supposed to bring ghosts back to life. It succeeds once in a thousand tries. This is typical of what prolongs the gloom. It is an underestimation of the power of archetypes to drag a partner into endless reiteration and a slow loss of light.

Ingmar Bergman was knowledgeable about this wintry fate, as shown in his movie "Wild Strawberries," among many others. He knew that a one-idea professor was going to go down, after a certain success of adding a paragraph to the system of his times. Such a professor is apt to get mean, also, especially to his wife, who is in a late bloom, out of sheer envy for her vitality.

She is apt to be amazed, over and over. Because she projects her own psychology onto him, she cannot believe he is being so petty. She will be hurt over and over again.

I spent about a year with a patient in this quandary, with little change in her readiness for him. Each instance of his meanness was grieved. She kept hoping she could bring him about, like a sailboat on a mistaken tack. I doubted she could do this, but she was going to try very hard.

Finally, with my help, a dream made its point. She dreamt of skiing like one of her daughters, youthfully, but she could not elude the shadow of grief, which turned with her at every turn. Next, she had her nose at a pane of glass, watching herself warm herself at a fire. She so much wanted a hearth. She was possessed, I told her, by a god of the hearth, that pressed her nose to the glass, where she would get hit over and over again. It was the god of her childhood, a childhood that was otherwise uncomforted.

I told her the god could not be denied. She must have him, and he her. She would keep putting things, like a mask, over the head of her husband, and be hurt, so long as she found his coldness amazing. Fortunately, she had many other sources of warmth, built up gradually in her long psychotherapy, which had the quality of this poem, "Allegro," by another Swedish writer, Tranströmer:

After a black day, I play Haydn,
and feel a little warmth in my hands.

The keys are ready. Kind hammers fall.
The sound is spirited, green and full of silence.

The sound says that freedom exists
and someone pays no tax to Caesar.

I shove my hands in my haydnpockets
and act like a man who is calm about it all.

I raise my haydnflag. The signal is:
"We do not surrender. We want peace." [Bly, trans. 1975]

A Case of Having a Fumbling Child

Here is an unlucky sequence. A pleasant, social child is hurt in junior high by a divorce, and protests by doing badly in school. She gets into a rut of truancy with similar pals. She is able to finish high school, but she successively proves that she cannot toe the line by herself, in college, or in holding a modest job. She lacks the virtues that are necessary for success for a young person. She has little interest in learning, and little ability to follow through. By 20, these may be irretrievable.

This is extremely painful for her mother, who is interested in many things, and well disciplined. How could a daughter turn out to be so much less than herself? In her liberality, this mother offers her daughter many chances, but the daughter fumbles them all, deceiving the mother to boot. Now the mother becomes bitter, as if the daughter is trying to take advantage of her, and even deliberately trying to make her feel bad. It might be so. Sometimes, it is the one power a daughter has over an accomplished mother.

Now we have a dangerous situation. Twenty-year-olds who are left behind can take drastic action against themselves, and, in passing, their parents. Such action is tempting, especially when she is drunk at three in the morning after rejection by a boyfriend takes away her last card to play. Now she is not even attractive.

Oddly, the mother will do best when she can face what is too late to remedy. For liberality, which agrees to new chances beyond the powers of the daughter to keep up, adds to the sense of endless failure. Then, the mother is apt to feel that nothing is possible, and this lack of faith altogether is very damaging.

Already, the young woman thinks of herself in all-or-nothing terms, and it is worse if her mother agrees with this point of view. In reality, she is capable, if she is held strictly to accounts. The nuns proved it having her in high school. The trouble is that there is no convent to send her to.

This is the tragedy of the children of the educated middle class. If they fall out of college, there is little to fall into. Some lower their sights, and take training courses. This works poorly when working is not habitual. If they fall all the way into chronic schizophrenia, the mental health center will keep them busy.

This becomes the challenge of such cases. Optimism is dangerous, when it fails to gauge the weakness of interest and of discipline.

Pessimism is dangerous, when it fails to see that there is more to life than success in the terms of your parents. Suicide in young people is apt to be imminent when they have lost faith altogether in themselves and when those who care about them have also lost faith in them altogether. The two great bonds are coming untied. See Havens (1965, 1967). Oddly, late middle age is similar in its predicament. Before finding a niche in society is much like after losing a niche in society. A mother of such a daughter has a very big job, and I have to be entirely accurate (accuracy is critical in such cases concerning where hope is to be put [Peter Miller, personal communication] about what to pose as the problem to this faltering mother).

After the conventional attempts of the daughter to get a life have fallen through, the mother is going to have to tolerate a great deal of helplessness. Even if she puts up a good front, she is also likely to feel despair. Both of these painful states can drive the mother to find a doctor who will diagnose the daughter, and, thereby, exculpate the mother.

I tell this mother that I agree it is not a good idea to be too positive with her daughter, for this enlists the stubbornness of the daughter against the mother's ideas for her. Rather, it is more probable that the girl would like to do things her own way. With an eye to this, I say two things. One is that she can be told that the conventional ideas for success, like school and/or work, probably won't work for her—yet she might not agree, and might want to prove that idea wrong. Two is that everyone needs to contribute something to have self-respect, but that many young people need all of their twenties to find out what that contribution will be in their own terms. She might not know, yet, for ten more years. In the meanwhile, the mother's job can be to give her some unearned fish (see Gustafson 1986, Chap. 15 about unearned fish to keep the dolphin from giving up in Bateson's experiments), and wait for developments. At the very least, this gets the mother off the daughter's back, yet it keeps the mother involved. It's the best chance. It avoids the considerable dangers of intrusion, and of abandonment (see Chapter 1 on the malignant basic fault).

A Case of Discovering That Women Come in a Few Types, or Jung's Theorem Reproved

This highly successful businessman came to me when his very nice and correct wife had come to the end of her patience with his philandering. We spent a year on his ensuing dilemma. If he stayed with her, this highly reliable friend, he was not going to have any more sexual adventures. Yet, if he followed these ladies of his adventures, he was not going to have a reliable friend.

He decided he was too youthful to give up his bliss, so he went on his own. Now his research began in earnest. Amazingly, he kept finding that there were more women like his wife, true companions through thick and thin. There were exciting women, whom he did not trust.

I told him that he had proven anew Freud's famous finding about good and bad women (1910), so to speak, but he was determined to continue his studies. Now he discovered a third category, arising from the fact that he liked to have a wife he could take to the country club. So there were those who presented well, who were not necessarily the sweetest friends, who were not necessarily exciting in bed. He had distinguished the virtues of class, of friendship, and of sexuality.

Of course, he might have distinguished other virtues as well, but these were the chief virtues relevant to his needs. The unfortunate thing was that any given woman was likely to have only one of the three necessary virtues. At this point, I was convinced that his studies were perpetual, and I told him why I thought they were so. He had proven Jung's theorem that women come only as types (of course, so do men, including himself). The 421st would only be like the previous 420. Obviously, he did want to jump to this conclusion.

His response was interesting, and indicated a change. He agreed he still wanted to believe in a combination of virtues showing up in a wife for him, yet he also brought me three dreams for the first time. I had been telling him for a year that his conscious standpoint (witness his research) was so far wrong, that only his unconscious could correct his conscious bias. I was relieved. I did not have to keep up the fiasco of his endless series of studies of female types (if he would go on himself), and I had something more useful to do for him.

Group Life

Group life is irretrievably a matter of types, whether it is scanned from the perspective of mating, or the perspective of working. God has given a principal virtue to every being, and held back all the other virtues to give to other beings. There is disappointment in this allotment for all of us, because we seek two virtues and sometimes three in our fellow beings.

Some of my friends complain that psychiatry is becoming little but positivistic research about the great biochemicals of the brain. This is indeed its regime, and all irrelevancies might as well put on their coats. My friends forget that everything is as it should be in this best of all possible worlds. I reply to them that they should please point out some other system of psychiatry that has more than one virtue. They just happen not to like the virtue of Ciba-Geigy Chemical Company. They could save themselves a great deal of grief by noticing that the academic battle is lost and going on to more interesting pursuits.

Group life is not our subject, per se, for I save that subject for the very end. Our subject is necessary suffering, and it is necessary to suffer a fall into the world of work where one virtue counts, and all others do not count (much). If one struggles, in amazement, against this fall, one suffers unnecessarily and for a very long time. It is a long series, proving Jung's theorem of types, just like the series of my businessman. The only difference is that the world of work is types of men, for the most part.

Falling Back into Nothing inside Oneself

We have been discussing the fall of man into the world, in Randall Jarrell's metaphor, from his mother's sleep. We could have put it more theologically. Man fell from the Garden of Eden, you will recall.

If the world is a fallen place, one might want to go back where one came from. Some kind of heaven, before or after this fallen world, is extremely appealing. In some countries, the machinery of oppression is so tight, it is difficult to imagine much room for the soul (psyche) to take flight, or much time before it must come back.

For example, in the recent Chinese movie "Raise the Red Lantern," the four wives in the traditional and rich Chinese household of the Chen family are driven against each other. The master has the red lantern posted at the door of the one who is currently in favor, while the other three then conspire to dislodge her, and bring the master back to them. The system is so tight because the women watch each other, and this too is abetted by servants who report to the master, all of this in a tight quadrangle of the four houses. Two of the wives, numbers three and four, take to the heavens above the courtyard. Number three has been an opera singer, so she has tasted some freedom, and takes to the roofs of the place to sing. She also takes the doctor as lover, and ends up hung for it, in these very heavens. Number four has been a university student, so she too rebels, and her flight to the heavens is also crushed, and she ends in madness. Only numbers one and two. who have stayed in place, last.

Part of the great longing for America has been to find some degree of freedom from such deadly arrangements, where you are finished if you go along, and finished if you depart. With some luck, many set up households with some latitude to get away from the department, or the extended family.

In theory, this allows a flight of the soul back to itself. Emily Dickinson (1862) writes, "The Soul selects her own Society—Then—shuts the Door. / To her divine majority—obtrude no more—." Sadly, there are not so many who experience themselves freely as a divine majority. Many are lost, when freed of their duties. Either it has been too long since their childhoods at play, or there never was such a childhood in the first place.

A Case of All Is One to Me

This woman was a competent teacher, with many burdens: her students, her children, her brothers, her parents, and so forth. Because she had a flash of wit, I imagined some delight in herself could create its world elsewhere. We spent several years of long, brief therapy, once a month, about her being taken advantage of, so she was less amazed, and more ready.

When the world took up less of her, she was more at a loss. She just didn't know what to do next. She had interests. None of them moved her, no more than any other interests. She had practiced indifference to herself so long, that she didn't know what she liked, or disliked. It was all one to her.

I replied that I did not believe that everything was the same to her, but I did believe *she* could not tell. Her education about herself had been put off for forty years. Did she want to begin? Actually, she was afraid. Anyway, Christmas would take every bit she had.

I do not know if she can begin. I do not know if she can keep a journal. I do not know if she can be in a writer's group. It may be too late. All I can do is to pose the problem. If you do not know what you like, and dislike, the way to begin is to practice. If you can't practice, you will not progress.

In one of his last papers, Freud (1937) pondered patients like mine who seemed to be very reluctant to make a change. He wrote that they display a peculiar "adhesiveness of libido." He said it was like working in "hard stone." He likened the situation to "psychical inertia." In any event, he concluded: "Even to exert a psychical influence upon a simple case of masochism is a severe tax on our powers" (p. 261). In other words, much suffering of this kind will not be relieved, or not very much. If you suffer from falling into dire arrangements in the world, then you can only back out of them if you have a world elsewhere to go to happily. If you cannot find such a world inside yourself, you will cling to the poor world you have got as the lesser evil. This will look like stickiness of character, as Freud observed, but it is actually a lack of meaningful pleasures. It is difficult to tell if the emptiness on the inner surface is a basic fault or a sheer neglect. See Chapter 1, "The Malignant Basic Fault." Still others have many solo pleasures, but no likelihood of sharing them. They cannot play along skillfully in group life.

Divergent Dilemmas

A somewhat complicated suffering, which is also necessary, occurs in individuals who do know how to enjoy themselves, and who do know how to earn their keep. The trouble is that these two things do not converge into one and the same project. So long as the individual expects them to come together, there will be continuing pain.

To a hopeful young person, it seems natural that virtues will unite in the various realms of his or her existence. In love, in work, in friendship. In Schumacher's terms (1977), this kind of young person regards the unity of happiness as a solvable problem, like the problem of how to construct a two-wheeled man-powered means of transportation: "I propose to call problems of this nature convergent problems. The more intelligently you (whoever you are) study them, the more the answers *converge*" (p. 121). Thus, the bicycle is the stable, convergent solution to the particular transportation problem defined. Yet it turns out that other problems in nature do not converge ". . . . the more they are clarified and logically developed, the more they *diverge*, until some of them appear to be exact *opposites* of the others" (p. 122).

Schumacher cites education as such a problem, which pulls for divergent replies. For example, some educators stress the virtue of discipline, while others stress the virtue of latitude for expression:

> . . . as we have seen, it is pairs of opposites that make a problem divergent [p. 125] . . . divergent problems cannot be solved in the sense of establishing a "correct formula"; they can, however, be transcended . . . Opposites cease to be opposites; they lie down together peacefully like the lion and the lamb in Durer's famous picture of Saint Hieronymus (who himself represents "the higher level"). [p. 126]

Thus, the opposition of discipline and expression, in education, is a perpetual tension. Fine teachers do not neglect either pole. In getting back and forth between them, they create some third thing. This is what Schumacher means by transcendence. Like Durer's painting, the creation resolves the tension, but never for long.

If a formula, as for teaching, sets in, there is always a neglect of one pole of the opposites. The discipline is steady, but the expression goes. It undoes this kind of happiness to try to stabilize it too much. It verges upon being a settled, or convergent problem:

> With a convergent problem, as we said, the answers suggested for its solution tend to converge, to become increasingly precise, until finally they can be written down in the form of an instruction. Once the answer has been found, the problem ceases to be interesting: A solved problem is a dead problem. To make use of the solution does not require any higher faculties or abilities— the challenge is gone, the work is done. Whoever makes use of the solution can remain relatively passive; he is a recipient, getting something for nothing, as it were. [Schumacher 1977, p. 125]

Thus, our hopeful young person who expects everything to come together is going to run into big trouble. If everything seems perfectly convergent, he will be dull. If everything will not come together, he will be very troubled.

The Weight of the Past

It is not so easy to be and stay happy, even when an individual is equipped with a trade, and capable of self-delight. Some of the difficulty comes from the past. It will not go away.

A Case of Transference That Resolves, and Dilemma That Persists

This young man came to me because he was exhausted by his successful work in graduate school. He surely had proven himself a diligent man. That performance was crafted for his father, a difficult taskmaster. Yet now he wanted to live more for himself, and he began to take some backpacking expeditions by himself. He looked very contented.

No longer having troubles to tell, he put his feet up on my couch. He could lay there in his self-delight, but not for long. He was restless about me. Surely, I would find this boring, or annoying? He had the feeling I was going to strike him at any moment.

These intrusions of father-feeling, of transference, settled rather readily, as he could tell I was actually enjoying his departures. They came up many times, and passed many times. Actually, the present was more difficult, because his dilemma could not disappear like transference.

Now he found himself sad, because he was free like Thoreau, but, unlike Thoreau, he was not so contented with being alone at Walden Pond perpetually. He lacked company. In graduate school, he had had pals, who were driven like him. He lacked ease. Now, how were company and ease to go together? Alas, we have one of Mr. Schumacher's divergent problems.

Company for men runs in packs, which are uptight. This virtue pulls to the right. Ease for men is apt to be solo. This virtue pulls to the left. In the social world we have got, these two virtues diverge and do not come together naturally.

This is hard to take, especially when boyhood converges company and ease on the playing fields, which are timeless. We men are apt to take that as the natural state of mankind, from which we are fallen. (Dylan Thomas [1953], as in his poem "Fern Hill," never could bear the fall from childhood grace and died of use of alcohol as anodyne.) Here is a necessary suffering.

I sometimes think that it would have been as useful to myself twenty years ago, as it is to my young patient now, to have someone clearly explain that my dream was convergent for these two great virtues, and that the social reality of men diverged them. Once the divergent dilemma is posed, and comprehended, the young man can take his necessary lack in the tight pack, and he can take his necessary lack in his solo discoveries, with less blaming and doubting of himself, because the lacks are built into social reality. (See Walter Hill's film "Geronimo," and Terrence Rafferty's equally beautiful review [1994].) This gives him more chances to transcend the opposition, by his thoughtful inventions. My patient had already begun this creation, for his ease on my couch did not lose my company.

A Case of Passive into Active, or Upsetting the Resident

The other great route for the intrusion of the past is the patient doing to others what was done to him, mostly unconsciously. This activity goes by many different names, such as identification with the aggressor (A. Freud 1946), projective identification (Klein 1959) or turning passive into active (Weiss and Sampson 1986).

This patient came to me, because he was upsetting his female resident doctor with his gallant interest in her. He did not mean to do this; he was just being his expressive European male self. Indeed, he was a little baffled that it should bother her. His admiration, his letters, and now his proposal to move into her apartment building—to him, this was all perfectly natural, but, being a gentleman, he would desist if she was uncomfortable.

She brought him to me for consultation. He expressed it perfectly, and added a little of sticking his face in my face to see how I minded. I told him, and her, that it was excellent that she could object, when uncomfortable, and as matter of factly as possible.

I did not do more than this. She could show him how to manage with having your limits run over, simply. He as a child had been so run over, and had been helpless. Now, he could watch her cope with it, in reverse.

I did not add, but I will add here, that he is left with one of Schumacher's divergent dilemmas. He loves to express himself without limits, and he loves to be loved. These two great things do not go together.

A Case of Tragic Divergence Built into the Family

A third way in which the past lays its load on us is in the way it poses the dilemma of family life itself. The Greeks were entirely familiar with the idea that some families set up their children for disaster. How is this accomplished? Here is a common situation in Europe (Freud 1910), which I encountered consulting in Germany.

The patient was a young man in his third marriage already, and barely keeping it up. His father had been a very practical man of business. His mother had been a romantic with a mysterious temple devoted to a previous lover.

In his two marriages, he had followed his mother's kind of fascination with young daring women, who turned out to be difficult, and soon he came home. Then he turned to his father's pole, and chose a practical and steady woman, who was, of course, steady. Now he came to me for help. He was depressed. It turns out there was a fourth woman, who was also very romantic, but he had had to back off seeing her to keep the third wife in tow. He felt this was a tragic mistake, and he was doomed to pine for her forever. Indeed, he had for several years, and promised to keep it up until doomsday.

I was impressed by his melancholy, which looked intransigent. It was quite like his mother's, which had lasted thirty or forty years. This was durable stuff. I told him it was, and would last well. He was stuck exactly as his parents had been, between virtues that would never be reconciled: romance without practicality and practicality without romance. These are untenable—for his parents, for him, for anyone. Naturally, he could not fly with his fourth lover, because of its sheer impracticality. Naturally, he could not be content with his third wife. The dilemma, as constructed—by himself, by his parents, or by their parents before them—was impossible to solve. It could never be made to converge. Practicality pulls to the right, and romance pulls to the left, ever diverging farther apart. See Freud (1910) for a graphic picture of this as typical for the male.

Actually, the man had other interests, and pleasures, and even a sense of humor, but just as soon as he got to enjoying them, he would drop back into melancholy over his lost lover! He was uncomfortable, obviously, in departing from the impossible dilemma of his parents, and retreated to it whenever something new was happening.

Beyond the Burden of the Past

The past is heavy, and it intrudes itself upon the very dilemmas we have in the present, which are difficult enough. When the past is cleared from intruding, there is still necessary suffering. I would like to illustrate this in the work realm.

A Case of Galbraith's Dilemma

I recall laughing so hard at Galbraith's (1981) portrait of his college days that once I missed a turnoff on the road by 40 miles. I had given it little thought in the meanwhile, until a patient came along who brought it squarely to mind. The patient was a student in agriculture, like Galbraith had been, and his complaints were about the same, as follows:

> That practical instruction in the agricultural arts lacked content and thus the capacity to occupy time was, in a general way rec-ognized. A practical solution was at hand, which was to fill up our hours with livestock judging, and as we passed through the college years, we became ever more involved in its mysteries . . . And as a further advantage, the standards of excellence were so subjective they could not be learned. [Galbraith 1981, p. 12]

Galbraith was assiduous, so he was chosen to go compete in livestock judging at the International Live Stock Exposition in Chicago: "If anything but luck had been involved, it had come from my studying not the livestock but the preferences of the deciding judges, our professors" (p. 12). Unfortunately, this was useless in Chicago, and he was benched as a spare.

Well, times have changed in agriculture, which is now scientific, but it seems that my patient was in Galbraith's Dilemma: if he did studies like his professors, he was acclaimed; if he went his own way, he was not. Pretty surprising result, for it appears that science has not altered anything but the form. Regimes will still have their way.

My patient had the following dream about his predicament: he dreamt that he was a class officer, who proctored exams, while taking them at the same time. Rather than ask for additional time to complete the exam, he wisely asked the professors just to elevate his grade by one letter! Next, he was tunneling in sand to Rockaway Beach, and came out to the ocean, which was spectacular at sunset. Across the bay, he saw his fellow proctors getting the students ready for the exam. Unfortunately, there was a high tide, and he could not get over there. Here is a beautiful painting from the unconscious of his divergent virtues. He can be an official, and get ahead, with spectacular simplicity. Or, he can discover, and be cut off by the tide across the bay! Perhaps, he can even transcend the opposition of these diverging virtues, for his painting shows that both have a place.

Holes in My Account of Necessary Suffering: Sin and Death (Mortality)

I might have hidden my two great omissions from this chapter, which were pointed out to me by my friend, Mike Moran (personal communication). They are, to wit, sin and death (mortality). That cover-up would weaken the greater theme of this book, which is, namely, selective inattention. My point of view is going to miss things, like any other point of view. We had best see it, and go on to a greater inclusiveness.

I laughed when he pointed it out to me, and immediately thought of early and middle Tolstoy, compared to Dostoyevsky (Bayley 1966). I am being like Tolstoy in seeing the soul as delighted in its own world, unless the world implodes too much or pulls the soul apart by unforeseen contradictions. This leaves out sin and death, which is Dostoyevsky's entire subject of the being rent by its own evil and obsessed with death, sickness, poverty, and all the other dire conditions of a fallen mankind (Bayley 1966).

Ironically, Tolstoy becomes a Dostoyevsky character when he comes apart at age 48 and never recovers. He becomes pathological, obsessed with his own sinfulness and the need for purification. Perhaps, I had better watch out. I am more inclined to think that Tolstoy's self-delight is durable if it can read the force fields in which it must choose its path. I will explain in Chapter 15, "Tolstoy's Fate," how he misread and fell. Once such a world is torn to pieces, a sterile equilibrium finds itself in preoccupation with the sinful and mortal flesh. Shakespeare's ostensible theme in his sonnets is his passing mortality (Shakespeare, Sonnet 87, in Hughes 1991), yet he retains his self-delight. For example, "Thus have I had thee, as a dream doth flatter / In sleep a king, but, waking, no such matter" (p. 81). Only a Shakespeare can keep these two halves together, of self-delight and mortality. The more driven and cornered by their mortal weakness, the more expressive become Hamlet, Macbeth, Othello, and Lear (Bayley 1981).

11

Visual Maps

In medical school, we asked patients many questions and wrote down their answers. In residency, we listened and hardly moved and certainly didn't take any notes. Nowadays, our residents do some of both. When they are doing pharmacological psychiatry, they write things down. When they are doing psychotherapy, they don't. The first is objective work, and the second is subjective work (Gustafson 1992).

I am doing a third thing, which has an objective, or outer surface and a subjective or inner surface. I am trying to help the patient get between the two worlds. For following him in his efforts, I find it indispensable to map his movements as we go along. This chapter describes how I sketch the hour, and how I provide pictures for the patient to take with him at the end of the hour.

There is some precedent in the field of psychotherapy for what I am doing. The existential tradition was concerned with moving into the patient's world(s), literally by moving into the patient's house, like Minkowski (1933), or more symbolically by moving into the categories or dimensions by which the patient constructed his world, like Binswanger (1963). (Havens [1973] summarizes the existential history, May, Angel, and Ellenberger [1958] is the best collection of essays, and Margulies [1989] the most recent example.) Winnicott (1971b) and other child therapists utilized drawings or other play materials to enter into the child's microcosm (Gustafson 1986, Chap. 7). Ryle (1994) also maps pictorially. Sullivan (1954, 1956) sat beside the patient and looked out with him at the social world he inhabited by discussing it with him as if it were projected on a screen before the two of them (Gustafson 1986, Chap. 6).

All of these efforts were attempts to go find the patient in his own locale, rather than obliging the patient to fit into the doctor's terms. They are quite opposite to the business of the doctor asking questions and obliging the patient to give answers. This type of objective-descriptive and dominant psychiatry has been described as a "Director Culture" (Freire 1970), which creates a blank (compliant) patient in a culture of silence about his own world. The subjective efforts, in contrast, map the patient in his own world. My sitting at a slight angle to the patient, and writing down things that he says, and drawing pictures of his world, are the opposite of a therapist-centered activity. I am trying my best to go with him.

Looking and Overlooking

In the upper left hand corner of the page, I draw a little eye that suggests that the patient is looking for something. In the upper middle of the page, I draw a second little eye that suggests that the doctor I am consulting to is also looking for something. (Of course, this would be omitted if I were not consulting to another doctor.) In the upper right hand corner of the page, I draw a third little eye that suggests that I am looking for what they overlook.

These eyes remind me as I go along what is necessary to address. The patient and his doctor are invariably looking for something, and they want me to help them find it. The challenge of the case, for any hour, is to reply to their search. The reply will be about what they overlook, which is indispensable to getting where they want to go.

Essentially, I am looking for holes in the attention of the patient and his doctor. I circle them, usually in blue, so I can find them easily and come back to them later, when it is my turn to comment on what is being attempted. In the meanwhile, I note down what is said, drifting from left to right, and from upper to lower parts of the page, with a black, ordinary ball point pen. Whenever something is more hopeful, I put it up, and whenever something is demoralizing, I put it down.

Whenever something is more objective or outside, I put it to the right, subjective or inside, to the left.

A Case of Veering from Every Painful Subject

A very simple mapping is the following. The patient was a young woman who had lost both her parents in a car accident. In her second session with a resident, it was not evident what she was looking for. The resident was looking to see how she was doing, and interviewed her about various topics that might be distressing. Listening to the audiotape, I noticed that they came near to about six painful subjects, and veered away from every one, usually by the resident changing the subject with further questions, as pictured in Figure 11–1.

I could meet the challenge of the supervision as follows: the resident sought to help the patient with her distress, but overlooked what the patient was looking for in the hour. The patient had no initiative in the hour, and the resident had all the initiative. Secondly, the very distress the resident sought to alleviate was veered away from whenever it was sounded. The map simply shows these holes in the interview.

Double Description

My mapping of looking and overlooking is already a double description (Bateson 1979), which is a reply to Bateson's question: "What bonus or increment of knowing follows from *combining* information from two or more sources?" (p. 67). There are many possible combinations of sources, such as the right eye and the left eye in binocular vision. Another is the eye of the patient and the eye of the doctor, which brings about a different kind of sight, which is often called insight.

I do not map my double descriptions onto a blank page. I did when I began, but I now map onto a double maximum curve, which is how I represent the shape of a dilemma. This is a theoretical construct, which I now take as a given. My justification is this entire book. That is, I can display my findings most lucidly, and parsimoniously, with a double maximum curve. If someone can show me a better construct, I will gladly try it out.

My double maximum curve shapes the space into which I map the interview, and introduces a number of assumptions at once, which I will make explicit:

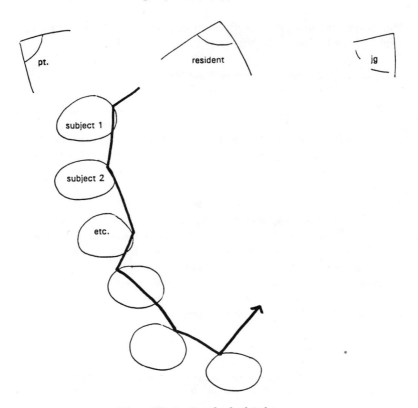

Figure 11–1. Overlooked Subjects.

1. The horns (maxima) are the virtues the patient seeks to maximize. The one on the right is conscious. The one on the left is unconscious, and opposite. Thus, a dotted line separates the conscious realm on the right (a little sun indicates daylight), and the unconscious or shadow realm on the left (a little moon indicates night)—the moon as the nearest celestial body was often the place of visions. Frye (1957) calls it "the point of epiphany."

2. The outside lines on the right and on the left are the slopes down which the patient drifts or slides or falls when attempting the virtue in question.

3. The chasms at the bottom of the slopes are the particular hells reached. Some are sharp abysses or basic faults, some more curved and gradual.
4. The cloudings over the slopes are what obscures the slope and its trend, namely, selective inattention. These bring about the holes in attention. I use a cumulus for an overpowering attitude, a stratus for delay, and a nimbus for subserving.
5. The space between the two maxima or horns represents some balance between the two, and is reached by steps. These are the ladders out of hellish regions. I often put a finger pointing to them, as in medieval paintings.
6. Some of these passages or tunnels or ladders reverse, suddenly, and go back downwards. For example, psychic inflation always reverses.
7. A few other symbols may be useful, such as my sign for the gap ({) between an ideal and the actual fall from the ideal.
8. My sign for self-blame or doubt (FH) with one, two, or three fingers.
9. A box, for attempted withdrawal by becoming static or fixed.

In Figure 11–2, I indicate the symbols as I have just enumerated them. The eye-signs and hole-signs previously discussed are also included.

The Case of Western Middle Class Man

(I have borrowed for this composite portrait from many sources, not the least of which is Bateson's [1971] essay, which purports to be about alcoholism, but actually is about Western man.)

This patient hardly ever comes for psychotherapy, yet his suffering is marked. His chief virtue is taking care of business (1). This wears or, more exactly, dries him out (2), as Henry Adams (1907) wrote: "No man, however strong, can serve ten years as school master, priest, or Senator, and remain fit for anything else. All the dogmatic stations in life have the effect of fixing a certain stiffness of attitude forever, as though they mesmerized the subject" (p. 102). This slope gradually drops him into a hell of pointlessness (3), yet he distracts himself from the drift by staying very busy in his stratus cloud (4).

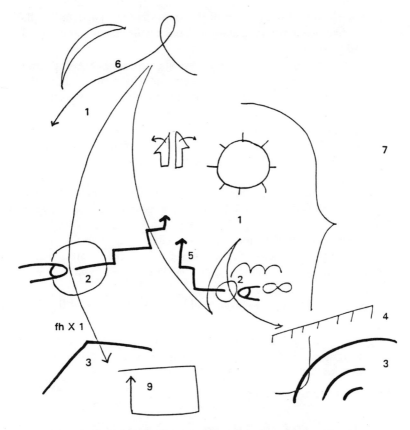

Figure 11–2. Symbols in a Gustafson Diagram.

The way out of such stiffening is to do the opposite, which could be any number of things, from drinking to Zen Buddhism. These loosen the grip on him of incessant competition (5). The opposites tend to run away with him into a psychic inflation, which has to reverse (6). Thus, he can't stop drinking, and gets wet rot, instead of the dominant dry rot. So, he goes back to his dominant and competitive attitude, in which he is never good enough (7), which gets him to blame himself (8), and he just drops out into watching sports on TV (9). Now he is safe from ruin, and can fulfill his conventional obligations.

The Physics of the Force Field

One of my students pointed out to me that my diagrams are similar to the famous Feynman diagrams of quantum mechanics in physics (Deborah Lynn, personal communication). Of course, it is an analogy between two different subjects that have points in common, and points of difference. I like the analogy for showing the power of the force field. I believe it is grossly underestimated, in nearly every case.

Feynman's diagrams in Figure 11–3 below show the interaction of quantum particles in their exchange of particles (energy), which are governed by the twelve conservation laws of physics (Zukav 1979, pp. 212–251), which generate statistical probabilities for the myriad possibilities. In the Feynman diagram, the coordinates are time, which moves upward, and space, but they can also be constructed with the coordinates of momentum and energy.

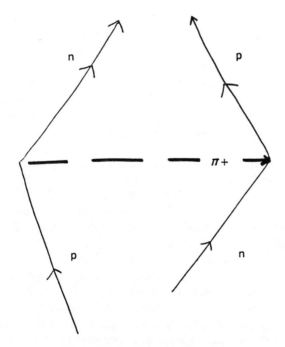

Figure 11–3. Feynman Diagram.

Gustafson diagrams show the interaction of a single subject with an extremely non-linear force field. By non-linear, I mean precisely that the forces do not act upon the subject in a continuously graded and regularly increasing manner, but suddenly, unevening, depending upon what region the subject is located in in the overall field. This is a similar point to the Feynman diagram, where, for example, the strong force that exchanges pions between protons and neutrons only operates at a distance of 10^{-13} cm, or at the distance of the diameter of a proton or neutron.

My diagrams are not dealing with such extreme contrasts in region, but region remains extremely powerful for the human subject. For example, Western man on the right slope has little chance of escape from his descent into dry, pointless rigidity. If he attempts a climb out of it, he is swept into the left region by psychic inflation, which has to reverse itself. This also is untenable. Peter Miller (personal communication) comments:

Reference to Feynman leads me to speculate about correspondence between forces in physics and in human experience. The weak nuclear force is a bit like our psychological process; strong nuclear like immediate interpersonal interactions; electromagnetism like the forces of the social system; and gravitation at once more comprehensive and more basic, the curved space which forms the structure of our interactions . . . the archetypes, the collective unconscious, or even our evolutionary biology.

Naturally, the reader is free to doubt if my diagram is right about the forces and to ask what forces they are that are so extreme. There are many names for them. The pull to the right could be called the power of group life in its basic assumptions, or the power of the increase pack, or the law of conservation of accommodation (Gustafson 1986, Chap. 17, Maturana and Varela 1980).

When there is no virtual space between the right and the left horn of the diagram, we have the extreme case of Western man depicted by Robert Louis Stevenson as *The Strange Case of Dr. Jekyll and Mr. Hyde* (1886). (See Figure 11–4.) While it is usual to regard the case as atypical, Stevenson himself presented it as a medical exploration of a typical state of affairs, just exaggerated, culminating in "Henry Jekyll's Full Statement of the Case" of himself:

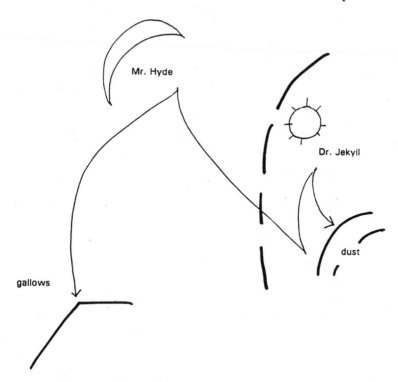

Figure 11–4. The Catastrophe of Western Man.

. . . with even a deeper trench than in the majority of men severed in me those provinces of good and ill which divide and compound man's dual nature. [p. 69] . . . I thus drew steadily nearer to that truth by whose partial discovery I have been doomed to perpetual shipwreck: that man is not truly one, but truly two. [p. 70]

Interestingly, Stevenson has Jekyll describe his correct life as dry, and his shadow life as not only wet, but oceanic:

Even at that time, I had not yet conquered my aversion to the dryness of a life of study. [p. 74] . . . I was the first that could thus plod in the public eye with a load of genial respectability, and in

> a moment, like a schoolboy, strip off these landings and spring headlong into the sea of liberty. [p. 75]

Finally, Stevenson notes again the lack of space-time between the correct right half and the free but terrible left half:

> A moment before I had been safe of all men's respect, wealthy, beloved—the cloth laying for me in the dining room at home; and now I was the common quarry of mankind, hunted, houseless, a known murderer, thrall to the gallows. [p. 83]

The story shows the huge power of the right and the left regions, when there is no region in between ("even a deeper trench"). There is the tragedy of dry dust on the right, and the tragedy of outright, if exciting, destruction on the left. The force field has no room and no time for anything else. Some may be able just to peter out on the right, but some find vitality on the left and have no resistance to its force. (In the language of chaos theory, these two regions are attractor sets. The right horn is lower and smaller because it is the small space of the conscious mind, while the left is the vast, oceanic unconscious.)

The shape of the force field depends on the way it is warped by the relevant forces, as pictured in Figure 11–5. Sometimes, there is ample room in the middle from an integration of opposites, like duty and pleasure, so that duty is often pleasant, and pleasure has its discipline of art. This then is a region of rejuvenation, which is a reservoir of vitality that increases in energy, rather than depleting like the region on the right, or exploding exponentially like the region on the left. Certainly the shape of double maximum curves is pulled upwards and downwards, as well as right and left. The right horn is pulled upward by the ambition of the ideal, and the right slope is pulled more steeply down by the lack of abilities to live up to the ideal. The left horn is pulled upward by the god, and the left slope is pulled more steeply down by the lack of abilities to live up to the god.

The existence of a region of rejuvenation is not the end of difficulty, for it is still subject to the huge forces in at least four directions that can get a sudden purchase on the subject. (See Chapter 7 on the relative autonomy of the ego from inward and outward drivenness.) Those who forget physics can get into a fast slide to the right or left, or an upward draft, or a downward slam, without (evident) warning.

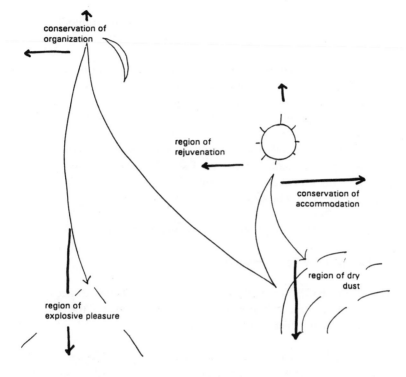

Figure 11–5. The Forces in the Field.

The Case of the Humanities Professor
in a Gustafson Diagram

The mid-life of a moderately successful professor in the humanities is
a taking stock. My patient had the usual situation. He wasn't happy
about the conventions in the literary business, which operate as a kind
of fashion. He was on his own with his favorite authors. Certainly, he
was rejuvenated by his own work, yet its excitements drew him strongly
into danger. This is why he saw me. Out of a huge series of dreams, I
can illustrate the force field we have been considering. Dreams can be
thought of as slices of the field, now in one region, and now in another
region.

The pull to the right into line with the law of accommodation, here with academia, was imagined in one dream like this:

> He was in a peculiar race (like the caucus race in *Alice in Wonderland*) in which you roll up moss on a spindle as you run along. A kind of Tarzan passed him on the right, as if showing how to do it really well, and ascended right into the jungle tops. This was called a Moss-Winding Race.
>
> There was another way to win the Race, which was to dig through yellow chalk cliffs head first (like digging a hole to China). This was like a birth-canal in reverse, but it would not give, and he would be stuck head first.

I will limit myself to the purely spatial commentary of these dreams. Obviously, he was feeling the pull into competition, upward. Yet he could hardly live with its downdraft, as follows:

> He was at a ball, in the bathroom for officers, all brilliant before the line of mirrors. Only as he got his turn, he discovered the ceiling was only five feet high!

Again, this is like a scene out of *Alice in Wonderland* (Carroll 1865), which is fitting as it was itself a story about academic life at Oxford. Now he turns deeply to the shadow side for renewal, which threatens to run away with him:

> He is brought a string of ten horses by two of his teachers in college. He is so excited, he rides off on the lead horse up a hill. Coming back, he gets off the horse to find his two dogs. When he comes out, the beauteous horse is gone. He wanders south and comes to a vast plain, where palominos are mating. But he cannot find his own horse, and wanders back. The horse show people tell him that all ten have been in the race, and are coming in now, and so they do. . . . Afterwards, he realizes a strange thing. His first teacher had had a head shaped like a horse's head, covered by a cloth in black and white checks, like the Purina feed boxes, while his second teacher had been a very old man of horses. This had seemed natural in the dream itself, as if taken for granted, and strange in the light of day.

Here is the psychic inflation so well and previously described by Jung, in which gods appear and threaten to run away with the professor. My patient called this his dream of Hermes Purina, in that it was a winged and tricky god like Hermes, but it was covered by that familiar black and white checked cloth of Iowa horse chow. So it was hiding under homely colors. About a week after this psychic inflation, he got pulled strongly into its downdraft, as follows: He saw a swimming pool, in which the little hermaphrodites were let in like goldfish, then to be swallowed in one gulp. Terrifyingly, he was fallen out of the sky with Hermes Purina, into the chthonic realm of the Titans who eat people up.

These are the forces that pull right and left, up and down, upon a poor professor.who has a reasonable capacity to enjoy himself. As his fellow professor Faust (Goethe 1832) once discovered, the region of rejuvenation is refreshing, but it is not so easy to content oneself modestly. Man is greedy, and thus is subject to the four winds. Yet, patient work in psychotherapy has its calming effects upon these huge forces. The double maximum curve is itself altered and made less sudden in its curvature, so the subject can ride it with more control, as is evident in a dream from about a year after the previous four dreams:

The patient was back in college, and it was quarter to four in the afternoon, when he woke up realizing there was only a quarter of an hour left in the class he had not gone to for the entire semester (obviously, the rebellious student in himself!). He ran up the hill to get to this last lecture, hoping to glean what was important for the exam in the final words of the professor.

Only he couldn't find a parking spot (now, somehow, he was in a car), and as he drove over the top of the hill (of this City of God, the university) he came to a dead end passage in which a car was stuck headfirst (like in his yellow chalk cliff dream we began with). His old professor came out of the car, shuffling like a shamas in black, and said, "No matter, I will take you down the street to the left and then around to the right to my house."

Just then the professor of the course he had been looking for showed up and told him: "I have done my part already, and the rest is up to you." She was huge, and bright-eyed like an Amazon.

He laughed at both, and decided he did not need the course of the one professor, and wasn't going to sneak around like the other one.

All of the forces alluded to in the four winds of the previous four dreams are here, but subdued: the ascent to academic glory, the urgency of it all, the fall from making it at the last minute, the sneaky Hermetic god promising to get him through to the left, and the Amazonian chthonic terror. At least he accepts the divergence between the fashion of the university and his own inclinations, without resorting to Hermetic powers. He just is not going to go over the top between the right horn of accommodation and the left horn of indirect and subterranean means. There is no such passage. You either take the course of fashion, if you want to occupy the citadel at the top, or you don't take it and don't go running up there in the last quarter hour of the semester! Or expect Hermes Purina to ride you around the left.

Drawings to Take Home

I gave the professor a drawing of his force field to take home with him, which appeared as in Figure 11–6 after this last dream of the University as Citadel. I try to pare down these take-home drawings to a minimum, when it is indeed tempting to put in a great deal. I prefer to let a series of such drawings make things complicated enough. Each particular drawing emphasizes a region of the force field, which preoccupies the patient.

For example, the disturbing region of this drawing/dream for my patient the professor was the chute in the center that was completely impassable. The same chute (but through yellow chalk to China) was in the first dream of the series, but it wasn't front and center. Now he was ready to face that region's implications: given the divergence of fashion to the right and discovery to the left, there was *no* center passage. In the literature of the "Prisoner's Dilemma" (Poundstone 1992), there is no saddle point:

> When the maximin and the minimax are identical, that outcome is called a "saddle point." Von Neumann and Morgenstern likened it to the point in the middle or a saddle-shaped mountain pass—at once the maximum elevation reached by a traveler going through the pass and the minimum elevation encountered by a mountain goat traveling the crest of the range. When a game has a saddle point, the saddle point is the solution of the game. [p. 54]

discovery

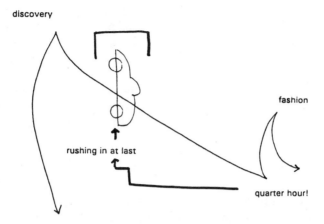

fashion

rushing in at last

quarter hour!

Figure 11–6. The Professor's Block.

My patient was discovering that his academic game had no saddle point, or compromise between them. Either you did fashion, or you had no place on the hill: period. Running up the hill at the last moment to meet its requirements was not going to do, nor slipping around the left. The tunnel through the region was a dead end, and was no place of rebirth. I let the drawing show that region in focus and allow the other regions to go into the background. This meets what the patient is looking for, but has overlooked consciously. This meets the challenge of the case for the hour in question.

Mood and Color

I have alluded in passing to color, but the reader might think I do most of these drawings in black and white. Not at all. Mood is color. If I want to be with the patient in his moods, and I do and I must, then I change colors as his mood undergoes its sea changes. Also, changes of mood often signal changes in region. These can be sudden, as from a brown and dull drift in the right region, to a sudden red flare of rage in the left region. I have gradually increased the number of colors. At first, I just added red to black for the kind of shift I just mentioned. Then, I put in sky blue for hopefulness in dreams; then, heavy black for abysses; then, heavy red for emergencies.

Next I felt the need for a set of magic markers with their deep saturation of color: such as purple for royal prerogatives, green for renewal, yellow for sunny, brown for banal, and so forth. I have since augmented these with the subtler and endless variations of a huge set of colored pencils. I like subtlety, as much as I like full saturation. We are back to the subject of opposites as the vehicle of truthfulness. In this, the painters precede us and teach us. Zbigniew Herbert (1991) has Vermeer break off his relationship with the great biologist Leeuwenhoek in a discovered letter as follows:

> If you absolutely require discoveries, however, I will tell you that I am proud to have succeeded in combining a certain particularly intense cobalt with a luminous, lemonlike yellow, as well as recording the reflection of southern light that strikes through thick glass onto a grey wall . . . Our paths part. I know I will not convince you, and that you will not abandon polishing lenses or erecting your Tower of Babel. But allow us as well to continue our archaic procedure, and to tell the world words of reconciliation and to speak of joy from recovered harmony, of the eternal desire for reciprocated love. [p. 150]

Like Vermeer, I need contrasts of color to pose the problems of reconciliation in living in the force field of the world. If we seek free passage in this force field, we have to be able to undergo profound changes of mood, and thus, of color, passing from one region to another.

The Professor Continued in Color

Two dreams from two successive nights of my patient illustrate the contrast in mood by color:

> He is racing on black ice in a race already won, but second place is open. A beautiful, willowy female in a black running outfit lopes along inside the track knowing she can take the race at any time like the hare with the tortoise. He, like the tortoise, puts down his head and goes all out and wins.
> He is on the western rampart of America, like it was the edge of a tall fortress on the Pacific, which was beautifully green, and

he wanted just to let himself slide off into the green world, but a beautiful lady with her husband pulls him back.

Black works here as grimness, about competition, which seizes him (as we noticed before). Green is ease and letting go (but dangerous). Seizure by the black drives the extreme opposite of the green. I can pose the problems of his particular force field in terms of the colors that will grab him.

Gustafson diagrams are like Freire pictures (Freire 1970), as well as Vermeer pictures. As we discussed, Freire pictures pose situations about which poor people in Brazil have tremendous feeling:

> . . . a group of tenement residents discussed a scene showing a drunken man walking on the street and three young men conversing in the corner. The group participants commented that "the only one there who is productive and useful to his country is the souse who is returning home after working all day for low wages and who is worried about his family because he can't take care of their needs. He is the only worker. He is a decent worker and a souse like us." [p. 111]

Freire comments on the dilemma projected onto the picture by the workers:

> On the one hand, they verbalize the connection between earning low wages, feeling exploited, and getting drunk—getting drunk as a flight from reality, as an attempt to overcome the frustration of inaction, as an ultimately self-destructive solution. On the other hand, they manifest the need to rate the drunkard highly. He is the "only one useful to his country, because he works, while the others only gab." After praising the drunkard, the participants then identify themselves with him, as workers who are also drinkers—"decent workers." [pp. 111–112]

A Gustafson diagram of this situation would look like Figure 11–7. I put the double danger of their situation before them, problem posing like Freire, only heightening it further with the double horns and with the contrasting colors. This has the marvelous effect, discovered by

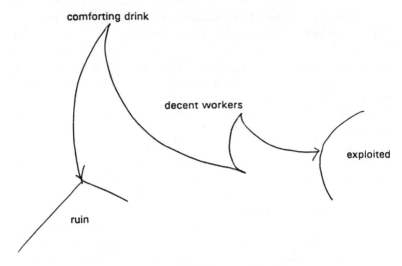

Figure 11–7. Freire's Dilemma of the Peasants.

Freire, of bringing them out of a culture of silence into their own expressive, what he calls "generative," language. They invent words never heard before, or use them differently for their own individual purposes. This happens when language has to travel a long distance between opposite terms, spaces, colors, ideas. For example, I just went down to my bird feeder and nearly ran into a nuthatch on the suet, which looked like a "seal of the air," in its grey and white, with a black hood. It didn't even run away, busy as it was with the stuff, but looked at me silly. My mind must have been in this state I am writing about, of connecting far-flung things, here a thing of the sea and there a thing of the air. Here are two more just for comparison and the sheer beauty of them:

> In Mississippi, coin record players, which are manufactured by Seeburg, are commonly known to Negroes as sea-birds. [Percy 1975, p. 64]

> William Carlos Williams . . . overheard a Polish woman say to her daughter: You bust your coat with your fifty sweaters. [Gustafson 1990, p. 422]

Generative language connects up its own interests, between terms that don't go together for anybody else. More than that, it is the vitality of being yourself. This is what I mean by the region of rejuvenation. "In contrast, imagine the failure of a moralistic educator, sermonizing against alcoholism and presenting as an example of virtue something which for these men is not a manifestation of virtue" (Freire 1970, p. 112). These reduce them back to the culture of silence, in the presence of the director culture of the educator (or psychotherapist or doctor or whatever official). It is all correct, and deadening.

12

Official Documents and Generative Letters

What to say and what not to say is extremely important in psychotherapy, for it is the very conclusion of the business. This is why many of us are reluctant to write anything down about what we do, for it exposes the conclusion to scrutiny. It will seem less daunting the more we practice.

I see two large purposes for dealing in writing with our patients, hour by hour, and these purposes each have their own language. The first purpose is official, and so is its language, and it is the documentation that will get us paid and defend us from review and even lawsuit. The second purpose is educational, and its language is generative (see Chapters 5 and 17 for discussion of generative language), and it will pose problems for our patients to ponder between sessions.

Official Language and Documentation in Medical Charts

Official language is operational. It specifies an operation to be carried out correctly. Its unit is the order, which is to be fulfilled. The word is from Latin, *ordo*, which means lines, and it has developed military, religious, architectural, biological, legal, and commercial variations.

Nowadays, an order is specified by a program, which is from the Latin *programma*, which means a public proclamation. Whether you order a highway, a pair of shoes, or a cognitive therapy of depression, there will be a program on a computer that specifies what this thing is that you will get. The program guarantees the uniformity of the object that is ordered.

The universality of such programs is an excellent development of Western culture, because we can rely on a kind of minimum standard in everything we purchase and use. The lack of such uniformity is evident in many second and third world countries, where the simplest activities like eating and drinking and sleeping and going anywhere can become adventures.

The field of psychotherapy is administered, increasingly, by programs, like every other field of our culture. You need an order authorizing you to perform the service. Thus, the first document in a medical-psychiatric chart is something like the Authorization for Mental Health Services. (In some mental health systems, there may not yet be such an explicit document.) The bottom line of this document is the "symptom or functional impairment for which the patient is seeking care." The "additional factors" point to what might make symptomatic relief difficult, and the "treatment plan" is to provide a rationale for relieving the symptom. In this way, the document has a singular logic, like any program that can be replicated simply.

All of this is entirely banal, but it has tremendous implications, because the entire justification of treatment is to relieve symptoms, like anxiety and depression. This obliges the psychotherapist to have a hypothesis about why the patient has anxiety or depression, and a rationale to relieve it, and soon! This pulls for bringing the anxiety or depression under control as fast as possible, which, in turn, pulls for the patient to comply with the regime prescribed. The simplest rationale is simply to attack the anxiety or depression with an antianxiety or antidepressive drug, or a behavioral or cognitive program.

Those of us who think that most anxiety or depression points to an underlying dilemma in the existence of the patient are not necessarily put in a difficult position by this document and its logic. There is a noble tradition in medicine that calls for facing underlying structural problems, and not simply getting rid of symptoms. The document obliges us to state our case, however, and very tersely. With practice, and with an adequate theory, this turns out to be routine. This is because there are only a few plots that persist in driving the patient to be symptomatic with anxiety or depression or something else.

For example, about half of the patients I get are being swallowed in their own subservience (Gustafson 1992, 1995), so they are depressed about its downhill probability, as they stand to be misused increasingly, and they are anxious about their own barely contained rage coming out and making it even worse. These are the two horns of their standard dilemma. My rationale for the treatment plan will be something like this: "Assist patient to face her own part in being badly, and depressingly, used, and to face her own anxiety about her anger."

The form is actually helpful. There are relatively simple and benign cases of subservience, in which such a treatment plan could be carried out in six or twelve sessions, and there are cases complicated by the findings on the form called "additional factors." Certainly, drug and alcohol dependence, organic findings on mental status, previous and lengthy treatments, and medical conditions warn us of some of the lengthening factors.

In practice, I supplement the form with a form of my own devising (Gustafson 1995, Chap. 2). (See Document 12–1, "Psychiatric Evaluation.") First of all, this document guides me to consider a medical physiological etiology for every case. Secondly, it guides me to consider the classical psychiatric syndromes that run chronic courses. Only thirdly do I propose what I find to be most common, which is a dilemma about the patient's existence. I do not want to get to the third conclusion until I have considered the first two conclusions. In the first session, the order in interviewing is the reverse of the order in the form. I hear the patient's story, which gets into his dilemma, and shift halfway through the hour to his medical and psychiatric differential diagnosis. Formally, I start from the medical and psychiatric, and then get to the psychological. (See Gustafson 1995, Chaps. 1, 2.)

There are two other considerations I always note formally, under the heading of psychiatric differential diagnosis on my own form. I call these the best news and the worst news (Gustafson 1986, Chap. 19). The best news is the most helpful relationship in the patient's history, and the worst news is the most difficult period of the patient's history. Without these two considerations, we are apt to underestimate first, strength, and second, depth of woundedness.

I reuse the Psychiatric Evaluation Form, whenever there is a recurrence of a possible medical problem or whenever there is a psychi-

MR#:

NAME:

DATE OF BIRTH:

DATE:

PSYCHIATRIC EVALUATION

A. *MEDICAL DIFFERENTIAL DIAGNOSIS, AND RECOMMENDA-TIONS* (All patients who have not had a medical evaluation since they have become symptomatic need to do so, as about one quarter of all psychiatric outpatients have undiagnosed and significant medical illnesses.)

☐ Referral necessary   ☐ Not necessary

B. *PSYCHIATRIC DIFFERENTIAL DIAGNOSIS, AND RECOM-MENDATIONS* (All patients should understand that there is a pharmacologic therapy for nearly all psychiatric conditions, which would be the primary recommendation of most psychiatrists. Referral for this perspective is available for all patients.)

C. *PSYCHOTHERAPEUTIC DILEMMA* (Stated in my letter to the patient.)

James P. Gustafson, M.D.
Professor of Psychiatry
University of Wisconsin Medical School

Document 12–1.

atric emergency. Not only will I have considered medical referral or emergency procedure, but it will be documented in the chart. Mental status is a useful component of the psychiatric evaluation, especially when drugs are being prescribed, for following their effects. From a legal point of view, the key to defense is that you have taken the danger seriously and thought through what action is possible, whether or not you succeed in preventing the actual catastrophe.

Two other documents could be called official, and they could also be considered educational, for they lie somewhere in between the two kinds of languages. These are The Family Therapy Worksheet (or Consultation Worksheet) and the genogram (Document 12–2). They are official in the sense that they record official facts about a family. They are educational in the sense that they point to the relevance of the family history for the subsequent fate of the patient. Thus, a chart that lacked them would suggest that the psychotherapist had given too little thought to the force of the family, while having them would suggest that he had at least considered its power.

Generative Language and Letters

Generative language is the language of fresh discovery. When two things are put together by a patient in a way he has never seen before, the words and phrasing are apt to be surprising and unconventional, and, thus, individual to him. Gerard Manley Hopkins (1966) called such seeing an "inscape," which has ". . . the unspeakable stress of pitch, distinctiveness, selving." Naturally, some have more gift for this kind of discovery than others. Hopkins was extraordinary, and Emily Dickinson was in the same class, as in her #328:

> A bird came down the Walk—
> He did not know I saw—
> He bit an Angleworm in halves
> And ate the fellow, raw, . . .

Here is an inscape, of a person enjoying himself immensely, not taking a man seriously, but despatching him like a bird would an Angleworm. He is free from conventional politeness, takes several more liberties, and takes off:

CONFIDENTIAL

University of Wisconsin Family Therapy Team
Telephone 263–6059

FAMILY THERAPY WORKSHEET

1. Date: _____

2. Person Calling: _____
   Address: _____
                 Telephone: _____

3. Referred by: _____
   Who said: "_____
   Kathy Moy said: "_____

4. For what PROBLEM (including "what is your part in the problem?"): _____
   _____
   _____
   _____

5. Do you want to work against the PROBLEM together or separately?
   _____

6. Who's in family:

NAME	AGE	EDUCATION	WORK	RELIGION
_____	___	_____	_____	_____
_____	___	_____	_____	_____
_____	___	_____	_____	_____
_____	___	_____	_____	_____
_____	___	_____	_____	_____

7. Marriage, Date: _____
   _____

8. Who else lives in household? _____
   _____

9. Who else involved in problem, knows about it? _____
   _____

10. HOW WE WORK: 1) Two hour consultation time (possibility of
    continuing, but only Fridays, 9:00–11:00 A.M., q. 3 or 4 weeks).

2) Set up: Videotaping; one way mirror; two interviewers, two colleagues for consultation; some days closed-circuit teaching, some days, not. 3) Financial: Cost; Insurance: U-Care limitations (if relevant). 4) Getting there: hospital registration; finding department. 5) If EMERGENCY requires canceling. 6) Questions? _____

_____
_____

11. Preliminary Hypothesis: _____
_____
_____
_____
_____
_____

12. GENOGRAM and Field of Power attached: _____
_____

Document 12–2.

And he unrolled his feathers
And rowed him softer home—
Than Oars divide the Ocean,
Too silver for a seam—
Or Butterflies, off Banks of Noon
Leap, plashless as they swim.

Dickinson's inscape has tremendous scope, from earth to sea to sky. Walker Percy (1975) calls this modern sensibility: ". . . it has the added advantage from my point of view of offering a concentrated field for investigation—here something very big happens in a very small place" (p. 66).

The Case of Foaming Stench in the Dumpster

This is the great marvel of the unconscious mind, how it can leap across any interval of space and time to find two things that belong together. For example, a patient of mine thinking of leaving her husband in the present had a dream image from twenty years previously in which she was retrieving a few childhood objects from a huge dumpster, up to her neck in foaming stench. She had actually had to get into a dumpster twenty years ago, but had not thought of the horrible experience until her dream called it up to her. The inscape proposed a different kind of leap from Emily Dickinson's, that biting the Angleworm in half might leave her back in the kind of mess she had had being alone.

Another word for this capacity of the mind to jump to far flung and even outlandish connections is the word epiphany. Epiphany means a manifestation of a god, but it can also mean a demonic epiphany (Frye 1957). Thus, it is the highest or the lowest point. In Joyce (1914), it means the great clarification (Michael Moran, personal communication). This capacity to fly or fall is extremely important to our purposes, because the operative and official and conscious mind lacks it and tends to just keep going as usual in the status quo. It cannot jump ahead to the lowest point where the slope is leading, and it cannot fly to what is longed for. It just operates on.

Thus, my patient placing herself in the foaming stench of the dumpster is providing herself with a demonic epiphany of hell itself, which is a very common motif of modern literature:

> the point of demonic epiphany, the dark tower and prison of endless pain, the city of dreadful night in the desert, or, with a more erudite irony, the *tour abolie,* the goal of the quest that isn't there. [Frye 1957, p. 239]

The hero or heroine ordinarily passes through the demonic point of epiphany like Dante at the very bottom of hell, in order to come out the other side to ascend the mountain of purgatory to the heavenly point of epiphany:

> At the bottom of Dante's hell, which is also the center of the spherical earth, Dante sees Satan standing upright in the circle of ice, and as he cautiously follows Virgil over the hip and thigh of the evil giant, letting himself down by tufts of hair on his skin, he passes the center and finds himself no longer upright, but standing on his head, in the same attitude in which he was hurled downward from heaven upon the other side of the earth . . . if we persevere with the mythos of irony and satire, we shall pass a dead center, and finally see the Prince of Darkness, bottom side up. [p. 239]

It is of huge importance that we understand this map, showing that the demonic point of epiphany can be passed through, or we will back off of it in fright, leaving the patient stuck and unable to go backward or forward. (See Chapter 1, "The Malignant Basic Fault," for the distinction between benign and malignant basic faults. In the latter, there is no passing through the point of demonic epiphany.) Thus, my patient's dream of baptism in the stench has many other landmarks of the turning point at dead center:

> The dream begins when she walks into a room where a very egocentric female colleague is sitting on the floor with a shattered ceramic leg in absolute filth.
>
> Then comes the descent further into the foaming stench, partly to get a brace for the colleague's leg.
>
> Finally, she and another woman try to get out through a window in the ceiling from the 1930s, with maybe a toehold, but only translucent, so she can't see through it. She thinks, "Some choice!"

Thus, she compares herself with two other women in hell, a first who cannot be saved from her shattered state, and a second who got out of marriage twice only to be taken advantage of further. Interestingly, she uses words in an otherwise silent dream at this last juncture and says, "Some choice!"

Her dream shows exactly how words can help. They can point to problems in a dark territory. She is doing this for herself in the dream, and I do it for her and for my other patients, after every session in a brief letter. I actually wrote her two brief notes about the dream. The first said: "Your unconscious has a lot of misgivings about women on their own, which you are obviously considering. Especially, why go back into a dumpster of liquified stench?"

Writing this chapter a few days later, I noticed the dream was in the triptych form of all epic dreams. (See Gustafson 1995, Chap. 13 for a discussion of epic dreams, and Chap. 3 for a discussion of female dilemmas.) Since I had commented on Act II of the triptych, and not Act I and Act III, I added a further note: "I thought about the dream further. It seems to me you are in a hell where you first compare yourself with the shattered _____ and wish to save her, and where you secondly compare yourself with _____ and see that climbing out of marriage through the ceiling (1930s window) can be futile if you end up in the same place. 'Some choice!'" I try to adjust the length of my remarks to the patient's readiness. When a patient gives me an epic dream, I take it as a sign that he or she is trying to encompass his or her entire dilemma at once. This patient's epic dream is a typical one, in that it poses both horns of her consideration, and the need for some third alternative besides the usual fate of women.

Problem-Posing Letters of Different Lengths

Problem-posing, as invented by Freire (1970), means pointing to a picture of something oppressive. If the picture is relevant, the subject will become excited like Bateson's (1971) dolphin and jump into language about the situation. It is as if a cloud lifts or is penetrated and much more can be seen, and talked about excitedly, as discovery. The subject can reach from one thing to something far-flung. The words that make this jump are called generative words or themes.

The jump that is made, like lightning across a dark distance, may show the slope the patient is sliding down. I am apt to use one ordinary sentence (problem-posing language can be quite ordinary and matter-of-fact in its pointing, but, when effective, elicits fresh and generative language from the patient) to pose the problem in a letter, and allow the patient to enjoy her eloquence. For example: "It is very surprising that liberal groups object to a hardheaded business manager." I am also apt to use one ordinary sentence to pose a problem on an inner slope that is perilous (as transference). For example, a patient who had begun to be less busy with bossing everyone around began to feel she could sit back on my couch, but the three-body problems of patient–family member problem were more comfortable than the two-body problems of just her and me (see Chapter 1 for primitive two-body transferences), so I needed to pose the alarm for her before she ran away: "Yes, the Navajo way (of silence) is a freedom, from having to talk and be busy, but naturally, it is a fearful thing to take this freedom and fear I'll be annoyed."

I also write one-sentence letters when the map of both fearful slopes has been sighted in the session: "The physics of the enclosed space-time diagram leave a fellow with little alternative."

I am likely to utilize a second sentence when I feel the pain of the emotions that have been set in motion by the vision need to be held.

For example, of a man who has glimpsed the futility of his sacrifices for others, I write: "The generous guy has a great deal of pain himself, for there is so much effort for so little satisfaction, and he is so much alone with it all. I am glad he can cry for himself (if he is not so glad and struggles mightily against his own grief)."

I need three sentences when a dilemma is more fully developed: one sentence for what is attempted and is impossible; one sentence for the improvement, which is dangerous; and one sentence for posing a way through the horns of the thing. For example, a new patient wanted to stop being angry at her fiancé, because it just drove him into more depression:

> You would like to get rid of your resentment at _____ and his mother, but it seems to be both harmful and necessary. It is harmful in putting him down further, and it is necessary to keep those fists up and not be naive about her (on a mission of great suspicion, as you put it). Clearly, your Reason underestimates the importance of your resentment, while I am confident your unreason could explain it to us (Jung's essay enclosed).

The reader may be asking him- or herself why I want to limit myself to one, two, or three sentences. I have two enormous reasons. The first is that it takes me about five minutes per letter, and so I am reluctant to give up more than a half hour a day for letters to six patients. The second reason is that I want the letters simply to point, like a bird dog, to what is being overlooked. In this, I follow Sullivan:

> One patient described this as follows: "I would suddenly become aware of a change in him, like the alertness of a pointer who has spotted a bird. It was a certain wave of thoughtful, kindly alertness, totally non-verbal. That knowledge of his already being where I didn't know . . . I was going, made it possible for me successfully to go through a number of rough spots." [M. J. White 1952, p. 132]

There is an exception to my policy of brevity, and that is the consultation where I am likely to see the patient only once. Ordinarily, I elaborate for the patient her dilemma, as in Document 12–3.

Dear _____:

Why do you keep getting drawn back into these dangerous situations with the likes of _____ and forget to take care of yourself? When you are FAR enough away and in the saddle as bitch, you are okay, but the trouble is that you are in love with love in your heart (romantic love, and love of family), so if you let men get NEAR to put the right words into your ears, you are hooked again as the love fish.

You are going to have a very hard time either way: If you keep your head and stay FAR, you will feel guilty as about your friend. If you get NEAR like your mother to the six black men in the dream, you will get shot in the head again. Your dreams keep sending the same horrid warning, and will continue until you get it—then, they will change to something better. You and Dr. _____ now have a pretty good idea how to read these warnings, but, of course, ideas are one thing, and feelings are another, and I really do not know if you can give up on _____ as the answer to your prayer? It could be too painful.

I hope I will get a chance to catch up with your work with Dr. _____ in the spring.

Document 12–3.

Psychiatry and a Case of Wallpaper Scissors

This business of flying ahead of the present position is for me the very business of psychiatry, which is about the psyche, which has wings that need to be used. Otherwise, it becomes flat, and stuck, and lost in a culture of silence. It becomes a mere type, which fits into the machinery. Often, a single detail that is a fragment of a dream will suffice to let loose the soul. For example, a patient dreamed that she was jogging, and passed a pair of scissors on the path, which did not seem peculiar until she woke up. I asked her about her history with scissors (see Gustafson 1995, Chap. 13 on dreams, for this method). To make an hour brief, she replied that her parents' house had allowed for only one pair of scissors and always in a particular drawer. This made her feel sad, and deprived.

Yet recently, she had been letting herself go a bit, and bought two pairs of scissors. Then, one got lost, and she bought two more! Recently, she came upon the lost pair, raking leaves. This made her laugh, because her son had been playing with them outside in the fall. So, a pair of scissors on the path meant a certain generosity toward children, and toward herself. It meant a different kind of household. Later, she decided the scissors on the path were wallpaper scissors, which she loves the heft of, and craft of. So, the dream is generating her entire new world, from her previous oppression. I noted this, as she was ending the hour, and she laughed and said I might cut her off.

All of this has the beautiful economy of a generative theme, which can telescope the oppression, the flight to something free, and the fear of being cut off. I simply acknowledged her individuation in a one-sentence note with a drawing:

> There is an entire world of meaning / in a pair of wallpaper scissors / passed on the path while running.

Michael Moran (personal communication) notes the parallel construction in "The Red Wheelbarrow," a poem by William Carlos Williams (1923). Without this play of her psyche, she tends to be flattened, like a playing card, in her subservience. So, the stakes are having a soul, or not. I keep the visual series of drawings in the back of the chart like an x-ray series, to follow the progression.

Wit

If I am often plain-spoken in my letters posing problems, it is because I like the flash of wit to come from the patient. My marvelous Webster's Collegiate Dictionary from 1943, which explains the nuances of words as well as any dictionary, says of wit:

> *Wit* is more purely intellectual than humour, and implies swift perception of the incongruous; it depends for its effect chiefly on ingenuity or unexpectedness of turn or application; *humour* implies, commonly, broader human sympathies than wit, and a more kindly sense of the incongruous, often blended with pathos.

Thus, my patient with the dream of the scissors is displaying a marvelous wit about the central dilemma of her own existence, which turns about this incongruous element of a scissors lying on the path. Without our work, she would have overlooked it, and missed a beautiful construction of her entire world.

I rely as much on humor in the sense of broader human sympathies and a more kindly sense of the incongruous as I do upon wit. Indeed, it is a subtle matter, when to be plain-spoken, and when to use wit, and when to let humor loose. Even when to pass by and say nothing.

Wit and Readiness For The Outer World

Wit is quickness, and I find that some patients need to borrow some for the outer world where trouble comes on fast. To a patient who was continually amazed at a series of mean women running things, I wrote: "You lose heart if you attack the Queen of Hearts where she has absolute dominion over the playing cards." Of course, I was alluding to her as an Alice who is naive. She is doubly mistaken, because she expects the Queen of Hearts to be interested in something beyond control, and because she thinks the other playing cards ought not to fall into this stupid game of power. A single sentence summarizes about forty years of her existence, because it is a series of the same mistake of overestimation of playing cards; quite like Alice. Of course, letters reflect my own preoccupations to some extent. The same week that I wrote the last letter, I wrote another about Alice, to an Alice, but with more allowance and length for the great pain she was undergoing as a Sunday school teacher in a church of mad parents:

> The great virtue of Lewis Carroll is to show how playing cards are terrifying, until you know what they are going to do, and decide in advance what you prefer to do back. Thus, every week will bring some new mad parent screaming like the Duchess, to which the liberal minister will respond pouring on oil of concern, and then, you, Alice. . . .

Here I am verging on humor, with its pathos.

Humor and Pathos

Humor is suited to coping with pain that keeps repeating itself, as a series. It is a chance to fly to the general conclusion, while also crying. I really want both, and they go very well together.

Thus, most of my men patients are forever vulnerable to being driven by winning. They are wired to the increase pack. While they may practice detachment, they had better be ready for these strong pulls into coming out on top. A patient of mine who grew up in the industrial culture of General Motors dreamt he was trying all night to get a flight back to Flint, but he could not get there. He had been unaware in meeting a very competitive colleague that he had been wanting to match him. His psyche of the night tried to fly there. I wanted him to grasp this as a perpetual series, so after this session I wrote to him, "Like the guy who made that movie 'Roger and Me,' you will always long to get some sense, company, and conversation out of the President of General Motors."

The next night, his psyche took a flight in the opposite direction which also surprised him. He dreamed that he was taking a train into the Lake Country in England, and ended up in an Underground Station in London. He had wanted to go away from the industrial machinery, to the lovely Lake Country, but the dream circled back to grimy and commercial London. There was also a beautiful painting in this dream, in red and gold, which was completed, he was told. This reminded him of a line from *Antony and Cleopatra* (Shakespeare 1607): "The barge she sat in, like a burnished throne,/Burned on the water . . ." (II, ii, 192–193). Here he was, flying off to the Lake Country, or to Alexandria, hoping for a different reception. I wanted him to grasp this also as a perpetual series. I wrote to him: "These are beautiful places you would fly to, and will countless times more, but they do not exist, for long, apart from the economy." The pathos is that he cannot live in General Motors, and he cannot live in a beautiful departure that is mostly of his imagination. The sooner he gets the humor of these two huge pulls, the less agony he will have in his existence. (See Walter Hill's poignant new film, "Geronimo," for this characteristic dilemma of man in the march of Western culture. If you join it, you are ashamed. If you oppose it, like Geronimo of the wind, you are going to get hunted down. A character who represents a beautiful compromise is Lieutenant Gatewood, but nobody thanks him and he is dismissed to a lonely post in Wyoming.)

Not Everything Is to Be Commented Upon

I conclude this chapter about writing, with its opposite, which is not writing. The only other statement of this kind I can recall is Balint's category, "Interpretations Thought Of, but Not Said," which he kept to himself, in his notes upon the case (Balint, Ornstein, and Ornstein 1972). Like every principle of psychotherapy, writing to patients may only be half right, and sometimes wrong. I have already mentioned psychiatric emergencies where my Psychiatric Evaluation will go silently into the official record of the chart.

I will give a few examples in closing. One patient who wrote to me asked me not to write her back. She said she felt freer to tell me about herself, if she did not oblige me to reply. Another told me to write and say very little. My learning made her feel inadequate, so I just ought to hold it back. Another said the same thing, and sent me a picture of myself and herself on a teeter-totter, with me on the left heavy end with a collage of my references, and with her thrust up in the air to the right by her lack of learning. To the lower right was just her, hiking, in a photograph. Finally, a fourth patient I saw with her husband told me she didn't like my letters, which reminded her of her father the journalist. I asked if she would like to take over the job, and she gladly did, and summarized the sessions for us.

PART III

A LIBERAL EDUCATION IN PSYCHOTHERAPY

My chief theme in concluding this book is the overwhelming dominance of group psychology in the life of mankind. I have seen very little reference to such a force in the literature on psychotherapy, yet it is the greatest thing to reckon accurately for this work. Man is a group animal, anxious above all else to fit in; yet to fit in and survive with his group, he is badly constrained and complains of the consequences. For this, he comes for help, worn out and worn down. He breaks out of the group, and becomes very anxious whether he will be let back in. For this he also comes for help. This is his central dilemma, and all others pale beside it in importance.

All animals have some kind of dilemma like this about the territory of their species. They stake out plots, and engage in plights to mate and bring up their young; yet they also cannot afford to be looking always in the direction of their own kind, nor can they be always showing off with their loudest calls and in their brightest plumage. They must also turn their heads to watch for their enemies, and they must also conceal their calls and their colors to be less conspicuous.

This latter half of surviving is called prey-vigilance, and it is opposite to the half that is playing to one's own crowd. Naturally, the lemma or assumption of prey-vigilance and the lemma or assumption of playing to one's own crowd for sexual and nutrient purposes are contradictory. You just cannot do both at the same time, which the birds on my feeder demonstrate by a continual oscillation between feeding and looking over their shoulders. They have been selected to oscillate like this because those who only fed were eaten, and those who only watched for enemies starved. Those who found some balance by oscillation between the two horns of their dilemma of survival did survive.

In his pre-modern days of hunting and gathering, and then agriculture up through the Bronze Age (to c. 1250 B.C., and the Age of Iron) mankind was more like the other animals than he has become as a modern creature. Because he was dependent on the non-human world of nature, he worshipped it as much as he worshipped the human crowd (Campbell 1964).

The Modern Force Field

Then, about 1250 B.C., came the men on horseback, who destroyed Troy (c. 1150 B.C.) and everything else in their path of the old way of balance between nature and man. Now nature was less fearsome than man himself, who came to destroy. Now man cannot take his eye off man. Rightly so. His peril comes with fitting in, or out, of the plans of man. This is the modern creature.

Marx argued (Ollman 1971) that man becomes a thing in capitalist schemes of production. He fits in as a piece, or he is out on the streets. Yet the transformation of man into thing began three thousand years before Marx with the men on horseback described by Simone Weil (1940) in the most profound essay on modern man ever written, "*The Iliad*, or the Poem of Force":

> The real hero of *The Iliad* (850 B.C.), its real subject, its center, is force: the force that is wielded by human beings, which subdues them, before which their flesh shrinks. . . . Force turns whoever comes under its sway into a thing. . . . For out of the power to transform a person into a thing, by making him die, grows another power, quite amazing in a different way: the power to make a person into a thing who is still alive . . . Who can tell how much—every moment—it has to bend and twist itself,

in order to conform? The soul was not made to dwell in a thing.
[pp. 104–105]

Here is one horn of the control dilemma of modern man, which impales him as a thing to have a place. This thing can be the wielder of the force, or the object of the force: "Such is the nature of force. Its power to transform human beings into things is double and cuts two ways: it turns to stone—in different ways, but to the same degree—the souls of those who suffer it and of those who wield it" (p. 109). Modern man can be the overpowering thing, or the subservient thing. (See Yeats [1914], "The Magi," or Ernst [1973], "Capricorn," or Camus [1957], "The Guest.") Or he can be the delaying thing, somewhere between these two, counting things. This third is the steward of power, and also becomes a thing. This is the crushing horn of being on the inside as a thing. Worse is the other horn, of being an outsider, or nothing at all and a nobody, with no company. Very, very few can stand this. Most come back in from the chill to be something after all. Yet we are greatly compromised to be included, and so we are back on the inside horn of the central dilemma of modern man. There is no way out of this terrain, which is shaped by the group psychology of modern man. This is his territory. The hundred years of psychotherapy that began with Breuer and Freud's *Studies on Hysteria* (1895) are always concerned with how to live with this dilemma. Consider again the five cases in the *Studies*, namely, Anna O., Frau Emmy, Lucy, Katherina, and Elizabeth von R. All are women subjected to the force of men as husbands and fathers and bosses. All are being strangulated, as Breuer and Freud say, by their own feelings in response. All are compromised. They can neither come out with their rebellion, nor can they stifle it.

It is no different for men, and it is no different a hundred years later. Yesterday, a resident presented two cases to me, both men. One was volcanic because he had to comply with his bosses. Spilling over, he came very near to the edge of being fired. The other shunned the competitive world in which his father was a big winner, and did not seem ready to come in out of the cold. Here you have it, the hot and the cold (Levi-Strauss in Charbonnier 1969), the inner and the outer horns of the perpetual dilemma of how to live with the force and the force field of modern man.

This map of the force field of modern man, in and out of his grouping, will allow us in this third and concluding part of this book to survey the problems of training, of art and of science in our field, and of some of the great debates about the nature of man as a group animal.

Training

Chapter 13, Training I, is concerned with the chief dilemma of the medical student who becomes a resident in psychiatry. His preoccupation, I find, in all four years of residency, is about getting involved without being taken for a ride. His tendency is to get this dilemma about half right. He enforces a protocol with a program for the patient to follow, which stays clear of being taken; yet he often misses a connection with the patient. Or he becomes a follower, an empathic follower, which stays clear of the lack of connection; yet he often ends up in collusion with the patient going nowhere. In other words, he is pulled to become the male thing or the female thing. Thus, he is oppressed, or perhaps more accurately, suppressed, by a myth that is a machine for the suppression (of the drift) of time. As Freire (1970) found in Latin America with his poor people trying to learn Portuguese, so I find with these young doctors that they come intensely alive when I pose pictures to them of their dilemma. This dilemma of involvement, without being taken for a ride, is their generative theme.

They are very technically oriented, as I certainly was in my days of residency. They desperately want a technique to cope with their recurring central dilemma. I offer them a map of it, in countless variations, and a wrench for adjusting the drivenness of the patient. At the right end of the wrench is the attunement of being with the patient in his turmoil. Just sharing it reduces its headlong and frantic quality. At the left end of the wrench is the drawing out of perspective, to look ahead where the patient's existence is going to go. This also gives pause and consideration, and loosens the drivenness onto one horn or the other. They wish to simplify their jobs to one thing, like attunement in the Rogerian or analytic sense, but this sacrifices their perspective about seeing ahead to where they will be taken on the ride with the patient. Conversely, standing way back to see the plot will miss the attunement and they will be cast out of the patient's existence. I therefore find it indispensable to offer them a wrench for adjusting both ends of the motor of drivenness. We cannot do without this double description to handle their continual dilemma.

It is interesting to put this learning problem in Piaget's (1968) terms of accommodation and assimilation. Accommodation means to adjust yourself to someone else's scheme. Assimilation means to fit others into your own scheme. The first de-centers yourself, to accommodate to someone else's perspective. The second centers upon yourself, making others fit into your terms.

The medical students and residents in psychiatry all tend to accommodate to the regime of psychiatry they are taught, simply because they will be tested upon it, and allowed to pass by if they are accommodating enough. Then, one of three things happens to them in their adjustment to theory (schema). The dominating ones tend to become directors, who fit patients into their terms, thus assimilating them into a standard practice, at the risk of losing touch with them. The empathic ones tend to become more existential doctors, who follow patients into their own worlds, thus accommodating to the patient's scheme or world view. A third group can't make up its mind and flip-flops between imposing theory and following the patients.

I'm attempting to involve them in the very process of liberal education, by which they alternate between accommodation to a writer's perspective, then take it apart to assimilate it to their own scheme, then back to accommodation to another writer, and so forth. I succeed to some extent, but the historical pull into fixing on a niche as overpowering, subservient, or vacillating is extremely powerful. As Marx argued (Ollman 1971, Weil 1940), the man becomes a thing that is a part of the social machine.

Chapter 14, Training II and III, is concerned with what additional help I can be to these young doctors and to those farther along in our field of psychotherapy. Some are serious enough about learning psychotherapy that they are willing to plunge into the study of the great predecessors in our field. My first book, *The Complex Secret of Brief Psychotherapy* (1986), covers this ground with Freud, Reich, Sullivan, Winnicott, Balint, and Selvini-Palazzoli. I now add Jung to that short list, and this is the reading material of my tutorials. I will explain in this chapter what I find indispensable about an education with these authors. Those who do not comprehend them are going to have big holes in their maps. Yet there is more to study, infinitely more, which I call Training III—the study of man himself in history, the subject of three of my previous books, *The Modern Contest* (with Lowell Cooper 1990), *Self-Delight in a Harsh World* (1992), and *The Dilemmas of Brief Psychotherapy* (1995). I will explain in this chapter why I find knowledge of history, literature, economics, and biology indispensable on a day-to-day basis with my patients. I simply cannot do without Darwin and Marx, and Levi-Strauss and Shakespeare, Max Ernst, and Yeats. Freud was educated like this a hundred years ago, but hardly anyone in our field seems to think it matters anymore. I will try to show why I think this is mistaken, and what can be accomplished daily and practically to meet the challenges of the cases by having the education.

Art and Science

Chapter 15, "Tolstoy's Fate," measures Tolstoy's great maps of man in *War and Peace* (1869) and *Anna Karenina* (1875–1877). I am first concerned with his vast canvases, which portray the pull into playing parts in the social machinery that is history on the march; second, with his characters who resist it in their self-delight, which is often tragic in its consequences; third, with the only character in these two great novels who finds a balance between the pull to the right of the machinery and the pull to the left of self-delight, namely, Kutuzov. I consider why Tolstoy could not maintain this balance himself.

Chapter 16, "The Science of Long-Term Psychotherapy," considers the evidence of science as a counter-current to the evidence of art. It is a spare field, simply because the resources necessary to the inquiry are monumental. Indeed, there is but one such work on the subject, which is the Menninger Psychotherapy Research Project, presented in encyclopedic form by Wallerstein's *Forty-Two Lives in Treatment* (1986). I outline the main lines of evidence, and supplement them with the partial findings of Malan, Luborsky and colleagues, Weiss and Sampson, Gaston and colleagues, and others. Nothing that would surprise Tolstoy or Simone Weil comes from these studies. As I wrote in summary of the studies of brief psychotherapy (Gustafson 1995, Chap. 15), the patients need an ally, a map, and places to land. Still, it is significant that these few studies we have confirm the findings of art. After all, it is possible that they would diverge, and it is for science to conduct the tests of the poetry of science (Maturana, in Gustafson 1986, Chap. 17). Finally, I consider chaos theory as a possible general theory for these findings on long-term psychotherapy. Specifically, is it a loose analogy or metaphor, or is it a tight analogy or metaphor that can be subjected to strict tests?

Man as a Group Animal

Chapter 17, "Jung's Individuation," begins from Freud's (1929) formulation of the dilemma of modern man burdened by the little room
allowed by the super-ego, but alarmed by the vast and uncontrolled id,
seeking the mediation of the ego as a balancing point between these
two disasters. The job is the adjustment of the compromise formations
between being good and subservient to the super-ego, and bad and wild
as the id. The tool is the pure interpretation of conflict (*Konflikt* in
German) between these extremes. Jung's terms for posing the dilemma
of modern man (in search of a soul, as he puts it in the title of one of
his books [1933]) alter the landscape and the address that is called for.
For him, the tamed man is locked in by his mask or persona on the
little social stage or box of conformity. The opposing term is the oceanic unconscious, which shows itself as a compensatory term to balance the aridity of the conscious mind. The key is to receive the unconscious as compensatory, as a continuous balancing, as a second eye,
to correct the distortions of the first eye.

Jung's own career shows how hard won is the ability to take the
unconscious as compensation to the conscious. In my terms, the pull
to the left of possession by a god is driven by the intolerable aridity of
the right. Conversely, the pull to the right is the force noted well by
Weil (1940), which drives everything before it. Both the left pull and
the right pull got Jung. The first was his romance with Sabina Spielraum
(Carotenuto 1982), and the second was his capture, temporarily, by
the Nazi psychiatry establishment, which got him to be in collusion
(Cocks 1985). As Weil noted, it is miraculous when a man can avoid
these fates for very long. Having gone down to the right in the force,
Jung then retreated into the mystical hocus-pocus of the East after 1940.
He just had no adequate map for the disaster of the world wars.

Chapter 18, "The Group Animal," utilizes a more adequate map
that is adumbrated in Lewis Carroll (1865), St. Exupery (1939, 1943),
Levi-Strauss (1955) (also,Charbonnier [1969] and Leach [1970]),
Canetti (1960), and Bion (1959), and which I have been relying on
throughout this book. In Bion's language, there are three pulls from
groups. The first is what he calls basic assumption dependency (baD),
or the pull into the assumption or myth that subserving the group will
get you taken care of by the group. The second is what he calls basic
assumption fight-flight (baF), or the pull into the assumption or myth

that fighting or fleeing with the group will save you. The third is what he calls basic assumption pairing (baP), or the pull into the assumption or myth that the uniting of opposites like male and female will create a marvelous new beginning like a child as savior of the group. The first is a machine (myth) for the creation of the female thing, the second for the male thing, and the third the child thing. They are the bondages in classical Indian philosophy (Campbell 1959) of *dharma* (duty), *artha* (power), and *kama* (love). In the terms of modern biology, these are the innate releasing mechanisms (IRMs) set off in us by group life (Campbell 1959), which bind us to its increase-mentality (Canetti, 1960).

Between the ages of 10 and 20 in Western society, under the most optimum conditions, the child is pulled out of his free-form naturalism into some kind of little box of being a proper citizen who pays his bills and causes no trouble. He is bound there by his myth or basic assumption, which obscures the drift into meaninglessness (St. Exupery 1939). He is trapped, but muffled. As Lewis Carroll (1865) shows in the education of Alice to the adult world of Oxford University disguised as a pack of playing cards underground, the adult is lost in the vain performances of these myths. He lives in a tiny world of increasing things, of which he is inordinately proud, smug, and turned off to every other consideration. Yet, he is obliged to play along or be cast out altogether.

If he is very blessed with good fortune, he will have family backing to play the game of increase successful in its endless forms from sport to reading to producing reports, and he will have backing to depart to his own world of *samodovolnost* or self-delight. Bachelard (1971) calls the first living in history on the horizontal, and the second the escape into the vertical of imagination. This back and forth is very difficult, because the pull to the right into the group is extremely powerful, and because of the pull to the left into the flight of the psyche to its own worlds elsewhere. Either, unbalanced, is disastrous. Either, gratified, sacrifices some of its opposite. Modern man is always in the dilemma of having to give up something, some of his beautiful vision to fit into the programs of increase, or some of his success for his own journey into the depth of his being.

In Chapter 18, I derive two further and crucial implications of this bimodal force field. The first is about stalemate and the second is about free passage. (See Chapter 7, Gustafson and Cooper 1990, for a preliminary discussion of this topic.)

Often, the double jeopardy of being in and being out results in the sterile compromise that Guntrip (1968) called the schizoid compromise, or, more down to earth, half-in and half-out. It is far enough in to have some kind of place, but far enough out not to be hurt so badly. It is not involved enough to develop, but also not far enough in to make a mark. Thus, it is sterile. Since it is such a common position, and since it is very stable in its slow drift into entropy, I mark it very carefully in this last chapter for its resistance to improvement in psychotherapy. Those who do not heed it well will misappraise its potential. After subservience, delay, entitlement, and basic fault, it is the fifth story or map of great practical importance.

Usually, in this fifth story there is a childhood fault, but group life then makes it very difficult to repair. If the child tries to get in, he is trapped in more intrusion by the group. If the child tries to get out, he is lost in more abandonment by the group.

So, the bimodal force field of modern group life is the great selection machine. Those who would transcend its rigors have to see it coming. Otherwise, their Pavlovian reflexes will pull them right under. I am reminded of the experiments with rats (W. T. Jones 1967), who could jump from electrified grids to safety on white spots (+) while getting shocked again on the black spots (–). If I were African-American, I would reverse the reward and shock, so you can see the social metaphor here. In any event, the rats became agitated when white was made grayer and black was made grayer, until, no longer able to discriminate safety from shock, they jumped high and to the right!

The actual ongoing experiment with us is that the insider white spots shock us to some extent and so do the outsider black spots to some extent. Society is thus like a high school that is going to hurt you in and hurt you out. Nevertheless, we don't have to be driven like the rats to panicky jumping if we can sit back from the force field and choose which paths in the field we prefer and which shocks we will take for our choosing. This gives us our balance.

13

Training I

According to the banking method of education (Freire 1970), which is the dominant method of psychiatry, medicine, and every other branch of education, we need only to make deposits in the residents or other students and they will reinvest the capital fruitfully in their own practices. Indeed, you can watch this banking process at work in any continuing medical education course on psychiatry or psychotherapy, whether it is about the latest class of serotonin-selective-reuptake-inhibitors or the latest class of protocols in cognitive behavior therapy. You can even assay the uptake and output with questionnaires and follow-up studies. In our residency, this is what is called education or training, no matter whether the specific topic is brief psychotherapy, community mental health, or geriatric psychopharmacology .

I have nothing against sound banking practices when it comes to depositing my money. I also have nothing against the exercise of breaking down psychotherapy into cognitive, behavioral, affective (dynamic and experiential psychotherapy concern affect or feeling), and willful (interpersonal and strategic psychotherapy develop will) procedures. After all, these are four of the chief faculties of the mind known to classical psychology of the nineteenth century. It is obvious that you can do something utilizing a fourth of the conscious mind (perception and memory are also faculties of the conscious mind that are not usually objects of psychotherapy. Of course, selective inattention poses perception as an object and psychoanalysis poses memory as its object), and the follow-up studies of modern psychotherapy prove just this.

Indeed, my own residency program teaches psychotherapy to second-year residents exactly in these terms as a technique utilizing one of the four mentioned faculties of the conscious mind. The residency program shown in this chapter is the very same one coast to coast with minor variations. I quote some from my own here, but I do not mean in any way to single it out. Psychiatry is a single paradigm in the United States, like all other bureaucracies.

Contemporary Models of Psychotherapy

Each model of therapy should address the following areas.

1. Underlying theory of behavior/personality (normality/optimality model)
2. Underlying theory of psychopathology (etiological model)
3. Theory of clinical intervention (mechanisms of change)
4. Processes of clinical intervention
   a. Therapeutic Operations (techniques and procedures)
   b. Therapeutic Contract (e.g., session frequency, role expectations)
   c. Therapeutic Bond (significance and functions of the relationship)
   d. Therapeutic Openness (e.g., defenses, involvement, experiencing)
   e. Therapeutic Impacts (in-session objectives for change)

Each presenter should plan to cover this material in four to five one-hour lectures. Presenters should make efforts to integrate case material (e.g., transcripts, audiotapes, videotapes) into their lectures inorder to illustrate the application of the conceptual material they are offering.

A. Foundations of Behavior Therapy
B. Cognitive Therapy (Beck, Rush, Shaw, and Emery 1979)
C. Psychodynamic Psychotherapy (Exploratory, Past-focused)

D. Interpersonal Psychotherapy
E. Experiential/Phenomenological Psychotherapy
F. Foundations of Brief Psychotherapy
G. Gustafson's Brief Psychotherapy

This education is highly operational in its language (Bridgman 1959). It specifies actions to take and in what order. It optimizes, etiologizes, mechanizes, and intervenes with its operations, contracts, bonds, openness, and impacts. In this exact sense of operational language, it is truly contemporary. It is fully programmable. Its language is borrowed from physical science, and so are its statistics (Bridgman 1959). All of this is typical of modern social science.

Noteworthy in our course is the final item, which sounds like something out of a nineteenth-century medicine show: "Gustafson's Brief Psychotherapy!" By this, my colleagues mean to say that I am not really part of the contemporary psychotherapy. In one sense, they are entirely right. I am not following the paradigm of isolating a faculty of the mind, giving it a lesson and measuring its movement in standard deviations.

Instead of being an idiosyncratic piece among the official pieces, I propose instead that I occupy what has been the center of the field for the last hundred years, as pictured in Figure 13–1.

MEMORANDUM

From: J. Gustafson
Subject: Contemporary Models of Psychotherapy (Gustafson's Brief Psychotherapy)

For my section of the course, I plan to center on the center of brief psychotherapy since Freud began the subject a hundred years ago with *Studies on Hysteria* (1895) with Breuer: which is how behavior, cognition, psychodynamics and experience (feeling), interpersonal difficulties and decisions (will) *fit together* in any given single case. For this, you need a relatively simple integrating concept, which was "conflict" (Konflikt) for Freud and is "dilemma" for me.

If you want to do this with me, you will need to read a little for each session, in preparation, whereupon I will briefly outline a few points, and we will discuss the dilemma posed for you by the work in question. An hour is very brief, so it will be difficult to show much video-tape, but I will show a little. I think it is better to *privilege* the discussion, so you can get an idea or two clear for yourselves.

1. Strangulated FEELING in Freud and Breuer, the case of Lucy in *Studies on Hysteria* (1895). Subservience Stories.
2. Befuddled WILL in Sullivan, *Clinical Studies* (1956). Delay stories.
3. Nasty Entitled BEHAVIOR in Winnicott, *Therapeutic Consultations in Child Psychiatry* (1971). Overpowering Stories.
4. Disastrous COGNITION in Balint, *The Basic Fault* (1967). Basic Fault Stories.
5. Benign and Malignant INTERPERSONAL DILEMMAS in couples, families, esp. teenagers and their parents, in Selvini-Palazzoli of Milan (1989) and Tiggemann and Smith (1989) of the Dulwich Centre, Adelaide, Australia.

Of course, my claim may be true while it is hardly trumpeted about. The field of psychotherapy is owned by its schools with their single faculties, and the only center that is granted is called eclectic. Eclecticism is merely a collection of the pieces.

The situation is like that in *Alice in Wonderland* (Carroll 1865), in which Alice's tears flood the poor animals, who are thinly veiled academics in the allegory. They want badly to dry off, being very uncomfortable with being all wet. The Dodo Bird proposes a Caucus Race in

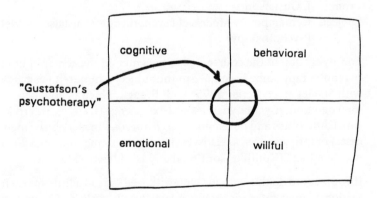

Figure 13–1. The Field of Psychotherapy.

which everyone runs starting from where they are placed on the course, running as they like and stopping as they like. Of course, it dries everybody off. Asked who has won, the Dodo Bird said at last, "*Everybody* has won, and all shall have prizes" (p. 21).

Dryness is popular and will prevail in academia for the foreseeable future. Caucus racing can be counted on to keep us all dry, and there will be countless contestants, named by their acronyms. Doubtless, I will be known for DT or dilemma therapy, which is a kind of NT or narrative therapy, which is itself a kind of ET or eclectic therapy.

Problem-Posing Education

If I am obliged to be a part of a banking curriculum on "Contemporary Models of Psychotherapy," I am not obliged to act like a banker. Thanks to academic freedom, I have room to conduct my part of the course as a seminar and not as a depositing lecture.

In this practice, I follow Freire (1970) and my other favorite teachers, whose chief aim is to bring the students out of a culture of silence into their most eloquent being. I need to confine myself to posing problems for the day's discussion, with not too many words or pictures, interviews or readings, or I will put them back under, into that passive state of numbness.

For example, the starting point or picture for the medical students in my class on interviewing is an interview conducted by two of them, with a follow-up in which I ask the patient if she or he wants anything from me in return for allowing the students to practice interviewing. In my seminars with residents, the starting point or picture is the reading for the day, hopefully brief. In my Brief Psychotherapy Clinic this year, the starting point or picture has been the chapters of this book and my previous book (1995), or a consultation to one of them with the patient present. In my workshops for professionals, the starting point or picture is a brief series of videotapes of the main stories to be faced in practice. In workshops for nonclinicians, I have begun to use short stories, taking *The Norton Anthology of Short Fiction* (Cassill 1986) as my text of psychiatry.

Whatever the starting point, which pictures a typical problem, the most important teaching principle is that I listen for their phrases, which are most *generative* for *them*. By the word generative, Freire (1970) means generative of their eloquence, which is out of the depths of feeling and thought and imagination. In other words, it is fertile for them, as opposed to dry. When I hear a fresh turn of phrase, I echo and amplify it to see if it catches on with others, so that a generative phrase for an individual becomes a generative phrase for the group.

This takes us out of the little box of the conscious mind and into the wet and fertile and vast unconscious mind. This would be alarming as well as exciting if I did not keep us tied to the technical problems of what to do with the patient. The group could become underconstrained once it slipped away from the rote methods of being overconstrained (Gosling 1979). I handle Gosling's Teaching Dilemma, by amplifying the generative themes to bring out the depths, while keeping us tied to the surface in terms of bringing us back to the implications of how we are to act with the patients. We swim freely and deeply in their generativity, which is spontaneous, coming up out of the ocean of the unconscious, yet we are tied to practical land.

What is astonishing to me is the coherence of the generative themes of medical students, residents in all four years, and psychotherapists in practice whom I meet all over the country in workshops. This coherence or unity of theme is what Freire (1970) found in Latin America with poor people who are badly oppressed in Cultures of Silence, who are talked at by the Director Cultures of the elite and educated from the big cities. This leads me to believe that medical students, residents, and psychotherapists in practice are also oppressed and that they are oppressed by similar situations in their practices. The same is true of teachers and artists and so forth in my seminars for non-clinicians.

The Medical Student, Resident, or Psychotherapist in Practice as an Oppressed Being

Medical students who are in groups to practice interviewing are pretty excited about their first interviews, and somewhat astonished by madness, when they come up to our inpatient ward with me for about twelve weeks. Since they will be held accountable for doing mental status exams, which are indeed useful for making organic findings, I have one student do the mental status exam. Since they are also held accountable for taking histories, which are indeed useful for seeing the terrible things overlooked by the patient, I have the second student take the history in his own way.

This year they spontaneously called the first kind of interview the dry interview, and the second kind the wet interview. The first is on firm ground and is a complete formality. The second falls into the deep, and usually has a lot of tears, when it is conducted with any sensitivity and clarity about the patient's pain. Many of my students connect very naturally, and the pain comes out, if they also miss a lot of holes in the story. Of course, they do not know what to do with all the pain but to go along with it. Then they give it back to me.

Most of the time the patient will want me to give a little further help, although there are a few patients, usually paranoid, or false self, who just want to get away as soon as possible, which I do not constrain. The help asked for by those who stay is about why the pain runs on and on, and what can be done to lessen the pain. This means putting it into perspective as a dilemma that has the topology now familiar to the reader. In these inpatient cases, the dilemma is always grievous either way.

What astonishes the students so that they are open-mouthed is the bizarre combination of a paltry and debased self, alongside a grandiose and even godlike self, which is routine in schizophrenia, mania, and hysteria, and surfaces in everything else when interviewed in depth. They cannot quite believe that these two things go together perfectly, as persona and shadow possession by a god. Their common sense tends to suggest that a person is either big or small, but, of course, their common sense is just familiarity with personae or masks. So, the oscillation between paltriness and sweeping powers shakes them.

First-Year Residents

First-year practice is all inpatient and tends to be entirely psychopharmacological. As Schmidt (unpublished) put it succinctly: "In this approach, our 'science' is the art of balancing neurohumors, with the brain nothing more than a great mixing vessel" (p. 3). This harkens back to the medieval medicine of humors, namely: blood, phlegm, choler (yellow bile), and melancholy (black bile). This, in turn, harkens back to the Greek medicine of air, earth, fire, and water.

The broken-down patients are stimulated with antidepressants and electroconvulsive therapy, while the anxious patients get anti-anxiety agents, the manics lithium and carbamazepine, and the psychotics antipsychotics. Many get combinations, because they are broken down and souped up.

If the medical students can enter into the dry and wet interviewing, the first residents generally stay on firm ground with dry interviews and little actual contact with the patients. Much of the day is spent, dryly, entering notes in the official record. This keeps the first-year residents, by and large, out of troublesome involvements. After all, they usually have no one to help them if they get in deep.

Some of them are drawn in, anyway, especially by the overpowering borderline patients. This is chiefly what they get exercised about in the little seminar I give them on "The Dilemmas of Management with Difficult Personalities on the Inpatient Service."

To: First Year Residents
From: Jim Gustafson
Subject: Seminar on "The Dilemmas in Managing with Dangerous Personalities"

———— tells me he has worked out the following dates with you for this seminar on Personality Disorders, which I construe to be relevant to you in terms of the four kinds of personalities which are most hazardous for you to manage with on inpatient services now and in the E.R. very soon to come. So this will be a timely transition for you.

I have found that this works best by a very brief posing of the *dilemmas* in managing with these people in a reading that *maps the likely situations you will find yourselves in.* These are all tricky, because all of these dangerous personalities have a highly inflated side to them and a crushingly deflated side to them. You need to be ready for both sides, or you will set them off unwittingly. They also pull you in, in different ways. Then in the seminar itself, we will discuss where you are apt to get in trouble and how you might come through all right. So I ask that you do this brief reading and think about how it has gone already for you, in advance of our discussion.

1. Paranoid Personalities.
   Reading: Ebert, R. (1987). Avoiding Murder by a Violent Patient. Psychiatric Times, December.
2. Borderline Personalities.
   Reading: Main, T. (1957). The Ailment. British Journal of Medical Psychology 30: 129–145.

3. Narcissistic, Manic and Inflated Personalities.
   Reading: Faulkner, W. (1939). Barn-Burning.
4. Antisocial Personalities.
   Reading: Porter, Katherine Anne (1993). Theft.

If they stay distant, they are pounded by complaints. If they respond by more contact, the situation gets worse. So, we discuss the dilemma of the malignant basic fault. The most pertinent map for them is in Main (1957). The second overpowering and malignant basic faulted type that gets to them is the paranoid patient, and the most relevant maps are Malan (1979, especially Chaps. 21, 22), Ebert (1987), and Sullivan (1954, 1956). Everything else is academic for them. Their task is survival.

Second-Year Residents

Second-year practice is outpatient. It is still heavily psychopharmacological at the mental health center and in our outpatient clinic. The first new thing is being on call in the emergency room, and the second new thing is a little outpatient psychotherapy. The first new thing is consuming. An entourage of borderline patients, who are very malignant and who are sent by everyone in the county, who wisely prefer not to deal with them—social workers, physicians, roommates, and so forth—circle the hospital continuously and take turns dropping in on the second-year residents. There are a few other patients who come to the emergency room, but few can vie with these for electrifying the residents.

They come in, usually complaining of something self-destructive, with huge charts that testify to the futility of treatment. The residents always have two bad choices. If they get very involved, it goes on for hours, and often ends up with a hospitalization that no staff upstairs in the inpatient service will appreciate. If they don't get very involved, the patient is menacing and threatens to go out and kill herself, or, at least, calls back several times that very night with the same threat.

There are two bad choices. When they call me as backup on the telephone, I help them decide which risk, under the circumstances, they prefer to run. This usually settles them down, nervously, awaiting the denouement. Of course, it is hard on the guts. Some naturally lean toward the far stance. They tend to suffer less. Some naturally lean toward the near stance. They tend to suffer enormously. Both positions are traumatic, and it takes an entire year of call for them to get used to this horrid dilemma. Even then, they hate it, which argues a certain clarity, especially if they can hate it cheerfully (that is, objectively) (Winnicott 1947). The net result of this traumatic year is to select the far position, which becomes the chief fate of psychiatrists.

As I write this, three typical events in the lives of the second-year residents illustrate the redundancy of their dilemma. The first and second events are in a conference called "Best of Call," for reviewing the quandaries of the week. I am there as a guest faculty, with the regular faculty members in charge of call supervision. A second-year resident presents a case of aspergillus (infectious) in a 60-year-old farm lady, which erupted into mania. The resident is angered from the word go, because the infectious disease team wants to dodge their own case, making it hers, when the chances of organic mania secondary to infection, steroid use, and antibiotic toxicity have not even been worked up with magnetic resonance imaging (MRI), spinal tap, and so forth. While angry, she has to "schmooze" the ID (infectious disease) resident to do his own workup, only to discover that the inpatient psychiatry nurses have no seclusion and won't take the patient. Fortunately, the ID resident is finally persuaded to do his own workup, and fortunately the head of our call services is willing to go over the head of the nurses to the director of the inpatient service to secure the admission. The dilemma is the usual: if the resident gets taken for a ride, by getting stuck with an organic case that may deteriorate rapidly, she is party to her own disaster; if she fights back, she courts the risk of angry interchanges with medicine and with nursing. In this case, she passed through the horns of the dilemma with help. Yet, the case selects her another step farther from getting involved.

The second case in "Best of Call" is a chronic schizophrenic at 3:00 A.M. with a crisis worker urging hospitalization. The resident decides not to hospitalize because the suicide threat is minimal and because the mental health center can re-evaluate at 8:00 A.M. So what to do between 3:00 A.M. and 8:00 A.M.? The resident says she was prepared to sit with the patient for five hours. The chief resident angrily retorts that that is not her job, and that we will be taken advantage of worse and worse if we allow crisis to slide their burden onto us, where it is the crisis worker's job to see the patient through from 3:00 A.M. to

8:00 A.M.! A third resident replies that crisis workers are themselves very angry. We are back at the usual dilemma, of being abused, or making others angry. I comment that the problem is ecological, for they will always test us to lessen their load, while we will be testing them back. It isn't going away. Again, it is the war of nerves that drives the residents further toward detachment.

The third event is that a faculty member of child psychiatry stops me in the hall to compliment me on my grand rounds on "The Central Dilemma of Brief Psychotherapy for the Last Hundred Years," and mentions that he cannot get the residents involved with children in actual cases. I reply that I have the same trouble with the residents in adult cases, except that by posing their dilemma I do get them involved, because their oppression is their *only* generative subject.

I would add that the faculty tend to be as lost as the residents over their most commonplace cases when they cannot anticipate the emotions of the residents that drive them in the usual dilemma. In "Best of Call," I broke some of the deadlock, by taking the discussion to the underlying anger set in motion by the referral from infectious disease. When faculty or residents can't face the feelings of connecting, they disconnect. This is the natural selection.

A little psychotherapy has the same result in terms of selecting for the far position. The residents have little idea of what they are getting into, and many of the patients are malignant. They are taken for terrible rides, which get worse with every extra effort, which only proves that involvement is a fool's mission. Some persist in connecting to patients, nevertheless.

Michael Moran (personal communication) reminds me that residents are also in danger of being eaten, so to speak, by whatever services they serve in. This induces a great mother hunger in them to be fed, and a great father hunger for help in defending themselves. The dilemma of being generous without being taken for a ride occurs with the duties of the services, as well as with individual patients. In this sense, my focus on the dilemmas with the cases takes the eye off the larger servitude; perhaps not. The structure is entirely parallel.

Third- and Fourth-Year Residents

Third- and fourth-year practice is very busy with duties: as senior residents on inpatient services, as consultants to medical and surgical services, and as would-be faculty doing research on the psychopharma-cologicals. It is a small wonder that they have an hour and a half a week to come to my Brief Psychotherapy Clinic and to follow a couple of outpatients in psychotherapy. Quite a few persist in this heroic effort to be there with a few patients. This oppression is hospital-wide. An older account of this is the novel of internship at Harvard called *The House of God* (Shem 1978), and a current account is the mock journal, *The New England Kernel of Medicine* (Bennett 1993). Bergman (1994) looks over the last twenty years of oppression of medical students and house officers.

The Generative Themes of the Brief Psychotherapy Clinic

In my clinic this year (1993–1994), we alternated reading and discussion of early drafts of this and my previous (1995) book, and consultations to the residents about their cases. Essentially, they went directly from reading any given chapter to the dilemmas of their own practice. I make big drawings of the dilemma being discussed. I am problem-posing back to them the worlds they are caught in.

They have been stunningly consistent in the first seventeen discussions of seventeen chapters. They develop about three or four variants per discussion, but they are all about the same obsession played out in different cases. This is the same dilemma we have seen in the first- and second-year residents. The difference is that they grasp it faster, with great outbursts of feeling, and with impressive clinical agility. Notice the following sequence of discussions. I am reminded of Bateson's (1971) dolphin in the mounting excitement of discovery of an entire series of new ideas. I have had to do less and less.

Allow me to summarize the first fourteen discussions by saying that they become most intensely expressive (generative) about variants of the borderline dilemma. They borrowed Semrad's phrase from me, ". . . no collusion with delusion," and they liked my term "the noble cause," similar to terms in Main's famous paper, "The Ailment" (1957). They enjoyed their own generative phrases, which were very down to earth. One dilemma was about being "stuck on a therapeutic bus with a bitch" in our fifth discussion. In the sixth came the term, "meat loaf," for somebody not getting that he was being trapped. "Lump-power" came out in the ninth, as well as "Humpty-Dumpty's Dilemma." The former meant a patient who commanded the doctor by acting as a complete lump. The latter meant the threat that Humpty-Dumpty was so fragile that he never came back together once fallen. In the fourteenth came a related metaphor of Cinderella waiting for the Prince in the Pumpkin who never came, which brought up the dilemma of how to deflate the Pumpkin.

Fifteenth Session: *Mother as Prisoner of Son the Monster*

In the discussion of Chapter 9, "Thirty-Year Psychotherapy," the case of a mother of a 14-year-old tyrant came up early and took the entire stage with fascination for everyone. I hardly said a word, but drew out what they said. The mother and son were in family therapy with one of the residents and a faculty member. The problem posed by the resident was that the mother was completely tyrannized by this boy.

She complained of this subjection, but she would do nothing to challenge it, saying, for example, that he could stay home from school because he *might* be sick. The boy did whatever he wanted, in the name of his possible sickness, like the boys in "West Side Story" who happily sing to Officer Krupke that they are "psychologically distoibed" and that he should call a "social woiker." It was obvious to us all that this mother was going to love this boy all the way to prison, in the usual fashion.

The mother was locked into a myth of being a good mother, which was drifting in a terrible way that she denied in the cloud of the myth. The resident felt confirmed in her view, which was fully externalized, but what to do? Could she explain this view to the faculty member, who seemed to be a prisoner of the myth as well by acting as if the family therapy was going to get somewhere by listening to the mother's complaints? The clinic discussed the danger of this discussion. If the resident went along with the pointless ride of the therapy, she would be very resentful. If she spoke up, to this superior, she might incur a great deal of anger. So, they posed this dilemma carefully to her in its double danger. The implication was that speaking up had better be carefully and tactfully addressed. For example, she might say to the faculty member, "Do *you* think there is any problem with the way we are proceeding?"

Sixteenth Session: *The Dilemma of a Therapeutic Bubble*

In a similar case, in which the patient drifted hopelessly and passed from one pair of residents to another for many years, the residents discussed their anger at being prisoners of the lump power of this patient who did virtually nothing but worry the residents about her ever-imminent suicide. Yet she was passed on as if the psychotherapy was going to change something for the better. It never did. So they were in collusion with a delusion. This was bad. Yet what did you do when the collusion was acting as a kind of bubble around the patient which, bursting, might be fatal? I did remind them of such a case (Margulies 1989, pp. 85–88), for I felt they were getting pretty exercised about being imprisoned with this lady and could act out dangerously to free themselves.

Seventeenth Session: A Case of Going over the Resident's Head after the First Session

Now discussing the use of drawing, we got into the dilemma brought up by one of the residents that drawing could draw you away from listening to the patient. He could be attuned, ear to ear, only if all other distractions were removed. Another replied that she got drawn in all too readily, so she liked drawing as a way of keeping back from the patient's feelings a little bit, and thus, keeping perspective about where the hour might be heading. After all, one could be drawn into attunement that was collusion with an impossible venture.

Here we were again in the usual dilemma, in slightly different words, namely the need and danger of attunement, and the need and danger of perspective through drawing of the plot of the story. Obviously, you could have too little or too much of attunement or perspective, as illustrated in Figure 13–2. Only a double description such as the dilemma map could keep track of this double task with its double challenge.

Well, immediately, this was verified in a shocking way. The very resident who said he had to privilege attunement, to keep from distraction, now showed himself in a dangerous situation, as follows. He had seen a patient once who came in for depression over his graduate career being at a standstill. Like so many graduate students in our university, this one had not kept up with the work, and was suspended by his department. Then he became depressed, and could do nothing. Then, his bitterness and blaming surfaced in terms of litigation against the department that had ruined his life.

Our resident listened, he felt, in reasonably good attunement. After all, this was what he was practicing. The next day he was called on the

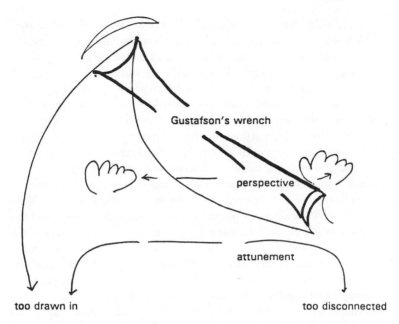

Figure 13–2. The Dilemma of Attunement and Perspective.

carpet by the chief of the department over a huge brouhaha brought by the patient for being badly taken care of in our department! He was humiliated, and very angry, at this strike at his competence that came so suddenly and without a hint of warning. Now, he was supposed to see this very patient at the end of our clinic for a second visit. How could he possibly stand to do it? He would be sitting there wanting to shoot the patient the entire hour, while waiting for the other shoe to fall.

Needless to say, this tale shook the seminar very hard, arousing a kind of underground tremor of fear and surfacing with outrage. Some said straight off that he could not go on like this. This patient played foul, and gave due warning that worse was coming. After all, he had proceeded to litigation against his own department. Why would he hesitate to fry this resident again?

Others took the opposite side. How was the first party warning of a malignant case so sure? After all, we had not even seen the patient. Wasn't this flying to conclusions on slight evidence? How did the dire warnings jibe with science?

The debate raged on. Where did Dr. Gustafson stand on this, after all? Would he see the patient in clinic for consultation next week? I said I would not. For me, the very investigation of the situation was a kind of dangerous operation in which the consultant was highly likely to be blamed for any recommendation felt to be negative by the patient.

I did not feel adequately positioned to investigate and defend myself from the likely malice ensuing from the investigation. Only the clinic director and departmental chairman had the kind of authority to defend themselves from the attack, and only they could look into it with the resident. *If* it turned out to be as malignantly blaming as it sounded, psychotherapy would only make it worse, and the patient would have to be told by our authorities that we could not prescribe a treatment that would make the patient worse and that, indeed, his kind of case did not do well with any kind of treatment. Even pharmacological treatment was improbable. *If* it turned out to be less malignant than it appeared at first hearing, then more could be offered. The dilemma was how to check out the probable malignancy of the case, while not endangering the doctor. I did not want to assume the case was inoperable on hearsay, but neither did I want to do a biopsy that would haul me into court for my cautionary recommendations.

Supervision

The clinic thus helps to surface the residents' common oppression in their common dilemma, and helps them find their way around in it more readily, with less danger. Yet, individual supervision is needed to get into depth for them as individuals with particular inclinations and particular dangers. The sequence of cases presented is always telling, because each individual resident tends to have his or her own trap over and over again. In this sense, they are all oppressed people getting into cages, unwittingly, but each tends to have his or her own special kind of cage. This needs to come into focus, for the resident to see it coming. It is not enough to have the clinic discuss "A Case of Going over the Resident's Head after the First Session." Residents long on attunement and short on perspective do benefit by such a discussion, but they also need to see themselves in a sequence of cases getting into the same fix of attunement. Then, it is possible they will jump like Bateson's dolphin out of the sequence to a grasp of attunement as a trap, in general—while not falling into the opposite error of perpetual distance.

When I first looked over my notes of three years of supervision, I feared being flooded with variations that would take an entire book to describe. This illusion was created by sitting too close to the material, where individual variations come into focus, obscuring the class of which they are a part, which came into focus when I stood back to a distance of three years and looked at the long row of faces. They divided, parted, even fell into two types with astounding simplicity.

The Attuned Who Lack Perspective

We have already adumbrated the first type from the last case presented of dangerous attunement. William James used to call this the soft-minded tendency. Like good mothers, the resident will get into the patient's corner all too readily, and are felt to be warm and supportive and even wonderful. Yet often, they are thus drawn into malignant fixes, and cannot get out. They ask too little of the patient and try to do it for them.

The Discerning Who Lack Connection

These are naturally the opposite, the tough-minded guys of William James. They are vigorous with the patients, like Teddy Roosevelt. Often the patients go away from them for lack of rapport. They see, often correctly, what the job is for the patient, but do not sit well beside the patient to help him bear it. They are more like the usual coaches in sport who make demands. They insist on compliance, and often do not get any.

Counter-Transference, versus a Personal Reaction as a Response to the Patient's Dilemma

The loose term in our residency vocabulary for having a personal reaction that gets in the way of helping a patient is counter-transference. This term, corrupted from psychoanalysis, sounds pretty important, and is used to cloud over a multitude of sins with a kind of pretty vagueness. (Orwell [1946] says that vague nouns are the chief stock in trade for language that is intended to hide things rather than reveal them.) I find it is more precise to pose the problem of having a personal reaction as a response to the patient's dilemma, rather than as a response to the patient's transference. After all, the patient is always in a dilemma that can be specified for a given hour. A transference is always something that can be inferred, even from little hints (Gill 1954), but it can be very subtle and faint and not the most important thing for a given hour. I understand that psychoanalytic seminars are often devoted to tracking the subtle shadows cast by the transference, as I have been in many such seminars myself called continuous case conferences. I found it an excellent exercise in attunement, but it runs the risk of putting a secondary consideration first. First is the patient's dilemma in living his life soundly. This is the challenge of the case, as Winnicott (1971) would say. Transference phenomena are means to meeting the challenge.

In other words, the resident finds herself driven by a force field. She falls into holes, or feels pushed away, and so forth. I explain that space-time is curved by force, and will compel her unless she can get an accurate picture of the effects on her. If she cannot see them coming, she cannot brace herself to withstand them. I draw her a map of the dilemma, as well as two sentences of summary of the problem and our hypothesis. She has it in pictorial and written form.

Psychotherapists in Practice, and the Routine Stalemates

As I conduct workshops around the country for psychiatrists and psychologists and social workers, I am often asked questions about cases they are stuck in. These come up when I show my own videotapes in a one-day conference, and they come up in great detail when I have a second day for them to bring in their own cases for consultation with me directly. In general, the stalemates are the same everywhere, from Australia to Holland, and from San Francisco to Missouri and to Maine. They are the very same stalemates as my students bring into my own clinic for consultation.

Sullivan (1954, 1956) used to say that being a consultant is ridiculously simple, because the therapist is always overlooking something in the dynamics that makes the entire difference to the outcome. All he had to do was to see the hole in the story, that the therapist could not face alone. In other words, the therapist is stuck in his own selective inattention that clouds over the key part.

What is the mechanism by which a therapist is in a cloud? There are actually two mechanisms, which are the opposite sides of a single coin. The first is that the therapist is so identified with the patient in her dilemma that he becomes lost in feeling with her and with a complete loss of perspective about how to get anywhere else. The second is that the therapist is so fearful of getting caught up in the patient's dilemma that he stays removed and is thus unavailable to the patient in bearing it. In other words, some therapists are too close in the attunement and some are too far away in the discernment. Let's take an example of excessive distance.

Too Far: A Case of Transference Fish

The patient is a young man harshly put down by his father. He is coming for help after a detour into drugs to struggle for a place as a good worker in college who will get a first girlfriend. He connects enthusiastically with his doctor, and is very grateful for the backing he has not had for a long, long time. Probably, he got it early from his mother, and this early connection is being revived and traded on. On the strength of it, he stands up to his boss in his part-time work, objecting to being passed over unfairly. He comes in triumphant, and tells the tale of his success.

His doctor is uncertain, and anxious that this will be a "fluff hour" in which nothing is accomplished. He tolerates the vaunting of the patient, which gradually trails off after three-fourths of the hour. The doctor then asks what problem the patient wants to talk about today, and the patient is vague. Both end up irritable, and far apart.

This is a routine problem, as pictured in Figure 13–3, in knowing what to watch for in hours in which the patient is full of success. There is always a lull coming, after the flush of victory. Into this lull will come a nice, big transference fish, such as "Are you annoyed with me?" "Am I bragging too much?" "Maybe you don't think it's that big a deal?" and so on.

Too Near: A Case of Mercurial Polio

The opposite problem is to be so much with the patient that you cannot see what's coming and why and how she keeps hitting the wall. Here is such a case, which was the chief subject of the eighteenth discussion of the Brief Clinic this year.

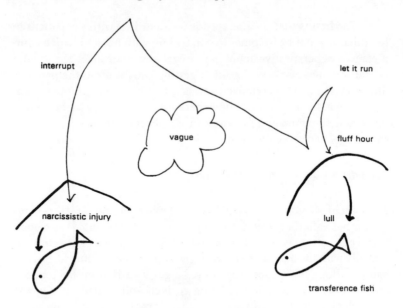

Figure 13–3. Success Hours.

The patient is a 50-year-old woman who is married to a minor tyrant. She acts as his doormat, and is hugely aggrieved. Yet she is the same in almost every other context. She explodes often, and is penitent, and is let back in. She is a walking catalog of physical ailments. Why, asked our resident, is she not getting better? Is this not a typical case of subservience (Gustafson 1992, 1995)? Something is missing here. Certainly, there is no lack of feeling. She feels the pain of complying, and being badly used. She feels the anger, which comes roaring out. The resident feels both with her, but it doesn't help. The two sides of her do not come together, in some kind of integration of being outspoken but still accepted.

Interestingly, there is something successful with A.A. (Alcoholics Anonymous), which aborts. She goes to meetings happily for a while and proceeds through the first three steps, but balks at steps four and five, of making a moral inventory and making amends. She runs away. She has many groups like this, where she gets a foothold, and runs away, so she lives in a kind of string of day hospitals.

Interestingly, she is also quite a celebrity in the hospital. Her last stunt was in the hospital gift shop, where she suddenly got the idea she might have polio, and collapsed in a near faint at the thought. She had to be revived by the emergency blue cart team. This made quite a stir, but she has pulled lesser versions many, many times. Her somatic pre-occupations also have a chronic, nagging channel, such as the idea that there might be mercury in her teeth poisoning her. This got a dentist to take out all of her fillings. She keeps the medical professions pretty busy.

The clinic got very involved in this discussion, with many allusions to similar cases. Many of the residents and psychology fellows seemed to be stuck in similar ones. They noticed two holes in the story, but they did not quite know what to do with them. One hole was the one pointed out by the presenter, namely, that the patient ran away from success with A.A. Several responded that she might feel much smaller being an actual and modest person, instead of this medical phenom-enon. A second hole concerned her anger. Why didn't she bring it out more constructively? The presenter replied that she had tried to strangle her husband several times.

It was my turn as consultant to see into the holes, to pose the problem of this stalemate. It seemed to me that the patient herself had the right diagnosis, but it was distorted in terms of primary process. She was indeed mercurial, but the answer was not to take the mercury out of her teeth. She also had polio, in the sense that her arms and legs went useless, but the answer was not in nursing her back to full strength. She was involved in a plot of huge power over her. She acted like a doormat, but was ready over the least little thing to explode in her mercurial manner. Doubtless, one of the ladies in the gift shop, irri-table as they are to everyone, had offended her. Her only circuit breaker to strangling the lady was to go limp, which convinced her she had polio, whereupon she fell to the floor, and the blue cart had to come running.

In other words, this is grand hysteria (Breuer and Freud 1895, especially "The Case of Frau Emmy"), or the ailment (Main 1957), and it is a tremendous superhighway that runs away regularly with the pa-tient. Since she offers herself as a doormat everywhere, her mercurial rage is always being set off, followed by her circuit breaker, followed by medical help rushing to her assistance. Once most of the nervous system has been recruited into this way of life, it is virtually impossible to elicit anything else. There are hardly any cells left to oppose it (Edelman 1979, 1982, 1985).

Yet, phenomenally, there is an alternative, and yet it aborts. Why? Surely, she balks at the moral inventory and making amends of steps four and five in A.A. because it is such a come down to modesty. As the Wizard of Oz (Baum 1900) says, "Get away from that curtain!" which, drawn back, reveals the tiny individual behind the huge facade. I felt it is even worse, for getting involved in her medical fantastic operations is, after all alienating, resented, and far away from being loved. Her longing must be great to be let in as herself, and yet it brings her too near. This is why she runs from A.A., and everywhere else she gets a little foot in the door. She fears being hurt. It is the usual Far/Near Dilemma of the malignant basic fault (see Chapter 1), as pictured in Figure 13–4.

Now, our presenting resident replied that the lady did try steps four and five with her pastor, who reprimanded her, and she felt very

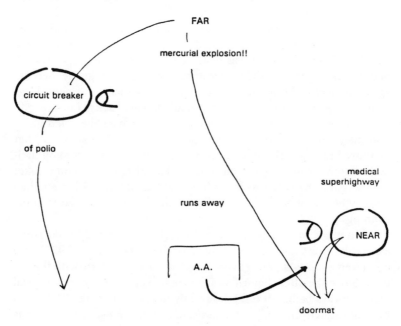

Figure 13–4. Mercurial Polio.

bad indeed. As one of our seminar participants astutely noted, she probably confessed to the very thing the pastor could not abide. She is a genius at getting far away.

Since we were discussing my Chapter 12 on writing things down, I was asked what note I would write this patient. My reply was this: "You get a new start with A.A., but you have to go away when you start to get near because it is too vulnerable." For me, this is the rate-limiting step, and so that is what I address. It gives the patient a chance to summon her stubbornness to prove me a little wrong. It also relieves the resident of saving a patient who is determined not to be saved.

Too Near and Too Far

In conclusion, I want to be careful to avoid a misunderstanding. Many residents and fellows and psychotherapists in practice are routinely too near, and miss the forest for the trees and run into all kinds of trouble as in this last case. Many, conversely, are too far routinely, and do not connect, and thus lose the patient as in the case of transference fish. Of course, the dilemma is how to be generous with those who can borrow, and how to stay back and see what's coming (badly) with those who are continuing to get in big trouble. You can hardly transcend this central dilemma of Training I if you are repeatedly stuck on one horn of it, the near or the far. If you can master the near horn you are prevailingly caught on, you can work on the far horn, and you might even get really reliable as a doctor.

14

Training II and III

A creature that is thoroughly oppressed can think of nothing but himself. He is self-referential, like someone ill trying to gather his powers to throw off the illness. This is why trainees are mostly available psychologically for their own generative themes that name their situation. Of course, this is not entirely true, like all psychological statements, for there is such a thing as curiosity, which can keep an independent existence apart from the life of the increase pack (Gilligan 1990). Some show this, and some have it very well hidden. This was our subject of Chapter 13, "Training I," the central dilemma of how to be generous without being taken for a ride.

More experienced psychotherapists can be little different than trainees, especially when they are still captives of the same dilemma of their training. Some are captured by the far orbit, after some bad falls in training in malignant situations. They give directions, now, to patients from far away, as across a desk. They tend to be cognitive, and behavioral, and strategic, but they can also be psychodynamic in their interpretations. Some are captured by the near orbit, providing empathy for feeling, especially pain, missing the perspective necessary to see what is going to happen next to their patients.

I have found a great deal more than this, as I have worked with experienced therapists in the last ten years in workshops across the country. Basically, I introduce myself by saying that our job is to see what our patients are looking for, to be with them in their distress, and to see what they overlook in the mechanics of the story that will keep it going. I outline the four (or five) kinds of mechanics of stories, illustrate and discuss them on videotapes, and point out that *any proposition I put forward is about half right*. This pulls strongly in them for participation in the story shown, yet it cannot help to remind them of occasions *when the story went wrong doing just what I recommended*. I will hear about it, straight out, and our discussion is lively about the holes in my own presentation. This is vital for me and for them.

　I find the strength of experienced therapists is in having a feel for the approach to different kinds of characters (stories). They are apt to be very keen about this, like experienced mothers, or experienced hunters. They have a nose, an ear, and an eye, for trouble, and a delight in breakthroughs.

　Generally, they have read very little. If I ask for a show of hands in a group of 100, only a few have ready the first important and extremely relevant map that began our field 100 years ago, Breuer and Freud's (1895) *Studies on Hysteria*. The same is true for Jung, or Reich, or Winnicott, or Balint, or Selvini-Palazzoli. My first of the three parts of this chapter concerns the Training II of catching up with 100 years of mapmaking. They tend to have a little cognitive mapping, a little behavioral, a little psychodynamic, a little strategic, or a little collection of the four kinds of maps, which makes them literally eclectic. I propose that they need maps that use all of the faculties, to grasp any particular story in depth. If the reader can catch up with a hundred years of mapmaking in a single day, that's (100×365) a speedup of 36,500 times! Very brief therapy.

　Generally, they have also read very little of history, and biology, and the arts, including literature, although there are some surprising exceptions. Their university education has rushed them through the technical things necessary to a degree in a specialty. They have not only missed out on the maps of our own field of the last 100 years, but also the maps of mankind pondering itself for three thousand years since the *Iliad* of Homer (c. 850 B.C.).

　The second part of this chapter, Training III, is on catching up on three thousand years of modern history. What is the pull to the right of the increase pack in Homer, Shakespeare, Rabelais, Montaigne, Tolstoy, Canetti, Levi-Strauss, and Kundera? What is this thing, territory, in its grip on man to hold him in its outer orbit? What is the pull to the left into the depths of his being in Campbell's descents of the hero, or in Yeats's towers, or in the possession of Shakespeare's tragic heroes by maddening obsessions? What is this thing, passion, in its grip on man to pull him down into its inner orbit? How is reading those two great pulls on the human being, noticed in history, biology and the arts, going to change our daily work?

Finally, and thirdly, I go to a recent workshop in the Midwest to show the generative themes of a fine group of experienced therapists utilizing my videotapes as pictures for surfacing their own concerns. In the holes in my presentation, they locate their own dilemmas.

Training II, or 100 Years of Mapmaking

Chaos Theory

In terms of contemporary chaos theory (Schmidt unpublished), I am characterizing the dilemmas of my patients as organized by two strange attractors plus a fraction of a third strange attractor, in the simplest cases. More complex cases can have as many as nine or ten strange attractors in certain phases, but tend to drop back down to a binary pair (Gustafson 1995). Thus, the classical symphonies like Tchaikovsky's Sixth, the Pathétique, move along in a binary opposition between two voices, complicate themselves to four or six in fugues, and can be fairly chaotic in brief polyphony that is only limited by the number of instruments in the orchestra. Such a musical score is similar to the psychological states of a complex being, which is why it is so attractive, as it were, by evoking the very music possibilities of such a soul.

A strange attractor is like a gravitational field that pulls the subject into its preoccupation. Thus, the subject tends to be in orbit around such a point. When there are two, or between two and three such points, the subject is in some kind of oscillation between the points. In general, the two dominant strange attractors for the human being are the outer one of territory, and the inner one of self-love or what I call, following Tolstoy's idea of *samodovolnost,* self-delight (Gustafson 1992). In psychoanalytic theory, this is called primary narcissism. See Balint (1968).

In the diurnal cycle, the human being sleeps in some kind of self-content, wakes into the territory of the daily struggle, and returns to his starting point. (Lewin [1973] demonstrated that dreams play on a screen like a movie screen, and he called this the dream screen. Lewin believed it was an equivalent to the mother, who comforted the child to sleep.) Along the way, he is capable of a great deal of back and forth between these two strange attractors. Le Corbusier's (1947) famous map of the diurnal cycle looks like Figure 14–1. I have added the two points of the two strange attractors that drive the cycle.

Now if I put the sleeping unconscious of self-content first and make it as huge as it actually is oceanic, and if I make the small conscious mind to come after, then the Le Corbusier map looks like the topography that I find most accurate for my patients, as in Figure 14–2. With such a topography, we can now understand the mapping of psychopathology of the last hundred years, starting from Breuer and Freud (1895).

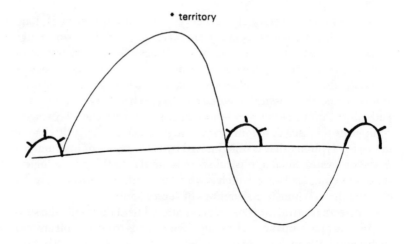

"This sets the rhythm of work for man."

Figure 14–1. The Diurnal Cycle of Le Corbusier.

uncs. self-content

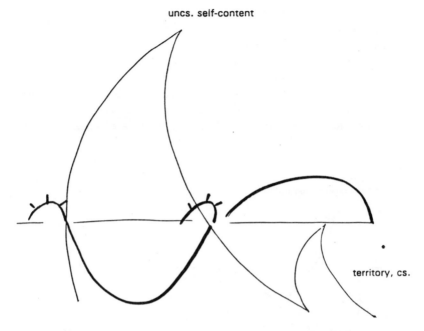

territory, cs.

Figure 14–2. Le Corbusier's Map Translated onto Dilemma Space.

Breuer and Freud, and Especially Freud

I wrote an unpublished book on this subject (Gustafson unpublished, a) before I published my first book with two chapters on Freud (Gustafson 1986), so what follows will be very schematic by comparison. Even the schema are of tremendous service, and are generally unknown. Essentially, Breuer and Freud (1895) discovered that women who are subservient in taking care of fathers, husbands, and bosses, develop tremendous pain. This is usually diverted into somatic preoccupations. When they suggested to these women that the somatic preoccupations were a diversion from their intense feelings about their situation, they were taken deeply into the shadow side of tears and rage as if they were riding a speeding train straight into the unconscious, as pictured in Figure 14–3. Scene after scene of their humiliations, and hurt, and self-denial flashed into view with tremendous intensity. Two of the five, Anna O. and Frau Emmy, were basic-faulted ("Dora" [1905] and "The Case of Homosexuality in a Woman" [1920] complete Freud's list of his published female cases. Both were basic faulted, malignantly, and turned out disastrously) and sank into an endless mire of injuries, while three of the five, Lucy, Katherina, and Fraulein Elisabeth, came through the train ride into the unconscious beautifully. The topography of subservience was mapped for all time. (See "A Case of Basilar Artery

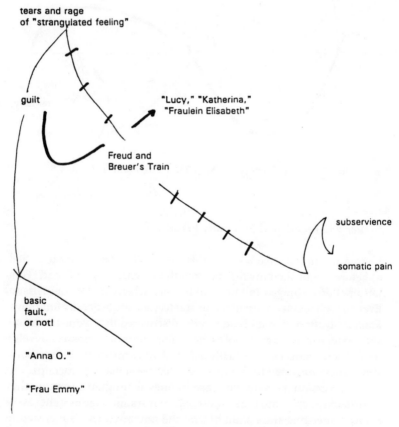

Figure 14–3. Studies on Hysteria.

Migraine" [Gustafson 1995] for the very same topography 100 years after Breuer and Freud.)

In the "Rat Man" (1909), Freud went on to map the topography of delay and overpowering in the German man, one benign and one malignant. Essentially, the Rat Man cannot decide between his lawyer career, and his beautiful love for his fiancée, Gisella. He comes to Freud in a delirium, from his oscillating orbit between the two great loves of his life. Freud skillfully poses his dilemma, in rat language generated by his prolific unconscious. He can make like a perfectly German rat of self-advancement, or he can be revulsed by these endless temptations. Yet his revulsion leads to poverty. He needs his rat-like connections to have a place in German law. Both horns of his dilemma are very dangerous. Freud poses it to him beautifully, and will not be diverted by his endless evasions, and somehow it comes out all right. This is the only case in which Freud's notes remain available. They show the tremendous vitality of the man's struggle. Yet there are gaps in how he worked it out.

The "Wolf Man" (1918) is similar in his violent interests, yet, after all, more entitled and malignant. He really cannot bear his weaknesses, and ends up getting Freud to take up collections for his financial support after analysis. This is certainly entitled, and overpowering. Later, Ruth Mack Brunswick (Gardner 1971) reanalyzes him by confronting all this entitlement, with wild and violent results, which somehow settle down. The fellow is a mix of obsessional delay, and malignant entitlement. Freud's attempt to deal with the first leaves the second.

Jung

Jung improves upon Freud in two big ways, which I will elaborate fully in Chapter 17, "Jung's Individuation, Compared to Freud." To be schematic, he discovers that entitled characters, equivalent to Freud's Wolf Man, are possessed by gods unwittingly. Jung utilizes the dream to demonstrate this cloud, for which they have selective inattention. Jung also altered the unconscious from Freud's picture of an id-driven pleasure-seeking machine of primary process. According to Jung, the unconscious is an adaptive instrument that balances the distortion of the conscious standpoint, by bringing up the opposite for comparison, often in caricature to make its point, absurdly. Thus, the Wizard of Oz (Baum 1900) is living in a cloud of glory as the pseudo-god that he is obliged to play, and his deliverance from this fixed role depends upon glimpsing the absurdity of the claim, by seeing the absurdity of its opposite of himself as a little quack. The story is like one of Jung's analyses of dreams, which, in sequence, deliver the protagonist from the psychic inflation of pretension.

Reich

Reich (1933) interposes the developmental history by which an Oz is possessed. Again, to be schematic (see Gustafson 1986, Chap. 4) he shows how the child lifts himself out of disturbing weakness, by identification with a powerful adult. Thus, a little boy with a cruel father takes refuge in identification with his uncle, an English lord (Reich 1931). Yet, he is now a prisoner of this new bearing, which makes him stilted in every way: bearing, voice, and gesture, which Reich sees as deriving from a "constant attitude" (here of English superiority to German sadism). The difference between Reich and Jung is that Reich sees the character being fixed by identification with an admired adult in the child's vicinity, while Jung sees the identification as having the scope of religious dimensions. It may be revealed to the child by a trusted adult, but it is a vision of a god that has the necessary power to possess the child forever.

Winnicott

Winnicott (1971) understood this kind of claim by a child, but put a different twist on it. He said it was a child's response to losing something crucial, whereupon he forced the world to give it back to him. Thus, the antisocial reaction of the child is a hopeful sign.

Yet, he must be stopped by the power of the parents, and somebody has to reach back to his pain of the loss. As with Jung and Reich, the problem is binary with Winnicott. The outer horn is the god-possession, the powerful adult identification, the drive to take back one's own, while the inner horn is the absurd weakness, the child's inferiority, the loss by the child. The means, to reach the full force of the dilemma, overlap also between Jung, Reich, and Winnicott. Jung prefers the dream, Reich the challenge to the constant attitude of superiority, and Winnicott play and drawings that culminate in the dream. I like to use all three means.

Balint

I will not belabor the crucial point from Balint that I elaborated in Part I of this book of how to distinguish between regression into the shadow horn of this dilemma, which is benign, versus regression, which is malignant. Balint's book (1968) is worth careful study in its latter two-thirds concerning his way of going with the patient as an indestructible and steady and yet equal presence.

Sullivan

This entire book is a testimony to Sullivan's (1954, 1956) central idea of selective inattention as the cause of the stories running away with the patients (Gustafson 1986, Chap. 6). The patients are in clouds, and unwitting over their participation in their own misery. What I have added to Sullivan's idea is my own idea of dilemma (Gustafson 1995). That is, Sullivan liked to argue that it would suffice to clear or dispel the cloud for the patient to see the terrain and make the necessary corrections of his course. See especially Chapter 10 in Sullivan's *The Psychiatric Interview* (1954), "Problems of Communication in the Interview." "The patients took care of that, once I had done the necessary brush-clearing, and so on . . . The brute fact is that man is so extraordinarily adaptive that, given any chance of making a reasonably adequate analysis of the situation, he is quite likely to stumble into a series of experiments which will gradually approximate more successful living" (pp. 238–239). This is simply not the case, when the patient is in dilemmas that are divergent, tragic, and malignant. It *is* the case in relatively convergent and benign dilemmas. It depends, thus, on the territory to be mapped. I knew this idea ten years ago, and knew it was helpful, but not sufficient. The terrain has the topography of dilemma, and there is great difficulty in giving up something to move through the pass.

Selvini-Palazzoli and White

I do not need to repeat the ground gone over in Chapters 3–6 concerning malignant and benign couples and families. I derived tremendous help from Selvini-Palazzoli and colleagues (1978, 1989) in creating these maps, and from Michael White (White and Epston 1990) in creating simpler ways through them. Selvini's (1978) idea of paradox is quite like my idea of dilemma, yet it obliged her to engage in a great deal of tricky counter-paradoxes, which I do not need for most of the benign cases of Chapters 4 and 6 on "Benign Couples and Families" that respond to an adequate map of their dilemma without guile or invariant prescriptions or the like from me. Yet, I believe Michael White makes it sound too easy to turn what he calls unique outcomes into new beginnings that are sustained. The dilemmas are often harsh, and the suffering necessary, as I showed in Chapters 3 and 5 on "Malignant Couples and Families." I wish to point out that Selvini-Palazzoli never proposed a method of family therapy for general use, but rather to solve the paradoxes of the most malignant families in Italy with psychotic offspring. Therefore, she accomplished precisely what she set out to do. Also, Michael White has aimed to help persons overcome certain drastic careers, starting with encopresis and going on to the in-the-corner lifestyle of schizophrenia. If his narrative method is heavily cognitive-behavioral, he has had considerable success challenging the drift of these careers. It seems to me that he gets very well through the selective inattention about where careers are taking people.

Conclusion to Training II

If I have been schematic in these last pages about my reading list for a tutorial of Training II, I do not actually mean that such an outline is the education. This would be as absurd as stating the dominant theme in a symphony of any great power along with its alternate theme, and claiming you understood the music. No, the music is the movement between the opposing currents in all its variations of theme, rhythm, and color. Every time I read one of these writers again with one of my students in the tutorial, I see much that I missed in the previous ten readings. That is the sign of music of any profundity.

I am hoping to introduce my students, and my readers of this book, to the practice of reading these authors over and over again. You make them your own only in this way. The students who ask for the tutorial (Training II) with me in our training program are usually those who have gotten the confidence to read and ponder reading and even write out their own opinions from a liberal arts education. They have had this practice in individuation. The majority have not and do not elect to take this tutorial with me. With this majority, I am confined to working at Learning I concerning their oppression, as discussed in Chapter 13.

Training III, or Three Thousand Years of Modern Self-Consciousness

As I said, current opinion about psychotherapy training would say absolutely nothing about history, literature, art, biology, and so forth. If Freud had such an education, it was just background, and really makes no difference to modern psychotherapy. Two of my favorite teachers of psychotherapy in my residency, Weiss and Sampson, are typical in this contemporary teaching of our subject (Gustafson in press, a). Their most recent book is called *How Psychotherapy Works: Process and Technique* (Weiss 1993). Their argument is very straightforward. A patient makes prominent his mistaken approach to things, testing the psychotherapist to see if he has a different and more useful approach. A patient has gotten distorted ideas from childhood, transferring them into the present where they do not fit, but hoping to find someone who can see what he overlooks. If my ideas were reduced to a single lemma or horn, they would look like this idea, which is close to Sullivan's monopathology of "parataxic distortion."

That's it. You need nothing more. You have a control-mastery theory, and you only need to practice using it. You certainly don't need a broad education about humanity of the last three thousand years. What use would it be and what difference would it make? These teachers were a great relief to me as a resident from many of the other faculty of the San Francisco Psychoanalytic Institute who engaged in various vague lectures about the art of psychoanalysis. Watching some of them through a one-way mirror or being in their continuous case conferences, I felt I was watching emperors without clothes. These others used big nouns like "art" to hide behind, grandly, as in the clouds (Orwell 1946). They didn't know what to do to be of help. We used to call Weiss and Sampson the Wizards, because they always had a hypothesis, and they were willing to venture a proposal of what to do, which could be proven wrong! This scientific spirit was very refreshing, and has stayed with me to this day and is evident in every consultation I take on with a trainee. My notes in the chart are brief and to the point of action:

Date, Consultation to Dr. _____
PROBLEM:
HYPOTHESIS:

I state the problem in one sentence, and my hypothesis about what to do in one sentence. It was all very matter of fact with them, and it is with me in these entries.

The only hint I had for years with Weiss and Sampson that something was wrong was that they never answered my letters from the field about when patients did *not* make prominent their difficulties or when patients were *not* trying to solve their problems. Driving to Indian reservations in Montana and Wyoming when I was Chief of Psychiatry for the Montana-Wyoming-Utah area of Indian Health Services, I could see for myself that a great deal of self-destruction was going on before my very eyes. I was not impressed with the operation of control-mastery theory in dispossessed Plains Indians, who had been robbed of their entire means of existence and driven into these empty corners. They seemed to be ruining themselves further, with a great deal of help from the white man's alcohol.

Some individuals were very constructive, and most were not doing very well. What was the difference, I asked myself (Gustafson 1976). It depended on having a vision, I decided. A few had a vision to live by, and they did. Others had had one and lost it.

Take basketball on the Crow Reservation (Smith 1991). It is marvelous fast-break basketball, which has many of the ancient qualities of buffalo-chasing. It gathers up young energy, beautifully. The entire reservation celebrates it, and it even defeats white men. Yet, very few Crow kids have ever made it into college basketball.

The most promising fall apart, and fall back into a dissolute or at least dissipated life of drinking and carousing and cruising, which replaces basketball after high school. It has a similar rhythm, but it destroys fast. It thus has an ephemeral life, through high school, and dies.

By "it," I mean the vision of basketball as a dance. The kids who prosper will need a vision that lasts longer, and some find it professionally as teachers, or in Native American or Christian religion as helpers (Gustafson 1976). Even armed with something for an entire life, the individual is still subjected to enormous forces that can pull him apart (Gustafson 1976). It is a situation familiar to many minorities, where the main body of the group is going to go to ruin. A given individual is in a terrible force field, with two steep slopes. If he goes along with the group, he surrenders his own chances for a different life in exchange for solidarity. If he resists in the name of a different vision, he loses his solidarity and comes under heavy attack as a sell out.

In other words, history on the American Plains has set up a terrible force field that is a given for young Native American people. They find their way through it, or they go down. This scenario brings me to my subject of Training III, or "Three Thousand Years of Modern Self-Consciousness."

A technical education in psychotherapy falls very short in these situations. No device will do, whether it is the technology of control-mastery, or behavior therapy, or whatever. The individual subject needs a vision to inspire him for a life, and he needs perspective on its raw hazards. This is the main line of modern self-consciousness since the *Iliad*.

It has an inside, and an outside. The inside is the inspiration of something beautiful and powerful. From the inside comes the feel of the thing that impels. From the outside comes the long view of where the thing leads. Homer can read from inside and from outside like no one else ever has:

> They have fallen into this predicament through the simplest of traps. At the outset their hearts are light, as is always the case when one feels the power with one and only the void against one . . . Unless one's spirit is cowed by the enemy's reputation, one always feels much stronger than he, when he is absent. [Weil 1940, p. 108]

And now the outside view:

> Achilles slits the throats of a dozen Trojans as casually as you or I would cut flowers for a grave. In exercising their power, they never guess that the consequences of their acts are going to make them cringe in their turn . . . nothing . . . is of a quality to induce . . . that brief interval in which thought might take place . . . that

momentary pause from which alone springs respect for our fellow creatures. [p. 106]

This is the great meditation of the last three thousand years, which continues down a long line of tremendous singers. Shakespeare gives the inside of Hamlet's sickening at the nearly universal falling in line with Claudius the murderer of his father, and he gives us the outside of Hamlet's cruelty in return, to Ophelia, Polonius, Gertrude, Rosencrantz and Guildenstern, Laertes, and so on. This is a direct continuation of the *Iliad*. Consider George Eliot's portrait of Doctor Lydgate in *Middlemarch* (1871). Lydgate has a beautiful inspiration of himself as the scientific doctor that drives him, outwardly, to overlook his standing in the little town that will bring him to his knees.

Literature gives us an adequate feel for what draws the individual in and for what forces are unrelenting in the world, and goes back and forth. A comic and contemporary version is James Thurber's story "The Secret Life of Walter Mitty" (1942), which begins from the inside secret:

"We're going through." The commander's voice was like thin ice breaking. . . . "We can't make it, sir. It's spoiling for a hurricane, if you ask me." "I'm not asking you, Lieutenant Berg," said the commander. "Throw on the power lights! Rev her up to 8,500. We're going through." [p. 1404]

Thurber drops us outside, just like this:

"Not so fast! You're driving too fast!" said Mrs. Mitty. "What are you driving so fast for?" "Hmm?" said Walter Mitty. He looked at his wife, in the seat beside him with shocked amazement. She seemed grossly unfamiliar, like a strange woman who had yelled at him in a crowd. [p. 1405]

Literature in this line from Homer to Thurber gives us practice in these extreme shifts, which are necessary to being with somebody in their vision, not too much, but rather outside with a different perspective.

Technical psychotherapy flattens the extremes. Its formula phrases never come along with the glory of a Mitty, nor do they reckon the rule of Mrs. Mitty, which abides no flicker of opposition. So, Mitty keeps his distance from the doctor, and Mrs. Mitty keeps finishing him off.

A Case of Being Crushed by the Wilcoxes

For example, a patient of mine married into the Wilcox clan of auto-motive manufacturers, like Margaret in *Howard's End* (Forster 1910). Like Margaret, she was from a Schlegel family of some depth. Schlegels are idealists, and do not reckon materialists like Wilcoxes very well at all. She took a huge pounding from Henry Wilcox, the auto magnate, so secretly shaky, so outwardly sure.

She got depressed, lonely, scared. She blamed herself for not fit-ting into the bone-crushing Wilcox clan. I could connect with her, because I could go inside to this experience of hers. My feel for it came from many sources, but Forster was certainly an important source I had read over and over since I first read it in college.

When I went on vacation, I was so worried about leaving her in the lurch, that I asked several different colleagues on different occa-sions to see her in my stead. No one ever worked. She always felt they were formulaic, and that she saw through them, and felt more alone than ever.

Gradually, I was able to help her externalize the Wilcoxes and what they would be doing next. I could bring them into focus from an outside perspective, very different from being with her in her interior world. In fact, the two perspectives were for her irreconcilable. It be-came my job to get back and forth with her until she could do it for herself. I certainly had my bearings on Wilcoxes from many sources, like Levi-Strauss, who said that the dominant engine in Western civi-lization is the steam engine, which "operate(s) on the basis of a differ-ence in temperature between their component parts, between the boiler and the condenser . . ." (Charbonnier 1969, p. 33). The idea is that society itself is such an engine in Western civilization, typified by Wilcoxes: ". . . it has had constantly to try, either within the society itself or by subjecting conquered peoples, to create a differential be-tween a ruling section and a section that is ruled" (p. 41). Wilcoxes head up, and heat up, and discharge onto their colder objects. So my Margaret was getting it, bad.

We went back and forth between her interior orbit up close in focus, and her exterior orbit out far in focus. I had to move freely be-tween two different lenses, a narrow angle, and a wide angle, each with a different grain, and a different extent of field. In the narrow angle up close, the Wilcoxes were completely out of focus. In the wide angle out far, she in her interior feelings was out of focus. (I am indebted to the ecologist, Tim Allen [Allen and Starr 1982, Allen et al. 1984], for showing me how one focus [grain, extent of field] hides another [grain, extent of field]. Koch's poem [1993] plays beautifully with the idea as a huge series.) That was why they couldn't see her at all! After much work, she could get back and forth, as in a dream like this:

> I am in a place run by my aunt selling beautiful ancient things. I try to buy back a doll of my grandmother, but I don't have the sixty-three cents my aunt requires. All I have are ancient coins. My aunt sees their value, and wants to take them all.

Here, her aunt is of Wilcox mind for market value, and of no mind for ancient values. Her dream warns her of the lack of backing from this aunt, and of the divorce proceeding to come. She can travel in her dream between her interior orbit of ancient value and the outer orbit where you'd better have the sixty-three cents!

Conclusion to Training III

I have dwelt most upon literature in Training III, and I suppose it is the center of what I would recommend for study, because it traverses the depth of inner worlds, to the cruel shallows of outer world. Yet, I do not think I could do without the intense study of inner dimensions in dreams, and poems, and in religion. Nor could I do without an extensive study of outer dimensions in history, in economics, and in the biology of territory.

I just had some correspondence with a friend who argued that I was giving little heed to sin in the interior world. I also just had some correspondence with another friend who argued for the power of land to shape the creature. We discussed entrenchment, and pitfalls, and flattery as bogus attention that is addictive in courts of power. Interestingly, these discussions were taken into my imaginative world of dreams .

> In one dream I was at an airfield in the country between Kansas and North Carolina with a helicopter blade strapped to my back. The air field was dry, brown, and barren. I decided I didn't want to do this flying anymore.

In a dream a few days later, I dreamt I was at the court of Versailles of Louis Le Gros and he was saying I was great.

In the first dream I am Icarus caught in the sin of flying too high. In the second dream I am deciding not to visit a famous therapist in Europe who will flatter me at Versailles. Thus, my reading and my discussions with my friends are taken into my unconscious world to strengthen its counsel to my small conscious mind. This is the lifetime education of Learning III, of catching up with man's self-deliberations of the last three thousand years.

Inner Vision and Outer Perspective

When I think back twenty-three years ago to my consultations for experienced therapists in the field of Indian Health Service (Gustafson 1976), and when I think back ten years to my study of the Milan family therapy team (Gustafson 1986, Chap. 16), and when I think back only last week to a workshop I did for experienced therapists in the Midwest, all falls in place in terms of myth. I mean simply this: patients need a myth as a vision that leads them up a purgatorial mountain. Yet, the myth is apt to be about half wrong in its predictions.

This typical situation puts experienced therapists in a difficult bind. If they are for the myth of the patient, they become as helpless as the patient in its grip. If they are against the myth, they are taking away something that keeps the patient going at all.

Out on the Empty Plains

As I wrote (Gustafson 1976), the mostly white therapists of the Indian Health Service made very shaky connections with their Native American patients. Only when the therapist and the patient shared a common vision, or ideology, or myth was there much of a bond. The three common myths were Native American, Christian, and professional, and the therapists were invited to become guardian spirits, or Christian confessors, or professional advisors.

The trouble was that the dilemmas of the patients were only half seen in such a directorial connection. A typical case (Gustafson 1976) would be a woman badly treated by her husband who was running around with other women. Should she go along, and forgive, or defy him and go her own way? Typically, the therapists were drawn by the shared myth of the patient to side with the patient on one horn of the dilemma, such as Christian forgiveness, or the opposite of professional self-advancement.

Of course, there is major suffering either way. Now I would say so, either to the therapist in consultation, or directly to the patient. This relieves them of the magical claims of the myth, while allowing the patient to stay more or less within her group. In other words, the patient needs some kind of vision: Christian, professional, Native American, or whatever, yet she also needs perspective on what it will overlook, to prevent her from being struck from the side.

In Milan

When I began to study family therapy in earnest over ten years ago in Italy, before beginning my family therapy team (my wife and I began studying *Paradox and Counter-Paradox* [Selvini-Palazzoli et al. 1978] hiking in the Italian Alps in 1982), I noticed that the families were often more skillful than the family therapists. Only the Milan team seemed to recognize this, and write about how tricky were the actual challenges.

For me, the most profound paper Selvini-Palazzoli and colleagues ever wrote was in 1977, called "Family Rituals: A Powerful Tool in Family Therapy." I did not like it for its powerful tool of family rituals. That is the half of it they would take off on to join the highly technical, interventionist style that has been in fashion in family therapy. I liked it for its historical clarity, concerning the socio-economic situation of the family (see Chap. 5), and for its clarity about their vision. It has an outer reckoning and an inner reckoning I had never seen in the field, only in novels.

For me, this is a typical situation in which family therapy is tricky and dangerous. I have seen many. The trouble is that the field takes the lesson to be a technological lesson of prescribing rituals. Actually, I do well when I get a strong grasp of the vision of the family, its regime, its myth, and I have the perspective from the outside to see what will never be brought into line with its will. There is always such a dilemma, and it can be tragic, and they cannot face it themselves.

Without this map, you blunder, by going along with the myth, or opposing it. You cannot bypass this kind of clarity by some kind of technical hocus-pocus. The family always smells it, and disqualifies you.

In My Midwest Workshop

I cannot do justice to a full day of discussions of videotapes that I showed these experienced therapists, but I can indicate the kinds of things that excited them. First of all, I had let them know that I supposed anything I pronounced was only half right. By that I was taking nothing away from what I showed myself doing. Rather, it might be done another way as well, and it might be quite wrong for their case, which might be similar. This gave them their opening, and they took it.

The first challenge was this. I showed a subservient young lady who was having a big physical reaction in the form of bizarre headaches. I showed myself saying, "That's always a distraction!" whereupon, the patient and I left the path of neurology she was on, and dived into her shadow of great psychic pain. One therapist in my audience raised her hand and objected that some of her patients would never tolerate this maneuver. I asked her what they would say. She replied that they would say ". . . so you think this is psychosomatic?" and dig in their heels.

I was very grateful for her objection. I agreed with her. There are many, many patients who need the myth of their ailment (Main 1957), which gives them their only place in the world. I would not think of trying to take it away from them. Some will not budge. I suggested this, instead. I never wanted to be in the position of deciding between psyche and soma, when the latter is legitimate and the former is illegitimate. I would say back to the patient, ". . . I have no idea if this is psychosomatic. Obviously you are in a lot of pain, and obviously you are upset. Shall we see what you are upset about?" I am leaving the myth in place, while also finding what it overlooks.

We were on our way, this the first in a series of myths that run their patients. Another was the teenager who says "I don't know" to all inquiries. Another, the dry delayers of long schooling, who do not know anything about the wetness of longing. Another, this great American desert for males of win/lose, which dries up any fertility of vision. Another, the alpha-male baboons. I will close with some detail on this theme so generative for them.

I was showing myself giving a corporate Napoleon a hard time from the word go. One of the women therapists objected, not to my doing this as a man, but to her doing it as a woman. Her men patients like this one would never take it from her. Rather than this front door approach of mine, she'd have to take a back door. When I asked her how she'd take the back door, she was not sure at first thought. I put the problem out to the entire assembly. I was problem-posing like Freire (1970) a picture of an alpha-male baboon and his female helper.

We had the most aroused discussion of the day, and the most educational for me in its richness of recommendations. We talked about male to male jocularity between powerhouses, like Larry Bird and Magic Johnson pushing away Charles Barkley in the commercial called "Nothing but Net." They felt my giving this Napoleon a hard time showed respect.

Yet a woman could not do it, without being felt to be a cutting bitch (see Hughes 1991). She'd have to come up alongside Mr. Powerhouse, and put aside his power plays, and note he was powerful, but needed help with something, as matter of factly as possible.

Afterwards, I thought of the reverse problem, of taking on alpha-female baboons. They would never take the pushing I gave Napoleon. They have a regime too brittle to bear slights from me. Yet, I must not let them run things. Interestingly, I have to move with them, as the women have to move with the alpha-men, respectfully, but firmly. Again, we are talking about myths, which must continue, but which do not work. This is the kind of subtle dilemma, which brings out the full expression of my audiences of experienced therapists. In other words, it is a study of a lifetime to stay clear of the double jeopardy of being drawn into myths or to foolishly oppose them (being hostage or outcast). You can only help patients when you can be with them either in or out, but not so much that you are equally lost in the force field. You can only help someone in psychic deflation or inflation or vacillation or basic fault if you have mastered each in yourself (Vance Wilson, personal communication). In this sense, Freud was absolutely right about the need for self-analysis, but he proposed wrongly that you only needed to master one story (Oedipus) in yourself.

15

Tolstoy's Fate

For me, Tolstoy has had more to teach about the dilemmas of living in the world than any psychologist. My maps are closest to his, yet his had weaknesses that were nearly fatal for himself. This is what he writes about, and what he enacts, this fatality that comes from lack of orientation.

Two Orientations

There are two orientations that are crucial on Tolstoy's huge canvas that portrays humanity on the move. The outer orbit is of the group that is a kind of living machine. In *War and Peace* (1869), Tolstoy sometimes emphasizes its machine quality, as when he opens with Anna Scherer's soirée in St. Petersburg as a spinning machine for the circulation and adjustment of status in the nobility. Tolstoy sometimes emphasizes its living quality, when he refers to the group as a swarm of bees. From either angle, the group compels. The guest at the soirée is bid to speak, and bid to cease, pulled in here, and pushed out there. Just so, the bee has to swarm and be killed in the autumn when bees do that. Almost no one can resist this kind of force. In this view, Tolstoy is very much of the view of Homer in the *Iliad* (c. 850 B.C.) (Weil 1940,

Steiner 1959) or Shakespeare in his tragedies (c. 1600), or, contemporarily, Levi-Strauss (Charbonnier 1969), or Canetti (1960). In his comic way, Lewis Carroll takes a similar view at about the same time, 1865, of the group as a pack of cards. (I will take up this group psychology thoroughly in Chapter 18, "The Group Animal.")

One fate in Tolstoy's histories is to be carried wherever the group is going. You go down in your role. Dolly is worn to pieces by the cares of her entire household in the opening scene of *Anna Karenina* (1875–1877). Andrew has to go to war, and dies of his war wounds, in *War and Peace* (1865). Karenin has to write his dispatches, and becomes all dry rot, like his later counterpart, the bureaucrat Ivan Illich (1886).

The other orientation that is crucial to Tolstoy's canvas of humanity is the inner one of *samodovolnost* (Bayley 1966), which is translated as self-delight or self-satisfaction. It is the wellspring of all vitality. Once it is gone, there is no more life, only a shell. Thus, Natasha has it and is immensely attractive, while Sonya lacks it and fizzles: "She is a sterile flower, you know—like some strawberry blossoms . . ." says Natasha of Sonya (Tolstoy, 1869, p. 1275). Some have it a little, and also fizzle out, like Koznyshev and Varenka, courting by picking mushrooms in a birch wood, but veering away from each other: "He repeated to himself the words with which he had intended to propose; but instead of those words some unexpected thought caused him to say: 'What difference *is* there between the white boleti and the birch tree variety?'" Varenka, tremulous, gives up on him by saying: "There is hardly any difference in the tops, but only in the stems" (Tolstoy 1875–1877, p. 513), as if to say she has a stem, but he lacks a stem, of any substance. This lack is fatal for Tolstoy.

The trouble with having self-satisfaction or delight is that it gravitates in two dangerous directions. One is into the role in the crowd, and one is opposed to the crowd. The outer orbit makes a smug personage, who takes himself to be one of a kind. Thus, Prince Shcherbatsky says of the Germans at the spas: "What is there interesting about them? They are as self-satisfied as brass farthings; they've conquered everybody" (Tolstoy 1875–1877, p. 213). Tolstoy says of a visiting foreign Prince:

> The Prince enjoyed unusually good health even for a Prince, and
> by means of gymnastics and care of his body had developed his

strength to such a degree that, in spite of the excess he indulged in when amusing himself, he looked as fresh as a big green shining cucumber. [p. 322]

More seriously, it leads young people to rush into untenable situations as if they had nothing to fear. Anna says to Kitty, about to have her debut:

"Oh yes, it is good to be your age," Anna continued. "I remember and know the blue mist, like the mist on the Swiss mountains . . . that mist that envelops everything at that blissful time when childhood is just, just coming to an end, and its immense, blissful circle turns into an ever-narrowing path, and you enter the defile gladly yet with dread, though it seems bright and beautiful. [Tolstoy 1875–1877, p. 67]

Equally heartbreaking is Petya's rush for glory in battle in his absolute confidence:

Denisov did not reply; he rode up to Petya, dismounted, and with trembling hands turned toward himself the bloodstained, mud-bespattered face which had already gone white.
    "I am used to something sweet. Raisins, fine ones . . . take them all!" he recalled Petya's word. And the Cossacks looked round in surprise at the sound, like the yelp of a dog, with which Denisov turned away, walked to the wattle fence, and seized hold of it. [Tolstoy 1869, p. 1174]

The inner orbit can be one of revolt against the crowd, and it always pays for going into opposition, mortally. Thus, old Bolkonsky is furious with his servants for sweeping the snow off the road for a visiting minister of the state courting his daughter and orders: ". . . Throw the snow back on the road!" From here on, he becomes more and more crazy, and cruel.

    The two most tragic characters of all are Anna Karenina and Tolstoy himself. In opposing the outer machinery, they underestimate its crushing power. Anna enters Petersburg on a train within her role as a great lady come to bring her brother, Stiva, into line about his marriage and to comfort his wife, Dolly. Opposing this engine, she dies under its wheels.

While Anna underestimates the cruel closure of the society against a woman who runs off from her husband with another man, Tolstoy himself underestimates the hold of the society on the peasants he would set free as partners in a new Russian agriculture, like his character, Levin:

> But the elimination of hostility and the establishment of "harmony," and class peace between the peasants and landowners were out of the question while private ownership of the land prevailed—their interests were diametrically opposed to one another. [Tolstoy 1875–1877, p. 828, commentary on *Anna Karenina*, by S. P. Bychkov]

Levin misses this, in his idealism, and so does Tolstoy. He sees more clearly in war, than in peace.

There are two disastrous fates for Tolstoy. The outer orbit of the swarming machine will swallow you up as a hostage to conventionality, or the inner orbit of rebellion will get you crushed by the swarming machine as an outcast to conventionality. You can perish inside it, or outside and under its tread.

Ambiguity

There are two confusing but common variations, which seem to defy this binary topography. That is, they appear outwardly conventional, but they are wildly and inwardly driven. One is the variation that prides itself on male realism.

Tolstoy is remorseless concerning the thinking of the generals, about which they are so smug, which has no connection with the actual swarming of the armies in the field. They are as madly solipsistic about papers as are professors, or bureaucrats.

> But strange to say, all these measures, efforts and plans—which were not at all worse than others issued in similar circumstances —did not affect the essence of the matter but, like the hands of a clock detached from the mechanism, swung about in an arbitrary and aimless way without engaging the cogwheels. [Tolstoy 1865, p. 1115]

Their verbal formulas do not connect to the world as it is in battle, but rather they obscure it (Sullivan 1956, Chap. 12). I like to picture them as in a cloud that is blue and pleasing to themselves on its inner surface, but brown and foolish to others on its outer surface. In this way, they are neither inward nor outward. All of the mad and professorial creatures in *Alice in Wonderland* (Carroll 1865) have this same nuttiness of inner vanity and outer ridiculousness, such as the White Rabbit, the Caterpillar, the March Hare and the Mad Hatter, and the Mock Turtle and the Gryphon.

The other variation that is confusing but common, appears to be the standard female altruism, yet it is madly parochial about its *idée fixe*. I like to picture it as in a cloud that is blue and pleasing to itself on the inside, while green and inviting to others on its outside surface. Anna Karenina is the most striking and memorable example in her tenderness with her son, Alyosha, with Dolly, with Kitty, and so forth, yet she is ferocious about having her way. Kitty picks this up at the ball, as follows:

> She had not come across Anna since the beginning of the ball, and now she suddenly saw her again in a different and unexpected light . . . She saw that Anna was intoxicated by the rapture she had produced [in Vronsky]. She knew the feeling and knew its symptoms, and recognized them in Anna—she saw the quivering light flashing in her eyes, the smile of happiness and elation that involuntarily curled her lips, and the grateful precision, the exactitude and lightness of her movements. [Tolstoy 1875–1877, p. 74]

The blue light begins to come through the inviting green, and is truly frightening. Vronsky begins to falter: "Every time he turned toward Anna he slightly bowed his head as if he wished to fall down before her, and in his eyes there was an expression of submission and fear" (p. 74). Kitty also begins to wilt and then die in her hopes for Vronsky. Anna is triumphant:

> She looked charming in her simple black dress; her full arms with the bracelets, her firm neck with the string of pearls round it, her curly hair now disarranged, every graceful movement of her small feet and hands, her handsome animated face—everything about

her was enchanting, but there was something terrible and cruel in her charm. [p. 76]

Lewis Carroll shows this ferocity in the Duchess and in the Queen of Hearts, but it is undisguised. Anna's cruelty comes blazing through like a sun that dispels the gentle clouds that hid it from us. Curiously, preparing for writing this chapter, I had a very striking dream myself about this doubleness of the female that is ordinary, but often missed:

I dreamt I had been the chief actor in a play. A new play was being cast in a day of tryouts, by a female director, who was no one in particular. I waited patiently as she filled the minor parts early in the day, and waited curiously for the major part to be given to myself. She finished her casting without any reference to me at all, and I was flabbergasted. I asked her what was wrong, and she replied that she had forgotten me. Could she not reconsider? I rejoined. No, she replied, that would spoil the pleasure of the arrangements she had already made!

Balance

Almost no one has balance for long in Tolstoy's view. The pull of self-satisfaction into an outer orbit in the crowd cannot be resisted. If it is resisted, it flies into an inner orbit that gets too far out and is badly punished. This is Tolstoy's determinism, his physics of fate that goes along with or goes under the crowd.

Generals are fools of this physics for Tolstoy. For example, Weyrother: "Weyrother evidently felt himself to be at the head of a movement that had already become unrestrainable. He was like a horse running downhill harnessed to a heavy cart" (1869, p. 279). Others are stupidly detached, like the Emperor, in his reply to Kutuzov's warning him of the disaster at Austerlitz via Count Tolstoy. Kutuzov tells Prince Andrew: "What do you think he replied? 'But, my dear general, I am engaged with rice and cutlets, look after military matters yourself!' Yes . . . That was the answer I got!" (p. 278). Only a few, but especially Kutuzov, have the balance to hold back from being drawn into glorious battles that cannot be won. He is like the great Chinese General Sun Tzu :

That is why it is said that victory can be discerned but not manufactured. [Sun Tzu 1988, p. 85]

So it is that good warriors take their stand on ground where they cannot lose, and do not overlook conditions that make an opponent prone to defeat. [p. 90]

Prince Andrew summarizes his trust in Kutuzov like this:

The more he realized the absence of all personal motive in that old man . . . only the capacity calmly to contemplate the course of events—the more reassured he was that everything would be as it should. "He will not bring in any plan of his own. He will not devise or undertake anything," thought Prince Andrew, "but he will hear everything, remember everything, and put everything in its place. He will not hinder anything useful nor allow anything harmful. He understands that there is something stronger and more important than his own will—the inevitable course of events, and he can see them and grasp their significance, and seeing that significance can refrain from meddling and renounce his personal wish directed to something else. And above all," thought Prince Andrew, "one believes in him because he's Russian . . . because his voice shook when he said: 'What they have brought us to!' and had a sob in it when he said he would 'make them eat horseflesh!'" [1869, p. 831]

This extraordinary man is deeply moved, yet he has no sentimentality about gaining or losing territory. He is free of its grip. This allows him to lose ground to Napoleon without fretting. He just goes to sleep in his tent, patiently, waiting for the tide from west to east to turn back east to west. Even Moscow he surrenders as indefensible with a shrug. It is a queenless hive. He will let the French dissipate there. They do, and end up fleeing, with Kutuzov following them out, refraining from a battle that is of no consequence to the tide that is running back to the West.

One looks in vain for such a noble character in the peacetime society. Count Rostov is a generous and lively man, but he is in over his head in convention that bleeds him, for lack of perspicacity. He hasn't the detachment to take a long view. Pierre is similar to Count

Rostov, but is a great fool of an endless series of enthusiasms. Later he becomes free like Kutuzov, as Bayley (1966) explains:

> By handing the work over to fate and the female he in fact obtained for himself—and in a sense for us too—the last perquisite of the male—freedom—the freedom that Pierre feels in captivity and in his final submission to Natasha, the freedom that comes from the recognition of necessity. [pp. 105–106]

Bayley uses the phrase most characteristic of Kutuzov in war, to fit Pierre in peace, namely, *the freedom that comes from the recognition of necessity*. As Bayley explains, this is the center of Tolstoy's perspective, its very balancing point.

Levin is the one attempting this in *Anna Karenina*, carrying on from Pierre. He certainly steers clear of everything that befell Pierre in the city, so he has detachment in that way. He has the great heart. Yet he fights in a country war, for liberating his peasants from the old system. Here he, like Tolstoy, lacks detachment.

The balance point glimpsed by Tolstoy more in war, less in peace, is a freedom that comes from the recognition of necessity. Let me explain that a little, as it will not be self-evident. Let us suppose, as I do and as Tolstoy did, that certain force fields draw a person in and down irresistibly. There are two: the swarm is the outer orbit, and the rebellion against it is the inner orbit. The first gets you lost in your own outer worlds, and the second gets you too far out on your own where you can't get back in. Thus, Anna has no balance, drawn down like a moth by the draft of Karenin, and up and out by the flame of herself with Vronsky. The forces here are Darwinian, a natural selection: outward by the group, inward by the urge to mate. She is drawn like the moth, lacking any freedom from the recognition of necessity.

Compare Shakespeare's famous hero, Prince Hal, in *Henry V*, who stays apart from the grim seriousness of most of the noblemen driven to the slaughter of one another without mercy, quite like Achilles and Agamemnon and all the others in *The Iliad*. He dwells apart with Falstaff in the tavern, from which he keeps a humorous perspective. Falstaff is his half-guide who counsels of these mad and serious men dead too soon: "I like not such grinning honor as Sir Walter hath" (5.3. 57–58). It would be baseness itself for Hal to stay with the "fat deer" and decline his responsibilities. Hal will not be pulled off to the left, any more than he will to the right. Says he to Falstaff, stopping the drift too far away, "I have procured thee, Jack, a charge of foot . . ." and soon "His death will be a march of twelve score . . ." and finally "Thou owest God a death." It is that balance *literally* is a matter of moving out of force fields where one has no resistance. This is the freedom that comes from the recognition of necessity. Hal like Kutuzov leaves the generals for the tavern or tent, and leaves Falstaff for the center stage.

A Day in Practice with Tolstoy at My Elbow

I hope the literary critics will forgive my forcing of Tolstoy into my practical field. For my patients, orientation is a matter of life and death. For Tolstoy's characters, it was as well. I am skipping everything else about him that is magnificent. I refer the reader to George Steiner (1959) for his comparison of Tolstoy to Homer, to the Norton editions of *War and Peace* (1865) and *Anna Karenina* (1875–1877) for appended collections of critical commentary by the best-known of Tolstoy's critics, *The Portable Tolstoy* (edited by Bayley), and John Bayley's *Tolstoy and the Novel* (1966), my principal guide to the center of Tolstoy.

I am a practical man, so I now take Tolstoy to work with me. Let us see what we see differently with Tolstoy at the elbow. I divide my findings, arbitrarily, into the three difficulties of orientation: the draw into the outer orbit, the draw into the inner orbit, and finding a balance point of freedom from the recognition of the necessity of the two orbits or force fields. Orientation is a matter of placing oneself in these fields, which operate on us with different strengths and selections depending upon which way we turn. We get different results from different postures in different places. Determinism operates, but we get a say over *which* determinism will pull us more or less. We can *point* ourselves differently, so different winds or streams catch us differently, like Prince Hal himself.

The Outer Orbit

Tolstoy's two novels could be taken simply as maps of the disaster of having to give up an amplitude of childhood for an adult harness. Thus, Tolstoy precedes Gilligan (1990) in posing this problem by over 100 years. His two novels are a huge presentation of his research on the question, so to speak. Some take the harness and are suppressed, while some refuse the harness and are driven beyond the pale.

My patients continually underestimate this force field of the outer world. Reading Gilligan (1990) and comparable feminist writers, I understand they want to be themselves and not go under. They are amazed at the lack of tolerance for this project, especially from men. I am continually in the position of pointing out that men by and large want to be approved of by women for their exploits and do not do well with having pointed out to them everything else they have neglected. This is no counsel of accommodation. I am simply saying something about the physics of these fellows that is highly predictable. It is just the nature of the territory. The patient is in a dilemma, thus, of what she chooses to do, given her nature and his nature.

A Case of Ill Humor

My patient is married to Karenin, who assumes himself right about everything, which, no doubt, has been a constant attitude from childhood and abetted by the high position he holds in the government. He is easily hurt at home, because he is less impressive there in his chair. He throws fits over the minor blunders of his wife and of his children. He is often crabby.

My patient has a hard time admiring this sort of performance. She is apt to let him know, and he behaves worse. She is in an awkward dilemma. If she lets him run on like this, she will hate him increasingly. If she objects, he hits the ceiling.

What she has finally discovered is that she can go away from him when he is like this, and he is apt to come after her, penitent. It is better to leave the house, than to be run down there, or attempt a stand. The force field there is pretty near impossible, unless she departs. This departure has the added virtue of making his self-centeredness less rewarding and thus less selected.

The Story from the Other Side: A Case of Quarrying Marble

Men become these self-centered and merciless creatures by a natural selection. They too lose a childhood. As my patient began to back off his heated and driven days in the corporate world of deadliness, he dreamt a huge dream about what had made him such a pile-driver like John Henry on the railroad:

He dreamt he was in his childhood backyard, which was filled with the bright colors of rocks of the kind you see in marbles that boys play with. Only these marbles were extremely dense and the size of beach balls. His parents were making him pick them up. But he was in a rage, throwing them with tremendous strength over the fence and into the street, where they rolled down the street with great force. As he did this, he caught the eye of a little boy of about six, across the street, who was eyeing him sympathetically .

I will not go over an hour of translation of this dream, except to say that marbles translated as something he did in a kind of private world of imagination as a boy. He is in a rage over having to give up play for dead serious quarrying of the huge marble of adult life. The most touching part is with the little boy across the street who is sympathetic, like a kind of Huck Finn he'd like to get back to.

The Inner Orbit

My very same patient continued in the next session to show why he fears the inner orbit even more. He had his feet up on my couch, feeling much eased by the last session, actually comfortable with himself. Now, we were moving into his inner orbit, quite as Freud proposed. The difference between myself and Freud I will spell out in Chapter 17 on "Jung's Individuation, Compared to Freud." In a sentence, I feel he mapped the inner orbit very well, the outer orbit badly. He was about half right and so is his procedure of analysis. I have my patients go into the inner world when we have cleared a disaster in the outer world as here. This is typical of my procedure.

Now, he began twittering his toes and thumbs, uneasily. I let him sit in it a while, before I asked him what was so uncomfortable. He replies that I must think him a sullen boy. Oh, really, I responded? Not really, he said, I am actually just taking it easy. Why would I take him to be a sullen boy? That was his mother, talking about his father. Father was sullen. He feared to be sullen. Father had been sullen, and not come through in the family business. He had resented its demands, and thrown it over, to mother's despair. This lad had felt driven by the comparison with his father never to be negative and never to ease up. He would prove his mother wrong about men. Lulls like this, which occur after mastering the outer orbit and easing up always have big transference fish in them, as here.

A Case of Romantic Sons

This patient had one of those Karenin husbands as well; alas, so many have him. She kept telling her sons about his cruelty, and they urged her to leave him. She argued back to her boys that she had no place to go. Oh, come with us, they said. We'll look after you. I have no money at all, she said. I cannot live with you indefinitely.

She felt terrible letting down her boys. She actually preferred giving this husband some further chances, but this alienated the boys. They would be mad at her. I told her she was going to suffer surely. If she stayed, as she was inclined, she'd have two mad boys. If she departed, she had an untenable existence with no prospect of earning a living.

The Region of the Equipoise

Tolstoy's determinism of the outer orbit and the inner orbit suggests a way to be relatively free of either orbit in the region of balance where the two cancel each other's effects, as pictured in Figure 15-1. I call this the region of equipoise, in which there is considerable equanimity as in Kutuzov, that is free not to be driven, or do anything at all. It is space like outer space where one swims more freely because the two gravitations have nullified each other. Small movements flow readily here, into large effects.

A Case of Huck on the Mississippi

Like so many women, this one had a swindler for an ex. On this day, she was enraged after visiting her attorney. She had joint custody, but she did all the care of the children. She had increased her income, only to find that she had to pay *him* for child care costs, because his income had plummeted since the divorce. This added insult to injury!

The trouble was that it was going to go on like this for the next fifteen years. She was stuck to a man who would drain her for all she could be drained for. This was her outer orbit.

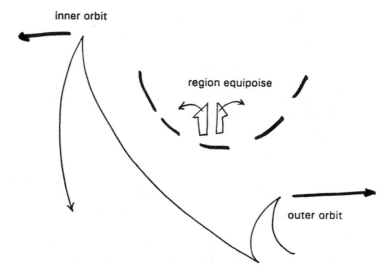

Figure 15–1. Equipoise and the Roman God Janus.

I noted she had forgotten about him on a nice trip to Minneapolis. Yes, she answered, but how horrible to get him back on her return. Well, there it was, I said. Huck is fine on the Mississippi, but he gets nailed on land every time. I imagine he's never gonna be ready for the land creatures, because it is so grand with Jim gliding under the stars on the Big Water. Well, we'll see, says she, taking my challenge. Poirier (1966) notes that Twain never did figure out how to get from the world elsewhere of the Big River back to land.

A Case of a Thirty-Mile-An-Hour Tailwind

My patient wanted out of the rat race, and managed to elect a freer existence, which paid enough. Now he dreamt that his son was riding a bicycle in a white suit with a thirty-mile-an-hour tailwind. In an intersection, he bounced off a black Cadillac crossing through, and barely survived. He had been a little depressed, being less important in the corporation. He had been flying high, the day before, riding his bicycle in a thirty-mile-an-hour tailwind out of control, scorning intersections. He had been kind to a local entrepreneur in his black Cadillac the day before by warning him of a scrape in a parking garage. The guy grunted, and gave him no thanks, and, in the dream, nearly kills his son, black on white innocence. Here we have the classical force field of Western culture, in its two tragic forms, of black dominance by sheer force, and romantic opposition in white with a tailwind to the right, where it is struck down, as it always is struck down. My patient had had some beautiful moments bicycle racing in the equipoise, flying like a bird, without too much eye for the record. Here, the gravitational fields of left and right pull him off course again. This may have to happen a number of more times to him, before he catches on in a more reliable way. He is not yet a Prince Hal. When he becomes something more of a prince, it will be like Pierre when he has had enough dire experiences to reckon the outer orbit and the inner orbit continually. Then he will have more time in the equipoise from the recognition of necessity, right and left. He will slip for less long into these terrible force fields, being better oriented, and ready to point away from them to let the opposite force pull him into the center.

Tolstoy's Near Destruction at 48 to 50: A Confession (1882)

How, you might wonder, could a man so well oriented spend two years in his midlife barely keeping himself from suicide? If we consider Tolstoy's crisis, we will be warned against thinking too much of his maps. In 1878, Tolstoy was 50 years old, hugely successful as the author of his two epic novels, and a successful landowner, husband, and father in Yasnaya Polyana. He was in despair, because his life no longer had any motive or meaning. His *Confession* (1882) shows the failure, in retrospect, after he has come through. Let us map it on Tolstoy's own topography, to see what got to him, to see what failure of orientation he overlooked, so that he went down. I will be somewhat schematic to get at the physics that is determinative.

Tolstoy explains his project, to use Sartre's phrase, as an author attempting to be a teacher about life. Disgusted with his dissolute life in the army and as a young and egotistical writer between the ages of 24 and 34, he marries Sofia Bers and begins a moral life like Levin at Yasnaya Polyana, which carries him from age 34, through his two great novels, to being a great success at 48 by 1876. He feels groundless, and empty. Why? And how?

He explains that his faith and his self-delight had been founded in a secular religion that drew him into outer orbit in the world: "This faith in the meaning of poetry and in the development of life was a religion, and I was one of its priests" (Tolstoy 1882, p. 671). He began to doubt its infallibility:

> My first cause of doubt was that I began to notice that the priests of this religion were not all in accord among themselves . . . There were also many among us who did not care who was right and who was wrong but were simply bent on attaining their covetous aims by means of this activity of ours. [p. 671]

His doubt deepened:

> I became convinced that almost all the priests of that religion, the writers, were immoral, and for the most part men of bad, worthless character, much inferior to those whom I had met in my former dissipated and military life; but they were self-confident and self-satisfied as only those can be who are quite holy or who do not know what holiness is. These people revolted me, I became revolting to myself, and I realized that that faith was a fraud. [pp. 671–672]

He remembers this time as if in a lunatic asylum:

> . . . thousands of us, contradicting and abusing one another, all printed and wrote—teaching others. And without noticing that we knew nothing, and that to the simplest of life's questions: What is good and what is evil? we did not know how to reply, we all talked at the same time, not listening to one another, sometimes seconding and praising one another in order to be seconded and praised in turn, sometimes getting angry with one another—just as in a lunatic asylum. [p. 672]

The contrast to the common people struck him down:

> Thousands of workmen laboured to the extreme limit of their strength day and night, setting the type and printing millions of words which the post carried all over Russia, and we still went

> on teaching and could in no way find time to teach enough and
> were always angry that sufficient attention was not paid to us.
> [p. 672]

All of this disillusion had already occurred long before his marriage. It corresponds to Levin's disillusion with city life in *Anna Karenina*, which led him into the country and into his work to establish peasant schools. This led into his marriage, where he threw his entire strength . . . "simply to secure the best possible conditions for myself and my family. So another fifteen years passed" (p. 675–676).

The old doubt began to reappear, bit by bit, to the point where he could think of little else. "What for?" became an incessant refrain:

> Or when considering plans for the education of my children, I
> would say to myself: What for? Or when considering how the peas-
> ants might become prosperous, I would suddenly say to myself:
> "But what does it matter to me?" Or when thinking of the fame my
> works would bring me, I would say to myself, "Very well; you will
> be more famous than Gogol or Pushkin or Shakespeare or Molière,
> or than all the writers in the world—and what of it?" [p. 677]

Now he had no ground to stand on at all . . . "But it was a long time before I could find out where the mistake was" (p. 699).

Barely keeping himself from the noose, he went on a long desperate search for his epistemological error, which he located at last as follows: "All our actions, discussions, science, and art presented itself to me in a new light. I understood that *it is all merely self-indulgence* and that to find a meaning in it is impossible" (p. 710, italics mine). In other words, self-delight drawn into the outer orbit of territorial gain becomes hopelessly lost in self-indulgence where it can never get enough notice, and is thus always angry.

Tolstoy sees that the poor are happier than the rich parasites of his circle, and resolves to join them in self-negation and hard work and thanks to God: "I quite returned to what belonged to my earliest childhood and youth. I returned to the belief in that Will which produced me and desires something of me. I returned to the belief that the chief and only aim of my life is to be better—that is, to live in accord with that Will" (p. 716). It was the only way he could limit the pull of his boundless energy to the right of ambition. He had to give up his worldly project, his very reason, to keep it from running away with him. Only then could he have peace, in subordinating himself to a project higher than himself. Kutuzov, you will remember, his own creation, could subordinate himself to saving Russia. Kutuzov could retain his reason for the project. All he had to do was keep pulling out of the driven region of the generals, into sleeping in his tent. Here was his region of equipoise, half in the world of the war, and half out of the world in his contemplation of the spirit of the Russian army. (Compare with the sterile half-in and half-out schizoid position below in Chapter 18, "The Group Animal.")

Tolstoy needed a similar project of huge scope for his tremendous faculties. He had it in writing the two novels, and in establishing his family for fifteen years. He foundered on what to do next. He had a holy war with the Russian agricultural system. Different from Kutuzov in his war, Tolstoy underestimated the enemy, so he was bound to come apart. His tremendous reason did not calculate that the peasants and his very own children could not afford to depart from the old regime. He was hopelessly off to the left in a rebellion in which few could follow him, despite all his powers. He renounced all his powers, and became a child again trying to do the Will of God. His own will had become untenable, trying to force the rural system to give way. According to his own map, you cannot rebel against any system, if you defy its mechanics willfully. He needed *something to depend on himself*, which was not illusory and not taking him off the deep end.

His dream at the conclusion of *A Confession* summarizes the situation in which his conscious mind was given correction by his unconscious mind as in a vision that constitutes a religious conversion. It is worth studying in detail (pp. 729–731), but I can abridge it without much violence to the text. The gist of it is that Tolstoy is suspended by plaited string lying on his back. As he discovers he can kick away the support for his feet to become more comfortable, he begins to slip from the legs, and so forth, until he looks down and discovers he is at the height of mountains peering into an abyss with little to hold him. Desperate, he looks up and begins to get calm and discovers he is secured from the waist by a single loop from a slender pillar. This is his new faith, which he will depend upon for the next thirty years.

Essentially, he has been up too high on illusions of plaited string, which is what Binswanger (1963) called *Verstiegenheit*, or extravagance, in English, which is the situation of climbers in the mountains who have climbed further than they can get down from. Essentially, he takes a fall back to a childhood position in which he has something to depend on like a belaying rope well-secured to a much lower place. There he will stay.

The Author's Dream In Reply

I became more anxious writing this chapter than any other, I think, because the forces involved are tremendous and the errors that are possible are as momentous as for Tolstoy himself. I felt the pull of the outer orbit that is huge (two years previous, I dreamt of riding atop a huge train along the Rhine River that went over a big bridge with an S-curve. The g's were so powerful that I could barely keep a grip), and I felt the pull of the inner orbit that would renounce the outer for a world elsewhere. (Two months previous, I dreamt of a big stage that was octagonal, with a viewing stand. Behind it was empty rooms, like my old fraternity on break. Obviously, I was on my own.) The dream that resolved it to bring about some equipoise for me was like this:

> I was standing on a huge wing dam which extended into the Mississippi River from the Wisconsin shoreline which is on the right bank facing north. Canoes were being put in where the dam met the shore. There you could touch them. The canoes then cascaded from the shore down to the big waters. As I walked out the dam to my left, I discovered that the canoes in the mainstream were thirty feet below me and out of reach. They could no longer hear me. They were brown.

To me, this was counsel against the illusion that got Tolstoy up too high. I could have a little influence on my students at the outset (as he did his peasants), but they soon were swept into the current where they could not hear me. If I was up high, I could get back to shore myself, and content myself with depending upon a modest influence to their departures.

Scale

My dream helped me with the problem of scale that defied Tolstoy. His very success in creating someone like Kutuzov in war naturally led him to want to be a Kutuzov in peace, himself. This was no more possible in Russian agriculture than it is in American psychiatry. The peasants and the students have to follow form.

If Tolstoy was disgusted with the self-indulgence of writers, then he could actually have reformed himself. This is a scale in which it is possible to have control. If the writer cannot do much to alter the world, he can at least alter himself. This is a much more modest scale, but a suitable scale for a craftsman/writer, to mend his own craft, writing.

16

The Science of Long-Term Psychotherapy

I will make this chapter briefer than the others, because its discovery is simple but important. Details would obscure its main line. The technology you will find in *Psychotherapy Research* (Gaston et al. 1994) is important as a defense of long-term work, but its complexity alters little in practice. (See also *The Journal of the American Psycho-Analytic Association 41*, Supplement 1993, entirely devoted to research on psychoanalysis.)

Historically, the consistent finding of the importance of therapeutic alliance to outcome (Frank 1971, Gaston et al. 1994, Luborsky et al. 1988, Malan 1976 a,b, Strupp and Binder 1984, Wallerstein 1986) has pulled psychoanalysis further into the direction it was already going. From an emphasis of interpretation in an austere relationship (Freud 1912, 1913, 1914, 1915), the shift is toward a more parental bond as the setting for interpretation. However, most of the change in classical technique had already been accepted (Greenson 1967) before the modern era of outcome studies. Suffice it to say that the trend is altogether clear, and the theoretical and research findings invite warmth of connection between patient and doctor.

Essentially, this emphasis lessens the distinction between psychoanalysis and psychoanalytic psychotherapy. Whereas the first had been

pure interpretation and the second more support, now both are inter-
pretive and supportive (Wallerstein 1986). The difference is a matter
of degree in the mixture of the two chief elements. In psychoanalysis,
the support comes more from the couch, whereas in psychoanalytic
psychotherapy, the doctor is going to be more openly supportive
himself.

Even this distinction breaks down, especially when the patient
needs more support (Gaston et al. 1994, Wallerstein, 1986). The only
difference becomes whether the patient is lying down or sitting up.

Alliance, Map, and Places to Arrive—And Slow
Development of Relative Autonomy of the Ego

I have argued for three concepts as the key to outcome in brief psychotherapy: the *alliance* is the connection that relieves the patient of being
alone with an overwhelming problem, and prepares to take him somewhere else. It is the vehicle for the journey. The *map* points out where
it is possible to go, and where it is dangerous to go or to continue to
drift. The *places* to arrive are niches where the patient has a chance to
use his virtues, as in love or work (Gustafson 1995).

Mostly, the studies of long-term psychotherapy find the same
as the studies of brief psychotherapy. What is added is clarity about
what takes a long time to crystallize. This slow development, in the
same therapeutic context of alliance, map, and places to arrive, is what
Rapaport (1959) called "the relative autonomy of the ego."

I will first illustrate this slow development in the only substantial study of long-term psychotherapy, the Menninger Psychotherapy
Research Project (Wallerstein 1986). I will supplement the Menninger
findings with what else is available. Finally, I will discuss chaos theory
compared to psychoanalytic theory, regarding this data.

The Menninger Psychotherapy Research Project

I certainly cannot do justice to this huge book (Wallerstein 1986) in a
few paragraphs, but I believe I can summarize the main trends of the
study without violence to the details. This is because the study is re-
markably consistent.

The patients were relatively difficult patients, mostly referred to
the Menninger Clinic from around the country, but they were also rela-

tively affluent to be able to afford this treatment. They were almost evenly divided between psychoanalysis and psychoanalytic psychotherapy, with an average length of five and two-thirds and four and a third years, respectively.

In general, these two treatments were equally successful (about 60 percent with very good and moderate improvements) and, as I have already said, similar in their mix of interpretation and support. About a quarter of the treatments failed altogether (26 percent). Paranoid, psychotic, alcoholic, and sociopathic characters comprised most of these, who were set in very bad ruts and only got worse.

The most interesting cases to me are three that were very disturbed, but, nevertheless, did very well: the Phobic Woman, the Medical Scientist, and the Bohemian Musician.

The Case of the Phobic Woman

This hysterical woman was alternately weak and clinging, and utterly overwhelming in her emotional demands. (See Weiss 1993, for summary of many intricate, empirical studies of the analysis of Mrs. C., who needed help with guilt about her omnipotence.) Her analyst met both of these trends very firmly, the first by encouraging her to attempt things she was frightened of, and the second by not letting her shout or otherwise run over him in the sessions. Gradually, she found middle ground between her psychic deflation of abject clinging and her psychic inflation of unlimited power (as if the analyst would come over at 2 A.M. for a session!). This middle-sized and competent being gradually emerged over nearly five years of analysis.

The Case of the Medical Scientist

This man had had nearly twenty years of alcohol and barbiturate addiction. Essentially, he used intoxication to let loose violently, in an unhappy marriage to which he was submitting. His seven-year analysis had to tackle the same trends. He'd act the part of the appeasing pupil to the analyst, while flagrantly disregarding reality from behind his facade. Gradually, he came to feel the analyst was "really in his corner" and could confide his love for him without being rejected. This allowed his shadow rebellion against both parents to surface in all its force. Gradually, a middle ground emerged in which he could compete with his famous father and tell off his bossy mother and wife who had owned him (one for the first twenty years, the other for the second twenty years). Importantly, he was able to divorce his wife and choose a better match for himself, and he was able to change his career to become an internist who practiced counseling in his medical practice, which he humorously called "barnyard psychiatry."

It is very important to add that he was determined to cure himself of his addictions, by holing up in a hotel room to withdraw, and he never demanded a "special status." As Malan (1976 a,b) has noted, this determination to get better is crucial to this kind of remarkable success. It is like the fight in kids from ruinous homes who are determined to get out of the house and find someone to help them (Werner 1989). When a patient with this determination meets a doctor who is ready to connect, a working alliance of considerable power gradually emerges that is more powerful than the futile subservience and the disastrous rebellion. (See Balint, Ornstein, and Ornstein [1972], and Gustafson [1976b] for very similar cases with this structure—the latter is also described in Chapter 1 of this book as "The Case of Danny Boy.")

The Case of the Bohemian Musician

This patient suffered as the artsy wife of a remote businessman, in endless somatic and hypochondriacal complaints (like one of the patients of Breuer and Freud [1895]). She tried to have her affair in the arts, while holding onto the security of the husband. This half-in and half-out arrangement collapsed when the husband would no longer abide it, and she became wildly disorganized, and panicky, and finally got hospitalized after driving over ninety miles an hour through a crowded suburban area. She went into a deepening depression in the hospital, and got twenty ECT treatments, as she was insistently suicidal. As her depression lifted, she "became a more difficult, angry and openly complaining individual."

Her doctor firmly gave back to her her dilemma (Wallerstein repeatedly uses this word) about having her way. She seemed to assume that she could force her way around, quite like her mother did her father. She did this with her husband, her lovers, her doctors, and so forth. The dilemma was to force things and pollute the relationship, or to choose something different, which would be unfamiliar to her, and, thus very fearful. Gradually, over three years of looking at her dilemmas in her psychotherapy with a supportive, but firm and clear doctor, she emerged with a middle position, in which she could share power. This capability was already there in her work as a music teacher, and now came to flower in a new marriage, with a sensitive man who shared her interests, but who was also orderly and practical. As Wallerstein (1986) puts it about so many of these cases, "the transference was transferred" from the doctor to the husband. The middle ground that crystallized slowly was both artistic and practical, whereas these two trends had been split, almost tragically, when she first came to the hospital.

Chaos, Catastrophe, and Psychoanalytic Theory

These three theories overlap up to a certain point, and, up to this point, make the same kinds of predictions. Then, they diverge, and something new under the sun comes out that has not been discussed in the field of psychotherapy. Since I think that chaos theory is the most general theory of the three theories, I would like to use three of its central ideas to illuminate this comparison: the ideas of bifurcation, fractal properties, and sensitive dependence on initial conditions (especially dimensionality). I am not going to attempt a complete statement of chaos theory (see Schmidt [unpublished] for the most comprehensive discussion).

Bifurcation

In all three of the cases I summarized from the Menninger study, there was a split in the patient's psychology between a familiar character or persona and an unfamiliar character or numina, as in *The Strange Case of Dr. Jekyll and Mr. Hyde* (Stevenson 1886). The patient tends to be in one of two orbits, as if revolving around two gravitational points of considerable power. In the language of chaos theory, these points are called strange attractors. Let us call the familiar point C, for normal control point, and the unfamiliar point R, for the romantic alternative. In these terms, the Phobic Woman clings to C, and is omnipotent at R; the Medical Scientist is the submissive pupil at C, and is flagrantly violent at R; and the Bohemian Musician is the bossy woman at C, and lost from all practicality at R.

Other languages can capture the same bifurcation of the patient's psychology, or course. In analytic theory, the controlling point, C, is dominated by the super-ego, and the romantic point, R, is dominated by id energy. In narrative theory (Gustafson 1992), the patients are caught in plots that operate as strange loops, doubling back on themselves: the first two are subservient (with a shadow side of overpowering), while the third is overpowering (with a shadow side of weakness).

Whatever language is used to describe bifurcation of the force field, the idea itself is critical to practice. You would not want to move the patient out of his dominant orbit (C), if you only propelled him into a higher energy orbit in which he was in less control (R). Thus, phobia, alcoholism, and hypochondriasis in the three cases are the dominant orbit (C), while omnipotence, violence, and impractical romance are the shadow orbit (R). Only a third thing that is crystallized slowly (three to seven years) will be stable in the middle-sized realm between psychic deflation and psychic inflation. The patient has to work through slipping back into (C) and (R) many times to regain his footing in the middle realm of ego autonomy.

In terms of catastrophe theory (Sashin and Callahan 1990), this middle realm is described as a container for affect. Without an ability to feel the emotions within the containment of the session, the patient jumps from low-energy enfeeblement (phobia, alcoholism, hypochondriasis) to high-energy action (omnipotent command, violence, impractical decisions), as pictured in Figure 16–1. As the patient utilizes the sessions as container, he gradually develops a container within himself (ego autonomy) in which he can feel, contemplate, and suspend impulsive action until it is integrated into decisions that balance the opposite concerns (dilemmas). Thus, the three cases nicely fit into bifurcated models of psychoanalytic theory, chaos theory, and catastrophe theory: the third state or orbit that is slowly crystallized is called the relative autonomy of the ego, or the third attractor (T for transcendence), or the container.

Notice what is missed without such a theory of bifurcation. In psychiatry and psychology, the dominant theory is that of disorder that is to be stabilized as order. Thus, phobia, alcoholism, and hypochondriasis are targets for treatments that are either pharmacological or cognitive-behavioral. Once you have gotten rid of the objective finding that has been targeted, you have completed the treatment.

In this perspective, which has only one to two dimensions (disorder, order), the three cases discussed will no longer show phobia,

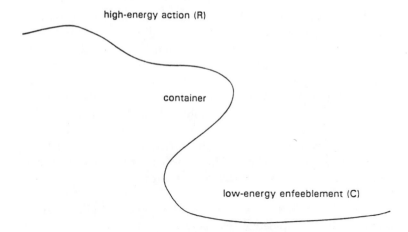

Figure 16–1. Catastrophe Theory.

alcoholism, or hypochondriasis after successful treatment of these low-energy states. However, there will be no mapping of the high-energy states that are so difficult for these three patients: the omnipotence, violence, and impractical decisions. The second half of the bifurcated field never comes into view.

Thus, in the famous meta-analysis of psychotherapy by Smith, Glass, and Miller (1980), the cognitive, behavioral, and hypnotherapies that are directive against the target symptoms show results that are about double the results of the less directive treatments. If you attack a target more vigorously, it disappears faster! Yet, the effects of all this targeting fall by half over two years (Smith et al. 1980). Obviously, there are other forces involved, which show their countereffects slowly over time, but this business of narrow windows of targeting never will bring the other forces into focus.

This is the chief limitation of the positivism (Comte 1830), that now dominates psychiatry and psychology. It allows for objective findings, but it has little interest in subjective findings. As Ryle (1994) argues, this is like grasping the procedures of the patient that are self-defeating (objective, paradigmatic), while overlooking the symbols of what is meaningful (subjective, narrative). The bifurcation between objective and subjective worlds is settled by eliminating the second world. The results are that phobic and alcoholic and hypochondriacal patients, like the three I have been discussing, are either compliant or non-compliant to treatment. If they are non-compliant, there is little access to the meaning that motivates them, and they are left either deflated for not living up to its romance, or inflated and out of control.

In a related field like sport, this would be an absurd reduction. A great tennis player, Jim Courier, dominated the game for about a year, with his superior (objective) mechanics (procedures), but somehow the meaning went out of his game, he started reading a novel between change-overs in a big match, and his game fell apart. Obviously, it takes objective mechanics and subjective meaning to continue flourishing. Either can falter.

In the theater, this is also obvious. For example, in Ibsen's *Hedda Gabler* (1890), the academic Tessman has played the narrow academic game, but feels empty of meaning, while his wife, Hedda, has played the romantic game and has no place in the world but to shoot herself. Either objectivity without meaning, or subjectivity without place, are what Ibsen called "life lies" (Gustafson 1992).

Tessman is lost in the objective horizontal of history, while Hedda is lost in the vertical of imagination (Bachelard 1971). Tessman is in the horizontal life-lie, gravitating around the control point (C), while Hedda is in the vertical life-lie, levitating around the romantic point (R). Schumacher (1977) calls Tessman's kind of life "the decapitation of the vertical" (see Gustafson 1986, p. 240), while Binswanger (1963) calls Hedda's kind of life "Verstiegenheit" or extravagance.

In other words, you can't make much sense out of the human being without a perspective that can bring his outer and objective world of performances into view, while also bringing into view his inner and subjective world of meanings. If you don't consider both worlds you are going to miss at least half of him.

The Fractal Property

This is the idea that a pattern has the same structure in micro- as well as macro-focus. Psychoanalytic theory and therapy depend upon this phenomenon. For example, a clinging gesture in the Phobic Woman will be isomorphic with her dominant attitude and with her dominant set of relationships and with her cultural beliefs. This redundancy is what allows the trend to be taken up on any level of analysis, from very small to very large. Conversely, the redundancy is what also keeps the trend from altering very much. You can change some of the bits, like one of her phobias, and she still retains the tendency to be phobic about other things.

A narrow target window will miss this wider class of redundancy, while settling for the elimination of a particular symptom. A theory that poses the difference between the item (a particular phobia) and the class (avoidance behavior in general) will be alert to this distinction between Learning I (the item) and Learning II (the class) (see Gustafson 1995, Chap. 15), that is, between what is relatively easy to do (and reverse), and what is relatively difficult and slow.

Sensitive Dependence on Initial Conditions (Especially Dimensionality)

Chaos theory postulates that a chaotic system will often magnify small differences in initial position or starting points. The repetition of the same function over and over again can drive two similar starting points farther and farther apart. Thus, two cases can look relatively similar in treatment, and have very different outcomes in long-term follow-up.

Suppose the Medical Scientist were paired with a similar case of twenty years of alcoholism, and even suppose the second patient had a similar determination to throw it off. Yet, if the second man had no profession to go back to, it might be very difficult to sustain the sobriety. Their fates might diverge, as is often true between those who have work and those who do not have work.

Divergence of Theory

Finally, I want to point to where chaos theory diverges from psychoanalytic theory, and predicts different outcomes. Analytic theory, I have argued, is a two-to-three-dimensional set of strange attractors (superego, id, and ego), which has considerable advantages over a one-to-two-dimensional set (disorder, order) prevalent in objective psychiatry and psychology.

Yet, a three-dimensional set is going to be inadequate for cases in which a fourth, fifth, and sixth attractor become important orbits in the patient's force field (see Gustafson 1995, Chaps. 10–12, on "Complex Stories"). How could that take place? I will go into this more fully in the next chapter on Jung's individuation, but the idea is simple enough to outline.

Any stability, say of the ego, is going to risk a new rigidity or stiffness. While it (T) may stay clear of the deflation (C), or inflation (R) prior to treatment, it may just stand relatively still. The new marriages of the Phobic Woman, the Medical Scientist, and the Bohemian Musician may be stable, but if they lack fresh currents, they will be dull.

Now, that repetition is going to sit better with some patients than others. Some like orthodoxy, for its comfort. Some find it stifling, and need continuous development. Like Ishmael in the opening of *Moby Dick* (Melville 1851), they get cranky being land-locked for too long, and begin to feel like knocking somebody's hat off. That is, until they undergo a fresh voyage. This is the pull of a new and fourth and fifth and sixth strange attractor, which unsettles the synthesis of the last voyage. Essentially, it is what an epic hero is all about, as we shall discover in the next chapter.

17

Jung's Individuation, Compared to Freud

Freud invented several strategies for unloosing the unconscious mind, and letting it into the confines of the conscious mind. The first method was following the train of associations from a neurotic symptom. By taking something like a nose distorted by an intrusion from the unconscious, as with Lucy (Breuer and Freud 1895) by the smell of burnt pudding, he could track backwards, to the left, and down into the depths of the country, like taking a train from the Vienna station into relatively unknown country.

The second method was the dream specimen come up from below and left on his doorstep like morning milk. He discovered how to take it apart into its components, which seemed to gather themselves from every corner of his 40-year-old life, into this incredible synthesis of the manifest dream (Freud 1900). Freud looked at this huge influx as wishes, which had been excluded by the attempt to be a proper child-citizen. He was already on his way to his later structural formulation of the id governing the unconscious, and the super-ego governing the conscious. The ego was to mediate. This binary system is deeply embedded in Western civilization, so Freud hardly invented its form. After all, a deity ruled the Christian world, and a devil lurked in the shadows. All of the civilizations that arose out of the Mediterranean basin have some such binary system of heaven and hell (Turner 1993).

The third method was what he called free association. The idea was to persuade the super-ego to relax its censorship, and let the id safely in with the motor system turned off. Lying on the couch was the literal means. Essentially, his psychotherapy of psychoanalysis was to let the id into the conscious mind, so that fresh compromises could be made between its wishes and the strictures of the super-ego. Freud believed that its wishes were largely those of a 5-year-old boy, a little Oedipus, who wished to claim his mother and kill his rival father to become king himself. These claims would be pressed upon the analyst himself, in the transference of the wishes and fears of the 5-year-old from his father of the past to this father of the present .

By the "Recommendations for Physicians on the Psychoanalytic Method of Treatment" (1912, 1913, 1914, 1915), all of this was codified quite simply as a set of dicta on how an analyst is to conduct himself in starting, working through, and handling transference. Its appeal has been great, and has continued with minor modifications to this very day.

I realize that advocates of self psychology would dispute this (Kohut 1971). I realize that advocates of the theory of unconscious plans (Weiss 1993) would argue that the unconscious is a constructive agent trying to correct the pathogenic beliefs of the conscious, and that Freud even thought this way himself (Gustafson in press, a). The main line of psychoanalysis remains free association on a couch, as a kind of limited freedom, as a playground for bringing out what has to be suppressed elsewhere.

The metaphor is chiefly military. The unconscious has to be let in to civilized territory, in order to be subdued. As long as it bangs around in the periphery of the empire, it will cause unruly trouble: ". . . one cannot overcome an enemy who is absent or not within range . . . We render it harmless, and even make use of it, by according it the right to assert itself within certain limits . . . into the transference as to a playground" (Freud 1914, pp. 163–164). The governing metaphor is the defense of the status quo, by rendering its instinctual rebellion harmless. It gives room to say anything. It has a modest practice as psychoanalytic psychotherapy, which consists chiefly of listening patiently, noting resistances, and occasionally a transference. (Its virtue is seen in Case 4, "A Case of Hamlet," described in my previous book [Gustafson 1995].) There are many grateful patients who have taken this opportunity, and many kind doctors who provide the space for it to flourish.

Jung's Individuation

For me, the great weakness of Freud's scheme is its formula that makes all cases the same, with minor variations. Freud's own cases do not suffer from his own formulation recommended to physicians. The four cases of *Studies on Hysteria*, Dora, the Rat Man, the Wolf Man, and a Case of Female Homosexuality, are all unforgettably individual (Gustafson unpublished, a). Yet his formula for his disciples has less room than Jung's. For some, this is a virtue. The subject is mastered, and its proprietor is secure.

For Jung, psychoanalysis was at first a great liberation, because it opened up the vast territory of the unconscious; yet, he found Freud's stake in him to be a heavy burden (Newton 1979). He became one of the rebellious angels. Jung's way of assimilating the unconscious, I find, has a great deal more latitude in it for what Jung called individuation. Individuation means the process of utilizing the unconscious as an opposing current to the conscious drift, in order to create a particular individual being different from all others. The two currents mix like melody and accompaniment to create the particular song. I would like to explain this capacity of Jung's ideas, which have become clouded over by Jungians. This institutionalization of Jung also needs explanation. He himself predicted the drastic reduction of scope, which is the work of disciples (Jung 1971, pp. 120–121).

The Unconscious as a Second Eye, to Compensate the First Eye of the Conscious: Natural Correction of Selective Inattention

Nothing could be more opposed to Freud's concept of the id-unconscious than Jung's concept of the compensatory-unconscious. Freud's is maladaptive, while Jung's is the key to adaptation. Jung believes the conscious mind to be a kind of blunt, one-eyed instrument. It is the province of the persona, or mask, which fits its owner into the hierarchy of social life, but a mask is also fixing its owner into a stock role, which affords little or no individual vitality.

The way out of this conventional trap is via the fertility of the unconscious, which has everything excluded by the stock role, but not only that. After all, Freud's id has the fertility of the devil, which is so appealing to Faust or to Dr. Jekyll. What is strikingly different about Jung's shadow is that it points to what is needed, to correct or compensate the stock persona. It points to what to face next.

In this precise sense, it corrects selective inattention. The conscious eye has its eye on something, while missing something vital. The unconscious eye will point unerringly. The most unforgettable illustration in Jung is the mountain climber who told him of a dream of ascending to heaven on a stairway off the top of a mountain. Jung begged him not to go hiking, but he went anyway and stepped right off a mountain to his death and dragged a companion with him (Jung 1933, pp. 14–15).

You could cite Freud's conception of the id in Jung's case to argue that the man could not resist his own wishfulness (id). You could cite Jung's conception to argue that the man's dream was trying to tell him that his conscious standpoint was dangerously off.

A similar difference in perspective could be illustrated by the Jekyll and Hyde story of Stevenson (1886). Is Jekyll the weak creature governed by his super-ego, and barely holding his monstrous id at bay? Is Jekyll a dry persona, who needs to plunge into the ocean of his unconscious to come to life?

The facts can fit both conceptions. What is the difference in perspective? Freud's perspective looks at the unconscious as a threat. Jung's perspective looks to the unconscious as having something needed.

If the unconscious takes over, it is surely a threat. The mountain climber climbing stairs to heaven is about to die. Mr. Hyde's dive into oceanic freedom is a summons to the police to come hang him. The unconscious only becomes a needed addition when it is placed alongside the conscious, to create a third thing. In this sense, Jung's idea is Hegelian: the thesis is conscious, the antithesis is unconscious, and the synthesis is the two taken together. Thus, the synthesis for the climber would be something about ectasis and being grounded, for Hyde something about staying dry and being wet (see Binswanger [1963] and Lewis Carroll [1865], respectively, for such synthesis to these two dilemmas).

Jung's argument is that the conscious deteriorates without its opposite, into excessive groundedness and dryness. Jung's argument is also that the unconscious deteriorates without the conscious mind. It possesses. Thus, the ecstatic climber is possessed by a godlike idea, as is Hyde. There are two possessions, an outward possession by a persona, and an inward possession by a god. Both cancel individuality. The persona or mask dictates the entire role. The god dictates the entire role.

How are we to become free of taking dictation? Jung's reply is that the unconscious can pull us away from the conscious, and the conscious can pull us away from the unconscious. We can learn to orient ourselves in such a way that we can use the opposing force to free ourselves from the force that holds us. This puts us into the equipoise region of relative freedom from being driven, as in Tolstoy's conception (see Chapter 15 and Figure 17–1).

A Case of a Perfect Schoolgirl

This woman had terrible parents, like so many other Children of the Garden Island (Werner 1989), and took refuge at school where she excelled. This saved her. It also became a dry trap for her as an academic. She became obsessed like Edward Casaubon in *Middlemarch* (Eliot 1871) with perfection of detail, dreading to show her work and

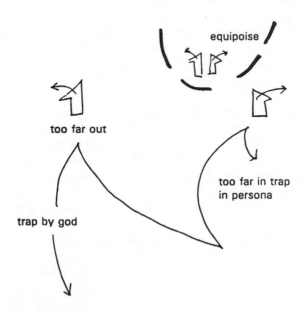

Figure 17–1. Unconscious/Conscious Balance.

have it criticized. This was like falling back into the hands of her cruel parents (the basic fault).

To make a long story short, I began to get her to bring out her unconscious in dreams. She showed a beautiful talent. Often, it was overwhelmingly painful, but she would point away from her pain to a box of children's blocks up high and to her left on a cabinet. This always pulled her through.

She became quite fertile, giving herself beautifully to her students and friends and colleagues. She had the opposite trouble. She got a tremendous amount done, but she got hurt trying to move mountains. She had too much faith. She would try to get a cruel colleague to lay off students, and she would try to get a misanthropic uncle to come in from the cold.

Her dreams helped her to face this. A series of them pointed out her selective inattention to fixed obstacles. For example, one such dream showed a patch of blue sky up and to the left, but a swath of her mother's hair blocked her way altogether. In brief, she had had to have faith in getting around this Grimm-like witch of a mother, yet now she had excessive faith that she could get around anybody similar to her mother. This is what Jung calls psychic inflation, and always points to possession by a god and loss of scale as happened to Tolstoy himself (see Chapter 15). The problem is to see which god has got you in its possession. Until it comes into focus, you can't point away from it, not knowing what *It* is. The deflation was very painful, and she cried, and looked at her children's blocks.

We began with her possessed by the persona of a perfect schoolchild. A persona is also based on subscription to a myth, a myth that fits you snugly into society. (This is our subject of Chapter 18, "The Group Animal.") She was possessed by a kind of Virgin Mother Mary. As she backed off the dry perfection, she became fertile. Then, as she gave up absolute fertility, she became more humorous and modest. This is what Jung meant by individuation. This is a long-term individual therapy at once a week, of a benign basic fault. It has lasted five years.

Summary of Jung's Individuation as Self-Regulation

Jung's idea of conscious/unconscious balance invites an orientation to self that is self-regulating. You don't need to depend upon an analyst. You already have an analyst inside of you that you are not utilizing. It is doubly clouded over, in Sullivan's sense of selective inattention. You do not realize how you are possessed by a persona pulling you to the right into the world, nor do you know how you are possessed by a god pulling you left and far out. These are the two strange attractors that dominate the life of man and keep him in thrall, unwittingly, so he just plays collective parts by dictation. Freud's (1909) Rat Man fits Jung's formulation beautifully, and achieves his liberation by bringing the rat persona and its variations *into focus*, as well as his opposite possession by a kind of god of German idealism (Gustafson in press, b.)

The Case of Mr. Lion

Mr. Lion was a fierce competitor. He was always pleased having his way, and always snarly when crossed. This was his persona, which is standard overpowering Western male. Naturally, he married Mrs. Lion, who was bent on taming him at home. They were soon bored with each other. After all, each repeated himself or herself this week, verbatim, from last week. Both were taking lion dictation.

This could have been the end of the story, as they might have gone into a long lion nap, caged in the myth of domestic bliss, captives of this machine for the suppression of time, but—lions love chases. Mr. Lion began a long series of chases of new lionesses. This revived him, until the new lioness began to repeat herself and began to notice Mr. Lion repeating himself. The chase was the pleasure, and the possession paled in attraction in a matter of weeks. He would promise fidelity to the new one, but he would be off chasing another. He was in love with the romance of the chase. He was actually dominated by this goddess.

This is the gist of what Jung meant by animus and anima. He lives a life of animus, and is thrilled by the anima. This is his dilemma: if he lets the animus rule him, he battles and sleeps, and remains a solid citizen. If he lets the anima take him over, he is a night cruiser, and forever needs new partners, and is a romantic rebel who brings a great deal of instability and pain to other people, especially women. Mr. Lion can live a correct life, and go sleepy, or he can live an incorrect life, and go chasing, as pictured in Figure 17–2. He can have stability, or he can have romance, but he has to choose. The two will not go together. Each has a physics that repels the physics of the other. Stability dulls out romance. Freud agrees: "We are so made that we can derive intense enjoyment only from a contrast and very little from a state of things"

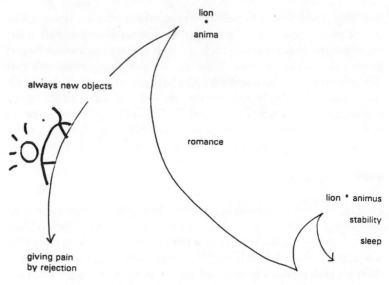

Figure 17–2. Lion Terrain.

(1930, p. 23). Romance wrecks stability. They are strange attractors that repel each other, and the poor lion is a prisoner of one orbit or the other. He is a purely collective animal, and he is going to be sad for sure.

There is a way out of this double orbit of official lionhood, which is the path of individuation. For if conscious stability bathes in its own unconscious depths, it will be ever fresh. If the swimmer keeps coming back up to land, he will not get too far out. If two people can do this, then stability/romance is a paradox that is continually renewed. John Donne is the great poet who mapped this triumph. Often, he used America as his symbol of discovery-in-stability as . . .

> License my roving hands, and let them go
> Before, behind, between, above, below.
> O my America, my new found land,
> My kingdom, safeliest when with one man manned,
> My mine of precious stones, my empery,
> How blessed am I in discovering thee!

To enter in these bonds, is to be free;
There where my hand is set, my seal shall be. [1988, from
"To His Mistress Going to Bed" (Elegy 19)]

Unfortunately, Mr. Lion is often unwilling to depart from his two orbits. Sadly, he is dull, or sadly, he is a heartbreaker and ends up alone. He is caged, or he is nowhere. In this sense, Freud's binary map fits him: he is either super-ego'd, or he is id-ed. Freud's map is a special case of Jung's.

Jung Meets Freud

To explain what individuation might look like in Mr. Lion, it is only necessary to study the case of that young lion, Jung himself, when Freud wanted to put him in charge of his church. Jung had dimly sensed that Freud had made a god out of his theory of sexuality: "I had a strong intuition that for him sexuality was a sort of *numinosum* [Roman local god]. Freud said to me, you see, we must make a dogma out of it, an unshakable bulwark" (1963, p. 150). For Jung to capitulate to being the chief lieutenant of the church dogma was crushing (Newton 1979). His spirit would have been extinguished. A great heat rose in him when Freud put down the remainder of the unconscious as nonsensical: "It was as if my diaphragm were made of iron and were becoming red-hot— a glowing vault" (p. 155). Jung did not get lost like Mr. Lion in a sterile subordination to a super-ego alternating with a glowing id. Rather, he let his fire come out and show the entire pantheon of gods in conflagration inside us. As I shall soon show, this led to many excesses in Jung when different gods owned him, and to subordinations when his persona owned him in public life; yet his path remained one of individuation, because he stayed dancing back and forth between god-possession inside and world-possession outside.

There are ever so many more dimensions possible for individuation on Jung's map. First of all, possession by a persona leaves little room, for this group only requires three types, which correspond to my overpowering, delaying, and subservient characters (Gustafson 1992, 1995) (see Chapter 18 also). The possession by the god has as many possibilities as Olympus and Hades, or the Hindu pantheon, or the North American realm of spirits. Clearly, Freud was so far off he saw only the possibility of possession by Oedipus. The baseline situation is one of three personae in the outer orbit, and one of thousands of gods in the inner orbit. This resting state is binary. Once the individual begins to emerge by going back and forth from thesis to antithesis, countless syntheses become possible in individuation. This is exciting.

Jung's theory of individuation is isomorphic to the current Freeman-Skarda chaos theory of olfaction. Greatly simplified, the Freeman-Skarda theory says that the olfactory brain rests in an oscillation between two strange attractors. When smells excite, it oscillates around as many as ten strange attractors in grasping a complex smell (Freeman 1991, Schmidt unpublished, Skarda and Freeman 1987) (I am indebted to Greg Schmidt for bringing the Freeman-Skarda theory to my attention.) Interestingly enough, I find classical Western music to have a similar resting structure, and structure of excitation. It is antiphonal or binary, as between melody and accompaniment, yet it splinters the two voices into as many as ten when it gets intense, as pictured in Figure 17–3. Listen to Samuel Barber's "Adagio for Strings," for example.

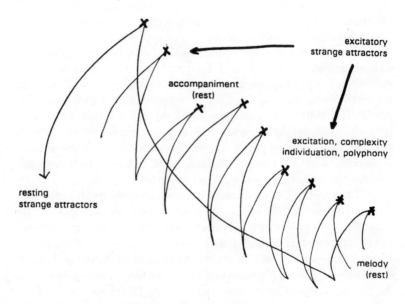

Figure 17–3. Polyphony.

Jung and Jungians, and Misunderstanding

One of the great pities about individuation is that it is liable to slip on a single point or two and wreck itself. The Greeks recognized this shakiness in their heroes and called the vulnerability *hubris*, which means insolence or excessive pride or excessive self-confidence. In general, hubris carries you too far to the right into battles that you cannot win and will destroy you, and hubris carries you too far to the left into going your own way and not being able to get back. Jung suffered on both scores.

I am not particularly interested in underscoring Jung's personal fallibilities (see Noll 1994, for a very thorough job of showing all of Jung's weaknesses, as part of the history of German Romanticism. Noll makes his entire influence into a mere cult, while seeing no substantial value in him at all), but in pointing to the weaknesses in his theory that derives from them. Conversely, his weaknesses of theory, or mapping, make the fallibilities inevitable. This mapping problem is what needs concern us, so we can learn something from his errors, and revise the holes of our own selective inattention.

There have been two major scandals about Jung, one concerning his love life with a former patient, and a second concerning his politics of fraternizing with the Nazi cooptation of psychiatry in Germany. The first has been pored over by Carotenuto (1982) and the second by Cocks (1985), so I need not go over the sordid ground.

Marital Dilemmas

The affair with Sabina Spielraum seems important to me because of the force with which the urge for doubling can press itself upon a self-confident hero. By doubling, I mean what Jung means as finding a double for oneself in scope and passion. Indeed, his most important essay on relations between men and women, "Marriage as a Psychological Relationship" (1925), is a brilliant mapping of the dilemmas that result from this urge for company. We profit from his difficulty if we can comprehend his essay.

The dilemma is ancient, and is the very subject of the beginning of the *Iliad*. Agamemnon refuses to give up Khryseis, his maiden prize of the war, and all the trouble of the Greeks ensues. He is going too far, and Apollo attacks him for his *hubris*. Agamemnon is shamed out of

Khryseis by Achilles in the council of war, calling for him to take a different prize. Agamemnon replies he will yield, but take someone else, like Briseis, who is possessed by Achilles. Now, Achilles goes wild in reply: ". . . we joined for you, you insolent boor, to please you, fighting for your brother's sake and yours, to get revenge upon the Trojans. You overlook this, dogface, or don't care, and now in the end you threaten to take my girl, a prize I sweated for, and soldiers gave me!" (Homer 1974, pp. 16–17). This speech drives Agamemnon to the very thing of taking Briseis from Achilles. It is an old trouble. The heroes of the early psychoanalytic movement fell into it similarly: Jung, Reich, Ferenczi, and so on. They did a great deal of harm, especially to women.

The important thing, it seems to me, is to comprehend the map and the forces involved, for the dilemma crops up for everyone to some extent. As Jung argues (1925), it is likely in any marriage that one partner will be more far-ranging than the other in interests. He or she will want company in such pleasures. Perhaps, the far-rangers were more apt to be men in the famous Victorian marriages (Rose 1984). Nowadays, the wider interests almost always are those of the women, while the men watch sports on television or dig away at their perpetual jobs.

In any event, the longing for company is apt to feel like an entitlement in those with many interests to share. Having so much to give, they want to give it. When their partners are dull and tuned into narrow bands, they grow very angry and they are apt to punish most cruelly.

Interestingly, the stay-at-homes are also wanting company in their narrow pursuits, and become very anxious about their partners roaming all over the countryside. They too feel entitled to keep the far-ranger at hand. They curb, or they rage, forcing their way.

The two entitlements are going to drive each other crazy, and so they do. This is the gist of Jung's dilemma of marriage. If the far-ranger (Mr. Lion) prevails, the stay-at-home is extremely anxious waiting behind. If the stay-at-home prevails, the far-ranger (Mr. Lion) is extremely depressed in his confinement. The dilemma becomes one of sailing between the two horns that will wreck the marriage. Of course, sometimes it is not possible to satisfy one, without disabling the other. In all cases, leaning too far to the left will be some hardship for one, while leaning to the right will be some hardship for the other. Many couples try to solve the problem by sorting out which pleasures are mutual, and which are perversely too wide or too narrow. This sets a second dilemma, between the horn of attempting too much together, and the horn of attempting too little together. Of course, these are the two great miseries of marriage, of being punished by the other's pleasure, or of drifting apart in separate pursuit of pleasures.

Political Dilemmas

If Jung foundered in his marital dilemma, and came through with a beautiful map for us, he also foundered in his political dilemma, and did not come through well and disappeared into the East. The gist of it (Cocks 1985, pp. 127–135) was that Jung tried to use his participation in the International General Medical Society for Psychotherapy to protect psychotherapy in Germany from extinction in the rising years (1933–1940) of National Socialism. This involved him as President of the International Society in cooperation with the German Society that increasingly espoused Nazi doctrines. By 1940, Jung had resigned. The damage was done. He had protected German psychotherapy from extinction by covering its Nazification with his prestige. Of course, it was a horrible dilemma.

To his credit, Jung moved, if slowly, from the right horn to the left horn. To his discredit, he took too long to see the damage of his utilizing his power as he did. He was romantic about "the youthfulness of the German soul," in 1933 (Cocks 1985, p. 128), which did not strike him as demonic possession by Wotan until 1936 (p. 133). (See Noll [1994] for Jung's long romance with the German *volk*.)

By 1940, as the war got underway, Jung became horrified (Jung 1963). From here forward, his tendencies to indulge in obscure religious symbolism ran away with him. You can see it in his essay "Individual Dream Symbolism in Relation to Alchemy" (1944 in *Portable Jung* 1971), completed in the war years, yet prepared in earlier versions in two lectures in 1935 and 1936. It is based on the fascinating idea of following the *sequence* of dreams as a kind of navigation in which the series of previous sighting points (dreams) helps you to reckon the next sighting point (dream). The sequence provides context for judging what the dream is trying to correct. In this sense, the selective inattention of the unconscious mind can also be compensated, just as the selective inattention of the conscious mind can be compensated, as he had argued before. The text used to demonstrate this use of sequence is four hundred dreams of a patient seen by one of Jung's pupils. It is a marvelous idea, and I have borrowed this use of sequence as context in my own practice of dream interpretation (to be discussed in my next book). However, the text becomes increasingly mad with obscure religious references, like Reich going off the deep end in *Character Analysis* (1933), which begins so profoundly and turns wild with psychic contact and vegetative current (p. 293). Jung is not becoming psychotic to leave this world, just densely obsessional (Eastern mandelas become a tremendous diversion into otherworldliness).

All of psychoanalysis has this same weakness, for all of psychoanalysis develops the inner world as its great interest, while the outer world becomes a limitation that gets in the way. The outer world is not known in its own right. It is always being underestimated, for the lack of a map of its actual structures. Reich is wounded by the Communist Party and Psychoanalysis, and Jung is wounded by getting drawn into German Romanticism. At least Freud (1930) in the same period knew that the world wouldn't allow very much individual liberty.

Jungians

I do not want to be sweeping in judgment, but I do want to indicate a tendency in the followers of Jung to weaken his chief weakness even further. It is a general tendency of disciples to take a complex thought with opposing currents, and make it go one way so all can join in it (Jung): "Naturally the disciples always stick together, not out of love, but for the very understandable purpose of effortlessly confirming their very own convictions by engendering an air of collective agreement" (*Portable Jung* 1971, pp. 120–121). Jung's own disciples have taken to romanticizing archetypes, as if they were an enticing idea to recommend to the uninitiated: "Come along on an inner journey, and see all the sights, which we know already, thanks to our master, Jung, who pointed them out to us!" Even the greatest student of Jung, Joseph Campbell, who could not be called a Jungian, falls into this facility when he calls upon his students in his famous catchphrase of "Follow your bliss."

Campbell is not facile about the profound journey of heroes, and what perils they actually face, and what a single blunder is apt to cost, in death. Better than anyone, he knows that the mysteries of the gods are beyond names, which are but the masks of god(s). Nevertheless, he gets enthusiastic (*en-theos* means full of the god) about the journey of the hero of a thousand faces. Always, this bespeaks a failure to grasp the crushing powers of the outer world. Most dare not go against it at all, and they know better, like Ophelia, Gertrude, Polonius, and Laertes. Claudius will finish them if they get out of line, and this they know.

Individuation with Eliot and Hardy

Individuation is harder than Campbell would have it, or Jung. George Eliot (1871) was a more accurate guide. Here there is no underestimation. Nor is there in Thomas Hardy in *The Mayor of Casterbridge* (1886), or in *The Return of the Native* (1878). Without our novelists of this quality, we would be perfect fools in our judgments of this subject.

Eliot and Hardy depict for us what lies in wait for the earnest young person who hopes to be herself or himself. The pull into stock roles is tremendous. The rebellion is fatal. The clever return on individual terms takes remarkable balance of character.

Let me reply with *Middlemarch* and bring in Hardy's two novels as supplement to my brief. If Eliot's portrait is of general import, which I find it to be, the society is dictated to by the banker, Bulstrode, the Mayor, Vincy, and the other notables with money and land, like Featherstone and Brooke. They are old farts, as my youngest daughter would say. That's the top end. Coming up are the eager young ones like Dorothea and Celia Brooke, Fred and Rosamund Vincy, Lydgate, Mary Garth, and so forth, to use Brooke's ample phrase. While the old ones are all cold calculation, the young ones are all warm clouds of illusion wanting to believe in their myths of advancing and coupling. In these clouds, they all make drastic mistakes.

Two Cases in Madison, of Marrying and of Advancing, a Dorothea and a Lydgate

This is a Middlemarch I live in, I am quite sure of it, as I watch what comes before me in my consulting room. Consider this Dorothea and this Lydgate.

Act I: Departure from the Regime of Stock Roles

(Acts I, II, and III are the three acts of the universal monomyth of rejuvenation by the hero [Campbell 1949]. See the conclusion of this chapter.) This Dorothea comes in her late twenties, shaken by how little distance she has come toward her great goals to be reached by 30. Her first marriage was to a mean man, and this took her five years to get out of. Her second marriage was to a kind man, and this she has just gotten out of because he only clings to her. Now she is free, and disheartened that she will ever have the family she imagined for herself.

This Lydgate is also in his late twenties, and is also shaken concerning his great goals to be reached by 30. He had never liked school for its stuffy domination, but he had been able to go teach English in Europe as a second language, where he had been able to create conditions that were very enlivening for his students. Now, he came back for a Ph.D., and found himself under egomaniacs again—the very equivalents of Bulstrode and Vincy and so forth—who gave four-hour monologues and who didn't show up and who dealt out arbitrary judgments. In helpless rage, he tried to talk with his fellow graduate students about this injustice, but he only made them very nervous, since they were eagerly bowing and scraping with the professors that would get them in somewhere. Our man was beside himself.

As a novelist-doctor, my first duty is to bring into focus what they have run aground on. Dorothea has struck the two chief possibilities of marriage, to a strong man and to a weak man, and neither will work, only equality. Lydgate has struck the chief characteristic of hierarchy, which is domination from the top, and currying favor from below. He cannot bear to knuckle under, and he dare not own his rage too openly. Neither will work. I pose to him the problem of owning his anger, which he seems to be terribly guilty about, judging from the proliferation of Gustafson's sign (one, two, or three fingers pointed perpendicularly to one's own head [Gustafson 1992], at every occasion he gets near it). Of course, this reaches back to his father, who would not countenance any opposition.

Act II: The Lull and Descent

I am always asked to help by somebody run aground on the usual structures of Middlemarch/Madison. They are always relieved to be with someone who can bring it into focus. Now comes a lull, as they are relieved of this outward source of great pain. I will usually notice the lull, and invite them to put their feet up on my couch. We are drop-

ping into psychoanalysis as casually as that. Always, there is a big transference waiting here about making themselves comfortable. Now it is
my job to bring into focus the forbidding presence.

Lydgate gets his feet up, and looks pleased, until his feet start
twiddling. This turns out to be his feeling that I think he is sullen. That
was what his mother said, when he played quietly by himself. When I
tell him I don't find him that way at all, he cries with great relief. Next
session he comes in with a dream about why he has to work so hard.
He is working hard, but he is terrified his father will explode at him.
When I tell him I am sorry he has to be so afraid, he cries again with
great relief.

Act III: The Re-Entry

This is always underestimated, as by Clym Yeobright, artist as returning native, or by Eustachia Vye aching to find her counterpart returned
(Hardy 1878), or Elizabeth-Jane and her mother coming back to re-
join Henchard, now Mayor (Hardy 1886). The structures of power do
not yield to these individuals, any more than they do to Dorothea or to
Lydgate.

It is a beautiful thing to pull back from the direct collisions with
the stock roles, of coupling and advancing, and it is a beautiful thing
to drop into the lull and get free of forbidding presences. It is a third
and difficult thing to come back to town as oneself without new slips
that get one punished or new departures that carry one too far out. The
third thing about individuation that lasts is to have an accurate eye out
for the pulls to the right and to the left. Dreams are by far the most
helpful, as they point unerringly to what will be overlooked by the
conscious mind eager to have its way. It will continually go back into
cloudiness. Listen to Helen Vendler (1994), professor of English at
Harvard, explaining the marvelous individuation of Shakespeare's
Sonnets as speech acts, all different and all defying paraphrase in their
design, and rhythm, and words. For example, in Sonnet 5:

Then, were not summer's distillation left,
A liquid prisoner pent in walls of glass,
Beauty's effect with beauty were bereft,
Nor it nor no remembrance what it was.

Vendler is aggrieved with her fellow critics for missing all of this: "Others are bound to continue grouping the sonnets in theoretical or generic or thematic clumps, if only because of that inveterate taxonomizing tendency—so inimical to aesthetic experience—in human mentality" (p. 49). Of course, this is the hurt of all individuation, which will be taken to pieces by the hierarchies. Different pieces will be taken by different search parties, depending on their object of increase.

Individuation must keep itself somewhat apart, but not too far. Let me close with two dreams that warned beautifully of this to Lydgate and to Dorothea, respectively. Their educations stand or fall on comprehending the dangers to right and left as they go along, as a single oversight can do considerable harm.

Lydgate's Dream of His Automobile

Lydgate dreamt he was back at the little college he came from to this University. He let the air out of the two tires on the right side of the automobile, and it rolled over and tucked the two wheels under it with a groan, like a huge buffalo, or perhaps a grizzly bear. He was nearly felled by its weight falling on him, but managed to push it back up and off of him, so it stood half-way erect. Then, he cast about for a way to repair it, as he thought he wanted to go back to the university after all. He found a bicycle pump, and that was little enough force for these big tires. He found a man with keys, and that was no help. He looked across the way at a regular service station, and somehow knew they would not know how to fix *these* tires, which were of a different order of things. He decided to stay in his little college after all, like Pascal in his room.

Here is a beautifully clear dream of deflation of huge grizzly or buffalo hopes for roaming all over the Western prairie. The man takes down his own claims, yet, obviously, he struggles to have them back. Surely, there will be more dreams in this series. He resolves here to stay in his room like Pascal, but he is a restless animal who can be seized with huge grizzly or buffalo ambition again.

Dorothea's Dream of Being Pippi Longstocking

Dorothea dreamt she was back in her hometown looking over a curious apartment. It was grafted onto a church! The thing was a duplex, church to the right, and apartment left and above. She herself was Pippi Longstocking, of all people! (Pippi Longstocking is a daring girl in a Swedish story about two little correct Swedish children, who discover Pippi living next door without supervision. Pippi claims her father is a famous pirate, and that she can do as she pleases.) She attempts to grasp this curious duplex by wandering about inside it and outside it. The church part is like a big suburban living room vacant of any interest whatsoever, while the outside is like a Swedish park in Stockholm that is perfectly in place.

The dream warns her of the myth of Pippi Longstocking, which is that you can be fully yourself, and regulation Swedes will be terribly glad of seeing you. All she had to do was live like a vacant church, and she would set them at their ease. Of course this is so, but the dream is a caricature of something she is incapable of doing to herself, which is making her inside into a suburban living room you could see anywhere and her outside into a perfectly appointed park in Stockholm.

Here is a dream about the temptation to play a persona that she could bear for very few minutes without exasperation. The dream ridicules the myth of being able to appear correct, while actually being a pirate's daughter. In actuality, she cannot play the part, which would be a duplex, or duplicity, so she will have to live apart, rather than in such a part.

Continuous Development

There is a cycle to individuation, in three movements: first, the departure from the stock role; second, the discovery in the lull (in which the conscious mind is suspended); third, the re-entry with this discovery, to fit it into the actual and continuing difficulties of the society. In Hegelian terms, the three movements are the thesis, the antithesis, and the synthesis.

Actually, the three movements for regeneration were not invented by Jung or Hegel. As Campbell shows so beautifully in his introduction to The Hero with a Thousand Faces (1949), the sequence is the same in all myths of the hero, from China to India to Europe to the Americas. Campbell calls this the monomyth. Because of its ubiquity, Campbell believes it has to be genetic, a universal route of renewal available to the human being stuck in stultifying circumstances. Act I is the departure from the dead regime. Act II is the discovery of the revitalizing substance or maiden or idea. Act III is the re-entry, which inserts the discovery into the body politic to allow it to flourish anew.

Of course, the new regime can and will become a dead crust. Again, a hero will be needed to break its thrall. In individual terms, some of us have a few such breakthroughs in the course of a lifetime. Some fewer hardly stand still, since the crust of each day is broken by the night journey, which brings new findings to fit in for the next day. This is what Jung meant by individuation, which is continuous development.

18

The Group Animal

The dominance of the group over the individual is hugely underestimated. Tolstoy suggests that it is missed because each of us is his own little observatory on the world. This gives us an illusion of sovereignty.

Having an individual doctor augments this illusion, by affording an audience for self-centered rambles. We are indulged, as patients. As doctors, we are drawn into finding the patient understandable, and lovable and forgivable. This pull into sympathy on this private little stage is apt to put the larger stage of the patient's work life and love life and society life out of focus.

In this way, we get too close. The extent of the field of viewing the patient is singular and the grain of the focus is so fine that we see him or her as a photograph up close in a family album. Here he or she seems particularly individual.

This connection is much sought after by the patient. It is good we can connect so, but we are also invited in to help to solve a problem. Usually, it is about anxiety and/or depression and their complications. The patient is in danger or in disillusionment. Anxiety and/or depression are the signals.

To see how the patient is in danger or disillusion, we have to be able to shift the extent and grain of our lens to see the patient on larger stages (Allen and Starr 1982). This is a wider angle, and a coarser grain, which are necessary to bring the pattern of misadjustment into sharp focus.

A third reason for underestimation of the dominance of the group, besides the solipsism of the individual soul, and the private scale of the consulting room, is the lack of calculation of the power of the forces involved. Often, I have read the relevant forces in the last twenty-five years of practice correctly, but I have not always measured their momentum accurately.

Freud (1937) repeatedly turns to the quantitative dimension to explain outcome in his last major theoretical essay. This discussion of forces in terms of libido and neutralized libido gave rise to a vast mechanics of libido that dominated much of psychoanalytic literature in the 1950s and 1960s with Hartman and Lowenstein and the so-called economic point of view. Even as a trainee, I knew it was mostly a waste of time. You could explain anything by proposing the cathexes of libido here, and there, and so forth, as in the medieval disputations about angels on the head of a pin. The quantitative problem was posed, but not in terms that could clarify technical practice.

Reading the Forces in the Schizoid Compromise

When I look back over ten or eleven years of consultations I have conducted and recorded on videotape, one miscalculation comes into focus and puts everything else into relative background. This is the problem that Guntrip (1968) called "the schizoid compromise" and claimed for it the chief form of psychotherapy stalemate. This gist of the compromise is what I would call the schizoid dilemma, as illustrated in Figure 18–1. These patients dread the nearness of intrusion and the farness of abandonment. What is even more important is that they stabilize in neither near nor far. They become adept at a third position, which is half in and half out, half near and half far. This is the schizoid compromise. It is truly a compromise, because it is also complained of, for its lack of intimacy, for its sad isolation. Actual nearness or farness are truly terrifying, and so half-near, half-far becomes preferable.

In terms of chaos theory, we can model this stabilization as a third strange attractor, which becomes the center of the dominant orbit. Occasionally, the patient gets into the influence of the near strange

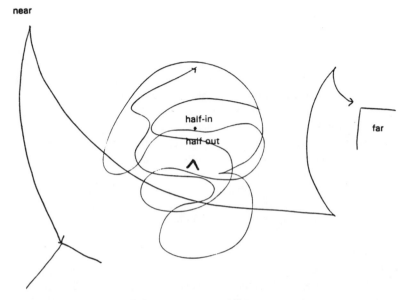

Figure 18–1. Schizoid Space.

attractor or the far strange attractor, but either is so traumatic in its terror, that the patient flees back into the stabilizing orbit of the near/far strange attractor.

How do we misread these dilemmas so readily? When we see them alone, we are apt to find them, often, very appealing, and so they give us pleasant views of possibilities of full engagement and of standing on their own, that is, of capability for near and for far. It is only in the force field of our consulting rooms that they show this appeal where they have our full attention and our full support. They gleam in this light.

Out on the larger stages of group life, in society and work and in love, they wilt into greyness. They dread to be known there and they dread to be left there alone. The forces overwhelm them, unless they stay near the strange attractor of half-in/half-out. This is overwhelmingly probable. The exceptions are brief, and only prove the necessity of coming back quickly to the only available stability.

This stability can suit the person to many grey occupations in which half-involvement is called for: policing, controlling, teaching, researching, bureaucratic, medical, technical, financial, accounting, legal, industrial, military, social work, and last but not least, psychology and psychiatry. It is a position that passes pretty well in the huge hierarchies that have become the bastion of our economy. If television and related distractions take up the remaining six hours of the day, it is a position that gets millions through life altogether.

The half-in, half-out position is selected by the strong force in the life of man: the need to feel secure by having a place. The other forces are relatively weak in the long run, although the urge to mate has its season of strength and can return in small bursts. In short, the particular person needs to be half-in/half-out to reduce his anxiety, and the firm needs him to be half-in/half-out to do its dull work. It is overwhelmingly probable that he will remain in this orbit. It is essentially the life of an official. "The Death of Ivan Illych" (Tolstoy 1886) is the grimmest version I know, and "The Secret Life of Walter Mitty" (Thurber 1942) and "The Catbird Seat" (Thurber 1953) are the two funniest versions. Gogol had a great eye for it as well, which is simultaneously grim and hilarious, as in "Nevsky Prospect" (1835) and "The Nose" (1836), and finally in his epic on the subject, Dead Souls (1842).

Any doctor who is foolish enough to think he is going to move a planetary official out of his orbit is going to have a long series of blunders. Often, their wives wish the doctor to move their husbands. Often, they wish the doctor to move themselves into a world in which they will have all the company they need to make up for their husbands and for their poor parents. Allow me to conduct a small parade of such cases, to show how they look promising when seen alone in the consulting room, and how futile they are when seen with the wider angle on the field of group life.

A Parade of Schizoid Compromises, or Officials

"The Necklace" (de Maupassant 1884): This brief story can stand at the head of the parade, for it has all the earmarks in a beautiful and unforgettable economy of plot. First, it has the charm of the protagonist when taken by herself: "She was one of those pretty and charming girls who are sometimes, as if by a mistake of destiny, born in a family of clerks" (p. 1024). Poor girl, she had to marry a little clerk for lack of any better offers, but she remains entitled: "Natural fineness, instinct for what is elegant, suppleness of wit, are the sole hierarchy, and make from women of the people the equals of the very greatest ladies" (pp. 1024– 1025). De Maupassant writes as if he shares her view. The irony is photographic. He has a picture of her world, which makes the actual hierarchy disappear into the background. He is playing the sympathetic doctor, and by this irony shows us how we are likely as well to get into collusion with such women.

Now, he will explode her myth of herself by taking her into the outer world. Her clerk husband brings an invitation to a ball. To make a brief story as brief as possible, she borrows a pearl necklace from a rich schoolgirl-friend, has a moment of ephemeral glory at the ball, loses the necklace on the way home, and she and her husband spend the next ten years in desperate and unending and ruinous labor to pay back the sum of money needed to buy a substitute set of pearls. Finally, spent, she meets the friend again and confesses the substitution, only to learn from the friend that the original necklace was made of paste. She has been completely taken by her fantasy of glory. She is quite typical, as the following series will illustrate.

The Case of the Therapist as Patient

Because her parents neglected her so, this patient became determined to look after others well. She did, and wore herself out. A little pretty still, she gets us to wish for her. She meets a man who used to have a girlfriend. Now, he has gotten rid of her and is really available, she imagines. She falls for him. He hasn't really gotten rid of this girlfriend. She decides, needing some compensation for her pain, to take a trip to South America. She buys the last available ticket for two thousand dollars on a special deal. She really hasn't any money.

She wants to know why this keeps happening to her. I draw her a little picture, shown in Figure 18–2. What she wants to know, at bottom, is whether she is hopeless, and ought not to come anymore. Well, I reply, *the plot is hopeless*, but I don't know about her. Obviously, she cannot afford to be *for herself* if this means being completely impulsive. She replies that she could be *less* impulsive if her twin sister were around to talk her impulses over with, but she is not. So now what?

My reply to her is that she has a twin sister inside of herself, which is her double to her conscious mind, of her unconscious mind. She has begun to turn to it a little, and now we will see if she can attend further. Of course, I have a dilemma myself, implicit in this reply. If I

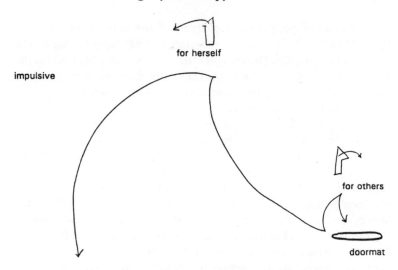

impulsive

for herself

for others

doormat

Figure 18–2. Helping Profession Syndrome.

collude with her false hope, she will have more foolish impulsiveness. If I deny hope altogether, I can push her over the edge now. I am not keen on optimism, nor pessimism. I chose to be altogether pessimistic about the plot, and very guardedly leave open a little room for her.

A Case of Dread in Asking for Help

As Guntrip (1968) showed so well, dreams are no panacea either for patients in this half-in and half-out orbit, for dreams can be utilized to distance the doctor in a kind of solipsistic world. For example, a patient of mine caught up like the last case in helping everyone else get looked after, dreamt as follows:

> She was in an airplane hangar getting a course on flying small planes. Busy assisting those around her, she missed some instructions . . . but was terrified to ask the instructor to repeat them to her.

Here is a typical dream for these patients. They are fine when others need them, but they are in terror needing something for themselves. This is true for her, with her parents, her former husbands, her friends, and with me (in the transference as it were). She is able to show directly her fear of needing me, in my consulting room. We can work on it. The same fear on the larger stage of family, friends, and romance, and work, and society, is much more difficult, for the instructors there are not necessarily going to adjust to her dread of them. Often, they are cruel, and often they are kind.

Her education has come very slowly. She has learned from me how to be ready for the cruel. She has a much more difficult time with half-decent relationships. Since everyone is so self-centered around her, they are nice when it suits them, and nasty when crossed. She never knows which. I think to myself that she'd do better to flip a coin when asking anything of them. Thus, she would stay mindful of her chances. This kind of readiness comes slowly. It is so hard to learn that people are motivated by fitting into their group and by pleasing themselves. The exceptions only draw one away from the rule.

I find it comes more readily to those who know how to enjoy themselves solo. This makes turning to others less momentous, as well as less impulsive. Those with a sport, or music, or nature, fare the best in getting an education about how to cope with other people. There is just less weight on it, so they can study it with less desperation.

The Case of Two Wounded and Well-Intentioned People

Of course, this case has millions of variations, but the variations are less important than the probable stalemate. Let us say that both had terrorizing mothers. The husband's chief line of defense is distance. The wife's chief line of defense is taking charge herself. She takes charge of him, and brings him to me. What is going to happen?

The best moments will occur in my office, and perhaps the only moments. He feels safer there, because I will step in if he is being run over. This is apt to be encouraging to her, for she is less abandoned. The trouble is that he is not likely to be willing to chance it when I am not there. This will make her furious.

From her point of view, he should come out of his mouse hole. The trouble is that he is also an elephant, disguised as a mouse. When he comes out, he is apt to make huge claims. For example, he will take charge of her householding, and run it down. This is wounding to her brittle dominion, she snaps; he is wounded, and flees back to his hiding place.

The dilemma is this: she rules, he hides, and both become bitter—she for the lack of company, he for the lack of the liberty to speak up. When he comes to show himself, he is himself a dictator and wounds her beyond repair. You see how difficult a stalemate we have here, pictured in Figure 18–3. Many, naturally, go nowhere, even with years and years of work. He cannot refrain from dictating, when he gets his opening. She cannot stop him, without getting wounded beyond repair.

Some can do this, and they take a turn for the better. I have some nice examples of husbands like this coming out of their corners, with some careful and measured steps. One enjoyed conducting trials of his wife in my office, in excellent humor, which made her laugh. His wife also could respond with indicting him in such a way that he could laugh back. It is possible to get somewhere with these, and it is possible to get absolutely nowhere.

Like Selvini-Palazzoli and colleagues (1989), I do best by putting the test to them as accurately as I can. I pose the problem of the husband's reaction needing to be carefully measured. I pose the problem

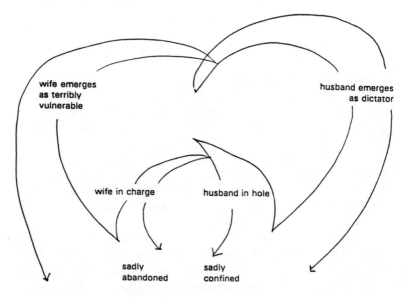

Figure 18–3. Spouse Cancellation.

of the wife's needing to let him know when she is over her head in response. Then, they manage the powerful currents, or they go too far. It is very chancy. (Sullivan [1956, pp. 243–246] has a great example of the force being handled in humor. He knew how to pose the problem, but it was also lucky how the two patients stumbled upon a humorous solution. This was a lesbian couple.)

A Case of Widening the Field

One of these brittle women like those Selvini-Palazzoli found so often in charge in Milan took in tow one of our female residents as a kind of lady-in-waiting to settle her down from her tempers. They made an excellent pair; I have come to think of them as Cleopatra and Charmian from Shakespeare's *Antony and Cleopatra* (1607). Now they became more ambitious. Cleopatra wanted Dr. Charmian also to fix her son who had rampages quite like her own, "clearing the board," and to fix her husband, who had headaches that were unintelligible to all the neurologists.

To make a long story short, Dr. Charmian brought in the entire family and found herself with big forces indeed. The husband confided to her that he was very angry with Cleopatra but feared to be put out of doors for it, and, lo, his headaches went away. Now, he flirted with Charmian, increasingly, which the Queen might not like, exactly. The Queen now showed her viciousness to the oldest daughter, which Dr. Charmian noted out loud. The Queen did not like this, either.

Dr. Charmian became quite anxious about her position in the court and consulted with me. I agreed she was getting herself into very hazardous waters. She served only with the Queen's pleasure, which was going to get quite scarce. Indeed, the Queen might feel quite helpless, if her husband flirted increasingly with Dr. Charmian, and if Dr. Charmian began to criticize her severity on the poor daughter. I told Dr. Charmian she might want to retreat to the smaller field of attending upon the Queen, who might feel quite ill herself at recent developments among these upstarts.

Smaller fields are often more manageable. See the Milan team on "Snares in Family Therapy" (Selvini-Palazzoli and Prata 1982) for a nice discussion on such hooking of the doctor to serve the dominant player in the family game. It is, after all, the classical role of the doctor in the family. Another example of this type of situation occurred to me the other day when I noted to a patient how her pain in being left as a child was like her pain being left in the present. She floundered, until I suggested that we confine ourselves to what she was looking at just now. This smaller field was bearable, while the larger field was not.

The Case of the Forest Ranger Ten Years Later

In my first book (1986), I described how a young man in college had been driven nearly to suicide by the persistent advice of a friend that he needed to be closer to other people, which he could not bear to be. Finally, I was able to convey to him that it was valid to enjoy the wide open spaces of being by himself, and he was able to put the friend at arm's length. I saw him again ten years later in a similar predicament, which I will now delineate.

He had been functioning pretty well, but he had found it necessary to take antidepressants to stabilize himself. He had contracted a medical condition that made taking the antidepressants a hazard, and his physician had insisted he discontinue them. He felt pushed to the wall, and became suicidal again.

I recognized his tremendous sensitivity to being told what to do from ten years previously. I was alarmed as before by his wild demeanor. I told him that I would talk with his medical doctor concerning his dictum that he could no longer take antidepressants. After all, he might be able to take them if he himself was willing to run the risks of the complications of his medical condition.

I talked with the doctor about the dilemma. I explained the patient's wild and desperate transference to the dictum against continuing antidepressants, and I appreciated the other risk of giving them. The doctor decided it was a great deal less dangerous to let the patient make up his mind about which risk he preferred. This is a classic story about managing medications. Often, the forces set in motion are transferences to intrusions like this, or abandonments, which no amount of medication can control.

This patient was very appealing in my consulting room where I give him plenty of room, yet he was nearly impaled in the world by being cornered by a doctor with a dictum, and by the patient allowing this to occur. His flaw had been nearly tragic, twice. After this one critical session, I wrote him a letter in which I said I hoped he would not let himself get pressed to the wall a third time.

Dilemmas and Related Concepts

After my parade of six schizoid compromises, seen individually, and seen at the mercy of group forces in the world, the reader may well understand how it is I have learned to reckon these forces the hard way, that is, by getting them wrong.

As I write this concluding chapter, I take walks with some of my patients around our beautiful marsh, rather than sit with them in my stuffy office. In this, I follow Freud's famous example (E. Jones 1955, pp. 79–80). I find it alters my perspective in a useful way. I see them out in the world ever so much more clearly than I would in my consulting room. I see them against the background of the marsh, the spring sky, and the capitol building in the distance. I see their faces against this background, and, interestingly, they are less beautiful and more flawed! The walking cure situates my patients in the world, better than the sitting cure.

Walking with my patients out in the world would not be an advantage if I were merely coming along with whatever myth was propelling them. We would be in a cloud together. For example, we might imagine that being half-in and half-out of the world was likely to lead to a new place.

Perhaps, this illusion would be propelled not only by the myth of the patient, but also by the myth of the doctor as well. We promise much. Some of us fight impasses, some of us provide safe places, and others create new stories. These correspond to what Bion (1959) called the basic assumptions of fight (baF), dependency (baD), and pairing (baP). Mobilizing an instinct like this can seem to take us anywhere, especially when there is an entire school of practice, publishing, and advertising as an advance and rear guard for such an army. This is what Kundera (1990) means by imagology. It is persuasive. It is the apparatus of group life in the late twentieth century.

Work and Love

There are two great dangers for our patients and for ourselves as their doctors. We can be taken in by myths and be mystified by them. We can be left out. In this sense, all dilemmas are about being in a group, or out of a group. Both are dangerous. We are always having to decide whether to be in or out with respect to any given opportunity. Often, we need to reckon the *size* of the trouble inside, and the *size* of the trouble outside. There is going to be trouble *either* way, and we need to gauge which is *more*, and *less*, for us.

A Case of Academic Darkness

My patient, a professor, was trying to decide whether to stay in his department or not. He had spent a great deal of time trying to persuade his colleagues to follow his political lead. He dreamt that he was going to his office in a quadrangle, to fix the two lights in his office. He found the two lamps with their sockets busted out. Worse, he found that his quadrangle was connected to another quadrangle, and another, and another, endlessly. His unconscious was being graphic. His lights weren't going to alter the darkness, and the darkness was not just his department, but an entire archipelago of departments. His dream diminished his light, while multiplying the darkness. It could not have been clearer about the scale of his difficulty as an insider, which his conscious mind had underestimated.

A Case of the Three Love Machines

Another patient felt a terrible failure at love, and put off discussing it with me for shame and for fear of feeling even worse about herself than she already did. At last, she got up her courage, and went over her history. Her first love was a Catholic boy who was very fond of her until he had sex with her. The second was a boy of puritanical background who was never interested in sex with her. The third was a boy who had gone to boarding schools, and was interested in sex with other men. He was cherubic at first, and sado-masochistic later.

I startled her by saying that she now had a complete education. She had been run over by the three love machines: sacred, profane, and diabolical! Now, she has a fair chance of reading the next one.

She had been so anxious to be included by a man that the results were terrible. She had spent some time being excluded, and the results were lonely. At last, she might be mature in her reckoning of which suffering she might prefer, and how much. Her detachment from this melancholia of self-blame came from an actual, accurate orientation to what was done to her, and what was her error of misreading their purposes. Of course, it was a big step in a series of steps. Here is a beautiful example of what Freud meant in "Mourning and Melancholia" (1917). Mourning becomes stuck as melancholia as long as the patient cannot sort out the blame.

The History of Dilemma as a Concept

The word dilemma is Greek, referring to something that has two lemmas or two preliminary assumptions. Its first known use was Latin, in the first century B.C., by Cicero (Chandler 1995, Craig 1993) (my thanks to Professor Denis Feeney for finding this), and in the fourth century A.D., by Saint Jerome. The idea was that a dilemma had two horns, that it had two divergent and preliminary assumptions. You could get hung up on either horn, or you could hang up your opponent there in argument. Thus, a standard argument in the Middle Ages would run: "You haven't lost horns, therefore you have horns" (Sherri Reames, personal communication). With all the love of public disputation, the concept of dilemma still remained peripheral. At least, the texts of medieval philosophy never accord it the honor of being in their indexes (Hyman and Walsh 1967).

It continues as an occasional use in the sixteenth and seventeenth centuries, as a problem with contradictions or with horns that hang up a person or an argument. (The Oxford English Dictionary cites: 1551 T. Wilson *Logike* [1580] 34b, "Dilemma, otherwise . . . called a horned argument, is when the reason consisteth of repugnant members, so that whatsoever you grant, you fall into the snare"), and so forth. Especially, it means a situation in which there are two alternatives, and both have their difficulties. In politics, posing the dilemma is a regular reply of presidents, senators, and representatives to queries of their constituents (Ian Gustafson, personal communication). See Eckholm (1993), for example. If you listen to ordinary conversation, you will find it cropping up now and again in this loose sense of two unpalatable alternatives: "I am in a dilemma about x. . . ."

Indeed, I have located a veritable host of words that mean about the same thing. Many of these I found in conversation and in texts of all kinds, and many in *Roget's Thesaurus* (1946):

dilemma	embarrassment
conflict	bewilderment
pickle	indetermination
predicament	divergent problem
quandary	confounded
catch (22)	confused
tangle	enigma
strange loop	difficulty
bolix	deadlock
being nonplussed	gordian knot
complex	maze
plight	slough
reversal	quagmire
conundrum	stew
paradox	imbroglio
contradiction	mess
snafu	botch
pass (as sorry pass)	hitch
corner (boxed into a)	stumbling block
fix	hard nut
puzzle	bother!
uncertainty	hard pressed
suspension (in)	disjunction
perplexity	catastrophe (as in catastrophe theory)

Heretofore, only two of these words on the list have gotten much service in psychotherapy, namely: conflict, and, to a much lesser extent, paradox. (Ryle [1994, 1990] uses dilemma in a reductive and merely cognitive sense as "false choices and narrow options" [1994, p. 99]. See Calahan and Sashin [1990] for a brilliant discussion of catastrophe theory. It overlaps chaos theory [Schmidt unpublished and Schmid 1991], and my topology of dilemmas. I will discuss the relation of these three theories in my next book, on dreams.) The latter is hardly heard after being in fashion in family therapy for a while. Conflict remains a fixed term of the psychoanalytic constellation.

Conflict versus Dilemma

Conflict was introduced in mid-career by Freud as a key term in his structural model of id, super-ego, and ego. By conflict, he means a very specific kind of conflict between id-satisfaction and super-ego-prohibition. A typical usage in his *New Introductory Lectures* (1933) runs like this: "Conflict is produced by frustration, in that the libido which lacks satisfaction is urged to seek other paths and other objects" (p. 358). Indeed, the course of conflict is what makes a patient suffer from neurotic symptoms:

> The rejected libidinal longings manage to pursue their course by circuitous paths, though not indeed without paying toll to the prohibition in the form of certain disguises and modifications. The circuitous paths are the ways of symptom-formation; the symptoms are the new and substitutive satisfactions necessitated by the fact of this frustration. [p. 358] . . . The pathogenic conflict is, therefore, one between the ego instinct and the sexual instincts. [p. 359]

The word conflict is from the Latin, *confligere,* which means to strike together. In colloquial use, it can refer to political conflicts, or social conflicts, or family conflicts. In Freud's use, it refers only to conflicts between sexual impulses and ego (or super-ego) prohibition.

It also is confined by Freud and his tradition to something that goes on inside an individual. Indeed, to say *internal* conflict is to be redundant. A patient is always said to *have* a conflict.

Compare dilemma as I use it in this book. I could use the term conflict to mean opposing considerations that strike together—instead of dilemma. I do not for a number of reasons. First of all, the word has been so coopted by psychoanalysis to mean internal conflict. I want a term that carries readily from inside to outside and back again. Secondly, the word is something one *has*—as opposed to something one is *in*. I want a term that denotes a territory that an individual has to live in one way or another. After all, one might have a conflict, resolve it, and no longer have it. A dilemma is something one remains in, as a territory to be lived. Thirdly, the word conflict refers in its Latin origin to action, to two things striking each other, as in combat. I am interested in such combat, but I want a term that is deeper. I want to indicate something that has roots that precede action, for my patients often are in dilemmas that throttle them long before they do anything about them. Thus, I like the idea of the very assumptions that they bring being antithetical. They are in trouble before they begin to feel, think, or act, because the ground they stand on is pulled apart.

It may be objected that dilemma has excessive cognitive connotations from medieval disputation. It has these connotations, no doubt. I find the ordinary person using the word long before I do to mean something that also is extremely upsetting, and dividing the will, and confounding action. In brief, it is cognitive, affective, willful, and behavioral—it disturbs all the usual faculties, and so serves my purpose as the central term of the drama of the lives of my patients. When I summarize my view after a session, I have never had a patient blink or falter over the word, either orally or in writing. Ordinary people know full well what it means in their lives, only they have just managed to overlook it because it is so hard to bear. My job is to face the dilemma with them.

Dilemma and Myth

To conclude, I want to be as clear as I can about the relationship of these two terms. The implications for me are profound. A myth is a story of a group about its heroes, their values, and the consequent struggles they must undergo. As I have taken pains to explain concerning Levi-Strauss's explication of myth, myth turns out to be mystification because it seems to make a clash of opposing terms, of good and of evil, come out all right. In this sense, a myth is a machine for the suppression of time. It has always been so, and will be so, as the Episcopalians repeat in their ritual: world without end, amen. A loyal insider to the group simply plays his part in the myth, without question, as hero, or as go-between, or as servant (an overpowering, delay or subservient character/story [Gustafson 1992]). An outsider has no place, whatsoever.

As Slater (1976) and many others have argued, a group or culture is likely to have a dominant myth, and an alternative myth. For us, there is the Frontier Myth of endless conquest in which we impose our terms on whatever land, peoples, or objects we come across in our expansion (C. Gustafson unpublished, a). Also for us, there is an alternative and cooperative myth in which we rally to support each other in the wake of wars, tornadoes, and floods. We are colonizers, first, and cooperators, second.

The culture or group may last a very, very long time in the terms of myth, and countermyth, as ours in America has for these nearly four hundred years. The trouble for individual beings, who become our patients, is that the myth is fine for the lasting of the group, while discarding a great many individuals. Indeed, a myth can have a period of flourishing, as for us when land was plentiful, and a period of decline, as for us when land is not plentiful. Whereas before we were all sheep of the Lord, we are now, and increasingly, sheep, and goats (Kozol 1967). The slope to the right is getting steeper by the week, and the goats need all their agility to keep from being pushed over the very edge to oblivion. Myths deteriorate in terms of keeping their promises, and their adherents become increasingly disturbed.

The Average Patient of Psychiatry

This is our situation, which is nearly an epidemic at the close of the twentieth century. The average patient of psychiatry who comes in for a visit is nearly always the same patient. She has been hurt by several self-serving men, and she has a job in which she is treated rather poorly, and her family seems more to blame her than help her. I know what she is going to say, before she gets two feet inside my office.

In other words, she believes in the romance (myth) of America the Beautiful, and it is letting her down very badly, in terms of mating (basic assumption pairing), earning a living (basic assumption fight-flight), and getting support (basic assumption dependency). My job, as I have explained so fully in this book, is to come to her defense, in seeing where the drift of her life is taking her, and in seeing where some opposite (and romantic) ideas (of a countermyth) will take her even worse. If she cannot rally, she will pass rapidly from hopeful childhood to sorry resignation. "Bright children do grow up to be dull. I wish I knew why. The century's mystery is that intelligent children become teenage louts, who grow up to be pompous dullards. I'd like to know why" (Davenport 1994). (I am grateful to Michael Moran [personal communication] for this reference.) I will pose to her her dilemma of letting it slide further, and her alternative of opposing this slide without arranging to be punished by her impulsiveness.

Thus, the concept of dilemma demystifies the myth which suppresses time. It poses time, and where it is going. It also poses alternatives, which are always myths as well, and where they are going.

Interestingly, dilemma is a plough that also relieves us of the burying of the past. Once a myth is demystified, and the countermyth is also demystified, a great deal of the past is no longer suppressed, but rather fully available as a file for review, as in the final case with which I conclude this book.

A Case of a Professor Assimilating His Unconscious

As I worked with one patient, a professor, and he became adept at utilizing his dreams, he had two remarkable dreams that summarized sixty years for him. The first was of his social life, and the second of his work.

In the first, he went to a party at a colleague's, which was like a visit to the Salvation Army. A rag-tag collection of people were performing very poor skits, for the general amusement. He left, in flight, with his wife, crossing over a frozen lake, through wire fences, and to a beautiful house, only the wife of his colleague came to remonstrate him for leaving her party. He and his wife ran out the door. Next he knew, his wife was holding up a grocery store, with a revolver, to get bus money, and soon he and she were fleeing over rooftops in Belfast and jumping into abandoned yards of old warehouses to flee the police!

As I said to him, after a long analysis of this dream, you get in too far, and then you get out too far. As if in reply, he dreamt four days later of his career at work. He had been in opposition for forty years, with little success. He dreamt he was the hero of Conrad's novel, *The Secret Agent* (1907), only he had decided to disassemble the plot. Behind a curtain wall in his college dormitory room, he had kept duffels of supplies for the revolution. Now, he took down the curtain, and unpacked the duffels, which only had camping gear, after all. For one last look, he climbed out his window behind the curtain, using clamps as in mountain climbing, but his wife walking by looked up, and he realized how silly he was attacking down the side of his own house—his own kitchen. He was biting the hand that fed him.

I didn't need to say anything about this dream to him, for he disassembled himself the countermyth of himself as secret agent. He could not be in, and he could not be out, and would have to be himself, in different proportions of in and out.

Conclusion

If the bimodal force field is as extremely powerful as I contend, it will be something to become oriented like my patient the professor and keep from making a complete fool of himself, or end up in a disastrous situation. It would be disappointing if that were all.

It is not all. As I was finishing up this book, I was drawn back to Raymond Carney's (1986) essay on Henry Adams. Here was the reply to my sense that group life swallows almost everything that is briefly individual (Ruth Gustafson, personal communication). Adams came to the same conclusion nearly a hundred years before I did (Shakespeare preceded Adams by three hundred years in *As You Like It* [1600]): "The individual, in Adams' conception of the situation, is born into a network of impersonal systems of meaning and social relations that make mere individual motives and intentions almost irrelevant and always marginal in their effects" (xxii). In a phrase, the individual is erased, and becomes a type that is governed by the force field in which he is set.

Yes, thought Adams, but he who reads the field, steps free of its mechanical action: "In meditation or in reflection is a kind of freedom, a margin for imaginative movement, room for vision and re-vision" (xxxii). Literally, as I read Carney's summary of the movement of Adams's thinking, I moved in the margins of his pages where I made my own notes and arrows, and there I lived freely. I took my liberty from the gravity of the text. This is the space that Adams meant can belong to us.

If the text is in but two dimensions per page and three dimensions for the thickness of the book, the reader can move in it as he chooses with all of his or her senses and past, present, and future interests, concerns, and dreams. This is surely a hyperspace of ten dimensions at least. We are free to move thus, if we are not driven by the bimodal space that makes us one-sided and serious and racing in the regime, or dallying in our imaginations, when the bell is ringing for us.

I have had many, many dreams about this realm of being free, and I conclude with just one. I was starting out from Poughkeepsie on the Hudson River looking west. My back was turned on Boston and New York. I felt like one of those pioneers, who had gotten free of the eastern seaboard, and looked into an incredible creation to the west. A freeway like a German autobahn ran due west, with the usual traffic. I found to my pleasure that I was riding west on a railroad with an invisible track that took me in a kind of sine wave along the line of the freeway as its axis, but with beautiful swinging to the right and to the left.

In other words, a liberal education in psychotherapy ought to free me from the horizontal of history into the vertical of the imagination with such scope afforded as the view of the open West in this dream. Yet, it need also bring me back down to earth. For I, my patients, and my readers will all have to reenter some regime which will have its own autobahn. The daily challenge is to get freely back and forth between the force field and the margins that belong to us.

References

Adams, H. (1907). *The Education of Henry Adams*. Boston: Houghton Mifflin, 1961.

Agee, J. (1938). *A Death in the Family*. New York: Avon Books, 1959.

Albee, E. (1964). *Who's Afraid of Virginia Woolf?* London: Jonathan Cape.

Alexander, F., and French, T. M. (1946). *Psychoanalytic Therapy, Principles and Applications*. New York: Ronald Press.

Allen, T. F. H., and Starr, T. B. (1982). *Hierarchy, Perspectives for Ecological Complexity*. Chicago: University of Chicago Press.

Aquinas, T. (1972). *An Aquinas Reader*. Edited by Mary T. Clark. New York: Fordham University Press.

Arendt, H. (1963). *Eichmann in Jerusalem: A Report on the Banality of Evil*. New York: Penguin.

Aristotle. (1934). *Poetics*. London: J. M. Dent & Sons.

———— (1991). *Art of Rhetoric*. New York: Penguin.

Asch, S. S. (1976). Varieties of negative therapeutic reaction and problems of technique. *Journal of the American Psychoanalytic Association* 24:383– 407.

Aurelius, M. (1986). *Meditations*, trans. Maxwell Stamforth. New York: Dorset Press.

Ba, M. (1980). *So Long a Letter*. Portsmouth, New Hampshire: Heineman.

Bachelard, G. (1971). *On Poetic Imagination and Reverie*. Selected and translated by C. Gaudin. Dallas: Spring Publications.

Balint, E., and Norell, J. S. (1973). *Six Minutes for the Patient*. London: Tavistock.

Balint, M. (1952). New beginning and paranoid and depressive syndromes. *International Journal of Psychoanalysis* 33:214. Reprinted in M. Balint, *Primary Love and Psychoanalytic Technique.* New York: Liveright, 1953.

———— (1957). *The Doctor, His Patient, and the Illness.* New York: International Universities Press.

———— (1968). *The Basic Fault, Therapeutic Aspects of Regression.* London: Tavistock.

Balint, M., Ornstein, P., and Ornstein, A. (1972). *Focal Psychotherapy, an Example of Applied Psychoanalysis.* London: Tavistock.

Balzac, H. de (1835). *Pere Goriot.* New York: Modern Library, 1946.

Bateson, G. (1971). The cybernetics of "self": a theory of alcoholism. *Psychiatry* 34:1–17.

———— (1972). *Steps toward an Ecology of Mind.* New York: Ballantine.

———— (1979). *Mind and Nature. A Necessary Unity.* New York: Bantam.

Bauer, J. (1978). *In the Troll Wood.* Text by Rudstrom. English version by O. Jones. London and New York: Methuen.

Baum, L. F. (1900). *The Wizard of Oz.* New York: Grosset and Dunlap, 1956.

Bayes, M., and Newton, P. M. (1978). Women in authority: a sociopsychological analysis. *The Journal of Applied Behavioral Science* 14:7–20.

Bayley, J. (1966). *Tolstoy and the Novel.* Chicago: University of Chicago Press.

———— (1981). *Shakespeare and Tragedy.* London: Routledge and Kegan Paul.

———— (1988). *The Short Story.* New York: St. Martin's Press.

Beels, C. (1991). An interview with Chris Beels. Interviewed by S. Madigan. *Dulwich Centre Newsletter* 4:13–21.

Ben Isiah, A., and Sharfman, B. (1949). *The Pentateuch and Rashi's Commentary.* Brooklyn, New York: S. S. and R. Publishing.

Bennett, H. J. (1993). *The New England Kernel of Medicine.*

Bennett, M. J. (1983). Focal psychotherapy—terminable and interminable. *American Journal of Psychotherapy* 37:365–375.

———— (1985). Focal behavioral psychotherapy for acute narcissistic injury: "De Mopes"—report of a case. *American Journal of Psychotherapy* 39: 126–133.

Berger, P. L., and Kellner, H. (1964). Marriage and the construction of reality: an exercise in the microsociology of knowledge. *Diogenes* 46:1–24.

Bergman, S. J. (1994). The house of God: a historical perspective. *Harvard Medical Alumni Bulletin,* Summer, pp. 33–35.

Bermel, A. (1982). *Farce.* New York: Simon and Schuster.

Bernstein, B. (1973). *Class, Codes and Control.* St. Albin, Herts, England: Paladin.

Bibring, E. (1953). The mechanism of depression. In *Affective Disorders, Psychoanalytic Contributions to Their Study,* ed. P. Greenacre. New York: International Universities Press.

Binswanger, L. (1963). Extravagence (*Verstiegenheit*). In *Being-in-the-World: Selected Papers of Ludwig Binswanger*, ed. L. Binswanger. New York: Harper and Row, 1967.

Bion, W. R. (1959). *Experiences in Groups*. New York: Basic Books.

Blake, W. (1987). *The Essential Blake*. Selected by Stanley Kunitz. New York: Ecco Press.

Bly, C. (1981). *Letters from the Country*. New York: Harper and Row.

Bly, R. (1975). *Friends, You Drank Some Darkness. Three Swedish Poets: Martinson, Ekelof, and Tranströmer*. Boston: Beacon Press.

Borges, J. L. (1971). The congress. In *The Book of Sand*, ed. J. L. Borges. London: Penguin.

Bourdieu, P. (1977). *Outline of a Theory of Practice*. Cambridge, England: Cambridge University Press.

—— (1984). *Distinction: A Social Critique of the Judgement of Taste*. Cambridge, MA: Harvard University Press.

—— (1988). *Homo Academicus*. Translated by Peter Collier. Stanford, California: Stanford University Press.

Brenman, M. (1952). On teasing and being teased: and the problem of "moral masochism." In *Psychoanalytic Study of the Child*, 7:264–285. New York: International Universities Press.

Breuer, J., and Freud, S. (1895). *Studies on Hysteria*. New York: Avon Press, 1966. Also *Standard Edition* 2.

Breytenbach, B. (1991). The exile as African. *Harper's Magazine*, May, pp. 39–44.

Bridgman, P. W. (1959). *The Way Things Are*. Cambridge, MA: Harvard University Press.

Broadway, J. (1993). A dream called Madison. *Wisconsin State Journal*, July 6, p. 1.

Brodkey, H. (1994). Dying: an update. *The New Yorker*, February 7, pp. 70–84.

Brodsky, J. (1986). *Less Than One: Selected Essays*. New York: Farrar, Straus & Giroux.

—— (1988). Uncommon visage: the Nobel lecture. *The New Republic*, January 4 and 11, pp. 27–32.

Brook, P. (1982). Freud's masterplot. In *The Question of Reading: Literature and Psychoanalysis*, ed. S. Felman. Baltimore: Johns Hopkins University Press.

Browne, T. (1682). Religio Medici. In *Seventeenth-Century Prose and Poetry*, ed. A. M. Witherspoon and F. J. Warnke. New York: Harcourt, Brace and World, 1963.

Buzzati, D. (1989). The falling girl. In *Sudden Fiction International*, ed. R. Shopard and J. Thomas, pp. 29–34. New York: W. W. Norton.

Byatt, A. S., ed. (1992). The TLS Poetry Competition. In *Passions of the Mind*, pp. 174–176. New York: Random House.

Callahan, J., and Sashin, J. I. (1986). Models of affect-response and anorexia nervosa. *Annals of the New York Academy of Sciences* 504:241–259.

——— (1990). Predictive models in psychoanalysis. *Behavioral Science* 35:60–76.

Calvino, l. (1972). *Invisible Cities.* Translated by William Weaver. New York: Harcourt Brace Jovanovich.

Cameron, N. (1961). Introjection, retrojection and hallucination in the interaction between schizophrenic patient and therapist. *International Journal of Psychoanalysis* 42:86–96.

Campbell, J. (1949). *The Hero with a Thousand Faces.* Princeton, New Jersey: Princeton University Press.

——— (1959). *The Masks of God: Primitive Mythology.* New York: Penguin.

——— (1964). *The Masks of God: Occidental Mythology.* New York: Penguin.

——— (1989). *An Open Life: In Conversation with Michael Toms.* New York: Harper and Row.

———, ed. (1971). *The Portable Jung.* New York: Penguin.

Canetti, E. (1960). *Crowds and Power.* Translated by Carol Stewart. New York: Continuum, 1981.

Carney, R. (1986). Introduction to *Mont-Saint-Michel and Chartres,* by H. Adams, pp. ix–xxxvii. New York: Penguin.

Carotenuto, A. (1982). *A Secret Symmetry: Sabina Spielrein between Jung and Freud.* Translated by John Shepley, Krishna Winston, and Arno Pomerans. New York: Pantheon.

Carroll, L. (1865). *Alice in Wonderland.* Illustrated by Michael Hague. New York: Henry Holt and Company, 1985.

Cassill, R. V. (1986). *The Norton Anthology of Short Fiction.* New York: W. W. Norton.

Chandler, C. E. (1995). Review of *Form as Argument in Cicero's Speeches,* by Christopher P. Craig, *Scholia Reviews* 4:1–5.

Chandrasekhar, S. (1989). The perception of beauty and the pursuit of science. *Bulletin of the American Academy of Arts and Sciences,* December, pp. 14–29.

Charbonnier, G. (1969). *Conversations with Claude Levi-Strauss.* Translated by John and Doreen Weightman. London: Jonathan Cape.

Chatelaine, K. L. (1981). *Harry Stack Sullivan, The Formative Years.* Washington, D.C.: University Press of America.

Cocks, G. (1985). *Psychotherapy in the Third Reich: The Göring Institute.* New York: Oxford University Press.

Colinvaux, P. (1983). Human history: a consequence of plastic niche but fixed breeding strategy. In *Environment and Population,* ed. J. B. Calhoun. New York: Praeger.

Comte, A. (1830). *Introduction to Positive Philosophy.* Indianapolis: Hackett, 1988.

Connell, E. (1945). The corset. In *The Norton Anthology of Short Fiction*, ed. R. V. Cassill. New York: W. W. Norton, 1986.

Conrad, J. (1907). *The Secret Agent*. London: Methuen.

Craig, C. P. (1993). *Form as Argument in Cicero's Speeches*. Atlanta: Scholars Press.

Dante. (1314). *Inferno*. Translated by Twenty Contemporary Poets. Edited by D. Halpern. New York: Ecco, 1993.

Darwin, C. (1899). *The Expression of the Emotions in Man and Animals*. New York: Appleton.

Davanloo, H. (1986). Intensive short-term psychotherapy with highly resistant patients. I. Handling resistance. *International Journal of Short-Term Psychotherapy* 1:107–133.

Davenport, G. (1994). *A Table of Green Fields*. New York: New Directions.

Deutsch, F. (1957). A footnote to Freud's "Fragment of an analysis of a case of hysteria." *Psychoanalytic Quarterly* 26:159–167.

Dickinson, E. (1960). *The Complete Poems of Emily Dickinson*, ed. T. H. Johnson. Boston: Little, Brown.

Dicks, H. V. (1967). *Marital Tensions*. New York: Basic Books.

Donne, J. (1988). To his mistress going to bed. In *The Essential Donne*, selected and edited by Amy Clampitt. New York: Ecco.

Donovan, J. M. (1986). An etiologic model of alcoholism. *American Journal of Psychiatry* 143:1–11.

Doyle, A. C. (1929). *Sherlock Holmes: The Complete Long Stories*. London: John Murray.

Durrenmatt, F. (1956). *The Visit*. New York: Grove Press.

——— (1962). *The Physicists*. Translated by J. Kirkup. New York: Grove Press.

Ebert, R. (1987). Avoiding murder by a violent patient. *The Psychiatric Times*, December, p.4.

Eckholm, E. (1993). Double sword for president—whose health is no. 1, businesses or workers? *New York Times*, August 23, pp. A1, A9.

Edelman, G. M. (1979). Group selection and phasic reentrant signaling: a theory of higher brain function. In *The Mindful Brain*, ed. G. M. Edelman and V. B. Mountcastle, pp. 51–100. Cambridge, MA: MIT Press.

——— (1982). Through a computer darkly: group selection and higher brain function. *Bulletin of the American Academy of Arts and Sciences* 36:20–49.

——— (1985). Neural Darwinism: population thinking and higher brain function. In *How We Know*, ed. M. Shafto, pp. 1–30. San Francisco: Harper and Row.

——— (1989). *Topobiology: An Introduction to Molecular Biology*. New York: Basic Books.

Eliot, G. (1871). *Middlemarch*. Harmondworth, Middlesex, England: Penguin, 1965.

Eliot, T. S. (1915). The love-song of J. Alfred Prufrock. In *The Waste Land and Other Poems*. New York: Harcourt Brace Jovanovich, 1958.

Ellmann, R. (1976). *The New Oxford Book of American Verse*. New York: Oxford University Press.

El Saadawi, N. (1975). *Woman at Point Zero*. Translated by Sherif Hetata. London: Zed Books, 1983.

Epston, D. (1989). *Collected Papers*. Adelaide, South Australia: Dulwich Centre Publications.

Erikson, E. H. (1954). The dream specimen of psychoanalysis. *Journal of the American Psychoanalytical Association* 2:5–56.

Ernst, M. (1973). *Inside the Sight*. Houston, Texas: Institute for the Arts, Rice University.

Estes, C. P. (1992). *Myths and Stories of the Wild Woman Archetype*. New York: Ballantine Books.

Fanon, F. (1963). *The Wretched of the Earth*. Translated by Constance Farrington. New York: Grove Press.

Faulkner, W. (1939). Barn burning. In *The Norton Anthology of Short Fiction*, ed. R. V. Cassill. New York: W. W. Norton, 1986.

——— (1942). The bear. In *The Norton Anthology of Short Fiction*, ed. R. V. Cassill. New York: W. W. Norton, 1986.

Flaubert, G. (1857). *Madame Bovary*. Translated by Paul de Man. New York: W. W. Norton, 1965.

Forster, E. M. (1910). *Howard's End*. Harmondsworth, Middlesex, England: Penguin.

——— (1924). *A Passage to India*. New York: Harcourt, Brace and World.

Foucault, M. (1961). *Madness and Civilization: A History of Insanity in the Age of Reason*. Translated by Richard Howard. New York: Vintage, 1973.

——— (1963). *The Birth of the Clinic: An Archaeology of Medical Perception*. Translated by A. M. Sheridan Smith. New York: Vintage, 1975.

——— (1975). *Discipline and Punish: The Birth of the Prison*. Translated by Alan Sheridan. New York: Vintage, 1979.

——— (1980). *Power/Knowledge: Selected Interviews and Other Writings*, ed. C. Gordon. New York: Pantheon Books.

Frank, J. (1971). *Persuasion and Healing*. Baltimore: Johns Hopkins University Press.

Freeman, W. J. (1991). The physiology of perception. *Scientific American* 264:78–85.

Freire, P. (1970). *Pedagogy of the Oppressed*. New York: Herder and Herder.

Freud, A. (1946). *The Ego and the Mechanisms of Defense*. New York: International Universities Press.

Freud, S. (1900). *The Interpretation of Dreams*. New York: Avon Press, 1965.

——— (1905). Fragment of an analysis of a case of hysteria. *Standard Edition* 7:3–122.

—— (1909). Notes upon a case of obsessional neurosis. *Standard Edition* 10:153–318.

—— (1910). A special type of object choice made by men. *Standard Edition* 11:163–176.

—— (1911). Psychoanalytic notes upon an autobiographical account of a case of paranoia (dementia paranoides). *Standard Edition* 12:3–84.

—— (1912, 1913, 1914, 1915). Recommendations for physicians on the psychoanalytic method of treatment. In *Freud, Therapy and Technique*, ed. P. Rieff. New York: Collier, 1963.

—— (1915–1917). *Introductory Lectures to Psychoanalysis.* Published in English as *A General Introduction to Psychoanalysis.* New York: Pocket Books, 1953.

—— (1917). Mourning and melancholia. In *General Psychological Theory, Papers on Meta-psychology*, ed. P. Rieff. New York: Collier, 1963.

—— (1918). From the history of an infantile neurosis. *Standard Edition* 17:3–124.

—— (1930). *Civilization and Its Discontents. Standard Edition* 21.

—— (1933). *New Introductory Lectures on Psychoanalysis.* New York: W. W. Norton.

—— (1937). Analysis terminable and interminable. *Standard Edition*, Volume 23.

—— (1938). *An Outline of Psychoanalysis.* New York: W. W. Norton, 1949.

—— (1989). *The Freud Reader.* Edited by P. Gay. New York: W. W. Norton.

Friedman, M., and Rosenman, R. H. (1974). *Type A Behavior and Your Heart.* New York: Fawcett Crest.

Frost, R. (1923). Fire and ice. In *The New Oxford Book of American Verse*, ed. R. Ellman. New York: Oxford Unviersity Press, 1976.

Frye, N. (1957). *Anatomy of Criticism. Four Essays.* Princeton, New Jersey: Princeton University Press.

Fussell, P. (1983). *Class.* New York: Ballantine Books.

Gabbard, G. O. (1994). *Psychodynamic Psychiatry in Clinical Practice.* Washington, D.C.: American Psychiatric Press.

Galbraith, J. K. (1981). *A Life in Our Times.* Boston: Houghton Mifflin.

Galdston, I. (1954). Sophocles contra Freud: a reassessment of the Oedipus Complex. *Bulletin New York Academy Medicine* 30:803–817.

Garcia, E. (1990). Somatic interpretation in a transference cure: Freud's treatment of Bruno Walter. *International Review of Psychoanalysis* 17:83–88.

Gardner, H. (1971). *Religion and Literature.* London: Faber and Faber.

Gaston, L., Piper, W. E., Debbane, E. G., et al. (1994). Alliance and technique for predicting outcome in short- and long-term psychotherapy. *Psychotherapy Research* 4:121–135.

Gedo, J. (1979). *Beyond Interpretation, Towards a Revised Theory for Psychoanalysis.* New York: International Universities Press.

Gill, M. (1954). Psychoanalysis and exploratory psychotherapy. *Journal of the American Psychoanalytic Association* 1:87–103.

Gilligan, C. (1990). Joining the resistance: psychology, politics, girls and women. *Michigan Quarterly Review* 29(4):501–536.

Gleick, J. (1988). *Chaos: Making a New Science.* London: Heinemann.

Goethe, J. W. von (1832). *Faust.* Translated by L. MacNeice. New York: Oxford, 1951.

Gogol, N. (1835). Nevsky Prospect. In *The Complete Tales of Nikolai Gogol*, vol. 1, ed. L. J. Kent, pp. 207–238. Chicago: University of Chicago Press, 1985.

——— (1836). The nose. In *The Complete Tales of Nikolai Gogol*, vol. 2, ed. L. J. Kent, pp. 215–239. Chicago: University of Chicago Press, 1985.

——— (1842). *Dead Souls*, trans. D. Magarshack. New York: Penguin, 1961.

Goldberg, A. (1975). A fresh look at perverse behavior. *International Journal of Psychoanalysis* 56:335–342.

Gosling, R. (1979). Another source of conservatism in groups. In *Exploring Individual and Organizational Boundaries*, ed. W. G. Lawrence. New York: John Wiley and Sons.

Gramsci, A. (1973). *Letters from Prison*, trans. L. Lawner. New York: Harper and Row.

Greenson, R. R. (1967). *The Technique and Practice of Psychoanalysis.* Vol. 1. New York: International Universities Press.

Grimm, J. L. K. (1819). *Grimm's Tales for Young and Old.* Translated by R. Manheim. New York: Doubleday, 1977.

Grinstein, A. (1968). *Sigmund Freud's Dreams.* New York: International Universities Press.

Guntrip, H. (1968). *Schizoid Phenomena, Object-Relations and the Self.* New York: International Universities Press.

Gustafson, C. (1994a). The myth of the American West.

——— (1994b). Piecing together person and place in *A Grain of Wheat* and *Nervous Conditions*.

Gustafson, J. P. (1967). Hallucinoia, the release of phantoms in schizophrenia. Thesis, Harvard Medical School.

——— (1976a). The group matrix of individual therapy with Plains Indian people. *Contemporary Psychoanalysis* 12:227–239.

——— (1976b). The mirror transference in the psychoanalytic psychotherapy of alcoholism. *International Journal of Psychoanalytic Psychotherapy* 5:65–85.

——— (1981). The control and mastery of aggression by doctors: a focal problem for the Balint Group with medical residents. In *Group and Family Therapy*, ed. L. Wolberg and M. Aronson. New York: Brunner/Mazel.

——— (1984). An integration of brief psychotherapy. *American Journal of Psychiatry* 141:935–944.

———— (1986). *The Complex Secret of Brief Psychotherapy*. New York: W. W. Norton.

———— (1987). The neighboring field of brief individual psychotherapy. *Journal of Marital and Family Therapy* 13:409–422.

———— (1989). A scientific journey of twenty years. *Journal of Strategic and Systemic Therapies*, July.

———— (1990). The great simplifying conventions of brief psychotherapy. In *Brief Therapy, Myths, Methods and Metaphors*, ed. J. K. Zeig and S. G. Gilligan. New York: Brunner/Mazel.

———— (1991). New narrative directions: so-called personality disorders and brief psychotherapy. *The Psychiatric Times*, November.

———— (1992). *Self-delight in a Harsh World: The Main Stories of Individual, Marital and Family Psychotherapy*. New York: W. W. Norton.

———— (1995). *The Dilemmas of Brief Psychotherapy*. New York: Plenum.

———— (in press, a). Review of *How Psychotherapy Works*, by J. Weiss. *Journal of Psychiatry, Practice and Research* 4:178–180.

———— (in press, b). The ecology of OCD. In *OCD*, ed. J. Greist and R. Dar. Washington: American Psychiatric Press.

———— (unpublished, a). Freud's unsolved problems, 1983.

———— (unpublished, b). Finding and going forward: the two great challenges of long-term psychotherapy, 1990.

Gustafson, J. P., and Cooper, L. W. (1990). *The Modern Contest, A Systemic Guide to the Pattern that Connects Individual Psychotherapy, Family Therapy, Group Work, Teaching, Organizational Life, and Large-Scale Social Problems*. New York: W. W. Norton.

Hegel, G. W. F. (1974). *Hegel, the Essential Writings*. Edited by F. Weiss. New York: Harper and Row.

Haley, J. (1966). Toward a theory of pathological systems. In *Family Therapy and Disturbed Families*, ed. G. N. Zuk and I. Boszormenyi-Nagy. Palo Alto: Science and Behavior Books.

Hardy, T. (1878). *The Return of the Native*. New York: Penguin, 1978.

———— (1886). *The Mayor of Casterbridge*. New York: Pocket Books, 1956.

Havens, L. (1965). The anatomy of a suicide. *New England Journal of Medicine* 272:401–406.

———— (1967). Recognition of suicidal risks through the psychologic examination. *New England Journal of Medicine* 276:210–215.

———— (1973). *Approaches to the Mind*. Boston: Little, Brown. Reprinted by Harvard University Press, 1988.

———— (1976). *Participant Observation*. New York: Jason Aronson.

———— (1986). *Making Contact: Uses of Language in Psychotherapy*. Cambridge, MA: Harvard University Press.

———— (1989). *A Safe Place*. Cambridge, Massachusetts: Harvard University Press.

Heller, J. (1955). *Catch-22*. New York: Dell.

Henry, J. (1963). *Culture against Man*. New York: Vintage.

—— (1973). *On Sham, Vulnerability, and Other Forms of Self-destruction*. New York: Random House.

Herbert, Z. (1991). *Still Life with a Bridle*. Translated by John and Bogdana Carpenter. New York: Ecco Press.

Herndon, J. (1965). *The Way It Spozed to Be*. New York: Simon and Schuster.

Hesse, H. (1943). *Magister Ludi (the Glass Bead Game)*. Translated by R. Winston and C. Winston. New York: Bantam, 1970.

Homer (1974). *The Iliad*. Translated by Robert Fitzgerald. Garden City, New York: Anchor Books.

—— (1963). *The Odyssey*. Translated by Robert Fitzgerald. New York: Anchor Books.

Hughes, T. (1991). *The Essential Shakespeare*. New York: Ecco Press.

—— (1992). *Shakespeare and the Goddess of Complete Being*. New York: Farrar, Straus and Giroux.

Hurston, Z. N. (1937). *Their Eyes Were Watching God*. New York: Harper and Row, 1990.

Hyman, A., and Walsh, J. J. (1967). *Philosophy in the Middle Ages*. New York: Harper and Row.

Ibsen, H. (1890). *Hedda Gabler*. In *Seven Famous Plays*. Edited by W. Archer. London: Duckworth, 1961.

Irving, W. (1829). *Rip Van Winkle. or the Strange Men of the Mountains*. New York: Scholastic, Inc., 1975.

Jacobson, E. (1953). Contribution to the metapsychology of cyclothymic depression. In *Affective Disorders, Psychoanalytic Contributions to their Study*, ed. P. Greenacre. New York: International Universities Press.

James, H. (1903). The beast in the jungle. In *American Short Stories,* ed. D. Grant. London: Oxford University Press, 1972.

James, W. (1902). *The Varieties of Religious Experience*. New York: Mentor, 1958.

Jantsch, E. (1980). *The Self-Organizing Universe*. New York: Pergamon.

Jarrell, R. (1941). The death of the ball turret gunner. In *The New Oxford Book of American Verse*, ed. R. Ellmann. New York: Oxford, 1976.

Jones, E. (1923). The God complex: the belief that one is god, and the resulting character traits. In *Essays in Applied Psychoanalysis*, ed. E. Jones. London: International Psychoanalytic Press.

—— (1955). *The Life and Work of Sigmund Freud*. Vol. 2. New York: Basic Books.

Jones, W. T. (1967). *The Sciences and the Humanities, Conflict and Reconciliation*. Berkeley: University of California Press.

Joyce, J. (1914). *Ulysses*. New York: Modern Library, 1961.

Jung, C. G. (1916). The relations between the ego and the unconscious. In *The Portable Jung*, ed. J. Campbell. New York: Penguin, 1971.

———— (1925). Marriage as a psychological relationship. In *The Portable Jung*, ed. J. Campbell. New York: Penguin, 1971.

———— (1933). Dream-analysis in its practical application. In *Modern Man in Search of a Soul*. Translated by W. S. Dell and Cary F. Baynes. New York: Harcourt, Brace and Company.

———— (1954). *The Practice of Psychotherapy*. Princeton, New Jersey: Princeton University Press, 1985.

———— (1963). *Memories, Dreams and Reflections*. Recorded and edited by A. Jaffe. Translated from the German by R. and C. Winston. New York: Vintage, 1989.

Kafka, F. (1883–1924). The judgment. In *F. Kafka, The Penal Colony: Stories and Short Pieces*. Translated and edited by W. and E. Muir. New York: Schocken.

———— (1946). *Metamorphosis*. Translated by A. I. Lloyd. New York: Vanguard.

Kaku, M. (1994). *Hyperspace*. New York: Oxford University Press.

Kernberg, O., Selzer, M. A., Koenigsberg, H. W., et al. (1988). *Psychodynamic Psychotherapy of Borderline Patients*. New York: Basic Books.

Khan, M. M. R. (1974). Dread of surrender to resourceless dependency in the analytic situation. In *The Privacy of the Self: Papers on Psychoanalytic Theory and Technique*, ed. M. M. R. Khan. New York: International Universities Press.

Klein, M. (1959). Our adult world and its roots in infancy. In *Envy and Gratitude and Other Works, 1946–1963*, ed. M. Klein. New York: Dell, 1975.

Koch, K. (1993). One train may hide another. *New York Review of Books*, April 8.

———— (1993). *Rose, Where Did You Get That Red? Teaching Great Poetry to Children*. New York: Vintage.

Kohut, H. (1971). *The Analysis of the Self*. New York: International Universities Press.

———— (1979). The two analyses of Mr. Z. *International Journal of Psychoanalysis* 60:3–27.

Korsch, B. M., and Negrete, V. F. (1972). Doctor-patient communication. *Scientific American* 227:66–74.

Kozol, J. (1967). *Death at an Early Age*. New York: Bantam.

———— (1985). *Illiterate America*. New York: Anchor Press/Doubleday.

Kundera, M. (1990). *Immortality*. Translated by Peter Kussi. New York: Harper.

Kuper, A., and Stone, A. A. (1982). The dream of Irma's injection: a structural analysis. *American Journal of Psychiatry* 139:1225–1234.

Laing, R. D. (1959). *The Divided Self: An Existential Study in Sanity and Madness*. London: Tavistock.

Laing, R. D., and Cooper, D. G. (1964). *Reason and Violence: A Decade of Sartre's Philosophy 1950–1960*. New York: Vintage.

Lapham, L. H. (1994). Morte de Nixon. *Harper's Magazine*, July, pp. 6–9.

Lawrence, D. H. (1982). *Birds, Beasts and the Third Thing*. New York: Viking.

—— (1933). The rocking-horse winner. In *The Norton Anthology of Short Fiction*, ed. R. V. Cassill. New York: W. W. Norton, 1986.

—— (1959). *Selected Poems*. New York: Viking.

Le Corbusier (1947). *When the Cathedrals Were White*, trans. F. E. Hyslap, Jr. New York: McGraw-Hill, 1964.

Leach, E. (1970). *Claude Levi-Strauss*. New York: Penguin.

Lemann, N. (1991). Four generations in the projects: one family's story. *New York Times Magazine*, January 13, pp. 16–49.

Lerner, G. (1986). *The Creation of Patriarchy*. New York: Oxford University Press.

Levi-Strauss, C. (1955). *Tristes Tropiques*. Translated by J. and D. Weightman. New York: Pocket Books, 1977.

Levy, S. (1994). Dr. Edelman's brain. *The New Yorker*, May 2, pp. 62–73.

Lewin, B. (1973). *Selected Writings of Bertram D. Lewin*. New York: Psychoanalytic Quarterly Press.

Lewin, K. (1947a). Frontiers in group dynamics. I. Concept, method and reality in social science; social equilibria and social change. *Human Relations* 1:5–41.

—— (1947b). Frontiers in group dynamics. II. Channels of group life; social planning and action research. *Human Relations* 1:143–147.

Lifton, R. J. (1971). Protean man. *Archives of General Psychiatry* 24:298–304.

—— (1986). *The Nazi Doctors*. New York: Basic Books.

Lloyd, A. S. (1972). Freire, conscientization, and adult education. *Adult Education* 23:3–20.

Lobel, A. (1980). *Fables*. New York: Harper and Row.

Lowell, R. (1986). Epilogue. In *The Harvard Book of Contemporary American Poetry*, ed. H. Vendler, p. 112. Cambridge, Massachusetts: Harvard University Press.

Luborsky, L., Crits-Cristoph, P., Mintz J., and Auerbach, A. (1988). *Who Will Benefit from Psychotherapy*. New York: Basic Books.

Main, T. F. (1957). The ailment. *British Journal of Medical Psychology* 30:129–145.

Malan, D. (1976a). *The Frontier of Brief Psychotherapy*. New York: Plenum.

—— (1976b). *Toward the Validation of Dynamic Psychotherapy*. New York: Plenum.

—— (1979). *Individual Psychotherapy and the Science of Psychodynamics*. London: Butterworths.

Malan, D., Balfour, F. H. G., Hood, V. G., and Shooter, A. M. N. (1976). Group psychotherapy: a long-term follow-up study. *Archives of General Psychiatry* 33:1303–1315.

Malan, D. H., Health, E. S., Bacal, H. A., and Balfour, F. H. G. (1975). Psychodynamic changes in untreated neurotic patients. II. Apparently genuine improvements. *Archives of General Psychiatry* 32:110–126.

Malcolm X (1964). *The Autobiography of Malcolm X.* New York: Grove Press.

Margolick, D. (1993). Lisa's bright shining future is laid to rest at Arlington. *New York Times,* July 17, p. 1.

Margulies, A. (1989). *The Empathic Imagination.* New York: W. W. Norton.

Marks, I. (1987). *Fears, Phobias, and Rituals, the Nature of Anxiety and Panic Disorders.* New York: Oxford University Press.

Masterson, J. F. (1975). The splitting defense mechanisms of the borderline adolescent: development and clinical aspects. In *Borderline States in Psychiatry,* ed. J. Mack. New York: Grune and Stratton.

———— (1988). *The Search for the Real Self: Unmasking the Personality Disorders of Our Age.* New York: Free Press.

Maturana, H. F., and Varela, F. J. (1980). *Autopoiesis and Cognition: The Realization of the Living.* Boston: D. Reidel.

Maupassant, G. de (1884). The necklace. In *The Norton Anthology of Short Fiction,* ed. R. V. Cassill. New York: W. W. Norton, 1986.

May, R., Angel, E., and Ellenberger, H. F. (1958). *Existence: A New Dimension in Psychiatry and Psychology.* New York: Simon and Schuster.

Mayman, M., and Faris, M. (1960). Early memories as expressions of relationship paradigms. *American Journal of Orthopsychiatry* 30:507–520.

McCorvey, N. (1994). *I Am Roe: My Life, Roe vs. Wade and Freedom of Choice.* New York: HarperCollins.

Melville, H. (1851). *Moby-Dick or, The Whale.* Edited with an introduction by Alfred Kazin. Boston: Houghton Mifflin, 1956.

———— (1853). Bartleby the scrivener. In *The Norton Anthology of Short Fiction,* ed. R. V. Cassill. New York: W. W. Norton, 1986.

Merton, T. (1948). *The Seven-Story Mountain.* New York: Harcourt Brace Jovanovich.

Miller, A. (1950). *Death of a Salesman.* New York: Viking.

Minkowski, E. (1933). *Lived Time: Phenomenological and Psychopathological Studies.* Translated by N. Metzel. Evanston, IL: Northwestern University Press, 1970.

Molière, J. B. P. (1666, 1669). *The Misanthrope and Tartuffe.* Translated into English verse by Richard Wilbur. New York: Harcourt Brace Jovanovich, 1954.

Murdoch, I. (1974). *The Sacred and Profane Love Machine.* New York: Penguin.

Newton, P. (1979). *The Accursed Correspondence: The Freud/Jung Letters.* University Publishing.

———— (1984). Samuel Johnson's breakdown and recovery in middle-age: a life span developmental approach to mental illness and its cure. *International Review of Psychoanalysis* 11:72–97.

Nietzsche, F. (1954). *The Portable Nietzsche*, ed. W. Kaufman. New York: Viking.

Noll, R. (1994). *The Jung Cult: Origins of a Charismatic Movement*. Princeton, New Jersey: Princeton University Press.

O'Brien, T. (1990). *The Things They Carried*. New York: Penguin.

Ollman, B. (1971). *Alienation: Marx's Conception of Man in Capitalist Society*. Cambridge, England: Cambridge University Press.

Ornstein, A. (1974). The dread to repeat and the new beginning: a contribution to the psychoanalytic psychotherapy of narcissistic personality disorders. *Annual of Psychoanalysis* 2:231–248.

Orwell, G. (1946). The politics of the English language. In *A Collection of Essays by George Orwell*. New York: Harcourt Brace Jovanovich.

Pascal, B. (1662). *Pensées*. Translated with an introduction by A. J. Krailsheimer. London: Penguin, 1966.

Percy, W. (1975). Metaphor as mistake. In *The Message in the Bottle*. New York: Farrar, Straus and Giroux.

Piaget, J. (1968). *Six Psychological Studies*, trans. A. Tenzer. New York: Vintage.

Pinter, H. (1977). *Plays*. London: Eyre Methuen.

Plato (1932). *Symposium*. Edited by R. G. Bury. Cambridge: W. Heffer.

Poirier, R. (1966). *A World Elsewhere: The Place of Style in American Literature*. Madison, Wisconsin: University of Wisconsin Press.

Popper, K. R. (1934). *The Logic of Scientific Discovery*. New York: Harper and Row, 1965.

Porter, K. (1935). Theft. In *The Norton Anthology of Short Fiction*, ed. R. V. Cassill. New York: W. W. Norton, 1986.

Poundstone, W. (1992). *Prisoner's Dilemma*. New York: Anchor.

Quammen, D. (1985). Has success spoiled the crow? In *Natural Acts: A Sidelong View of Science and Nature*. New York: Schocken.

Rafferty, T. (1994). True west. *The New Yorker*, January 10, pp. 81–83.

Rapaport, D. (1959). The structure of psychoanalytic theory: a systematizing attempt. In *Psychology: A Study of Science*, ed. S. Koch. New York: McGraw-Hill.

Reich, W. (1931). Character formation and the phobias of childhood. *International Journal of Psychoanalysis* 12:219.

——— (1933). *Character Analysis*. New York: Farrar, Straus and Giroux, 1949.

Reider, N. (1953). A type of transference to institutions. *Bulletin of the Menninger Clinic* 17:58–73.

Renoir, J. (1974). The grand illusionist turns 80. *New York Times*, September 15.

Rice, A. K. (1965). *Learning for Leadership*. London: Tavistock.

Riker, W. H. (1993). Campaign rhetoric. *Bulletin of the American Academy of Arts and Sciences* 46:37–48.

Rilke, R. M. (1907). The panther. In *Translations from the Poetry of Rainier Maria Rilke*. Translated by M. D. Herder Norton. New York: W. W. Norton, 1938.

——— (1938). *Translations from the Poetry of Rainer Maria Rilke*. Translated by M. D. Herder Norton. New York: W. W. Norton.

Rose, P. (1984). *Parallel Lives: Five Victorian Marriages*. New York: Random House.

Rosenfield, I. (1986). Neural Darwinism: a new approach to memory and perception. *New York Review of Books*, October 9, pp. 21–27.

Rosenhan, D. L. (1973). On being sane in insane places. *Science* 179:250–258.

Rostand, E. (1898). *Cyrano de Bergerac*. Translated by A. Gertrude Hall. New York: Doubleday.

Ryle, A. (1990). *Cognitive-Analytic Therapy: A New Integration in Brief Psychotherapy*. New York: John Wiley and Sons.

——— (1994). Introduction to cognitive analytic therapy. *International Journal of Short-Term Psychotherapy* 9:93–110.

St. Exupery, A. de (1939). *Wind, Sand and Stars*. Translated by Lewis Galantiere. New York: Harcourt Brace Jovanovich.

——— (1943). *The Little Prince*. Translated by Katherine Woods. New York: Harcourt Brace Jovanovich.

Saint Jerome (1953). *Saint Jerome lettres*. Translated by Jerome Labourt. Paris: Societe D'Edition Les Belles Lettres.

Sashin, J. I. (1985). Affect tolerance: a model of affect-response using catastrophe theory. *Journal of Social and Biological Structure* 8:175–202.

Sashin, J. I., and Callahan, J. (1990). A model of affect using dynamical systems. *The Annual of Psychoanalysis* 18:213–231.

Schatzman, M. (1963). Paranoia or persecution: the case of Schreber. *International Journal of Psychiatry*, pp. 51–91.

Schmid, G. B. (1991). Chaos theory and schizophrenia: elementary aspects. *Psychopathology* 24:185–198.

Schmidt, G. L. (unpublished). The chaotic brain: a unifying theory for psychiatry.

Schrag, P. (1994). California's elected anarchy. *Harper's*, November, pp. 50–59.

Schumacher, E. F. (1977). *A Guide for the Perplexed*. New York: Harper and Row.

Selvini-Palazzoli, M. (1980). Why a long interval between sessions: the therapist control of the family-therapist suprasystem. In *Dimensions of Family Therapy*, ed. M. Andolfi and I. Zwerling. New York: Guilford Press.

——— (1985). The problem of the sibling as referring person. *Journal of Marital and Family Therapy* 11:21–34.

——— (1986). Towards a general model of psychotic family games. *Journal of Marital and Family Therapy* 12:339–349.

——— (1988). *The Work of Mara Selvini-Palazzoli*. Northvale, New Jersey: Jason Aronson.

Selvini-Palazolli, M., Arolli, L., Diblasia, P., et al. (1986). *The Hidden Games of Organizations.* New York: Pantheon.

Selvini-Palazzoli, M., Boscolo, L., Cecchin, G. F., and Prata, G. (1977). Family rituals: a powerful tool in family therapy. *Family Process* 16:445–453.

——— (1978). *Paradox and Counterparadox: A New Model in the Therapy of the Family in Schizophrenic Transactions.* New York: Jason Aronson.

Selvini-Palazzoli, M., Cirillo, S., Selvini, M., and Sorrentino, A. M. (1989). *Family Games, General Models of Psychotic Process in the Family.* New York: W. W. Norton.

Selvini-Palazzoli, M., and Prata, G. (1982). Snares in family therapy. *Journal of Marital and Family Therapy* 8:443–450.

Sendak, M. (1967). *Higglety Pigglety Pop! or There Must Be More to Life.* New York: Harper and Row.

Shakespeare, W. (1599–1600). *As You Like It.* In *William Shakespeare: The Complete Works,* ed. A. Harbage. Rev. ed. Baltimore: Penguin, 1969.

——— (1600). *Hamlet, Prince of Denmark.* In *William Shakespeare: The Complete Works,* ed. A. Harbage. Rev. ed. Baltimore: Penguin, 1969.

——— (1600). *The Life of King Henry the Fifth.* In *William Shakespeare: The Complete Works,* ed. A. Harbage. Rev. ed. Baltimore: Penguin, 1969.

——— (1604). *Othello the Moor of Venice.* In *William Shakespeare: The Complete Works,* ed. A. Harbage. Rev. ed. Baltimore: Penguin, 1969.

——— (1605–1606). *King Lear.* In *William Shakespeare: The Complete Works,* ed. A. Harbage. Rev. ed. Baltimore, Maryland: Penguin, 1969.

——— (1607). *Antony and Cleopatra.* In *William Shakespeare: The Complete Works,* ed. A. Harbage. Rev. ed. Baltimore: Penguin, 1969.

——— (1608). *Coriolanus.* In *William Shakespeare: The Complete Works,* ed. A. Harbage. Rev. ed. Baltimore: Penguin, 1969.

——— (1611). *The Tempest.* In *William Shakespeare: The Complete Works,* ed. A. Harbage. Rev. ed. Baltimore: Penguin, 1969.

Shapiro, D. (1976). The analyst's own analysis. *Journal of the American Psychoanalytic Association* 24:5.

Sharaf, M. (1983). *Fury on Earth: A Biography of Wilhelm Reich.* New York: St. Martin's Press/Marek.

——— (unpublished). Nobody cries in Texas.

Shazer, S. de (1987). Minimal elegance. *Family Therapy Networker,* October, pp. 57–60.

Shem, S. (1978). *The House of God.* New York: Dell.

Shorris, E. (1994). A nation of salesmen. *Harper's,* October, pp. 39–54.

Skarda, C. A., and Freeman, W. J. (1987). How brains make chaos in order to make sense of the world. *Behavioral and Brain Sciences* 10:161–195.

Skynner, A. C. R. (1981). An open system, group-analytic approach to family therapy. In *Handbook of Family and Marital Therapy,* ed. A. Gurman and D. Kniskern. New York: Brunner/Mazel.

———— (1986). What is effective in group psychotherapy. *Group Analysis* 19:5–24.

———— (1987). *Explorations with Families: Group Analysis and Family Therapy,* ed. J. R. Schlapobersky. London: Methuen.

Slater, P. (1976). *The Pursuit of Loneliness: American Culture at the Breaking Point.* Boston: Beacon Press.

Smith, G. (1991). Shadow of a nation. *Sports Illustrated,* February 18, pp. 62–74.

Smith, G., and Tiggeman, J. (1989). Seeing teenagers separately: new stories in the family. *Dulwich Centre Newsletter,* Winter, pp. 3–9.

Smith, M. L., Glass, G. V., and Miller, T. I. (1980). *The Benefits of Psychotherapy.* Baltimore: Johns Hopkins University Press.

Snyder, G. (1990). *The Practice of the Wild.* San Francisco: North Point Press.

Sophocles (1954). *Oedipus the King.* Translated by D. Grene. In *Sophocles I. The Complete Greek Tragedies,* ed. D. Grove and R. Lattimore. Chicago: University of Chicago Press.

Spiegel, D. (1994). Compassion is the best medicine. *New York Times,* January 10, editorial.

Spies, W. (1991). *Max Ernst: A Retrospective.* Munich: Prestel-Verlag.

Steiner, G. (1959). *Tolstoy or Dostoevsky: An Essay in the Old Criticism.* New York: Alfred A. Knopf.

Stevenson, R. L. (1886). *The Strange Case of Dr. Jekyll and Mr. Hyde.* New York: Puffin Books, 1985.

———— (1892). The lantern-bearers. In *Across the Plains.* London: Chatto and Windus, Piccadilly.

Stewart, I. (1993). The topological dressmaker. *Scientific American,* July, pp. 110–112.

Strachey, J. (1934). The nature of the therapeutic action of psychoanalysis. *International Journal of Psychoanalysis* 15:127–159.

Strupp, H. H., and Binder, J. (1984). *Psychotherapy in a New Key: Time-limited Dynamic Psychotherapy.* New York: Basic Books.

Sullivan, H. S. (1954). *The Psychiatric Interview.* New York: W. W. Norton.

———— (1956). *Clinical Studies in Psychiatry.* New York: W. W. Norton.

Sun Tzu (1988). *The Art of War,* trans. Thomas Cleary. Boston: Shambhala.

Terkel, S. (1972). *Working.* New York: Avon.

Thomas, D. (1971). *The Collected Poems of Dylan Thomas.* New York: New Directions.

Thoreau, H. D. (1854). Walden. In *The Portable Thoreau.* New York: Penguin.

Thurber J. (1942). The secret life of Walter Mitty. In *The Norton Anthology of Short Fiction,* ed. R. V. Cassill. New York: W. W. Norton, 1986.

———— (1953). The catbird seat. In *Thurber Country.* New York: Harper and Brothers.

Tiggeman, J., and Smith, G. (1989). Adolescent 'shock therapy': teenagers shocking their critics. *Dulwich Centre Newsletter*, Winter, pp. 10–16.

Tolstoy, L. (1869). *War and Peace*. New York: Modern Library, 1966.

——— (1875–1877). *Anna Karenina*. New York: W. W. Norton, 1970.

——— (1882). A confession. In *The Portable Tolstoy*, ed. J. Bayley. New York: Viking.

——— (1886). The death of Ivan Illych. In *The Norton Anthology of Short Fiction,* ed. R. V. Cassill. New York: W. W. Norton, 1986.

Tomm, K. (1988). Interventive interviewing: part III. Intending to ask linear, circular, strategic, or reflexive questions? *Family Process* 27:1–15.

Travis, D. (1994). Mathematics and photography. *Bulletin of the American Academy of Arts and Sciences* 47:23–45.

Tsurumi, W. (1994). A final exit for Japan's Generation X. *Harper's Magazine,* January, pp. 20–22.

Turner, A. K. (1993). *The History of Hell*. New York: Harcourt, Brace.

Twain, M. (1885). *The Adventures of Huckleberry Finn*. New York: Collier, 1962.

Vendler, H. (1985). *The Harvard Book of Contemporary American Verse*. Cambridge, Massachusetts: Harvard University Press.

——— (1994). Shakespeare's sonnets: reading for difference. *Bulletin of the American Academy of Arts and Sciences* 47:33–50.

Voltaire (1759). Candide. In *The Portable Voltaire*, ed. B. R. Redman. New York: Viking, 1949.

Vosnesensky, A. (1966). *Antiworlds: Poetry by Andrei Vosnesensky*. Translated by Patricia Blake and Max Hayward. New York: Basic Books.

Wamboldt, F., and Wolin, S. J. (1988). Reality and myth in family life: changes across generations. *Journal of Psychotherapy and the Family* 4:141–165.

Wallerstein, R. S. (1986). *Forty-two Lives in Treatment*. New York: Guilford Press.

Weber, M. (1904–1905). *The Protestant Ethic and the Spirit of Capitalism*. Translated by Talcott Parsons. New York: Charles Scribner's Sons, 1958.

Weekley, E. (1967). *An Etymological Dictionary of Modern English*. New York: Dover.

Weiden, P., and Havens, L. (1994). Psychotherapeutic management techniques in the treatment of outpatients with schizophrenia. *Hospital and Community Psychiatry* 45:549–555.

Weil, S. (1940). *The Iliad*, or the poem of force. Translated by Richard Ringler. In *Dilemmas of War and Peace: A Source Book,* ed. R. Ringler. London: Routledge, 1993.

Weiss, J. (1993). *How Psychotherapy Works: Process and Technique*. New York: Guilford.

Weiss, J., and Sampson, H. (1986). *The Psychoanalytic Process*. New York: Guilford.

Werner, E. E. (1989). Children of the Garden Island. *Scientific American*, April, pp. 106–111.

West, M., Sheldon, A., and Reiffer, L. (1989). Attachment theory and brief psychotherapy: applying current research to clinical interventions. *Canadian Journal of Psychiatry* 34:369–374.

White, M. (1984). Marital therapy—practical approaches to long-standing problems. *Australian and New Zealand Journal of Family Therapy* 5:27–43.

———— (1989). *Selected Papers*. Adelaide, South Australia: Dulwich Centre Publications.

White, M., and Epston, D. (1990). *Narrative Means to Therapeutic Ends*. New York: W. W. Norton.

White, M. J. (1952). Sullivan and treatment. In *The Contributions of Harry Stack Sullivan*, ed. P. Mullahy. New York: Science House.

Williams, W. C. (1923). The red wheelbarrow. In *The Norton Anthology of Modern Poetry*, ed. R. Ellman and R. O'Clair, 2nd ed., pp. 318–319. New York: W. W. Norton, 1988.

———— (1950). The use of force. In *The Norton Anthology of Short Fiction*, ed. R. V. Cassill. New York: W. W. Norton.

Wilson, Z. V. (1986). *The Quick and the Dead*. New York: Arbor House.

Winnicott, D. W. (1947). Hate in the counter-transference. In *Through Pediatrics to Psychoanalysis*. New York: Basic Books, 1958.

———— (1971a). *Playing and Reality*. London: Tavistock.

———— (1971b). *Therapeutic Consultations in Child Psychiatry*. New York: Basic Books.

Witkin, G. (1991). Kids who kill. *U.S. News and World Report,* April 8.

Woolf, V. (1927). *To the Lighthouse*. New York: Harcourt Brace Jovanovich, 1981.

———— (1938). *Three Guineas*. New York: Harcourt Brace Jovanovich.

Yalom, I (1975). *Theory and Practice of Group Psychotherapy*. 2nd ed.. New York: Basic Books.

Yates, F. A. (1966). *The Art of Memory*. Chicago: University of Chicago Press.

Yeats, W. B. (1914). The magi. In *Selected Poems and Two Plays by William Butler Yeats*, ed. M. L. Rosenthal, p. 49. New York: Macmillan, 1962.

———— (1918). *Per Amica Silentia Lunae*. London: Macmillan.

———— (1939). The long-legged fly. In *Selected Poems and Two Plays of William Butler Yeats*, ed. M. L. Rosenthal. New York: Macmillan, 1962.

Zukav, G. (1979). *The Dancing Wu Li Masters: An Overview of the New Physics*. New York: Bantam.

Credits

Index